EMMA GOLDMAN

EMMA GOLDMAN
AN INTIMATE LIFE

ALICE WEXLER

PANTHEON BOOKS   NEW YORK

Part of this book appeared originally, in slightly different form, in
the spring 1982 issue of *Raritan: A Quarterly Review*.

Library of Congress Cataloging in Publication Data

Wexler, Alice, 1942–
Emma Goldman: an intimate life

Bibliography: p.
Includes index.
1. Goldman, Emma, 1869–1940.   2. Women revolutionists—
Biography.   3. Women revolutionists—United States—
Biography.   I. Title
HX843.G6W49   1984   335'.83'0924 [B]   83-47752
ISBN 0-394-52975-8

Manufactured in the United States of America

Designed by Terry Antonicelli

First Edition

For John
and for Nancy, Maryline, and Milton

Since woman's greatest misfortune has been
that she was looked upon as either angel or devil,
her true salvation lies in being placed on earth;
namely, in being considered human, and therefore
subject to all human follies and mistakes.

Emma Goldman

C O N T E N T S

PART SIX: Prisoner and Deportee

ACKNOWLEDGMENTS

I first wish to thank David Schickele, who initially awakened my interest in Emma Goldman and whose enthusiasm and insights into Goldman's life have continually stimulated and encouraged me. For nearly a decade, Richard Drinnon has been a constant source of assistance, support, and inspiration to me; his eloquent biography of Goldman, *Rebel in Paradise*, has been the essential foundation for my own efforts. Paul Avrich has answered innumerable questions, provided invaluable leads and contacts, and generously shared with me the fruits of his vast research into the history of anarchism, particularly in relation to Alexander Berkman and to Max Baginski. I owe a special debt of gratitude to two people who read this manuscript in its entirety at an early stage. Blaine McKinley's detailed critical response and his knowledge of American anarchism have been extremely important to this work; his helpfulness in providing information, answering questions, engaging in arguments, and sharing ideas from his work in this area have greatly enriched both this book and the process of writing it. The astute suggestions and sensitive criticism of Christine Stansell, who read an early version, were also important to me. I am grateful to Candace Falk for directing my attention to the dramatic contents of the Goldman-Reitman correspondence in the Ben Reitman Papers of the University of Illinois at Chicago. For Falk's account of her 1975 discovery of the previously unknown letters now contained in Supplement IV to this collection, and for Falk's analysis of the Goldman-Reitman relationship and its implications for the concerns of modern-day feminists, see her book, *Love, Anarchy and Emma Goldman*, Holt, Rinehart and Winston, 1984. Exchanges of insights and ideas with Falk were helpful in the development of my thinking about the Goldman-Reitman relationship and its importance in Emma Goldman's life. I especially wish to thank Lillian Hellman for her illuminating reflections on this relationship and for her generous assistance at a critical stage of this book. Drs. Nancy Wexler, Maryline Barnard, Milton Wexler, Gerald Aronson, and Alan Z. Skolnikoff helped to clarify the sexual and psychological dynamics of Goldman's life. Richard Poirier, Fawn Brodie, Charles Strozier, Sarah Stage, Steven Axelrod, Kay Trimberger, and Eli Zaretsky provided valuable criticism and suggestions for parts of the manuscript. Conversations with Karen Rosenberg, Lynn Rogoff, Marty Blatt, Rise Axelrod, Stephanie Kay, and Paul Berman have also been helpful. I wish to thank Josef Purkart for translating Goldman's early letters to Max Metzkow from German into vivid English; Sharon Salinger for a translation from the Hebrew, Winifred Frazier for her unpublished paper, "Emma Goldman and the World of Culture," presented at the 1978 meetings of the Modern Language Association; Laura Farabaugh of Nightfire (San Francisco) and Jim Huggins of the Freedom Bookshop (London) for providing copies of rare Goldman pamphlets and of *Mother Earth*; William Nowlin; Scott Giantvalley; Donald Wyrick, Warden of the Missouri State Penitentiary in Jefferson City; and members of the Pacific Street Film Collective.

Relatives, friends, comrades, and the children of comrades have generously shared recollections of Goldman. I am grateful to Ian and Betty Ballantine for an afternoon of vivid reminiscences; to Miriam Commins Berman of Rochester, who at the age of ninety-three called up memories of the McKinley assassination as if it had occurred yesterday, and who provided useful background about the family of her great-aunt; to Federico Arcos for sharing both his recollections and the wealth of archival material that he has collected; to Ahrne Thorne for many illuminating conversations about Goldman and about Yiddish anarchism generally; and to Daniel and Bertha Malmed for reflections on Goldman's relationship with Leon Malmed. Hilda Adel, Kay Boyle, Nan Britton, Miriam Hapgood DeWitt, Esther and Sam Dolgoff, Sonya Farber, Bernardine Szold-Fritz, Eva Langbord, Federika Martin, William Arthur Mendelsohn, Joan Norlander, Otto A. Steen, Clara and Sidney Solomon, Mollie Steimer, and Sarah Toback also shared memories of Goldman and those close to her.

As befitted her tumultuous life, Goldman left copious records in two continents. Librarians and archivists at many institutions have generously opened doors to this mass of material. I wish to thank especially Rudolph de Jong, Thea Duijker, and Mieke Yzermans of the International Institute for Social History, Amsterdam; Mary Ann Bamberger and Mary Lynn Ritzenthaler of the University of Illinois, Chicago; Edward C. Weber of the Labadie Collection, University of Michigan; Patricia King and Eva Moseley of the Arthur and Elizabeth Schlesinger Library on the History of Women in America, Radcliffe College; Zachary M. Baker at the Yivo Institute for Jewish Research; Cynthia Huggins of the Newberry Library; Larry Nauken of the Rochester Public Library; Hilja Kukk of the Hoover Institution at Stanford University; and Helen Tuntland of the Hochstein School of Music. A grant from the National Endowment for the Humanities funded part of the research for this book. Permission for the use of quotations from Emma Goldman's letters and papers has been granted by Ian Ballantine, Miss Goldman's literary executor, who controls all rights in the property of Miss Goldman. Alfred A. Knopf, Inc. graciously gave permission to quote from *Living My Life*. The editors of *Raritan: A Quarterly Review* kindly allowed me to reprint a revised version of "Emma Goldman in Love," which appears here as chapters 10 and 13. Katherine S. Inglis gave permission to quote from the letters of Agnes Inglis.

Sara Bershtel brought an incisive critical understanding and elegant style to the editing—and more than editing—of this manuscript. I benefited as well from the judicious criticisms and suggestions of Helena Franklin, also of Pantheon Books. The faith, warmth, energy and wisdom of my agent, Frances Goldin, helped negotiate all phases of this book. My typist, Clara Dean, miraculously transformed hieroglyphics into text. The generous services of Susan Spivak also helped make this book a reality. I wish to extend my special appreciation to Drs. Edward A. Kravitz, Anne B. Young, Allan J. Tobin, and David Housman. Most of all I wish to thank John Michael Ganim, who illuminated endless travels through streets and archives, theaters and prisons in pursuit of an elusive subject.

INTRODUCTION

"Her name was enough in those days to produce a shudder," recalled her friend Margaret Anderson, editor of the avant-garde *Little Review*. "She was considered a monster, an exponent of free love and bombs."[1] Almost from the moment she entered the anarchist movement in 1889 at the age of twenty, Emma Goldman enjoyed a notoriety unequalled by any other woman in American public life. The government thought her one of "the ablest and most dangerous" anarchists in the country.[2] Singling her out as a special target of persecution, Washington kept up a running battle with Emma Goldman until it finally succeeded in deporting her, along with several hundred other immigrant radicals, on December 21, 1919.

Goldman was one of the most respected members of an international radical movement that had emerged in the mid-nineteenth century alongside the socialist movement in partial opposition to Marxism. The anarchists were socialists, but of a particular kind. Anticapitalist, they also vehemently opposed the state and all forms of centralized authority. Rather than capturing state power, the anarchists sought to destroy it; instead of state control of the economy, the anarchists proposed self-management and workers' control; in place of building mass political parties to elect socialists to office, they formed small militant groups to spread anarchist ideas by means of newspapers, lectures, and demonstrations. Emma Goldman defined anarchism as "the philosophy of a new social order based on liberty unrestricted by man-made law; the theory that all forms of government rest on violence, and are therefore wrong and harmful, as well as unnecessary."[3] She spent much of her life in America working for this vision, which for her encompassed an ideal of sexual and personal freedom as well as social revolution.

Emma Goldman's life, intense and fast-paced, seems to have encompassed the activities not of one woman but of many. She first attracted national attention as the lover of Alexander Berkman, who tried to assassinate steel magnate Henry Clay Frick during the Homestead Steel strike of 1892. After Berkman went to prison, Goldman quickly rose to eminence within the movement, her fame as a charismatic platform speaker extending far beyond the small circles of anarchist militants. On her annual cross-country lecture tours, which began in the late nineties, large audiences turned out to hear her ringing denunciations of capitalism, militarism, and government and her perhaps even more controversial defense of atheism, sexual freedom, and homosexuality. Later, aided by the great love of her life, the Chicago hobo-turned-physician Ben L. Reitman, she raised funds for the Industrial Workers of the World (I.W.W.), campaigned for birth control, organized legal defense for imprisoned radicals, and opposed the draft during World War I, for which she spent twenty months in prison. For twelve years she published an anarchist magazine, *Mother Earth*, and also produced two volumes of essays. She lectured extensively on *The Social Significance of the Modern Drama*—the title of her second book—insisting that radical art was potentially even more subversive than outright political agitation. At a time when many reformers and feminists wanted to "purify" politics by outlawing prostitution and alcohol and by imposing upon men the rigid sexual code demanded of women, Goldman argued that restriction and prohibitions created social problems rather than solving them. The solution, she insisted, lay in more freedom for both sexes, as well as an end to "industrial slavery." Admired by many eminent Americans—including Eugene O'Neill, Lincoln Steffens, Eugene Debs, H. L. Mencken, the painter Robert Henri, and especially Roger Baldwin, founder of the American Civil Liberties Union, who regarded her as a major influence on his life—she was hated and feared by others for her outspoken attacks on conventional values and her public defense of political terrorists. Indeed, many people remained convinced that she had inspired the assassination of President William McKinley, despite the absence of any evidence linking her with that act. Although Goldman was an early and ardent defender of the 1917 Bolshevik Revolution, she turned against the regime after spending two years (1920–1921) in the war-torn Soviet Union. Denied reentry into the United States, she remained active as a writer and lecturer in exile, mainly in France, England, and Canada. In her late sixties, she visited Spain and worked on behalf of the anarchists during the Spanish civil war. She was in Canada, struggling to assist refugees from fascist Spain and Italy, when she died in May of 1940.

Despite a lifetime committed to anarchism, Goldman was almost as controversial within the movement as outside it, especially during her thirty-three years in America—the height of her importance as a public figure—when her work ranged considerably beyond the concerns most immigrant anarchists thought appropriate. Her comrades admired her courage and charisma as a speaker and organizer, but many criticized her outspokenness about sex, her unconventional personal life, and her attraction to middle-class "American" audiences. They thought that a revolutionist should stick to economic, political, or antireligious subjects, while Goldman insisted on talking about literature and drama as vehicles for changing social attitudes. Her impatience with opposition and her sometimes imperious behavior further deepened tensions between her and her comrades.

To isolate the historical Emma Goldman from myth, fiction, and controversy is no easy task. Besides the political argument she generated, there is the demonic legend that surrounded her during her years in America: an image created partly by a hostile government and sensationalizing press, but one that she herself exploited to popularize her ideas. Certainly she was one of a very few radicals with a fine grasp of public relations. In addition, there is her own myth of herself as earth mother and as tragic heroine, which she dramatized in her massive autobiography, *Living My Life* (1931). This memoir is the starting point for any biography, but we should note that it was written as Goldman approached sixty, long after most of the events it describes had taken place and with few available records of these events—apart from letters she had written to friends, mainly after 1917—to correct the vagaries of memory (her papers had been confiscated by the Justice Department in 1917 and were never returned). Written, moreover, from exile in the south of France, the autobiography was aimed at an American audience in the hope that it might facilitate Goldman's reentry into the United States and perhaps even yield an income that would ease her desperate financial straits: a perspective that may have led her to play down her European childhood and adolescence in order to emphasize her American identity. In addition, the memoir was heavily edited by Alexander Berkman, Goldman's most intimate lifelong friend, and in certain ways was almost a joint effort. We know from Berkman's diaries the extent to which he changed, cut, and polished the manuscript. "The Mss., after I correct it, looks worse than an ordinary battlefield," he boasted one day. "Some pages: half of it crossed out by me, the other half every word, literally, changed by me."[4] Sometimes Goldman's constant litany of complaint made him laugh aloud; he managed to delete the worst excesses. Neither Goldman nor Berkman deliberately tried to eliminate painful episodes or idealize the central character of *Living My Life*. Still, like any autobiography, Goldman's is a partial account, both of the anarchist movement in America and of her life within it.

One hesitates, however, to examine the Goldman legend too closely. The anarchists were so embattled a movement and Goldman herself was so relentlessly pursued and persecuted that her human limitations seem relatively insignificant in comparison with the injustices inflicted upon her and the tremendous courage with which she defended her convictions. Moreover, Goldman's heroic legend was a great part of her power as an inspiration to others; indeed, her public persona was perhaps her most original creation. Goldman wished to live her life as a heroine: to invent herself as mother earth, martyr, messiah, "a voice in the wilderness," as she often described herself. Within a small community, she largely succeeded—succeeded so well, in fact, that even she did not know where the myth ended and the woman began. Even to herself, the son of a close associate told me, the private Emma Goldman always remained an enigma.[5] To glimpse the "all too human" (as Goldman described it) personality behind the heroic exterior is likely to be a disheartening experience, as it was for some of her close associates. Yet while the historical Emma Goldman was more problematic, more contradictory, and less romantic in certain ways than the ebullient figure of legend, the reality of her life was no less heroic and in many ways more interesting and moving.

In both her public and private writings, Goldman often raised questions about her own motivation that offer a compelling challenge to the biographer. In her memoirs she wondered if her thirty years "on the firing line" had "served only to fill my inner void, to find an outlet for the turbulence of my being," or if it was "really the ideal that had dictated my conscious course?"[6] Privately, she put it even more forcefully. "Did it not occur to you," she wrote to a skeptical member of her family, "that my external activities may have been an escape from my emotional dissatisfaction deeply hidden in my inner life?"[7]

That Goldman viewed her life in this way suggests the tremendous difficulty faced by women in public life during the pre–World War I decades in assuring not just their critics but even themselves that their commitments to public life were legitimate. But Goldman's questions also provide a starting point for exploring the inner life of a political figure—one who left a record of her moods, feelings, and fantasies that was remarkably rich, voluminous, and uncensored for a person of her active temperament and in her public position. Goldman wrote so much—"she wrote down every mood, every feeling," an anarchist comrade of Goldman's reminded me—that one must be careful not to extrapolate from momentary expressions of feeling a defining strand of her character.[8] Yet it is precisely this expression of conflicting thoughts and emotions that defines much of her fascination—for her contemporaries as well as for us. Others have celebrated her impressive consistencies. What attracted me from the start were the conflicts and contradictions that Goldman saw at the center of her own character and that she could never wholly untangle.

When I first learned about Emma Goldman, I found her both admirable and irritating. As I studied her memoirs and vast correspondence, I was often dismayed by her self-deceptions and vanities, her frequent scorn for other radicals and feminists. Gradually, however, I found my vexation changing to empathy. My own mixed feelings about her, I learned, were widely shared by many of her contemporaries in the anarchist movement, even those who were devoted to her. There are few women in public life who have left so complete and intimate a record of their inner lives as Emma Goldman, or so poignant a document of "subjective discontent," as the radical journalist Agnes Smedley once described it.[9] I have always imagined that, in revealing her emotions so fully and in raising so many questions about her own motives, Goldman wished to invite the collaboration of future biographers in sorting out her complexities. In any case, I have taken those questions as my starting point in the present portrayal of her life.

PART I

YOUTH

C H A P T E R

I

"MY LONE AND WOEFUL CHILDHOOD"

Emma Goldman often claimed that she was born a rebel. "Environment," she would insist, "can only bring out what is inherent in human beings. It can never put anything in sterile ground. If I had not been born with the love for freedom and the intense hatred of injustice, I do not believe that I would have become what I am."[1] She was an anarchist "of the Topsy variety—I was just born so."[2] In her autobiography, Goldman accorded little attention to the events of her early years, partly in order to stress her identity as an American, but also because she regarded her childhood and adolescence as prelude to her real life as an activist. Yet while she dismissed this period as "insignificant," her few recorded childhood memories suggest the powerful legacy of those early years, which her mentor, Johann Most, believed "had made me what I was."[3] Despite her own recurrent assertion that "Anarchists and rebels are born not made," she herself persuasively described the conditions that led her to grow up "largely in revolt."[4]

Goldman's attitude of revolt was shared by many young Russian Jews who, in the latter part of the nineteenth century, were beginning to rebel against the oppression they suffered under the regime of the Czars. When the Russian Empire annexed the Baltic provinces and most of Poland during the late eighteenth and early nineteenth centuries, it acquired a large population of Jews who had previously enjoyed a relatively autonomous social and cultural existence. In contrast with the fairly tolerant attitude of Poland, the government of Russia had a long history of hatred for the Jews. Upon gaining the new regions, it launched a contradictory policy that oscillated between exclusion and forced conversion to Christianity ("Russification"). Most Jews were required to live within the western provinces of the empire, a region of some 386,000 square miles extending from the Baltic Sea to the Black Sea, designated as the Pale of Settlement. By the end of the nineteenth century, about ninety-four percent of the Jewish population of Russia—approximately 4,900,000 people— lived within this region, comprising nearly twelve percent of the total population of the area.

Within the Pale of Settlement, the rights of the Jews to move and to work were severely restricted. They had to live within specified towns or cities, and even then were subject to frequent expulsions. Generally excluded from occupations such as government service and agriculture, they functioned as middlemen between the aristocracy and landowners, on the one hand, and the peasants on the other. Jews were often innkeepers or proprietors of shops in which agricultural produce from the countryside was exchanged for manufactured goods from the cities. Often they were simply traders who bought livestock and produce from the peasants at weekly fairs and then sold these goods locally. In the larger cities, Jewish manufacturers produced textiles, leather goods, and tobacco; Jewish craftsmen tended to be tailors, cobblers, cabinet makers, or metalworkers. With the beginnings of industrial capitalism in the late nineteenth century, Jews swelled the urban working class. In general, the economic position of the Russian Jews steadily deteriorated throughout the nineteenth century. If a small elite became doctors, lawyers, bankers, and wealthy industrialists, a large number had no discernible means of support and came to be known as "luftmenschn," men who lived on air.

While the residential and occupational policies of Czar Nicholas I (1825–55) aimed at containing the Jews within a narrow sphere, his educational and military policies attempted to bring about conversions to Christianity and forcible assimilation of the Jewish population. The most savage of these policies was the "cantonist" system, imposed in 1827, which made Jewish boys subject to military service under special conditions not applied to non-Jews. Theoretically draftable at age eighteen, in practice Jewish boys were literally kidnapped as children—aged twelve, or even younger—and sent to special institutions where they received military training. As soldiers, they were required to serve in the army for twenty-five years. The real purpose of the cantonist system was not military but social: to separate Jewish children from their cultural milieu and force them to convert to Christianity. Similarly, the official government schools and the later Jewish "Crown" schools (much like the government schools but without their heavily Christian emphasis) aimed, overtly or covertly, at assimilation. Graduation from the official elementary and secondary schools, moreover, did not bestow civil equality. Jewish graduates were not permitted to enter the universities, and they suffered the same occupational and residential restrictions as nongraduates.

Against this background of persecution, the accession to power of Czar Alexander II in 1855 seemed to promise a new era of liberalization for Jews and non-Jews alike. The serfs were emancipated in 1861. The hated cantonist system was abolished. A limited number of Jewish students were permitted to enter the high schools (*Gymnasien*) and universities. Furthermore, university graduates were made eligible for government service and were permitted to move freely beyond the Pale, as were wealthy merchants, medical workers, and certain classes of skilled artisans. Areas of the empire previously closed to Jewish residence, such as the city of Kiev, were now opened. Other cities were forbidden to restrict Jewish residence to specified ghettos. A general relaxation of censorship applied also to Hebrew and Yiddish books and newspapers, stimulating the growth of the Jewish press and intellectual life.

This period of liberalization caused many Jews to regard Alexander II as a great liberator. But it proved to be brief. Following the Polish uprising of 1863, and particularly during the 1870s, official hostility toward all non-Russian minorities, including the Jews, intensified. By the late 1870s, some restrictions on residency had been reinstated, censorship was gradually tightened, university quotas reduced, and occupational restrictions extended. The fervent hopes for complete emancipation and equality cherished by many Jews at the start of Alexander's reign slowly faded.

Within the communities of the Pale, two distinct movements were beginning to transform traditional Jewish cultural life: one oriented toward Western Europe, the other toward Russia. By the middle of the nineteenth century, the Jewish Enlightenment, or "Haskalah" movement, was introducing modern secular literature and philosophy from the West, particularly Germany, into the towns and cities of the Pale. While not rejecting a Jewish cultural identity or the Yiddish language, the "maskilim," or followers of the Enlightenment, challenged the religious orthodoxy that governed the everyday life of the Jews. They sought above all to modernize Jewish cultural life and to introduce into the rigidly traditional Jewish educational system the literature, philosophy, and science of the West.

Many of the sons and daughters of the "maskilim," however, rejected their Jewish identity altogether. As they entered the Russian gymnasia and universities, fleeing the towns for the cities, they sought to identify themselves with a secularized Russian culture. They spoke Russian and regarded themselves as Russians; they were inspired, not by Western European liberalism, but by Russian radicalism. In their view, the emancipation of the Jews would come about only through the revolutionary transformation of all of Russian society.

Into this world in transition, Emma Goldman was born on June 27, 1869, in the Russian province of Kovno (today Kaunas, in the Lithuanian Soviet Socialist Republic) to a petit bourgeois Orthodox Jewish family of declining fortunes. Of her paternal great-grandparents, Aaron and Katie Ruttenberg, we know only that they were from somewhere within the Russian Empire. Probably they lived within the provinces of the Pale. Emma's paternal grandmother, Freda Ruttenberg, was born in 1824.[5] She married Solomon Goldman, by whom she had at least four children.[6] Freda and Solomon Goldman owned a rather successful business, manufacturing and selling mattresses in the city of Kovno.[7] Eventually widowed, Freda Goldman left Kovno when she was in her sixties, emigrating to America with her son (Emma's father) and settling first in New York City, later in Rochester, where she died at the age of ninety. Emma remembered her as a resilient, courageous, and spirited woman—very Orthodox, and devoted to her family, including her radical granddaughter, whom she regarded as "a good Jewish daughter" because "she gave everything to the poor."[8]

Emma's father, Abraham Goldman, was born to Freda and Solomon Goldman in January of 1845, probably in the town of Siauliai (Shavl in Yiddish) in the present-day Lithuanian Soviet Socialist Republic, some seventy-three miles north of the city of Kovno and within the province of Kovno.[9] Siauliai was a town in which the approximately 2,500 Jews formed a majority of the population in 1847. At some point Abraham moved with his parents to the city of Kovno, where he lived until his marriage. In her autobiography, Emma described her father in his youth as "handsome, dashing and full of vitality." He had been an ambitious, energetic young man, "dreaming of the large city and the big things he could do there." "Highly educated," according to his granddaughter, and fluent in four or five languages, he had cherished hopes of becoming "a man of learning" or "a man of the professions." Instead he found himself, as a Jew, excluded from any real opportunity to advance, except, wrote Emma, by exploiting the peasants, which he refused to do. "The failure of his life, the lack of opportunity to put his abilities to good use, had embittered him and made him ill-natured and hard towards his own." He was inclined to vent his frustrations on his family. Emma believed that her parents' unhappy marriage, which she attributed to her mother's sexual coldness, intensified her father's harshness. "His violence and hardness had only been symptoms of an intensely sexual nature that had failed to find adequate expression."[10] A photograph of the young Abraham Goldman shows a proud, handsome, hopeful man with a high, thoughtful forehead, a determined mouth, dark, wavy hair, a curly beard, and slightly stooped shoulders that hint at slackness—or possibly the illness that, although she never identified it, Emma indicated had made him an invalid for the last thirty years of his life.[11]

An Orthodox Jew, Abraham Goldman was conservative in his politics and social views, maintaining staunchly traditional convictions

7

about the proper roles of sons and daughters. Hot-tempered and impatient, he reacted harshly to his daughter's early rebelliousness, so that from the outset his relationship with Emma was tense and difficult. Like many Jewish fathers, he attached a higher value to sons, for whom the world of scholarship and learning was exclusively reserved. Daughters were to marry and have children. Traditional Jewish culture, however, in no way forbade, and even encouraged, economic activity on the part of women. Since study of the Torah was the most admired occupation of men, many Jewish wives took an active or even exclusive role in supporting the family so that their husbands might study. Cultural tradition and the exigencies of poverty, in which most East European Jews lived, had fostered generations of assertive, energetic women, used to making their way in the world and to decision-making within the family. But this worldliness had as its end the family, not the self; however capable, women in this world could not become the scholars or professionals to which Jewish tradition accorded the highest prestige. Emma felt that her father, full of frustrated intellectual ambitions that he hoped his sons could fulfill, had been disappointed at the birth of a daughter. "As long as I could think back," she reported bitterly, "I remembered his saying he had not wanted me. He had wanted a boy, the pig woman had cheated him."[12]

Somewhat older than her father, Emma's mother, Taube Binowitz Goldman, was born in the town of Jurbarkas (or Jurburg) in the southwestern part of what is today the Lithuanian Soviet Socialist Republic, some forty-five miles northwest of the city of Kovno and a few miles from the border with East Prussia.[13] Jurbarkas, in fact, was one of the larger Jewish communities in Lithuania and was strongly influenced by the proximity of the Germans across the border. The Binowitz family seem to have been somewhat more educated and affluent than the Goldmans. Taube's father, Maurice Binowitz, was either a lawyer or a physician; he evidently made a great impression on the young Emma, who described him as "a linguist and a man of attainments."[14] Taube's four brothers, all lawyers, married non-Jewish women and converted to Christianity in order to practice in St. Petersburg.[15] In her autobiography, Goldman described one of Taube's brothers as "a very distinguished lawyer" who was arrested, imprisoned, and even in some danger of exile to Siberia because he had had "advanced ideas and talked them." According to Emma,

Taube had traveled to St. Petersburg and personally secured his release. Although she never indicated any closeness to this uncle, Emma sometimes speculated that she might have "inherited" her revolutionary tendencies from him.[16]

A second sibling of her mother's who made a mark on Emma was an aunt who "went on for years indifferent to everything around her, including her children." When similar symptoms appeared in another member of the family, Emma thought they might have been hereditary.[17] This observation is significant, since Emma herself struggled against depression all her life.

At the age of fourteen or fifteen, Taube Binowitz had married her first husband, Leon Zodikow, a physician also from Jurbarkas. The couple lived in their native town, where two daughters were born: Helene in 1860 and Lena in 1862. Shortly thereafter the family moved to the city of Königsberg, where the parents of Leon Zodikow were living. Zodikow died of tuberculosis in 1864 or 1865, leaving his widow with a small legacy.[18] Taube's actions during the next few years remain obscure. Apparently she left her two small children with Zodikow's parents while she herself went off to St. Petersburg.[19] A few years later she married her second husband, Abraham Goldman —a marriage arranged, according to Emma, "in the traditional Jewish Orthodox fashion, without love."[20]

Taube Goldman was by all accounts a remarkable woman, who worked alongside her husband to support the family, managed the finances of the family business after they had emigrated to America, and played an active role all her life in local community and religious affairs. In America she would become a powerful figure in philanthropic work within the Jewish community of Rochester, New York, respected by Jews and non-Jews alike. Photographs of the young Taube show her as handsome in a small, round, solid way, with deep-set dark eyes and a square determined chin, her compact features crowned by a massive braid. Emma described her as "strong and self-assertive," and thought "no statesman or diplomat excelled her in wit, shrewdness or force of character."[21] Though she probably had no more than a few years of elementary education, Taube read avidly and impressed observers as a literate, educated woman. Emma often insisted that her parents had had nothing to do with her radicalism, but she did believe that she had "inherited" from them "my ability to think for myself and a considerable mental capacity."[22] Indeed,

Emma suggests in her memoir that it was her mother who first awakened her own great sensitivity to the spoken word. Years later she still recalled her mother's gift of making the books she had read come alive for her children, and the excitement of Taube's vivid storytelling. "We children used to hang on her very lips," Emma wrote.[23] Taube's character also reflected qualities particularly associated with the Lithuanian Jews by their neighbors; she was quick-witted, pungent, even sharp in her speech, impressing acquaintances with her forcefulness and intelligence rather than her warmth. At times she was capable of an imperiousness that inspired associates to call her "the Duchess," and Emma herself observed, with a mixture of admiration and bitterness, that her carefully groomed mother had always been "the grand dame par excellence."[24]

As a small child, Emma experienced her mother as cold and without tenderness, unwilling to give her daughter the affection for which she longed. Although not as given to fits of violent anger toward the children as Abraham, Taube "never showed much warmth," according to Emma, except toward her youngest and favorite son.[25] Popular with her neighbors and coworkers, Taube committed her deepest energies to projects other than her children. While Emma was hurt by her mother's distance, Taube's independence and energy made her a powerful model for her daughter. As she grew older, Emma came to admire Taube's activism, and it seems likely that in her own dedication to public life on a national and international level, she was both emulating and outdoing her mother. Taube, for her part, gradually grew more accepting of Emma, and despite their political disagreements, defended her daughter loyally against all detractors.

Although both of Emma's parents were Lithuanian Jews, Abraham, born and raised in the province of Kovno, seems to have been more attached to the religious traditions of his forebears. Taube, who had grown up close to the Prussian border, identified with the more secular, cosmopolitan culture of the German Jews, sharing their contempt for the poorer, more traditional, less educated Russian Jews—and indeed for Russia itself. Both parents evidently observed Jewish ritual, attending synagogue on Saturdays and holidays; Emma later described herself as "devout" until the age of seventeen, implying that she had received a traditional religious education.[26] Still, she recalled little discussion of religion at home—"I got my idea of God

10

and devil, sin and punishment, from my nurse and our Russian peasant servants," she would say.[27] Taube, "very German" according to her daughter, set the cultural tone of the household by hiring German-speaking nursemaids from Königsberg, speaking often in German to her children, and in general attempting to surround them with German cultural influences.[28]

If the differences between her parents enriched Emma's childhood by exposing her early to distinct cultural perspectives, they may also have intensified the strife which, according to Emma, characterized the marriage. In retrospect, Emma recalled that her parents quarreled and fought constantly. Her father, she believed, had really loved her mother, but found her cold and unresponsive—perhaps, Emma speculated, because Taube remained emotionally attached to her first husband, who had died. In any event, she recalled hearing remarks of her mother's that convinced her of "what a purgatory my parents' intimacy must have been to them both."[29] The considerable conflict and tension in the home were further exacerbated by a close, even claustrophobic attachment between family members. "That's what it means to be a Goldman," Emma once remarked with irritation, "devotion to distraction."[30] What most angered her was that while family members were obsessed with each other's most minor physical ailments, they seemed incapable of responding to deep emotional needs. Let a "loved one suffer spiritually, let him eat his very heart out with some soul struggle, and he will receive neither understanding nor help from his people. . . ."[31]

Helene Zodikow, born May 5, 1860, in Jurbarkas, was the eldest of the five children Taube was to bear between 1860 and 1879.[32] In many ways Helene, nine years older than Emma, was more a mother to her little sister than Taube. A gentle, self-sacrificing, affectionate girl, Helene conveyed an impression of sadness even when she was very young. A photograph probably taken when she was in her twenties shows a slender, serious, dark-eyed young woman with compact Binowitz features, her wavy hair parted in the middle and pulled back softly into a bun. Helene was protective toward Emma and often intervened in the battles between Abraham and his most rebellious daughter. From her, Emma could always be sure of love and sympathy. Emma, in turn, was devoted to Helene, who "meant more to me than even my mother. . . . It was always Helena who gave me affection, who filled my childhood with whatever joy it had. She

11

would continually shoulder the blame for the rest of the children."[33] Although she often defended Emma against her father's anger, Helene was timid, according to her sister, and unable to stand up for herself. When she was sixteen, Helene evidently fell in love with a Lithuanian boy. Her parents forbade them to marry because he was not Jewish, and Helene accepted their decision. In Emma's typically romantic view, this sacrifice had cost Helene whatever capacity for passion or joy there was in her nature. Emma resolved that she would never allow either her parents or anyone else to victimize her in that way.

Like her mother, Helene was intelligent, well-read, and fluent in five languages, including Lithuanian and Lettish—unusual even for those Jews who lived in the regions where these languages were spoken. Helene also shared her mother's talent for diplomacy, combined with a warmth and empathy lacking in Taube, which led many people to seek her out for emotional support and psychological counsel. Although fairly conservative in her social attitudes, as a young woman Helene read some of the forbidden revolutionary literature circulating among Russian students during the 1870s and 1880s. It was Helene who first introduced Emma to these books. Although Helene may have attended high school, financial necessity forced her to go to work while still a young woman. In St. Petersburg and later in America, she worked as a photographic retoucher, a common occupation for young unmarried women.

With her second half-sister, Lena Zodikow, Emma had a more tense and distant relationship. Born August 16, 1872, Lena resented Emma because Abraham, shortly after his marriage to Taube, had unwisely invested—and lost—the inheritance Leon Zodikow had left his daughters.[34] This, at any rate, was Emma's interpretation of her half-sister's early hostility toward her. Lacking Helene's motherly attitude to the younger children in the family, Lena was livelier, more assertive and outgoing and less conventional than her older sister. When Lena emigrated to America at the time Emma was about eleven, their early emotional distance was reinforced by several years of physical separation. Later, however, they grew friendlier toward each other. Lena had the strong intellectual interests and great respect for education characteristic of the entire family, and this formed a bond between the sisters, despite Lena's conservatism. When Lena was in her seventies, Emma remarked that she was "amazingly alert for a woman who had led such a secluded and insular life. She reads a lot and what is more she understands what she reads. . . . But human beings and their foibles are beyond her."[35]

Whether Emma was the third or fourth child in the family is unclear. Her autobiography mentions that she was the fourth child delivered by her mother, and her niece, Miriam Berman, also recalled that the first child born to Abraham and Taube had been a son, Louis, who died.[36] Yet Emma elsewhere says "a baby brother of mine who died at the age of six" was born between herself and her brother Herman (born in 1872). At the age of fifty she still remembered "so distinctly the astonishing questions the child would ask—who made the rain, what is in the sky—what is God—and so on. Always looking out with great big blue wistful eyes—and no one to satisfy the child's curiosity."[37] The only other specific reference she made to this brother was when, in the outline for her autobiography, she notes "first contact with death through little brother."[38]

In the world of Goldman's childhood, the death of a sibling was not an uncommon occurrence. Still, a sensitive child might well feel guilty about the death of a sibling rival, as if her own aggressive hostile feelings had caused her brother's death and turned her into a murderer and a monster. The guilt of the survivor echoes at moments in the pages of Goldman's autobiography and correspondence, as if the adult Goldman's sense of responsibility for the suffering of others was first awakened by this childhood loss. At the same time, she evidently determined to make reparations for this early failure by becoming the greatest rescuer and mother of all children.[39]

With her surviving brothers, Herman and Morris, Emma Goldman's relations were quite straightforward. Herman, born in September of 1872, was closest in age to Emma, but the most unlike her and the farthest from her emotionally. As the eldest surviving son, Herman evidently bore the brunt of his father's wish for a professional man in the family. Yet he hated school, had no intellectual interests or ambitions, and failed to aspire to medicine or law. His real love was machines. Eventually Herman became a highly skilled machinist, much to the disappointment of his father.[40]

Emma had a more intimate relationship with her baby brother Moishe (later Moe or "Morris,"), born in August of 1879. Emma described Morris as "like my own child, only more understanding, much closer than children usually are with their mother."[41] Later she would also describe him as "more my lover than brother," someone with whom she could share her innermost thoughts and feelings.[42] Morris eventually became a doctor, realizing his parents' dream of a professional son. Emma was proud of her brother and his achievements, while Morris, like Helene, was gentle and affectionate, greatly admiring his courageous sister and remaining loyal and devoted to her, though he did not share her politics.

Soon after Emma was born, the family moved from the city of Kovno to the Lithuanian town of Papilė, located about ninety-four miles northwest of Kovno and a few miles south of the border with the Latvian province of Courland, in a landscape of gently rolling countryside cut by the Venta River. Emma always placed Papilė (which she referred to by its Yiddish name, Popelan) within Courland, perhaps to indicate her own identification with the German culture of that province and with the more westernized, assimilated, and generally cosmopolitan Courland Jews.[43] In any case, for the first seven or eight years of her life, Emma lived in this small, predominantly Jewish town. There her father managed the government-subsidized stagecoach, a position to which he was annually elected by the local inhabitants, and also ran an inn: both fairly typical occupations for Jews in that part of the Russian Empire. Emma recalled this period in the gloomiest terms. The family's large, chaotic house was cold and uncomfortable; her mother and older sisters toiled all day; officials and drunk, quarrelsome peasants crowded her father's inn. Despite the presence of Russian peasant servants and German nursemaids, she recalled spending most of her time by herself, without even dolls to comfort her in her loneliness. Only the family servants remained in memory as friendly companions, and even these were repeatedly snatched away from her by her exhausted and irritable parents. One of the German nursemaids from Königsberg, Amalia— adored by Emma—became pregnant (like several of her predecessors) and was fired by Taube. (Later Emma would insist that this incident had "cured" her of any notions that motherhood must be confined to marriage.[44]) Another servant, "Petrushka," a young peasant who supervised the Goldmans' cows and sheep, awakened the six-year-old Emma's passionate love by playing with her in the meadows near her house, entertaining her with his flute and carrying her gaily home on his shoulders. Later Emma would associate her first erotic sensations with Petrushka's games of "horse": he would throw her up into the air, catch her, and press her to him, filling her "with exultation, followed by blissful release." In her autobiography, Goldman called the loss of Petrushka, dismissed by her father after an argument, as "one of the greatest tragedies of my child-life." Dreams of Petrushka, she would write, led to a confrontation with her mother, whom she found leaning over her bed one morning tightly holding her hand and threatening to whip her "if I ever find your hand again like that. . . ."[45]

From this earliest period of her life, few other memories survived, most of them observations of a harsh, often frightening world that she later recalled in the context of her early moral education. One such memory concerned talk about the beating of peasants by Czarist officials and her own horror when one day she came upon "a half-naked human body being lashed with the knout."[46] Another involved the gathering of military officials and doctors at her father's inn to induct local youths into the army. The brutality of the officials; the anguish of the mothers desperate to keep their sons out of military slavery; her own mother's attempts, intermittently successful, to prevent the drafting of some men—all inspired in her, she would later write, a hatred of militarism and a determination to fight it. Witnessing the annual elections for stagecoach manager and her father's defeat on one occasion " 'because we are Jews, dear child, and the other man gave more vodka' " saved her, she insisted, from putting any trust in politics. She had "looked behind the scenes, so could never be deceived by the Punch and Judy show which beguiles and misleads the stupid public."[47]

At the center of Emma's retrospective self-portrait stands a lonely, unhappy waif, surrounded by "hard and cold stone cliffs," comforted only at moments by servants subject to the whims of her parents and by a beloved older half-sister who was herself little better than a galley slave. However Goldman may have exaggerated this picture, it does help account for her later sense of herself as a starving being, and for her passion to feed and mother other people, which seems to have been partly a way of giving to others what she had always longed for herself.[48] Throughout her life, she would use the imagery of hunger and thirst to describe her longing for love, sex, affection, even intellectual stimulation. "I am so starved and famished for a kindred spirit," she would write friends from prison. "You can imagine how hungrily I am looking forward to your coming." To her lover Ben Reitman, she would confess her "terrible hunger for your love, an insatiable thirst for it." "My soul, my body, my very spirit, are starved, absolutely starved for affection, devotion and care," she would plead. "Shall they perish of hunger? Or will you give them food?"[49] The deprivations of her earliest years, when "I was left to myself most of the day," seemed to leave her with so profound a sense of alienation that no amount of love or recognition could ever entirely vanquish it. Surrounded by people, she would nevertheless complain of feeling lonely. The effort to overcome this alienation— and also that of others—would become one of the defining themes of her career. Throughout her life, Goldman would struggle to fill her gnawing sense of inner emptiness—with heroes, friends, words, ideals; to melt "the ice crust over my heart and soul" that haunted her worst moments.[50]

Sometime in 1875 or 1876, when Emma was six or seven years old, her father evidently decided to send her to live with her grandmother in Königsberg so that she could attend a private Jewish elementary school. Besides the better educational opportunity, Königsberg also seemed to offer a more interesting and cosmopolitan milieu. As the capital of Prussia, Königsberg was a major Baltic seaport, connected to the coast by a deep-water channel twenty miles long that cut a broad swathe through the city. The old part of Königsberg had grown up around the thirteenth-century castle of the Teutonic knights who were its original founders. Seventeenth-century canal houses lined the channel, and a large and imposing synagogue reflected the power and prestige of the local Jewish community. Indeed, by the middle of the nineteenth century Königsberg had become, along with Berlin, a center of the Jewish Enlightenment, producing a number of distinguished rabbis, scholars, doctors, and leaders in the movement for Jewish emancipation.

For the young Emma, however, life in Königsberg seemed initially even narrower and more restricted than in Papilė. Her father had dispatched her with ominous threats of punishment, promising to come personally to Königsberg to thrash her if he should hear any complaints. Forced in her grandmother's crowded household to

1 6

share a bed with an aunt—an arrangement she hated—Emma began to miss Papilė's spaciousness and felt "stifled and alone in the world." Soon she made friends with other children at school and became less lonely. But after a month her grandmother went away, and Emma's "purgatory" began when an unscrupulous uncle decided to take her out of school and put her to work as a servant, using the school money sent by Abraham for the support of the household instead. Bullied and abused for weeks by her uncle, with her aunts too terrified to defend her, Emma finally summoned up courage, she tells us, to protest an especially unreasonable order, whereupon her uncle slapped her and kicked her down a flight of stairs. She was rescued at last by the neighbors and then by her father, who embraced and kissed her for the first time in four years and took her home.[51]

Soon afterward, however, for reasons that remain unclear, the entire family moved to Königsberg; Goldman's memoir mentions only that the parents had "lost everything" in Papilė. Emma's half sister Lena indicated, years later, that they moved because Abraham Goldman needed the baths at Königsberg for his health.[52] Emma, upon returning, again enrolled in a school—now a public school (*Volksschule*), since her parents were too poor to afford "decent" schooling for herself and her brother Herman. She managed to complete six years of school, including three-and-one-half years of *Realschule*, or high school, where the regime was harsh, the instructors brutal, and learning almost nonexistent. In retrospect, Emma recalled this experience with bitterness. Her religious instructor beat his pupils, the geography teacher sexually molested them in secret, the curriculum bored her, and the school days were enlivened only by plots hatched by the more daring pupils, of whom Emma, according to her own account, was a ringleader.

A sensitive German teacher, however—a young woman evidently suffering from tuberculosis—stood out in Emma's memory as an inspiring exception. This teacher befriended Emma, invited her to her home, and prevailed upon her friends to give Emma music and French lessons gratis. As an adult, Goldman still recalled the excitement of attending her first opera, *Il Trovatore*, with her teacher, who may also have significantly influenced her literary tastes. This woman loved the popular sentimental German romances churned out by such now-forgotten writers as Eugenie Marlitt, Berthold Auerbach, Paul Lindau, Paul Heyse, and Friedrich Spielhagen. Marlitt, Goldman recalled, was her teacher's favorite, so she also loved Marlitt; the two of them would read together "and would both grow tearful over the unhappy heroines."[53] Still, this teacher evidently encouraged Emma to prepare herself for the *Gymnasium* and took seriously her pupil's aspirations to study medicine. According to the autobiography, Goldman passed the entrance examinations for the *Gymnasium* but failed to secure the necessary certificate of good character from her religious instructor, who had announced prophetically before the class that "I was a terrible child and would grow into a worse woman. I had no respect for my elders or for authority, and I would surely end on the gallows."[54] She did not enter the *Gymnasium*.

Besides her disappointments in school, these years in Königsberg also saw a worsening of Goldman's relations with her father (though the vagueness of the memoir makes it difficult to date these events with any precision). She describes her father, frustrated by his financial insecurity, as increasingly irascible, ready to unleash his anger in bitter, often violent outbursts against his daughter. The autobiography describes an incident, for example, in which Abraham lashed Emma with a strap until stopped by her younger brother Herman, who ran up and bit his father on the calf. While Emma was comforted by her sister Helene, her father raged outside the door, threatening loudly to "kill that brat" if she would not obey. Goldman recounts another scene in which her father, enraged by a low mark for behavior on her monthly report from school, smashed her head with his fist, pounding her and pulling her about, shouting, " 'You are my disgrace! You will always be so! You can't be my child; you don't look like me or like your mother; you don't act like us!' " Once again Emma was rescued by the faithful Helene, who took some of the blows intended for Emma; Abraham eventually grew tired, dizzy, and fainted. There were also punishments in which Emma was forced to stand for hours in a corner or to walk back and forth with a glass of water in her hand, threatened with a whipping if a drop should spill: a trick she eventually mastered, but which made her ill with anxiety for hours after. Although we cannot know how representative or how realistic these memories are, Goldman clearly felt rejected and unwanted by her father. Her own feelings toward him in her childhood—and perhaps even in adulthood—were powerfully ambivalent: "I loved him even while I was afraid of him," she would write. "I wanted him to love me, but I never knew how to reach his heart. His hardness served only to make me more contrary."[55]

At some point—the date remains unclear—Abraham Goldman was evidently offered a position as manager of a cousin's dry-goods shop in St. Petersburg. He decided to accept. Leaving his wife and three children in Königsberg (he may have been accompanied by Helene), he departed for the Russian capital and, after a time, sent for the rest of the family. Emma tells us that she had not wanted to leave Königsberg, despite her unhappiness there; but since the possibility of advanced education in that city was denied her, she resigned herself to the move to St. Petersburg. Within a year, she says, it "changed my very being and the whole course of my life."[56]

CHAPTER

2

"THE DISTANT SPECTER OF REVOLUTION"

A t first, moving to St. Petersburg in the winter of 1881–1882 did not dramatically alter Emma Goldman's prospects. For Jews in the imperial capital—which had been opened to certain categories of wealthy or educated Jews only during the previous twenty years—life was apt to be harsh. The grandeur of the city—with its majestic palaces and domed churches looking out onto the Nevsky Prospekt, the main thoroughfare—contrasted sharply with the dismal one- and two-story wooden tenements housing the city's working-class residents, including most of the seventeen thousand Jews who formed about two percent of the total population in 1881. Although the St. Petersburg Jewish community was the wealthiest and most powerful in all Russia, including influential bankers, industrialists, and journalists as well as scientists, artists, and physicians, most were garment workers, shoemakers, metalworkers, or simply impoverished "luftmenschn." The beauty of St. Petersburg, its network of canals and bridges giving it the atmosphere of Amsterdam or Venice, formed for Goldman a magical setting whose treasures, for the most part, remained beyond her reach.

Soon after her arrival, Emma enrolled in a Russian high school, but withdrew after six months in order to go to work. Whether the decision was one of choice or necessity remains unclear. At times she said that she had wanted to go to work in order to become independent; her memoirs, on the other hand, state that the family's precarious financial status made it imperative for her to contribute to the family income.[1] The dry-goods shop briefly managed by her father had failed even before she had arrived in the capital; using funds borrowed from Taube's more affluent brothers, Emma's parents had then invested in a small grocery store, which at first yielded little return. Helene went to work in a photo-retouching shop. And Emma began knitting shawls at home, an occupation she hated. Later, she secured work in a glove factory owned by her father's cousin, and after that she was employed in a corset shop in the Hermitage Arcade.

Emma's memories of her "tortured adolescence" were dominated by images of her angry, abusive father hurling curses at her and beating her. As Emma tells it, her father was obsessed with the idea that she was becoming "loose": when he saw her in the Summer Garden with a mixed group of boys and girls, he became enraged and, when she arrived home, pounded her with his fists, yelling that "he would not tolerate a loose daughter." A traditional Jewish father of his time, Abraham wanted to marry her off at the age of fifteen—not usually young in that milieu. "Girls do not have to learn much!" he would shout. "All a Jewish daughter needs to know is how to prepare gefüllte fish, cut noodles fine, and give the man plenty of children." She, on the contrary, wanted "to study, to know life, to travel," and announced that she would never marry for anything but love. Emma imagined herself "stricken with some consuming disease! It would surely soften Father's heart." Outwitting him and escaping the house with her sister to attend a forbidden dance, she dreamed of dancing herself to death—"what more glorious end!" Or again, she decided to end her life by consuming "quantities of vinegar."[2]

Painful as these conflicts were, one cannot help sensing a certain pleasurable excitement in Emma's descriptions of them, as if the scenes and battles with her father—the few occasions when he actually paid attention to her—had an almost erotic intensity that she would seek to recapture in later battles, both political and personal. Hers, she would write, was a "turbulent nature, which could find expression only in the clashing of wills, in resistance and the surmounting of obstacles."[3]

From this period, Goldman's memory of being "driven to first sexual experience—horror of it" stands out in particularly sharp relief. While working at the corset factory, she and the other girls were approached as they left work each day by young Russian officers and civilians. While the other girls had "sweethearts," only she and a Jewish girlfriend resisted the men's advances. (Emma does not explain why, though religious differences may have been the reason.) A young clerk at a nearby hotel began to court her. Indifferent at first, she gradually started to respond to him and for several months they met at a local pastry shop. One day he invited her to the hotel where he worked and took her inside a large room, offering her a glass of wine. "Suddenly I found myself in his arms, my waist torn open—his passionate kisses covered my face, neck, and breasts. Not until after the violent contact of our bodies and the excruciating pain he caused me did I come to my senses. I screamed, savagely beating against the man's chest with my fists." Suddenly she heard the voice of her sister Helene in the hotel hallway, and both she and the man fell silent until Helene left. "I rose mechanically, mechanically buttoned my waist and brushed back my hair. Strange, I felt no shame —only a great shock at the discovery that the contact between man and woman could be so brutal and so painful." At home, Emma found Helene distraught. "The shame I did not feel in the arms of the man now overwhelmed me. I could not muster up the courage to tell Helena of my experience."[4]

Undoubtedly this experience deepened the ambivalence about men and sexuality that plagued Goldman throughout her life. "After that I always felt between two fires in the presence of men," she wrote many years later. "Their lure remained strong, but it was always mingled with violent revulsion. I could not bear to have them touch me."[5] Undoubtedly this episode also strengthened her determination to resist her father's marriage plans. Her unhappiness at home was already nurturing her enduring hatred of conventional family life and of the enforced intimacy of marriage. She would come to hate prolonged physical proximity—"in the same house, the same room, the same bed"—because it made her feel watched, spied upon, imprisoned, and because she associated such claustrophobic physical closeness with emotional isolation. She longed for love, but her longing would always be undercut by her fear of becoming dominated or dependent. Even as a young girl, Emma did not dream of marriage and motherhood.

But if Emma struggled without success both to win her father's love and to escape his domination, she now began the political education that would eventually transform her life. She had arrived in the Russian capital at a critical historical moment. In March of 1881, Czar Alexander II had been assassinated in St. Petersburg by members of the most powerful terrorist organization in Russia, Narodnaya Volya, or The People's Will. Emma had learned of this event in Königsberg, where she had come across a large poster announcing the death of the czar, " 'assassinated by murderous Nihilists.' " Her mother had explained that Alexander II was a "good, gracious Tsar   the first to give more freedom to the Jews." Like many Russian Jews, Taube believed that the reforms enacted by Alexander during the first years of his reign were the prelude to complete emancipation. She regarded the Nihilists as "cold-blooded murderers . . . who ought to be exterminated, every one of them!" Taube's vehemence aroused Emma's interest, and eventually she found herself sympathizing with the Nihilists, without quite knowing why. When she learned of their execution, "I no longer felt any bitterness against them. Something mysterious had awakened compassion for them in me. I wept bitterly over their fate."[6]

The revolutionists whom Emma mourned were leading figures in the Russian socialist movement known as Populism, of which The People's Will was the last terrorist manifestation. Emma always called them "Nihilists," a name originally used pejoratively by those hostile to the radical movement, but later adopted by the radicals themselves, although technically Nihilism referred to one particular element within the broader Populist movement—the rebels of the 1850s and 1860s for whom the element of personal revolt was paramount, as distinct from those who were primarily political and social radicals.

The assassination of the czar in 1881 climaxed several decades of mounting radical activity directed against the czarist autocracy. Populism had first emerged as a Russian response to the European revolutions of 1848 and was strengthened by the growing contradiction between Russia's nascent industrialization and expanding urban intelligentsia, on the one hand, and the extreme poverty of the Russian masses, on the other. All wealth and power in Russia were concentrated in the hands of a tiny landed gentry, which lived off a vast, exploited population of illiterate and impoverished peasants. Presiding over this empire of misery was the czar, whose absolute if inefficient rule was supported by a powerful secret police, a huge, chaotic bureaucracy, and the Russian Orthodox Church. In revulsion against the growing poverty and injustice around them, intellectuals such as Alexander Herzen and Nikolai Chernyshevsky—nourished by radical thought from Western Europe—began to evolve a specifically Russian version of socialism. Believing that the Russian peasants were inherently socialist in spirit, they argued that Russia could bypass capitalism in the march toward socialism, if only the enslaving institutions of autocracy could be destroyed. They called for a decentralized agrarian socialism organized around the traditional autonomous, self-governing peasant commune, with collective ownership of land, factories, and workshops; and for universal education and suffrage, complete freedom of speech and the press, sexual equality, and a democratically elected constitutional government with a high degree of regional autonomy.

From an early emphasis on self-education in loosely organized discussion circles and study groups, the Populists moved toward more organized forms of agitation and propaganda work among the peasants and workers—what they called "going to the people"—and, finally, toward highly disciplined, conspiratorial terrorism, including the destruction of property and assassination of state officials. A growing number of mass arrests in the mid-1870s had resulted in two spectacular political trials in 1877 and widespread repression, which hardened the conviction of many that only sustained violence against the state offered any hope for radical change. In January of 1878, a wave of antigovernmental terrorism began when a young woman named Vera Zasulich marched into the office of Governor-General Trepov of St. Petersburg and shot him at close range, wounding but not killing him. (This was the man whom, years earlier, according to

Emma, Taube Goldman had persuaded to free her brother from prison.) During the next three years, Narodnaya Volya carried out a series of assassination attempts against government officials and the czar himself. After several failures, the Executive Committee of that group succeeded in assassinating Czar Alexander II on March 1, 1881. The young assassins were tried and publicly executed one month later, on April 3.

The assassination of Alexander II was followed by savage reprisals and repression. Most of the revolutionists of the seventies were arrested, imprisoned, exiled to Siberia, or executed. Through mass arrests, tightened censorship, stricter control over the universities, and the elimination of newly established courses for women students, the imperial administration of Alexander III sought to crush all progressive tendencies. The Jews became particular targets. When a wave of pogroms swept southern Russian in the summer of 1881, the government tacitly supported the mob violence, encouraging the use of Jews as scapegoats for the increasing unrest within the empire. New anti-Semitic legislation—the May Laws of 1882—undid the modest gains won during the early years of Alexander II's reign and severely curtailed Jewish residency, occupational, and educational rights. This renewed persecution by the state and repeated waves of anti-Semitic violence over the next three decades drove nearly one third of all the Jews living within the Russian Empire—approximately two million people—to emigrate.

What survived during this decade of repression, however, were clandestine reading circles, which circulated forbidden radical literature and kept alive the memories of the revolutionists of the sixties and seventies. Emma, "too young to understand and grasp the theories that carried Russia's youth onward," nevertheless absorbed their spirit, "the white flame of Russian idealism," from the student friends of Helene.[7] From her Russian teacher, she learned that Governor-General Trepov was not kind and humane, as her mother had told her, but tyrannical, a monster who ordered the Cossacks to beat and arrest protesting students, who tortured prisoners and robbed and flogged the peasants. Above all, she learned during these years about the women who played important roles in the Russian revolutionary movement, and she first glimpsed the models of independence that she would gradually emulate.

Emma found one image of new womanhood in the heroine of Chernyshevsky's famous novel, *What Is to Be Done?*, which exerted a powerful influence on Russian radicals of the 1860s and after. Evading the censors and finding its way into print in 1863 (while its author was in prison), *What Is to Be Done?* tells the story of Vera Pavlovna, a young woman of the gentry whose family expected her to marry young, bear many children, and observe the rituals of her class. Instead, she yearns for independence and a life of social usefulness. Through contacts with the radical "new people"—or Nihilists—she escapes into a chaste "fictitious marriage" with an idealistic young medical student, which enables her to carry out her dream of organizing a sewing cooperative. Eventually she falls in love with the best friend of her husband; the latter, rejecting jealousy as an outmoded bourgeois obsession, graciously absents himself so that she can truly "marry" the man she loves. Content in her true marriage (her former "husband" also marries), Vera then decides to enter medical school in order to become a doctor among the poor. *What Is to Be Done?* helped to popularize among Russian youth the notions of communal living arrangements, of making "fictitious marriages" in order to free young women from their families to work or study, and of organizing cooperative enterprises. Chernyshevsky did not invent these ideas, nor that of "going to the people." But he did effectively publicize such experiments, inspiring thousands more to imitate his fictional models in real life. Moreover, the two central characters, Vera Pavlovna and Rakhmetov—the archetypal revolutionary "new man," hard but humane, wholly dedicated to the cause of helping The People—inspired many followers.

Even more important than fictional heroines were women revolutionists such as Vera Zasulich, Sophia Perovskaya, Gesia Helfman, Vera Figner, and Catherine Breshkovskaya. They "had been my inspiration ever since I had first read of their lives," Emma wrote later in her memoirs.[8] While the terrorists were not specifically feminist (the Russian feminist movement of the seventies and eighties was primarily a genteel, upper-class affair, concerned with securing access for women to higher education and elite professions), they were strongly egalitarian in practice. Women functioned at all levels of the movement, including the leadership. One of the most revered of the terrorists, Sophia Perovskaya, was among those hanged for her role in assassinating the czar; another conspirator, Gesia Helfman, was pregnant at the time of the trial and was sentenced to prison, where she died shortly thereafter. The prominence of women in the Russian revolutionary movement was an altogether unique phenomenon within the context of the nineteenth-century European Left. The movement itself was perhaps the only setting in which women were treated as equals, the vocation of revolutionary the only one that allowed women the full use of their talents.[9] Moreover, the revolutionary ethic of sacrifice for the cause appealed both to the traditional value of female self-sacrifice and to women's hunger for action, equality, and social commitment. Vera Zasulich astutely captured the complex appeal the movement held for women when she recalled her own youthful excitement as "the distant specter of revolution appeared, making me equal to a boy: I, too, could dream of 'action,' of 'exploits,' and of the 'great struggle,' . . . I too could join 'those who perished for the great cause of love.' "[10] Emma Goldman —inspired by these women, excited by the atmosphere of "revolutionary mystery" that pervaded St. Petersburg, and shocked by the anti-Semitism she observed all around her—now imagined herself as Judith, "cutting off Holofernes' head to avenge the wrongs of my people."[11]

But by the time Emma arrived in Russia, the revolutionary movement she might have joined was all but destroyed. Belief in the imminent possibilities of a major transformation of society had dissipated among the intelligentsia.[12] In this decade of disenchantment and pessimism, with the revival of the "sacred institutions of Holy Russia—the Church, the State, property and the family," Emma felt stifled and discontented; her hopes remained fantasies of revolt and revenge, unconnected to any plan of action. When, late in 1885, Helene, who was then twenty-five, arranged to leave St. Petersburg to join her sister Lena in Rochester, New York, Emma promptly decided that she would go, too. She could not bear to part from her adored Helene, and she was desperate to escape from her father. According to her autobiography, Abraham refused to let her go, even when Helene offered to pay her sister's fare. Staging a dramatic scene, Emma "pleaded, begged, wept. Finally I threatened to jump into the Neva, whereupon he yielded."[13] She and Helene secured second-class passage from Hamburg on the S.S. *Geilert*, arriving in New York on December 29, 1885.[14] They were processed through Castle Garden, where, according to Emma, "the scenes were appalling, the atmosphere charged with antagonism and harshness."[15] They arrived on New Year's Day in Rochester, the city that would become a permanent home to all the Goldman clan except for Emma herself.

CHAPTER
3

"A
GREAT
IDEAL,
A BURNING
FAITH"

For a romantic young girl filled with idealistic dreams who had grown up in the great capitals of Königsberg and St. Petersburg, Rochester was not a promising destination. Straddling the banks of the Genesee River in the middle of upstate New York, Rochester in the eighties radiated stolid conservatism and civic pride. The flour mills and plant nurseries that had dominated the city's economic life in the earlier part of the century were giving way to clothing and shoe manufacturing establishments, as well as to such industries as optics and photography. By the 1870s, a community of German Jews had become relatively prosperous in this city of predominantly Irish, German, and English immigrants, and had come to control the expanding garment industry, which was by now the largest and most important in the city. At first the German Jews welcomed the East European Jews who began arriving in the eighties, seeing them as sources of cheap skilled and unskilled labor.

By the late eighties, however, the new arrivals who continued to pour into the city—many of them refugees from the pogroms—were received with less enthusiasm by the German Jews, who feared a threat to their own recently secured social position. For these newly arrived immigrants, living and working conditions in the congested downtown Jewish district were grim: three or four families plus a shop were crowded into each of the one-and-a-half-story houses that lined gloomy streets unrelieved by sunlight or patches of garden. The limited social and cultural life available to the Jews of this provincial world centered around the synagogue, the fraternal or charitable organization, and various clubs. After the splendors and the mysteries of St. Petersburg, Rochester on the Genesee was crushingly dull.

In her autobiography, Goldman narrates the story of her entry into this barren new world. She boarded with her sister Lena, who was now married to Samuel Cominsky, a Russian Jewish roofer and tinsmith, and who was expecting her first child. Emma sewed overcoats for ten and a half hours daily, earning two dollars and fifty cents a week, in the factory of Leopold Garson, a prominent German Jewish manufacturer and philanthropist who nevertheless rigidly controlled his employees and refused Goldman's request for a raise. Disgusted, Emma decided to leave Garson's for the smaller, less pressured shop of a Mr. Rubenstein, where she met a fellow immigrant, Jacob Kersner. Kersner, a few years older than Goldman, belonged to an aristocratic Russian Jewish family that had been driven out of Odessa by the pogroms. Well educated, he had completed the gymnasium in Russia in preparation for the university when his family was forced to emigrate. In America, like many immigrants, he had had to take up work as a tailor, though for a time at least, he maintained his intellectual interests and may even have had leanings toward radical politics as well. Feeling lonely, bored, and restless, attracted by Kersner's intellectual bent and by his Russian, Emma decided, she tells us, to marry him.[1]

Another event may have helped to precipitate this decision. In the fall of 1886, as a result of growing anti-Semitic persecution and harassment of the Jews in Russia, Taube and Abraham Goldman decided to follow their daughters to America. They arrived in Rochester—accompanied by their sons, Abraham's mother Freda, and one or more of his sisters—probably in September of 1886, just nine months after Emma and Helene. Emma had left St. Petersburg partly to escape the authority of her father and her claustrophobic household. The arrival of her family, which again reduced her to the status of a mere daughter, may have intensified her desire to marry as a way of maintaining her independence. Indeed, Goldman wrote in her autobiography that even before the wedding she had become disillusioned with Kersner, whom she had discovered to be more commonplace and less intellectual than she had imagined. Still, she decided to go through with it, and in either November of 1886 (Lena's date) or February of 1887 (Emma's date), she and Kersner were married by Rabbi Kalmon Bardin according to Orthodox Jewish ritual.[2]

Thirty years later, Goldman still recalled the great disappointment of her wedding night. Her husband was impotent, and her own desire was mixed with a dread of being touched. Her autobiographical account puts the blame for the failure of the marriage squarely on her husband, whom she depicts with no trace of sympathy. He was weak, obsessed with card games, and conventional to boot, insisting that his wife quit work, since it was "disgraceful" for a married woman to work outside the home. Later, when Emma tried to leave, he threatened suicide to force her to return to him. In 1893 Kersner was sentenced to three years in Auburn Prison on charges of grand larceny. Eventually he would change his name and disappear into the industrial wilds of Chicago, where he died in 1919.[3] Unhappy in her marriage almost from the start, dismayed by the harshness of life in America, still filled with memories of the revolutionary Russia she had known only through books, Emma was "saved from utter despair by my interest in the Haymarket events," which she began to follow avidly in the newspapers.[4]

The Haymarket drama unfolded in Chicago, the mostly highly industrialized American city of the mid-eighties, at the height of the campaign for the eight-hour workday and at a moment of mounting labor and radical militancy. The first year of Goldman's American residence, 1886, "witnessed a more profound and far more extended agitation among the members of organized labor than any previous year in our history," concluded one contemporary report.[5] The sources of sharpening class conflict lay in the dramatic changes in American society that had occurred since the Civil War as industrial productivity soared, manufacturing intensified, and huge corporations began to dominate economic and political life. By the turn of the century the names would be familiar: Rockefeller, Carnegie, Vanderbilt, Gould, Morgan, Huntington, Crocker—to cite but a few. Yet while these families acquired huge fortunes and built palatial mansions on Fifth Avenue or Lakeshore Drive, more and more workers found themselves barely scraping together a living from ten, twelve, or fourteen hours' daily labor. Despite billowing increases in the national wealth, poverty in the America of the "Gilded Age" was becoming increasingly visible and widespread, particularly in the dismal Eastern mining and mill towns and congested cities where tenement-filled slums festered and spread. In 1890, about one percent of all families earned twenty-five percent of the national income, while fifty percent of the families earned less than twenty percent of the national income. Not only low wages and an unequal distribution of wealth but also irregular employment and spells of unemployment plagued many workers. In the mid-eighties, the average worker was idle about one-quarter of all possible working time during the year, while unemployment soared from about one million in 1885 to as high as two million in 1886.

Intensifying and complicating the industrial situation was the rising tide of immigration—five and one-quarter million people arrived in the 1880s, three and three-quarters million in the 1890s. To the American-born and those who had arrived earlier—mainly Protestants from northern and western Europe—these newcomers, mostly Jews and Catholics from southern and eastern Europe, appeared strange and alien. They huddled by necessity as well as choice in the ghettoes of Boston, Pittsburgh, or New York, or in mill towns such as Paterson, New Jersey, and Lawrence, Massachusetts. They took whatever jobs they could find, usually the least-skilled, lowest-paying, most soul-destroying ones, and they transferred their own cherished dreams of education and advancement to their children while they themselves struggled to survive. Often they became the scapegoats for mounting industrial strife, blamed for importing "alien" radical doctrines into America and thereby stirring workers to unwarranted protest.

As workers began to organize into the National Labor Union, the Knights of Labor (1869), and later the American Federation of Labor (1881), employers increasingly mobilized the authority of the police and the courts, which defended their interests against those of the workers in most disputes. Union membership was grounds for instant dismissal from a job; the blacklist and the "iron-clad oath" were used to isolate union activists and frighten employees away from unions. While the courts increasingly used the injunction against strikers and punished the boycott as conspiracy in restraint of trade, employers were allowed to hire private police forces like the Pinkertons and in general to use state and federal militia to discredit and smash strikes.

While the majority of immigrants were conservative, deeply attached to the religious and ethnic traditions from which they had come, a few did indeed bring with them European revolutionary ideas, for which they continued to agitate in this country. Despite their small numbers, they were highly visible both in the labor movement and in the Left. With its large working-class immigrant population, many of whom were German, Chicago by 1885 had become the center both of a militant workers' movement and of a revolutionary movement with strong labor connections. The latter boasted about three thousand members and five newspapers, and agitated vigorously for the use of terrorism against capitalism and the state. In the atmosphere of the 1870s and 1880s, when strikes were suppressed with extreme police brutality and labor and socialist candidates for political office were frequently victims of electoral fraud, the call for violent and extralegal tactics by workers gained a small but vocal following. In Chicago, the leading social revolutionaries, as they called themselves, differed in their political views: while Albert Parsons, editor of the influential *Alarm*, and August Spies, editor of the *Arbeiter Zeitung*, accepted in 1885 that elections were useful in educating workers about their rights, others, such as Samuel Fielden, rejected any participation in electoral politics. But all the Chicago radicals opposed the wage system and the state power that upheld it; and nearly all defended, in speeches, pamphlets and the radical press, the use of arms and explosives.

Until about 1886, their rhetoric of violence was not taken too seriously by the press. But in that year the emergence of a powerful national movement for the eight-hour workday began to increase tensions in the city. As the movement was gradually endorsed by growing numbers of unions around the country, the American Federation of Labor set May 1, 1886, as the date initiating the eight-hour day. Long before that, workers in many plants began negotiating with employers for the change. Indeed, the eight-hour day was won in many plants without the necessity for a strike, but thousands of workers unable to secure this demand prepared to walk out. Tension deepened in Chicago, the center of the agitation, as May 1 approached. Both police and employers expected trouble, but when it came, it stemmed from an incident entirely unrelated to the eight-hour campaign.

Early in February, a dispute at the McCormick Harvester Company over the discharge of several workers engaged in union activities resulted in a lockout; the plant was shut down. Workers declared a strike, and Pinkerton operatives were called in to protect strikebreakers hired early in March. However, things remained calm. May 1 came and went with no troubles reported anywhere in the city. But on May 3 a clash broke out among the striking McCormick workers, scabs who were leaving the plant at the end of the day, and nearby police. One striker was killed and an undetermined number injured. A meeting was called for the evening of May 4 at Haymarket Square to protest the police action. The organizers and the speakers at the meeting, active social revolutionaries, included Albert Parsons, August Spies, and Samuel Fielden. A slight drizzle fell the night of the meeting, and the turnout was smaller than anticipated. Still, from the wagon which served as a speakers' platform, the organizers spoke in English and in German, protesting the events of the previous day but not calling for any specific acts of reprisal. The mayor, Carter Harrison, who had generally taken a fairly tolerant stand toward the activities of the radicals in his city, appeared briefly; observing no disturbances, he left, stopping by the police station to say that no action would be necessary. All at once, in Haymarket Square, a battalion of some one hundred eighty police appeared. To the police command that the meeting disperse immediately, the speakers replied that they would finish, then leave. Suddenly a bomb exploded in the midst of the police, killing seven officers and wounding about seventy others. In panic, the police opened fire, killing and wounding an undetermined number of spectators.

At once, all radicals in Chicago, particularly the foreign-born, became the target of a virtual reign of terror. Known socialists and anarchists, as well as many labor activists, were hunted down, arrested, grilled, and sometimes tortured by police eager to uncover a vast underground conspiracy. Revolutionists of all stripes were damned in the press as vipers, serpents, fanatics, and monsters. Ultimately, eight men stood trial for the bombing, in an atmosphere of anti-anarchist and antiforeign hysteria. The prosecution did not even attempt to prove the guilt of the defendants in actually throwing the bomb; only two of the accused had been present at the Haymarket when it exploded. Instead, the men were tried for their revolutionary ideas; by continually urging the use of dynamite and explosives in their speeches and papers, they were, alleged the prosecution, indirectly responsible for the Haymarket bombing and therefore legally culpable. With a blatantly biased judge and a jury handpicked for its conservative, antilabor views, the defendants were found guilty. Three were sentenced to prison terms ranging from fifteen years to life; one, Louis Lingg—the most ardent advocate of violence, who was actually engaged in making bombs—committed suicide in prison. Four men—Albert Parsons, Adolph Fischer, August Spies, and George Engel—were hanged on November 11, 1887. The person who actually threw the bomb has never been identified.[6]

In Rochester, Emma Goldman anxiously followed the events of the Haymarket case in the local newspapers, which were filled with denunciations of the Chicago anarchists, as all were called in the press. A tremendous amount of public attention was focused on the Chicago defendants—and on anarchism—throughout the trial. Their speeches in court, the stories of their lives, and the details of their deaths were all reported at extravagant length. Soon Emma and Helene began attending socialist meetings in downtown Rochester— meetings that Emma found "dull" and "colorless" until one night she heard a well-known German socialist speaker, Johanna Greie, defend the Haymarket men in a presentation dramatically different from the hostile accounts in the daily press. Greie convinced Emma of what she had surmised all along: the Haymarket defendants were innocent. Around this time, too, according to her autobiography (elsewhere she said it was after she had left Rochester), she began reading the militant anarchist newspaper, *Die Freiheit*, published in New York by Johann Most, and hungrily devoured "every line on anarchism I could get, every word about the men, their lives, their work. I read about their heroic stand while on trial and their marvelous defence. I saw a new world opening before me." The executions on November 11, 1887, were the final influence "that crystallized my views . . . and made me an active Anarchist."[7]

Many years later (no contemporary accounts have survived), Emma spoke of her conversion to anarchism not as an active, reasoned choice, but rather as an epiphany. It had come to her during sleep, like a call from God or fate or destiny. And it was a call she was prepared to hear. Her emotional description of her feelings on the night of the Haymarket executions may have exaggerated the suddenness of her conversion for dramatic effect. The events of the day had thrust her into "a stupor; a feeling of numbness came over me, something too horrible even for tears." At her father's house that evening, she had paid no attention to the conversation of her elders until she heard a visiting relative sneer in a shrill voice: " 'What's all this lament about? The men were murderers. It is well they were hanged.' With one leap I was at the woman's throat. Then I felt myself torn back. Someone said, 'The child has gone crazy.' I wrenched myself free, grabbed a pitcher of water from a table, and threw it with all my force into the woman's face. 'Out, out!' I cried, 'or I will kill you!' " The terrified woman left, and Emma "dropped to the ground in a fit of crying." She was put to bed, fell into a deep sleep, and awakened the next morning "as from a long illness, but free from the numbness and the depression of those harrowing weeks of waiting, ending with the final shock. I had the distinct sensation that something new and wonderful had been born in my soul. A great ideal, a burning faith, a determination to dedicate myself to the memory of my martyred comrades, to make their cause my own, to make known to the world their beautiful lives and heroic deaths."[8]

Perhaps the eighteen-year-old Emma had fallen a little in love with these Haymarket men. Clearly she felt deeply the injustice done to them; clearly she admired their courage and conviction. But neither her outrage nor her admiration alone explain her conversion to anarchism, since these feelings were shared by many who did not become anarchists. Like any deep commitment, hers was strongly overdetermined, deriving its strength from many sources. She identified intensely with the Chicago radicals. She, too, had felt persecuted by unjust authority and had dreamed of becoming an avenger, like Judith. She, too, was a German-speaking immigrant, part of the exploited working class for whom they spoke. Disappointed and angry at the harsh realities of American life, she responded eagerly to their politics of revolt; their defense of "force" resonated with her own fantasies of "cutting off Holofernes' head." Their lives and deaths, moreover, must have recalled those of the revolutionists whom she had admired in St. Petersburg. To Emma, recently arrived from Russia and filled with memories of pogroms and political trials, the Haymarket events must have seemed all too familiar. She could easily conclude that republican America precisely resembled czarist Russia, that in both "the keynote of government is injustice."[9] And as if in answer to her dashed hopes and disappointments, she now discovered a revolutionary movement in which she could translate her anger and her newly acquired ideals into action.

Goldman's descriptions of this event suggest that the martyrdom of the Haymarket men—the persecution they suffered and their deaths on the gallows—was also an important part of their appeal. For Goldman, becoming an anarchist meant embracing a kind of martyrdom—hostility, persecution, possibly death—even while fighting against it. The very outrage aroused by the word *anarchist* seemed to enhance its appeal for her, as if, by becoming an anarchist, she could fulfill the bitter prophecies hurled at her by her father, yet prove that anarchists were not criminals but idealists. In anarchism Goldman seemed to seek some fulfillment of her adolescent fantasies of suffering and sacrifice, of earning her father's love through her own pain, while living out her active and even violent dreams of becoming an avenging Judith. Years later Goldman seemed to acknowledge this aspect of the movement's attraction for her when she observed that "if nothing else would speak for anarchism, the martyrs it gave to the World would be its justification and its beauty."[10]

Goldman also wanted, like Johanna Greie or her Russian revolutionary heroines, to play a starring role on a worldwide stage, to participate in dramatic events that attracted the world's attention. Socialism did not offer Emma such a stage, for it seemed to her "generally uninteresting," too "colourless and mechanistic." Anarchism, on the other hand, with its scenario of villains and heroes, its rhetoric "shooting forth flames of ridicule, scorn and defiance," appealed to her love of theater as well as of justice. The vivid, violent language of Most's paper, *Die Freiheit*, "fairly took my breath away." Here was the exciting drama she had long been seeking.[11] By her own account, Goldman's initial attraction to anarchism was deeply emotional. "I felt more than I thought," she admitted in 1901. "I was an Anarchist from sentiment, not from reason."[12] Though she later acquired a thorough knowledge of anarchist history and ideas, she was always frankly less interested in abstract theory—"Just mere theories do not move me," she would say—than in the claims of her own feelings, which were deeply engaged by the Haymarket drama. "It is not enough to grasp our ideas," she would insist later in her life. "It is necessary to feel them in every fiber like a flame, a consuming fever, an elemental passion."[13]

Had Haymarket never occurred, Emma Goldman would no doubt have found her way eventually into the anarchist movement. But this one dramatic event acted as a catalyst, galvanizing her imagination and propelling her directly toward the movement to which she would dedicate her life. Indeed, although the Haymarket affair intensified the popular stereotype of the anarchist as a wild-eyed terrorist and weakened existing links between anarchism and the labor movement, the Chicago events also stimulated widespread discussion of revolutionary ideas and may even have acted as a stimulus to radicalism in general.[14] Far more workers and intellectuals would be drawn to the socialist unions and the Socialist Party than to anarchism during the next three decades, but the anti-anarchist hysteria stirred up by Haymarket by no means destroyed the anarchist movement; it continued with unabated vitality, albeit on a small scale, until World War I. For Emma Goldman, paradoxically, the Haymarket events were tremendously liberating. Soon after the executions, she divorced her husband and left Rochester for New Haven, where she worked briefly in a corset factory and met local anarchists and socialists. Exhausted and strained by work—and perhaps also by her continuing inner struggle to free herself from her family—she returned to Rochester, this time to the home of Helene. Kersner found her and threatened suicide, she later reported, if she would not remarry him. She did, but the marriage again failed. Finally, she left for good.

After her departure, Emma and her family moved in quite different directions—although by no means destroying the ties between them. In her youth, she tended to identify her family as "well-to-do"; later in her life, she emphasized their poverty and frustrations: her father, she wrote in her memoirs, was "one of the mass of the exploited and enslaved for whom I was living and working."[15] In truth, though not wealthy, within the Rochester Jewish community the Goldman clan was a respected family of small business people, professionals, and skilled workers whose members shared the energy, talent, and strong cultural interests of Emma herself. Taube Goldman in particular was an influential figure in Jewish charity and philanthropic work: a president of the Hebrew Ladies' Relief Society, which aided indigent East European immigrants; a founder of the Bikur Cholim Society, a group of women who raised money for a Jewish Home for the Aged; a vice-president of the Jewish Children's Home, which opened in 1914; and an active participant in the Associated Hebrew Charities. Taube Goldman's death in 1923 was observed in an admiring obituary in the *New York Times* and by one of the largest Orthodox Jewish funeral processions to take place in Rochester.[16] Abraham Goldman's furniture store was rather successful, and he enjoyed an excellent reputation in the Rochester business community. When he died in 1909, he left an estate of $3,500, a considerable sum for that time.[17]

Helene and her husband, Jacob Hochstein, who had been a teacher in his native Minsk and whom Emma described as a talented scholar and musician but a poor businessman, owned a printshop and later opened the first steamship agency in Rochester, which eventually became quite successful. Hochstein remained an intellectual and an idealist. He had radical sympathies and played an active role in the Rochester branch of the socialist Workmen's Circle. He and Helene had frequent gatherings of friends to discuss books, exchange ideas, and listen to music played by Hochstein, himself a gifted violinist, and their children, whose musical education he encouraged. One son, David, began a promising career as a violinist, achieving international recognition at an early age before he was killed in action during World War I at the age of twenty-six.[18]

Lena and her husband, Samuel Cominsky, sent all six of their children to college. A son, Saxe Commins, became one of the most distinguished editors in American publishing; a friend and editor of Eugene O'Neill, William Faulkner, and Sinclair Lewis, among others, he was editor-in-chief at Random House for many years.[19] A grandson, Ian Ballantine, was an early promoter of mass paperbacks in America, opening the first American office of Penguin Books in 1939, helping to found Bantam Books six years later, and starting

Ballantine Books in 1952. Among the descendants of Taube and Abraham Goldman were many professionals and intellectuals: doctors, nurses, teachers, editors, publishers, scientists, and musicians.

While Emma Goldman continued to define herself in opposition to her family after she left Rochester—"I never realize the abyss between their lives and mine as much as I do when I come face to face with them" she complained—her relations with them grew closer over the years. She remained distant from her brother Herman, who advanced from the position of machinist to that of superintendent in the Willsea Works in Rochester, a company that made and repaired highly specialized machinery. But she kept in close contact with both sisters and with her baby brother Moishe, who graduated from Columbia University's College of Physicians and Surgeons. And while she developed affectionate ties to a wide circle of nephews and nieces, one especially beloved niece, Lena's daughter Stella, would become a kind of daughter to Emma herself, working as assistant, agent, and secretary to Emma before and during World War I. Goldman's difficult relations with her father were never wholly resolved, but she would eventually boast of her family's clannishness, calling them "not merely blood relations [but] friends who have stood by me through every difficulty. And the devotion they have given me is beyond anything words can describe. . . ."[20]

When she left Rochester in the summer of 1889, however, such thoughts must have been far from her mind as she imagined with excitement the heroic new world awaiting her. Now she was going to live like Vera Pavlovna, "to do what I like, live as I like, without asking anyone's advice, without feeling the need of it."[21] She would follow her Russian heroines Vera Zasulich and Sophia Perovskaya; she, too, would "go to the people" and dedicate her life to a great cause. At the age of twenty—no longer so young by the standards of her world—she had finally escaped the family claim.

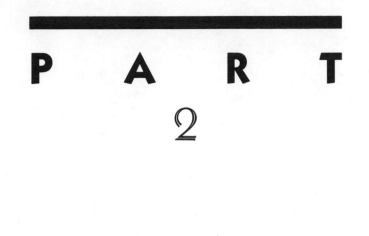

PART

2

INTO
THE
MOVEMENT

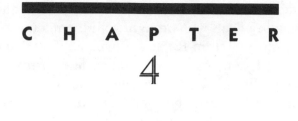

CHAPTER
4

EDUCATION
OF
AN
ANARCHIST

E mma Goldman arrived in New York on a steamy day in August of 1889, carrying her sewing machine, five dollars, and a handbag containing three addresses: those of her aunt and uncle (who ran a photographic studio at 45 Canal Street), a friend, and the office of Johann Most's *Freiheit*. Leaving her past behind, "cast off like a worn-out garment," the twenty-year-old Goldman briskly faced a new world armed with "youth, good health, and a passionate ideal. Whatever the new held in store for me I was determined to meet unflinchingly."[1]

Briefly disheartened by the unfriendly reception of her relatives, she rented a room of her own on Suffolk Street and plunged into the life of Manhattan's Jewish immigrant district on the Lower East Side. Formerly a German neighborhood, the East Side now drew impoverished Jewish workers from the *shtetlakh* and cities of Eastern Europe, bewildered refugees from Russian pogroms, and displaced intellectuals and radicals who brought with them a reverence for the revolutionary movement in Russia. If living and working conditions in the decaying tenements were crowded and dismal, the streets, cafés, and theaters bustled with intensity. Indeed, not only European emigré intellectuals but also the American-born were attracted to the vibrant cultural life of the Lower East Side, which became, writes one historian, "a kind of Left Bank, whose ad hoc university was scattered through the various tenement assembly rooms in which lectures and meetings were forever taking place."[2]

During the eighties and the nineties—the first two decades of mass Jewish migration from Eastern Europe—most efforts to organize the swelling immigrant working class met with disappointment and frustration, despite hard-fought strikes and the widespread attraction of socialist and anarchist ideas. Still reeling from the shock of migration, too exhausted to attend meetings, most immigrants were too overwhelmed by the effort to survive to engage in political work, even within the immigrant world. A growing minority, however, became increasingly politicized. Many were radicalized by their first contact with the harsh conditions of city sweatshops and slums in the United States. Some who had been involved in the Russian revolutionary movement and later in specifically Jewish radical movements like the Bund would become leaders in the anarchist, socialist, and labor movements in America. At the time of Goldman's arrival in New York, the distinctions between anarchists and socialists were not strictly drawn, and all radicals—who constituted a tiny fraction of the immigrant community—cooperated during strikes and protests.

The anarchist movement at this time was shifting from the predominantly German immigrant membership of the eighties to the largely East European Jewish membership of the nineties and after. The classical organizational form of anarchism was the small propaganda group dedicated to spreading anarchist ideas through lectures and the publication of newspapers and pamphlets. Industrial centers such as Paterson, Buffalo, and Pittsburgh all had active anarchist circles. New York boasted several such groups—the Jewish Pioneers of Liberty (later called the Knights of Freedom), the Autonomie group around the influential Austrian journalist Joseph Peukert, and the rival *Freiheit* group around Johann Most. While working in a corset factory and later doing piecework at home, Emma joined the

Freiheit group, determined, she said later, to study, "to make passion bow to wisdom."[3] She immersed herself in anarchist literature and history, eagerly devouring the radical periodicals from Europe that piled up in the *Freiheit* office on William Street and learning both from personal contacts and from her reading the theoretical basis of the politics to which she would devote her life.

Anarchism in America was made up of two major strands. The individualist strand, of predominantly native origin, rejected government authority but accepted private property, exalting the claims of the untrammeled individual. The collectivist strand, of primarily immigrant origin, rejected both government and private property, calling for various forms of stateless socialism. The essential anarchist idea, that is, hostility to government authority, had found expression in the lives and writings of a wide variety of Americans—from the dissenters of colonial New England to nineteenth-century individualists such as Josiah Warren and Steven Pearl Andrews and writers such as Emerson, Thoreau, and Whitman. But an organized revolutionary anarchist movement having strong connections with labor had emerged in the United States only in the 1870s, with a largely immigrant membership and intellectual origins in Europe.

The European anarchist movement had emerged partly out of a struggle within the First International between the followers of Marx, on the one hand, and those of the French printer-propagandist Pierre-Joseph Proudhon and his successor, the Russian revolutionist Michael Bakunin, on the other. The anarchist followers of Proudhon and Bakunin shared the Marxist opposition to capitalism, but held sharply different convictions about revolutionary strategy and tactics. Instead of a highly centralized revolutionary movement aimed at building mass political parties, the anarchists called for a decentralized movement of relatively small, militant, semiautonomous groups. Rather than trying to capture state power, these groups would aim to destroy it. Bitterly opposed to any participation in parliamentary politics, the anarchists during the 1870s and 1880s urged a vigorous propaganda of word and deed, including insurrectionary tactics by secret conspiratorial groups and individual acts of revolt—destruction of property and even assassination—to dramatize social evils and galvanize the masses. While both Marxists and anarchists aimed ultimately at a stateless socialist society, Marxists insisted on the need for a transitional period of expanded state control, while the anarchists envisioned the immediate implementation of stateless socialism.

There were further theoretical disagreements. Bakunin envisaged the earliest social revolutions, not in the highly industrialized countries, as Marx had predicted, but in the more backward peasant societies. While Marx stressed the revolutionary role of the industrial workers, Bakunin emphasized that of the peasants, the students, the "lumpenproletariat" scorned by Marx, and even, to some extent, the intellectuals, despite Bakunin's deep distrust of all experts in power. Against the Marxists' insistence on the determining role of objective conditions in shaping consciousness, anarchists emphasized the power of consciousness—of ideas and will—in changing material conditions.

Bakunin himself appeared to many as the very embodiment of revolutionary will. A physically massive, Wagnerian figure of volcanic, contradictory passions, with the aristocrat's bonhomie and a fund of enormous energy, Bakunin swept through Europe in the 1860s and 1870s, rushing from one barricade to the next, celebrating in his life and his work a mystique of action for its own sake that at times degenerated into romantic paeans to violence and apocalyptic destruction. Enamored of science yet distrustful of all rigid theoretical systems, Bakunin insisted that the role of the revolutionist was primarily to lead people to revolt; once they had thrown off oppressive state power, they would invent their own socialist forms of cooperation and organization. Goldman greatly admired Bakunin the man; she thought he "towered mountain-high over Marx who was after all hopelessly middle-class, the typical German professor who knew a lot about books but absolutely nothing about life. With Bakunin it was just the reverse."[4]

In the United States, the spirit of Bakunin prevailed during the 1880s among those radicals, predominantly German immigrants, who were moving away from the parliamentary politics of the Socialist Labor party (SLP) in the direction of anarchism. Some members of the SLP grew increasingly impatient with tactics they regarded as hopelessly ineffective. These dissidents began in 1880 to form Social Revolutionary clubs, first in New York, later in Chicago, Pittsburgh, and elsewhere, affiliated with the Bakuninist International Working People's Association (organized in opposition to the Marxist International Workingmen's Association). Members of these clubs also began organizing armed workers' groups as an instrument of self-defense for labor. Although the members of the Social Revolutionary clubs and of the armed groups were at first very far from any sense of unified purpose, they generally shared a disgust with the reformism of the Socialist Labor party and favored Bakuninist ideas of insurrection and armed struggle—tactics the SLP vehemently opposed.

By the time Emma Goldman entered the anarchist movement in 1889, the influence of Bakunin was beginning to give way to that of Peter Kropotkin. The most distinguished theorist of communist anarchism, he would soon dominate the thinking of the movement in America. A more scholarly and elegant writer than the unsystematic Bakunin, whose insights emerged in brilliant aphorisms and scattered fragments, Kropotkin wrote numerous articles, which reached the United States during the 1890s in such journals as *La Revolte*, *The Nineteenth Century*, and *Freedom*; many were later collected in his books, including *The Conquest of Bread*; *Fields, Factories and Workshops*; *Mutual Aid*; and *The Memoirs of a Revolutionist*. In contrast with Bakunin's fascination with violence and destruction, Kropotkin, possessed of a benign, almost saintly character, emphasized throughout his life the constructive, creative possibilities of anarchism. Kropotkin trained as a geographer, and his early scientific work took him to remote villages in Siberia; his admiration for the independence of the people he encountered and his observations of the damage caused by administrators imposed from St. Petersburg helped shape his later vision of the autonomous, self-governing anarchist commune. While Bakunin had envisaged a society of collectives in which people would be compensated according to the work they performed, Kropotkin's more utopian vision foresaw a society of residential communes loosely federated together, in which people would be compensated simply according to need. Such a society would be based strictly on the principle of voluntary cooperation, although critics have noted that while opposing formal law, Kropotkin was willing to admit the covertly coercive power of public opinion and informal group pressure as a form of social control in an anarchist world.[5] As a scientist, however, Kropotkin was convinced of the inherent human drive for cooperation and strove to prove that anarchism was based on science as well as idealism. He argued eloquently against the prevailing notions of Social Darwinism that attempted to justify cutthroat competition as biologically adaptive. Instead, Kropotkin insisted that a spirit of cooperation and "mutual aid" was equally important to evolution and progress; there was no inherent conflict between the individual and society, since human beings were naturally social and rational beings. Anarchism, then, aimed for "the most complete development of individuality combined with the highest development of voluntary association in all its aspects, in all possible degrees, for all imaginable aims."[6]

Emma Goldman would always publicly identify Kropotkin as her principal teacher; privately, however, she was more critical of what she regarded as his naïveté and discounted his influence on her thinking. Kropotkin, she said once, had lived "mostly a book life and has little knowledge of the World or people. That's how he managed to retain his idealism, his faith in the people." Though Goldman met Kropotkin several times and corresponded with him, she felt he did not like her and thought her too " 'loose.' I guess I have never made much fuss of him, have gone my own way and developed on independent lines."[7] While Goldman accepted Kropotkin's vision of communist anarchism, she did not share his reverence for "the people." She was, moreover, always more interested in the "spirit of revolt" than in the forms of a future utopia, more impelled to criticize the present than to imagine the future, less interested in science and more interested in sex than was her mentor.

Soon after she entered the anarchist movement, in fact, Goldman was drawn to the critiques of sexual repression that helped shape the strong emphasis on personal liberation characteristic of her politics. At first she drew her ideas about sex from European sources: from Chernyshevsky's version of woman's emancipation in *What Is to Be Done?* and from Freud, whose lectures she would attend in Vienna in 1896. At this time Freud was a young neurologist just beginning the investigations that marked the birth of psychoanalysis. *Studies in Hysteria* was published the year before, and Goldman later wrote that Freud's lectures made clear to her for the first time "the full significance of sex repression and its effects on human thought and action." Subsequently, she discovered the ideas of English sex theorists such as Edward Carpenter, author of the popular *Love's Coming of Age*, first published in England in 1896, and Havelock Ellis, whose *Studies in the Psychology of Sex* began appearing in 1897. These

4 8

English "sexual modernists" celebrated the pleasures of sex apart from procreation and called for a freer, less rigidly heterosexual morality: ideas which Emma embraced with enthusiasm.[8]

By the late nineties, she had also discovered the American "free lovers," whose views were presented most articulately in the weekly *Lucifer the Lightbearer*. This paper was published from the early eighties until 1907, first in Kansas, later in Chicago, by the former Congregational minister Moses Harman and his daughter Lillian, whom Goldman met in 1897. Inspired partly by nineteenth-century utopian and communitarian ideas, the free lovers were small groups of outspoken critics of repressive Victorian sexual values who began in the 1870s to campaign for freer, more tolerant attitudes toward sex. Far from the wild proponents of promiscuity and license they were often thought to be, the free lovers were in fact extremely conscientious advocates of a new morality unregulated by church or state. They urged that, liberated from such "invasive influences," sexuality would return to a "natural" state of self-regulation, free from both the excesses and the inhibitions generated by external controls. Though they opposed legal and religious marriage on principle, they saw freedom as a way to "purify" sex by bringing it under the control of reason. Drawing feminist connections between "sex slavery" and "wage slavery," they urged greater autonomy for women, including "voluntary motherhood," though not necessarily mechanical contraception. Despite their Victorian preoccupation with self-control, they did move toward a greater acceptance of female sexuality. To discuss such issues in print in the 1870s and after, however, often meant direct confrontation with the Comstock Law. This law—a sweeping collection of statutes passed in 1873 in response to pressure from Anthony Comstock, powerful head of the New York Society for the Suppression of Vice—virtually outlawed all frank public discussions of sex, as well as all abortion and contraceptive devices and information, on the grounds that they were indecent, immoral, and obscene. Thus free speech became an urgent concern for the free lovers, some of whom suffered barbarous treatment—repeated legal harassment and imprisonment—for their efforts.[9]

Goldman also found strong support for the idea of personal rebellion in Max Stirner's *The Ego and His Own*, a book first published in Germany in 1844, which circulated widely during the 1890s. At its

4 9

best, this work boldly attacked conventional morality and psychological repression, damning the "spooks"—religious commands and prohibitions, sexual taboos, ideas of obedience to family and state—that served to alienate people from their feelings. For Stirner, as later for Goldman, it was not the institutionalized embodiments of authority so much as the idea of authority—belief in the legitimacy of power—that perpetuated injustice and lack of freedom. Celebrating the free, uninhibited, self-sufficient individual—the "egoist"—Stirner anticipated Nietzsche in declaring the death of God and calling for a society of powerful, self-sufficient personalities, cooperating minimally in pursuit of mutual self-interest.[10]

Later Goldman was ecstatic to discover, in Vienna in 1895, the writings of Nietzsche, which she would often quote in her letters and lectures. Indeed, in the years before World War I, when the Nietzschean idea of the superman had become highly controversial, she would defend his thought in her speeches and publish frequent excerpts in her magazine. There was much in his writings resonant with anarchism—his hatred of the state and religion, his reversals of conventional morality and calls for a revaluation of values, his attacks on all fixed, rigid, theoretical systems. Yet Kropotkin despised him as "a philosopher in carpet slippers" and regarded his individualism as that of the "bourgeois who can exist only on condition of the oppression of the masses. . . ."[11] Goldman, however, was attracted by the individualist strand in Nietzschean thought. She, too, admired the strong, heroic, nonconformist individual and was capable of Nietzschean tirades against "the rabble" and the "common herd" that at times appeared to undercut her defense of labor. She would later scornfully dismiss the "shallow interpreters of that giant mind" who criticized Nietzsche as a hater of the weak while ignoring the fact that he "also called for a state of society which will not give birth to a race of weaklings and slaves." In her memoirs she would insist that Nietzsche's aristocracy was "of the spirit" and that he was therefore an "anarchist, and all true anarchists were aristocrats."[12]

Both Stirner and Nietzsche remained controversial figures among the Kropotkinite anarchists. The individualist wing of the movement, however, enthusiastically claimed Max Stirner as the prophet of a new society of "egoists." By the nineties, individualist anarchism in the United States found its most influential voice in the weekly *Liberty*, published by the Bostonian Benjamin J. Tucker for nearly three decades. Sharing the communist anarchists' opposition to government, voting, and electoral politics, the individualists nevertheless accepted the institution of private ownership while decrying its abuses, tending to look backward in time toward an idealized vision of yeoman farmers and independent craftsmen and artisans. Though economically conservative, the individualists were social and political radicals whose commitment to absolute individual freedom made them strong defenders of civil liberties and eloquent critics of censorship, militarism, and imperialism. Goldman disliked both Tucker and his followers, whom she thought too cold in spirit, but she read and admired *Liberty* and absorbed from its pages, as well as from Stirner, Nietzsche, and such American writers as Emerson, Thoreau, and Whitman, the extreme individualism that distinguished her thought from that of most other immigrant anarchists.[13]

The man who now began to instruct Emma Goldman in anarchist ideas—Johann Most—ironically had at best a cloudy vision of them himself. Nevertheless, he profoundly influenced her life and her career. At the time of their meeting, Johann Most was a man of forty-three—the same age as her father—and more subdued in appearance than his fiery reputation would suggest. Physically he was a slender, unprepossessing man about five feet four inches tall. Usually dressed in a business suit, he had neatly trimmed hair and a full graying beard that partially covered the disfigured right side of his face—evidently the result of a badly performed childhood operation that had left one cheek deeply scarred.

In the seven years since his arrival in the United States, Most had managed to bring new life and unity to the quarreling anarchist groups. He had also, at the 1883 Pittsburgh Congress, which he helped organize, supported those anarchists who advocated violence as a weapon of revolutionary struggle. The Pittsburgh Manifesto issued at the Congress unambiguously emphasized the use of force to destroy existing authority and bring about social revolution. In the *Freiheit* Most kept up a relentless call for insurrectional deeds and violent acts of protest by individuals, even going so far as to print instructions for manufacturing bombs and other explosives. Though he eventually absorbed the teachings of Peter Kropotkin and identified himself as an anarchist communist, in the late eighties and early nineties Most's views were a confused, ill-digested amalgam of the ideas of Marx, Proudhon, Bakunin, Kropotkin, and the Russian terrorists. More notable for his ferocity than his cogency, he was still a forceful, arresting speaker whose vitriolic oratory and sardonic wit aroused his listeners to frenzies of enthusiasm. He also excelled as a militant polemical journalist; *Die Freiheit*'s wit and invective enjoyed an ardent following among immigrant radicals on the Lower East Side.[14]

Despite his unremitting opposition to all forms of authority, Johann Most was himself an autocrat—vain, theatrical, domineering, short-tempered, intolerant of difference, given to fierce rages and smoldering resentments. He apparently attributed his hatred of existing society to the bitterness of his childhood. Born in Augsburg, Bavaria, the illegitimate son of an impoverished clerk and a governess who had died when he was nine, he blamed his inability to pursue a longed-for career in the theater on his facial disfigurement. Despising his abusive stepmother, unsuccessful in realizing his ambitions as an actor, he had first turned to bookbinding, then to politics. He spent ten years as a socialist agitator, including five years in an Austrian prison and a brief term as an elected socialist representative to the German Reichstag. Imprisoned a second time for antigovernment agitation, he left Germany in the wake of the antisocialist laws of 1878. As an exile in London, he began publishing the *Freiheit*, moving it increasingly in an anarchist direction, which eventually led to his expulsion from the German Social Democratic party. After serving eighteen months' imprisonment in England for an editorial celebrating the assassination of Czar Alexander II in 1881, Most accepted an invitation from Justus Schwab, a leading New York social revolutionary and proprietor of a famous saloon, to visit the United States in December of 1882. He subsequently settled in New York, becoming the model for the classical anarchist villain parodied in the American press: the monster with a dagger in one hand, a torch in the other, "and all his pockets brimful of dynamite bombs."[15] As in Germany and England, Most continued to suffer harassment and renewed imprisonments for his advocacy of violence. Even after he publicly repudiated "propaganda of the deed," he continued to be persecuted for his earlier views.

The bitterness of Most's life moved Emma deeply. Her portrait of him as the caustic yet human revolutionary—"very lonely among thousands"—is one of the most sympathetic in her memoir and suggests her own identification with him. Certainly she admired his fierce resistance to the persecution he suffered all his life. She was also thrilled by his remarkable voice, "his sparkling wit and biting sarcasm" on the lecture platform.[16] He recognized—as she told it— her talent for dramatic oratory and saw in her the makings of a great public speaker: an heir to himself. During the next two years, Johann Most taught Emma Goldman how to speak. The particular hallmarks of her early style—her aggressive, combative stance toward her audiences, her use of ridicule and sarcasm, her tendency, in the words of Margaret Sanger, "to berate and lash with the language of scorn" —were all the legacy of Johann Most.[17]

Intellectually, however, Most's was a less crucial and lasting influence on Emma, though he did teach her the history of European revolutionary movements and introduced her to the classics of anarchist literature. She was always more fascinated by Most's personality than by his ideas, more thrilled by his language than by his arguments. For a time she accepted his defense of individual terrorist acts, but in later years she would complain that his obssession with violence had done enormous damage to the anarchist movement.[18] Initially adopting his views on the futility of trade-union action, she quickly rejected that position and strongly sided with those anarchists who urged support for all labor struggles, including the eight-hour day campaign of which Most was contemptuous. Within a year or two, Goldman left the *Freiheit* circle and joined the Autonomie group of Most's hated rival, Joseph Peukert. This group was more Kropotkinite than Bakuninist; according to Goldman, it emphasized decentralization within the movement and the autonomy of groups —even opposing the appointment of a chairman at meetings—and stressed the absolute freedom of the individual, ideas that she found more to her liking than Most's enthusiasm for "centralization and control."[19]

Emma's tensions with Most were personal as well as political. Libertarian in theory, Most could in practice be intolerant and dictatorial. He did not welcome independent thought in his followers. Among anarchists, he was especially notorious for his conservative views on women and sex, his hatred of all theories of sexual liberation, and his desire for conventional domesticity. When he fell in love with Emma, he wanted to make her his wife, the mother of his children. Even though he had launched her as an anarchist speaker, he wanted to subordinate her to himself. Emma had no intention of giving up her hard-won independence. Moreover, she felt no physical attracion to Most, whom she considered more a father figure than a lover. When she refused his demands for "closer contact," he grew angry and resentful.[20] His rage was intensified by her alliance with Peukert and by his jealousy of Alexander Berkman. Eventually he withdrew entirely from their friendship and refused to see her at all.

Berkman, a compositor on the *Freiheit* who first took Emma to hear Most speak, would indeed become her most intimate lifelong friend and the man who most profoundly influenced her life. He had arrived in the United States from Russia early in 1888, two years after Emma, but had almost immediately become active in anarchist circles in New York City. In contrast with Emma's precarious petit bourgeois upbringing and her Prussian education, Berkman's early life in Vilna, St. Petersburg, and Kovno had been distinctly Russian, far more prosperous and privileged. He was born in Vilna in November of 1870, the youngest of four children. His hated "bourgeois father," Joseph Schmidt Berkman, was a successful wholesaler of uppers for shoes, and his "aristocratic" mother, Yetta Berkman, came from the wealthy Natanson family. The Berkmans soon moved to the capital, St. Petersburg, where they enjoyed such prerogatives of wealth as servants and a summer home in a fashionable suburb of the city. Growing up in the seventies in St. Petersburg, the center of the rapidly escalating revolutionary movement, the young Berkman was intrigued by the aura of secrecy and mystery surrounding certain topics at home. Shortly after the assassination of the czar in 1881, when Berkman was eleven, the police searched the family house; later, Berkman's favorite uncle, Maxim, disappeared from sight. The boy could pry out of his evasive parents only that there was some connection between the infamous Nihilists, so vehemently denounced by his father, and the fate of Uncle Maxim. In fact, Mark "Maxim" Natanson, who eventually escaped from exile in Siberia, played an important role in the revolutionary movement as a founder of the Chaikovsky Circle and leader of the Socialist Revolutionary party.[21] Though later in his life Berkman, like Emma, often insisted that he had not acquired any of his revolutionary tendencies from his family, his memoirs show that Mark Natanson was his hero and idol, an important early model of ideal manhood.

With the death of Berkman's autocratic father, the family lost their right of legal residence in St. Petersburg (which had been based on the father's status as a wealthy merchant) and moved to Kovno, where Berkman continued his studies in the classical *Gymnasium*. Restive under the influence of another of his mother's brothers—his rich and conservative uncle Nathan—Berkman began to spend his time with local university students home from St. Petersburg on vacation, "reverently listening to the impassioned discussion of dimly understood high themes, with the oft-recurring refrain of 'Bazarov, Hegel, Liberty, Chernischevsky, v naród.' To the People!"[22] Although Berkman, like Goldman, was too young to participate in the revolutionary movement of the seventies and only learned about it secondhand, his residence in St. Petersburg and Kovno, the stories about Uncle Maxim, and his contacts with university students politicized him at an early age. Forbidden to associate with the household servants, he formed a friendship with a factory boy whom he taught to read. Berkman fought his first rebellion defending a family servant girl against his proud and haughty mother. Fascinated by "secret associations, forbidden books," he simultaneously discovered the "mysteries of sex" and announced in school that "there is no God," for which he was promptly demoted one grade.[23]

In the late eighties, a series of events triggered Alexander Berkman's decision to leave Russia and come to America. His relations with his mother became increasingly strained. He criticized what he regarded as her imperious treatment of the family servants; he was irritated by her equivocal answers to his questions about Maxim. When she became seriously ill, probably in 1887, their relationship had been tense for some time. In his memoirs, Berkman wrote that he had felt vaguely guilty about her illness, afraid that his insistent questions about Uncle Maxim had been the cause. Before he could beg her to forgive him, she died.[24] After her death, he hinted at his feelings when he inserted into his *Prison Memoirs* a sentimental deathbed scene worthy of a romantic novel. He portrayed himself as yearning to embrace his mother and plead for forgiveness just at the moment when death snatched her away from him forever.

At the age of eighteen, Berkman was an orphan, no longer bound to Kovno by ties of home or family. When his older brother Max was denied admission to universities in Moscow and St. Petersburg because he was Jewish and decided to enroll in a German university,

Berkman made up his mind to accompany him. Max subsequently changed his mind, upon being admitted to the medical faculty at Kazan University (where he died two years later of tuberculosis). But Berkman left Russia anyway, traveling first to Hamburg and then to New York, where he arrived in February of 1888. Finding rooms on the Lower East Side, he secured employment variously as a cigar-maker, a cloakmaker, and a printer. The student, with his classical *Gymnasium* education, was abruptly transformed into a worker.

The young man whom Emma Goldman met in November of 1889 was of medium height and muscular build, with "the neck and chest of a giant," Emma recalled. Steel-rimmed glasses lent his face a scholarly look. Years later Emma particularly remembered his strong jaw, high studious forehead, intelligent eyes, and the intense, "almost severe" expression on his face. Also memorable was his "uncompromising fervor," which at times verged on intolerance and self-righteousness.[25] In his own autobiographical account, written some twenty years later, Berkman portrayed himself at nineteen as a convinced Russian terrorist who modeled himself after the character of Rakhmetov in *What Is to Be Done?* As Berkman described him, Chernyshevsky's ideal revolutionist was "a being who has neither personal interests nor desires above the necessities of the Cause; one who has emancipated himself from being merely human, and has risen above that, even to the height of conviction which excludes all doubt, all regret; in short, one who in the very inmost of his soul feels himself revolutionist first, human afterward." For Berkman, to be a real revolutionist was to be "a man, a complete MAN."[26] And the most sublime demonstration of revolutionary dedication and of manhood was a great act of sacrifice. "Could anything be nobler than to die for a grand, a sublime Cause? Why, the very life of a true revolutionist has no other purpose, no significance whatever, save to sacrifice it on the altar of the Beloved People." The revolutionist, he felt, had "no right to live or enjoy while others suffer."[27]

Berkman had agreed "absolutely" with the famous *Revolutionary Catechism* (1869) of Bakunin and Nechaev, which stressed the necessity of total self-sacrifice for the revolution. The *Catechism*, however, urged that the revolutionary steel himself for acts of destruction.[28] Berkman's idea of terrorism emphasized self-immolation far more than destruction: for him, the value of an act of terror against an agent of oppression lay above all in the death of the terrorist. To Emma Goldman, Alexander Berkman appeared as the embodiment of the serious revolutionist. In her positive moments, she revered him for his uncompromising intensity; in more negative moods, she regarded him as "an obsessed fanatic to whom nothing but his ideal and faith existed."[29] Yet despite her criticisms, Emma always looked up to the more educated Berkman, constantly compared herself to him, respected his views even when she did not agree with them, and cared desperately about his opinion of her. For his part, he admired her energy, courage, and loyalty, not only to the radical movement, but also to himself. Though he often seemed puzzled by her emotional reactions and could criticize her sharply on occasion, he trusted and depended upon her as one "Immutable" in his life.[30]

Soon after they met, Emma Goldman and Alexander Berkman (Sasha) became lovers. Together with another young woman, Helen Minkin, and Berkman's cousin and inseparable companion Modest Stein—"Fedya" in her memoirs—they moved into an apartment on Forty-second Street where they shared everything. Berkman worked as a cigarmaker and Helen Minkin in a corset factory; Emma kept house and made silk shirtwaists at home, while Fedya painted, supported by the others. The four lived together in a state of exuberant enthusiasm, although Emma and Sasha argued frequently about revolutionary ethics. She found him too hard, too puritanical in his insistence that the true revolutionist sacrifice everything for the cause. She believed that a movement for freedom should not demand self-denial and asceticism from its adherents. To her, anarchism meant individual liberation as well as social revolution. She wanted flowers, music, theater, "beautiful things"; he insisted that it was wrong to spend money on such "luxuries" when the movement was starved for funds and the people lived in poverty. She retorted that beautiful things were not luxuries but "necessaries."[31] Emma found an ally in Fedya: less dedicated than the others, he was "somewhat inclined to sybaritism; not quite emancipated from the tendencies of his bourgeois youth," according to his cousin. In his youthful fanaticism, Berkman would occasionally berate Stein for such extravagances as spending twenty cents for a meal when the needs of the movement came first. In fact, Stein eventually became a successful commercial artist, making courtroom drawings for major New York newspapers, later going to Hollywood to do graphic portrait work, and leaving the anarchist movement altogether.[32]

If Berkman grew impatient with his cousin's aestheticism, Emma found herself attracted by it. Soon she and Fedya became lovers as well. His appreciation of "beautiful things" and his easygoing tolerance made him a less intense and demanding companion than the strenuous Berkman. "He never expected me to live up to the Cause," she wrote in her autobiography. "I felt release with him."[33] Berkman evidently accepted their relationship without protest—Emma hints in her memoirs that he, too, had other involvements—and the commune continued to flourish. It was augmented at some point by an additional member, Fritz Oerter, mentioned by Goldman in the notes for her autobiography—"my life with F.O."—but omitted from the final manuscript.[34]

The first three years of Goldman's life in New York, then—from the summer of 1889 until the summer of 1892—were full of exciting experiments on all fronts, political and personal. Goldman seems to have seized hold of experience all at once, plunged voraciously into all forms of activity. There may also have been a slightly driven, desperate edge to all this. Looking back on those early days in the movement, Goldman recalled that it had taken some time for her to free herself from the oppressive "phantoms" of her youth. Her sex life always left her feeling dissatisfied, "longing for something that I did not know."[35] "Life," she admitted to a friend, "was a book with seven seals."[36] Her beloved Alexander Berkman attracted and repelled her at the same time—awakened her passion and admiration, but also irritated and angered her. Fedya shared her aesthetic interests, yet proved too yielding for her "turbulent nature." She found a more satisfying outlet for her energies in the meetings, lectures, demonstrations, and conferences that seemed to fill all available moments. In the summer of 1890, just a year after her arrival in New York, she engaged in her one effort at organizing during a strike. She was invited, she tells us, by Joseph Barondess, a charismatic and flamboyant young East Side labor leader, to assist in the strike of cloakmakers that had erupted in May of that year. The New York cloakmakers were among the worst paid of the city's garment workers, often laboring fourteen or fifteen hours a day for nine dollars in weekly wages. A newly formed Dress and Cloakmakers' Union had won some benefits in a series of strikes in New York and other cities in the early months of 1890. But these successes began, in mid-May, to provoke retaliation from a number of New York City employers, who began locking out those employees most active in the new union. The lockout grew into a strike, which lasted nine weeks and involved some four thousand workers. Unusual in this strike were the large parades, demonstrations, and mass meetings organized to mobilize support for the strikers and to encourage other workers to join the union. Goldman recalls in her autobiography that an outside representative of the striking workers, one Thomas Garside, had persuaded the workers to agree to a compromise settlement with the manufacturers, though she herself had opposed the pact.[37] In fact, although it was initially accepted by both the manufacturers and the head of the Cutters' Union (which represented a small number of employees), Garside's proposal was overwhelmingly rejected by the workers at a mass meeting on July 16, 1890. The strike continued, and on July 25, the manufacturers accepted the demands of the Cloakmakers' Union. Both union leaders and strikers considered it a great triumph, and from this strike Joseph Barondess emerged as an important leader, both in the union and in the Jewish community generally.[38]

Although a distance of forty years could easily have blurred Emma's memory of this event, the distortion reflects her later skepticism about the ability of large organizations to act effectively, and her tendency to highlight the role of individuals. Labor organizing did not appeal to Goldman, although many anarchists were union organizers and Emma herself spoke often in support of various strikes and helped to raise strike funds. She never joined a union, however, and by 1890 she was already moving toward the independent stance that would characterize her career as an agitator. She disliked any limitations on her own freedom to act. She would not be a leader, she later explained, because leaders must be diplomatic, must make concessions to their followers and to the will of the majority. "I bow to nothing except my idea of right."[39] Although she was highly effective, Emma's experience as an organizer seemed to deepen her determination to move outside the ranks of labor: to establish herself in an independent position from which she could work on labor's behalf.

On first coming to New York, she had alternated between doing piecework on silk shirtwaists at home and working in a sweatshop. Later, she and two friends attempted to follow the model of Chernyshevsky's Vera Pavlovna, setting up a cooperative dressmaking shop in New Haven, where Berkman had secured work in the printing shop of a comrade. When that experiment ended in failure, she joined Modest Stein in working at a photography shop in Springfield, Massachusetts. That shop was so successful, she tells us, that she, Stein, and Berkman decided to set up their own independent establishment, a studio in nearby Worcester, fully equipped and ready for the customers who never arrived. Undaunted, the three then hired a wagon and solicited customers in the countryside, with disappointing results. Although engaging in business was "against our principles," the movement's need for funds overcame their scruples and they opened a lunchroom and ice-cream parlor in Worcester. This enterprise was beginning to achieve promising returns when an unexpected series of events in July of 1892 persuaded them to close it down and return to New York.

CHAPTER

5

ATTENTAT: "THE CONSCIOUSNESS OF GUILT"

I n June of 1892, a lockout of workers at the Carnegie-owned steel plant in Homestead, Pennsylvania, suddenly erupted into a bitter strike when management, headed by Henry Clay Frick, proposed to cut wages and institute an open-shop policy. Despite his hostility to unions, Frick had prior to this time been willing to bargain with representatives of the Amalgamated Association of Iron and Steel Workers, which was strong at the plant and, indeed, was one of the most powerful unions in the country. Its members were primarily highly skilled workers who, despite long hours and exhausting labor, did not regard themselves as badly off. The contract governing wages and prices that had been in effect at Homestead since 1889 was due to expire on June 30, 1892. Negotiations for a new contract had begun in January of that year between representatives of the union—holding out for maintaining the same wage scales and representatives of management, who demanded a pay cut for certain

Homestead workers. Meanwhile Andrew Carnegie wrote to Frick from England, indicating his desire to operate the plant as nonunion upon expiration of the current contract. Frick disregarded Carnegie's proposals and continued to meet with union representatives. By June, however, no agreement had been reached. Frick requested a further meeting with the representatives of the Amalgamated on June 23, abruptly announcing that after this meeting, management would bargain individually, not collectively, with its members. Once again, at the June 23 meeting, no agreement could be reached on a new wage-scale, but the union expected that negotiations would continue. Two days later, management announced that there would be no more meetings. Frick closed the plant, locking out the workers, who subsequently declared a strike. Frick then prepared to protect strikebreakers by calling in Pinkerton guards. On July 6, three hundred armed Pinkerton employees were loaded onto two barges in Pittsburgh in the middle of the night and towed ten miles up the Monongahela River to Homestead. Informed of the plan, armed workers were waiting on the shore. A pitched battle broke out at dawn, and intermittent gunfire continued for the next twelve hours. During the battle, seven Pinkertons and nine strikers were killed. Many more on both sides were wounded.[1]

The battle of July 6 brought Homestead to the front pages of newspapers all over the country. Though the conservative press criticized the workers for using armed resistance to the Pinkertons, newspapers like the *Chicago Herald* and the *New York World* defended the strikers and pointed out the disparity between Carnegie's prolabor pronouncements and the willingness of his company to assault striking workers. In Congress, the events of July 6 initiated extended debates about the right of owners to dispose freely of their property versus the right of workers to bargain collectively through their unions for fair wages, reasonable hours, and decent conditions of work. Senators who spoke in Congress on July 7, the day after the confrontation, condemned the use of Pinkertons; John Palmer, a Democrat from Illinois, went further, arguing for the first time on the Senate floor that large corporations such as Carnegie Steel had the character of public establishments, and that "the owners of these properties must hereafter be regarded as holding their property subject to the correlative rights of those without whose services the property would be utterly worthless."[2] In short, public opinion strongly supported the workers.

From their lunchroom in Worcester, Emma Goldman, Alexander Berkman, and Modest Stein anxiously followed the events at Homestead in the newspapers. "To us," Emma recalled later, "it sounded the awakening of the American worker, the long-awaited day of his resurrection. . . . We saturated ourselves with the events in Homestead to the exclusion of everything else." For Berkman, the heroism of the strikers recalled the great Russian revolutionists and martyrs. "It is the spirit of the heroic past reincarnated in the steelworkers of Homestead, Pennsylvania." Prior to the July 6 battle, Emma, Sasha, and Stein had decided to go to Homestead to agitate among the strikers; they planned to distribute leaflets, to "bring them our great message and help them see that it was not only for the moment that they must strike, but for all time, for a free life, for anarchism."[3]

The battle of July 6 electrified the three young anarchists, but in Alexander Berkman it stirred something deeper even than outrage or revolutionary fervor. To him it was the "psychologic social moment" for an *attentat*—the assassination of a powerful agent of oppression. This act, aimed at Henry Clay Frick, would "strike terror into the soul of his class" but, most important, it would dramatize the struggle of labor at Homestead. The purpose of an *attentat* would be "to call attention to our social iniquities; to arouse a vital interest in the sufferings of the People by an act of self-sacrifice; to stimulate discussion regarding the cause and purpose of the act, and thus bring the teachings of Anarchism before the world." In Berkman's view, murder and *attentat* were "opposite terms." "The killing of a tyrant . . . is in no way to be considered as the taking of a life. . . . To remove a tyrant is an act of liberation, the giving of life and opportunity to an oppressed people." Far from being indifferent to the moral implications of his act, Berkman was preoccupied with them. "It is impossible to confound law with right; they are opposites," he wrote in his *Prison Memoirs*. "The law is immoral: it is the conspiracy of rulers and priests against the workers, to continue their subjection. To be law-abiding means to acquiesce, if not directly participate, in the conspiracy. A revolutionist is the truly moral man: to him the interests of humanity are supreme; to advance them, his sole aim in life. Government, with its laws, is the common enemy. All weapons are justifiable in the noble struggle of the People against this terrible curse."[4]

Berkman's decision to assassinate Henry Clay Frick placed him squarely within the anarchist tradition of individual acts of terror that had developed in Europe during the 1870s and 1880s in the aftermath of the Paris Commune of 1871 and the assassination of the Russian czar in 1881. At this time, the severe political repression in most European countries had persuaded some revolutionists, including even Kropotkin, of the futility of striving for legal political reform, and had encouraged tactics of "illegalism" and violence. In the United States, too, the harsh suppression of strikes had encouraged support for armed retaliation by workers, a position strongly advocated by Johann Most. In France, particularly, a series of sporadic explosions and assaults in the 1880s intensified between 1892 and 1894 with a wave of dramatic terrorist attacks, including the assassination of French President Sadi Carnot in 1894. After a series of murders and bombings beginning in March of 1892, one of the most celebrated of the anarchist terrorists, Ravachol, was executed on July 11, 1892—a little over a week before Berkman's attempted *attentat*.

Aware of the precedents for his act within European anarchist tradition and of anarchist belief in the apocalyptic value of an act of self-immolation and assassination, Berkman drew his primary inspiration from the Russian revolutionary ethic of sacrifice for the cause. He identified with the Nihilist heroes of his adolescence. "Inexpressibly near and soul-kin I feel to those men and women, the adored, mysterious ones of my youth, who had left wealthy homes and high station to 'go to the People,' to become one with them, though despised by all whom they held dear, persecuted and ridiculed even by the benighted objects of their great sacrifice."[5] Berkman, setting out to assassinate Frick, would actually take the name of Rakhmetov, the revolutionist-hero of Chernyshevsky's novel, *What Is to Be Done?*

Berkman's vision of himself as the Russian Rakhmetov suggests his remoteness from American traditions of protest. His account of Homestead, like Goldman's, has a strangely abstract, literary quality. Their difficulty in finding someone to translate their German propaganda leaflet into English was symbolic of the great distances separating them from "the people" they proposed to liberate. Berkman's action was also, of course, an act of suicide—the first act of "voluntary Anarchist self-sacrifice in the interests of the people" in America.

He emphasized this point in his *Memoirs*, insisting that he had wanted "to die for the Cause."[6]

Berkman planned to assassinate Frick and then blow himself up with a nitroglycerin cartridge, following the example of his Haymarket hero Louis Lingg. He traveled by train to Pittsburgh, where he stayed for several days with comrades, and then to nearby Homestead, where he gained entrance to the office of the manager by posing as the head of an employment agent for strikebreakers. He fired his revolver, not at "Mr. Frick, but the person who had oppressed labor."[7] Observing that the man still lived, Berkman also managed to drive a sharpened steel file into Frick's buttocks and leg before being apprehended, arrested, and dragged off to jail. But both of Berkman's aims were frustrated. Frick did not die, and Berkman was forced to relinquish the capsule of explosive which the local police spied in his mouth.[8] His trial took place September 19, with Berkman acting as his own counsel, despite his limited English. His failure to use any of his rights to challenge the jurors or make objections later severely limited his rights of appeal. Despite his youthful bravado in court—he announced contemptuously that he expected no justice and grandly identified himself with "those who were murdered at Chicago"—he was nevertheless devastated by his twenty-two-year prison sentence (which exceeded by fifteen years the usual maximum sentence of seven years for attempted manslaughter).[9] Carl Nold and Henry Bauer were both convicted as accomplices and sentenced to five years in prison for having sheltered Berkman prior to the assassination attempt—of which they had known nothing. Far from inspiring the workers at Homestead or anywhere else, as Berkman had hoped, his act was almost universally condemned, even by many anarchists. It did not break the strike, as has sometimes been claimed; instead it blurred the important issues that had been dramatized by the battle of July 6 and deepened the association between anarchism and terrorism.

It also polarized the anarchist community in New York. The majority were hostile to Berkman, and only a few, most notably Emma Goldman, defended him.[10] One of the most outspoken critics was Berkman's former mentor, Johann Most, who had always, as Goldman put it, "proclaimed acts of violence from the housetops." Now he attacked both Goldman and Berkman in the pages of the *Freiheit*, implying that the attempt had been a newspaper fake or had been designed to arouse sympathy for Frick.[11] Just released after a year's imprisonment in the aftermath of Haymarket, and jealous of Berkman's relationship with Goldman, Most may have been inspired partly by fear of another prison term and by resentment of Berkman —"that arrogant Russian Jew"—but soon he, like Kropotkin, reversed his previous defense of the *attentat* altogether.

Most's attack on Berkman enraged Goldman, who demanded proof of his charges in an issue of *Der Anarchist*, the paper put out by Peukert. When Most failed to answer her challenge, she resolved to confront him publicly. To his next lecture she brought a horsewhip, and as he stepped out onto the platform, she loudly demanded that he prove his accusations against Berkman. When he dismissed her scornfully, she jumped up and lashed him with her whip, breaking it over her knee and hurling the pieces at him. If Goldman felt excluded or even upstaged by Berkman's act, her dramatic gesture certainly won her some notoriety of her own and, according to one historian of the movement, provoked "the greatest scandal in the history of anarchism."[12] Later she regretted her theatrics, which intensified hostilities within the already badly divided movement, and wondered how she could have acted so harshly toward a man she had once idolized. But when Max Nettlau confessed to her in 1932 that he had always believed that she had horsewhipped Most "for personal insults or slander written or spoken against you yourself," she replied primly that while Most had indeed slandered her, this was not what had impelled her action. "I had so little personal life then," she insisted, "that nothing anyone had done against me really mattered. But A.B. and his act mattered everything to me." Since Most had always called for acts of violence, "his attitude toward A.B. was too great a shock for me to reason about." Besides, she insisted further, at the age of twenty-three, one does not reason.[13]

Indeed, Goldman's feelings about the Homestead events were so mixed that she could never quite sort them out. For many years afterward, both Goldman and Berkman remained extremely guarded about her role in the attempted assassination. Until Goldman wrote her autobiography, neither of them gave any public indication that she had been an accomplice to the act. Just one year afterward, when Emma herself was tried on unrelated charges, she stated in court in reply to the questions of the prosecuting attorney that while she admired and respected Berkman, she did not approve of his action.[14]

The 1911 portrait of her by her friend Hippolyte Havel stated only that the police "exerted every effort to involve Emma Goldman in the act of Alexander Berkman," a version that was repeated almost verbatim by Frank Harris in his essay twenty years later.[15] In his own *Prison Memoirs*, Berkman too was careful not to implicate Goldman, indicating only that she knew of his act, visited him in prison, and staunchly defended him afterwards.[16]

Forty years after the fact, in her autobiography, Goldman decided to turn the spotlight on her own role in the Homestead events and frankly portrayed herself as Berkman's accomplice: she had wanted to accompany him; only the lack of a few dollars and Berkman's insistence that she remain behind to explain his action to the world had prevented her from doing so. Her memoir describes at length how she helped him test explosives and how—imagining herself in the role of Dostoyevsky's saintly prostitute Sonya Marmeladov—she dressed up in cheap finery and paraded with the whores down Fourteenth Street, trying unsuccessfully to sell herself to raise money for Berkman's gun and a new suit. Ostensibly portraying Berkman as a heroic figure, her memoir subtly belittles him, showing him as cold, rash, calmly willing to exclude her from "his last great hour," and indifferent to the risks to innocent people as they tested bombs in a crowded tenement apartment. (Berkman indeed protested that she had painted him "exclusively hard, without other sides of my character."[17]) She, on the other hand, was troubled by uncertainties about the moral legitimacy of their actions. While Berkman coolly conducted his experiments, she was tormented by dread "for Sasha, for our friends in the flat, the children, and the rest of the tenants. What if anything should go wrong—but, then, did not the end justify the means? . . . What if a few should have to perish?—the many would be made free and could live in beauty and in comfort. Yes, the end in this case justified the means."[18] While the autobiography strongly suggests her ambivalence, Goldman insisted in private correspondence that she had wholeheartedly supported the attempted assassination and that both she and Berkman had been "of the generation and period that believed implicitly in the notion of the end justifying the means."[19] Even privately, however, she evaded the critical question of whether she had been prepared to kill for the cause, observing rather that she had been willing "to give my own life for an act, and though it was bitterly hard, I was also willing that

Berkman should give his." She had been motivated, not by "the humane promptings of a girlish heart," as another correspondent thought, but by "my religiously devout belief that the end justifies all means."[20] In the absence of contemporary evidence, such inconsistent testimony seems to support Ben Reitman's conclusion that Goldman "probably acquiesced in Berkman's act."[21]

The evidence regarding Goldman's feelings immediately following Berkman's action at Homestead is similarly inconclusive. Years later she would stress her deep feeling of relief at learning of his failure to kill Frick, since Frick's recovery meant "the saving of AB's life."[22] At the time, however, Berkman believed her reaction to be one of disappointment. In the first letter she wrote to him in prison, he sensed bitterness and almost resentment. "Why do you speak of failure?" he angrily replied (in a letter of October 19, 1892). "You, at least, you and Fedya, should not have your judgment obscured by the mere accident of physical results. Your lines pained and grieved me beyond words. Not because you should write thus; but that you, even you, should think thus. Need I enlarge? True morality deals with motives, not consequences. I cannot believe that we differ on this point."[23]

But Berkman, too, was distraught over "the mere accident of physical results" and hoped at least to carry out the second part of his plan. To this end, he insisted that Emma come to see him immediately. She agreed to a visit arranged by Berkman through a special request to the prison inspector (since prisoners were routinely denied visitors during the first three months of their sentences.)[24] Berkman wanted her to bring him "the gift of Lingg"—a cartridge of dynamite. Emma, for undisclosed reasons, did not bring it. "An embrace, a lingering kiss, and the gift of Lingg would have been mine," he wrote her afterward. "To grasp your hand, to look down for a mute, immortal instant into your soul, and then die at your hands, Beloved, with the warm breath of your caress wafting me into peaceful eternity —oh, it were bliss supreme. . . ."[25] Such morbid fantasies alternated with a powerful desire for life and with a new dependence upon Goldman—"the true Russian woman revolutionist"—whose help he needed to survive. "I clutch desperately at the thread that still binds me to the living—it seems to unravel in my hands, the thin skeins are breaking, one by one," he wrote her in October of 1892. "My hold is slackening. But the Sonya* thread, I know, will remain taut and strong."[26]

At first, however, the Sonya thread nearly broke altogether. Emma's initial plan, not mentioned in the autobiography, was to flee the country early in November of 1892, even if that meant not seeing Berkman again.[27] Emma did not leave and became Berkman's most faithful supporter during the fourteen years of his imprisonment. However mixed her feelings in the immediate aftermath of the July events, she soon dedicated herself to securing a commutation of his sentence, maintaining contacts, supplying news from the outside, and assuming a kind of maternal responsibility for his welfare. Other comrades gradually ceased to write or to care, "but you are never disappointing," he told her.[28] Attempting to describe, long afterward, her feelings during the early months of Berkman's sentence, she would stress her "consciousness of guilt," her painful longing "to give up my freedom, to proclaim loudly my share in the deed."[29] She told Theodore Dreiser that she had "regretted ever since that I did not share the consequences with him—it would have been easier than it was being on the outside."[30]

Although she admitted in her memoirs "the doubts that had been assailing me since Sasha's act," she seemed to find such doubts intolerably painful.[31] Publicly at least, she almost always praised both Berkman and all other anarchist assassins of the nineties, even while insisting that "the tremendous pressure of conditions," not anarchism, was responsible for acts of political violence. Just when such anarchists as Kropotkin were beginning to repudiate the tactics of the *attentat* as sterile and self-destructive, Emma fiercely defended them, describing political assassins contradictorily as the victims of desperate circumstances—men recoiling violently from a violent society—and as men of superior will and conscience. Such confusion may have had its origins partly in her need to see Berkman as a hero, to idealize his act and all similar acts, in order to endure her own "consciousness of guilt." Not only did she continue to defend his act for many years, she also accepted his idea that "true morality deals with motives, not consequences," clinging to this romantic notion long after Berkman had abandoned it. Goldman did not advocate

* Sonya was the name of Berkman's sister; it was the code designation for Emma.

assassination and may even have discouraged young hotheads in the movement who plotted similar acts, but she could not, for a long time, bring herself to criticize them or even to analyze them concretely. As she herself later admitted, the aftermath of 1892, when Berkman and she were harshly criticized by many anarchists as well as by labor and the Left generally, inspired in her a growing disdain for those who refused to acknowledge the nobility of Berkman's act. Increasingly, she would celebrate the lonely romantic rebel, while viewing with dimmed enthusiasm the masses who failed to appreciate him.

Homestead profoundly influenced Goldman's life and her complex relationship with Berkman: a relationship woven of love and guilt, of anger and tenderness, of frequent irritation and lasting mutual admiration.[32] For fourteen years Emma would be haunted by the consciousness of her lover behind bars, acutely aware of the disparity between his suffering and her freedom. She often wondered if it was "for the purpose of testing me by fire" that he had been sent to prison. She would tell him that his sentence was "as much my Calvary as yours," as if to remind him that she had suffered, too.[33] As the years passed, Berkman seemed to regard Emma's strong loyalty, which flagged only for brief intervals, with a kind of wonder, astonished at the depth of her commitment, gratified that his own youthful perception of her character had proven to be correct. For her part, Emma would turn loyalty to Berkman almost into a religion. She never relinquished the heavy "burden of responsibility" she felt for his welfare, as if she owed him a debt that could never be repaid. Yet interwoven with her concern was resentment—a feeling that he did not fully appreciate her sacrifices—which sometimes led her to oblique insults or belittlement. Both her anger and her admiration surface throughout the autobiography, where she acknowledged the enduring legacy of that one dramatic moment of their youth. "Often," she wrote in her memoirs, "I wanted to run away, never to see him again, but I was held by something greater than the pain: the memory of his act, for which he alone had paid the price. More and more I realized that to my last breath it would remain the strongest link in the chain that bound me to him."[34]

C H A P T E R

6

"THE
STRENGTH
TO
STAND
ALONE"

Loyalty to Berkman did not, however, preclude the development of an independent identity of her own. Indeed, Berkman's incarceration almost certainly hastened it, by throwing her more than ever on her own resources and forcing her to define her position vis-à-vis his act. It also deepened her determination to resume work in the movement. With her lover in prison, she would now live for them both; she would keep his memory alive and, by working to spread anarchist ideas, would vindicate his action.

At first, however, she was stunned and overcome with grief. Her health deteriorated; she lost weight, developed a cough and hemorrhages of the lungs, and was eventually diagnosed as having tuberculosis. Moreover, she found herself a pariah: hunted, she tells us, by the police trying to implicate her in Berkman's act; locked out of her apartment by a roommate terrorized by police raids; forced to spend nights in a Second Avenue café or riding back and forth to the

Bronx in a streetcar; driven to seek refuge in a brothel, the only place willing to rent her a room.

In the midst of her despair, at a meeting to discuss ways of securing a commutation of Berkman's sentence, Goldman met Edward Brady, a gentle, tender, motherly man ten years older than she, who fell in love with her and helped nurse her back to health. Goldman later described Brady—who had spent a decade in an Austrian prison for publishing illegal anarchist literature—as a reserved, serious, literate man: "never much of a talker," as she put it. His interests were as much literary and philosophical as political and economic; he seemed to her "the most scholarly man I had ever met"; he introduced her to the classics of Shakespeare, Rousseau, and Voltaire, while also teaching her the refinements of French cooking.[1] Still active in the anarchist movement, Brady also introduced Emma to the famous First Street saloon of Justus Schwab. Schwab, who had originally invited Johann Most to America in 1882, now ran, with his wife, "the most famous radical centre in New York," where one could meet "French communards, Spanish and Italian refugees, Russian politicals and German socialists and anarchists who had escaped the iron heel of Bismarck."[2] Besides these emigré intellectuals and activists, many American-born radicals and writers congregated there: men like the radical journalist John Swinton; the writer Ambrose Bierce; James Huneker, the music and literary critic-enthusiast, who was already beginning to campaign in America for such European writers as Ibsen and Nietzsche; and Sadakichi Hartmann, the elusive writer–photographic performer–critic who would later contribute to Goldman's magazine *Mother Earth*. Emma, with her characteristic aplomb, made the place her headquarters and used it as a kind of office, granting newspaper interviews there and inscribing that famous address—51 First Street—on the personal cards that she had printed.

In her autobiography, Goldman wrote that during the early months of 1893, her friendship with Brady had gradually deepened into love—a tender, soothing kind of love, which did not, of course "eliminate Sasha from my mind." An older, more experienced lover than Berkman, Brady became an important source of support for Goldman, intellectually and emotionally. But for all his political radicalism, Brady, like Johann Most, remained conventional in his personal life. He believed that woman's destiny was motherhood, and wanted his lover to bear his children and be a "wife," in fact if not in law. He wanted to possess her, to cage her, to deny "the beloved the right to herself." His was "a love that throve only at the expense of the loved one." As she reported in her memoirs, he felt that her devotion to the movement was inspired by her "unsatisfied motherhood seeking an outlet," or worse, that it was "nothing but vanity, nothing but your craving for applause and glory and the limelight."[3]

By this time, the twenty-five-year-old Emma had definitely decided not to have children. Seeking relief several years earlier from severe menstrual pain, she had been diagnosed as having an inverted uterus. Only surgery, her physician had told her, would correct her condition and make conception possible. "I would never be free from pain, or experience full sexual release, unless I submitted to the operation," she wrote later. Despite the continuing pain, she decided, she tells us, to forgo the operation. To devote herself to the movement, "I must remain unhampered and untied."[4]

But if her decision expressed a realistic choice of public commitments over private satisfactions, she presents it in her autobiography as a sacrifice, almost a form of martyrdom. "Years of pain and of suppressed longing for a child—what were they compared with the price many martyrs had already paid. I, too, would pay the price, I would endure the suffering, I would find an outlet for my motherneed in the love of all children."[5] Perhaps she felt constrained to justify her untraditional choice in terms of traditional values, as if it were permissible for a woman to remain childless only if she perceived it as a sacrifice. She may even have believed Brady's analysis of her thwarted motherhood, for she never denied his claim. But her memoir suggests a deeper ambivalence about maternity, a fear of the "helplessness of motherhood" and of the intimacies involved in the mother-child relationship. Having children of her own, she worried, might somehow add to the world's store of "unfortunate victims," as if she were doomed to inflict upon her own children the unhappiness she herself had suffered as a child.[6] Perhaps the thought of having children reawakened painful memories of her own early years, her own cold, distant mother. Perhaps she felt that she did not know how to mother, or that she would repeat her mother's mistakes.

Ed Brady did not accept her decision. He grew increasingly dissatisfied with her immersion in political work, her frequent absences from home for meetings and lecture tours. He wanted her to give up public life, considering it too dangerous for a woman, and urged her to take up writing or a profession. Goldman, torn between her love for Brady and her deepening commitment to the movement, saw in his demands an effort "to rob me of all that is more precious to me than life."[7] The conflict gradually led to painful battles between them, followed by reconciliations that grew less and less satisfactory. They finally separated in 1897.

As Goldman's romance with Ed Brady flowered, the financial panic of 1893 deepened into the worst industrial depression the country had ever known. Businesses collapsed, banks failed, and the number of unemployed mounted precipitously (from an estimated 800,000 in the summer of 1893 to some three million the following December), many of them taking to the roads and rails in search of work. For the first time, the federal government was bombarded with demands for direct relief for the growing armies of the jobless and homeless. By August of 1893, the growing ranks of the unemployed in New York were becoming increasingly angry. Many of these people were recent immigrants, primarily East European Jews, who were crowded into the miserable tenements of the Lower East Side. As the crisis worsened, labor leaders such as Samuel Gompers of the American Federation of Labor and Joseph Barondess of the Cloakmakers' Union petitioned the New York State Legislature for financial emergency relief and public projects to put the unemployed back to work. By mid-August, the efforts still had not yielded results. Protests organized by both socialists and anarchists became more frequent, and the regular lectures and meetings of the immigrant district grew sharper in tone. At the end of July, Goldman had returned to New York from Rochester. She had not fully recovered her health when she became involved in collecting food, setting up soup kitchens, and organizing mass meetings and "hunger demonstrations." She was not present on August 17 at Walhalia Hall on Rivington Street when a full-fledged riot erupted. Windows were broken, furniture smashed, and bottles thrown. The fracas catapulted the anarchists, blamed for causing the trouble, into the newspaper headlines. The next day, August 18, Goldman spoke in German at the Golden Rule Hall next door and, according to the *New York Times*, told people:

"If you are hungry and need bread, go and get it. The shops are plentiful and the doors are open."[8] On Saturday, August 19, another mass demonstration, called by the Jewish Clothing Workers' Union, took place at Union Square, this time without any disturbances. The following day, Sunday, August 20, one hundred delegates representing one hundred thousand organized workers met at the International Labor Exchange to set up committees to lobby city and state officials for more public works employment and direct relief for the unemployed. By this time, Goldman had been presented in the newspapers for several days as one of the leading instigators of the unrest on the Lower East Side.

On Monday, August 21, a series of meetings during the day culminated in another hunger demonstration, intended to show the rich the sufferings of the poor. Union Square bristled with policemen. A crowd of some three thousand people listened in the rain to several other anarchist orators before Goldman, scheduled to speak last, was introduced, to tremendous cheers and ovation. Her arguments characteristically blended astute strategy with divisiveness. She ridiculed the efforts of labor leaders and socialists to organize mass support for unemployment relief and public works, and warned her listeners not to have faith in leaders or politicians, who would only cheat and betray them. Instead, she urged the jobless to take direct action by demonstrating their misery in the streets: a strategy that Gompers himself would subsequently endorse. Several versions of the controversial conclusion of her speech at Union Square that night have been recorded; her exact words may never be known. Newspaper reporters and detectives sent to cover the meeting claimed that she told the audience that if they could not get bread or work peacefully, they should "take everything" and take it "by force."[9] She herself, at her subsequent trial, stated that she had only meant to urge her listeners to march past the homes of the wealthy and demand food from them directly, rather than petitioning the state, as the socialists and labor leaders proposed they should do. "Workmen, you must demand what belongs to you," she quoted herself as saying. "Go forth into the streets where the rich dwell, before the palaces of your dominators . . . and make them tremble."[10] But although she insisted at her trial that she had urged demonstrations, not expropriations, a sympathetic comrade, Voltairine de Cleyre, agreed that she *had* urged expropriations, and Emma later recalled telling her audiences, "Ask for work. If they do not give you work, ask for bread. If they do not give you work or bread, then take bread."[11]

In any case, if she did exhort hungry people to take the bread they needed from the shops, she was not alone: even according to biased press reports of the August meetings of the unemployed, Goldman's speeches were not the most inflammatory. They were, however, the most persuasive, and for this reason she was carefully watched by the police, who took her words seriously while dismissing those of other, often more incendiary radical speakers. At the age of twenty-four, Emma Goldman was already considered a professional agitator. Her powerful presence on the platform could arouse an enthusiastic response from her listeners. That she was a force to be reckoned with is suggested in a nasty *New York Times* headline, meant to reassure worried citizens about the explosive situation on the Lower East Side: "THEY ARE A MILD LOT THERE—EVEN RAINDROPS PUT THEM TO FLIGHT—BUSINESSMEN OF THE DISTRICT ARE DISGUSTED WITH THE WAY THE DOINGS OF THE IGNORANT UNWASHED HAVE BEEN MAGNIFIED—THE DANGER IS IN LEAVING PERSONS OF THE EMMA GOLDMAN TYPE AT LARGE."[12]

Goldman was arrested in Philadelphia on August 30 and charged with "inciting to riot." Brought back to New York, she was indicted on September 5. She may have anticipated this outcome, for her name had been much mentioned in the newspapers for over a week prior to her arrest and the police chief had publicly threatened to arrest her should she continue speaking. She may even have welcomed the event as a way of feeling closer to Berkman and of demonstrating her solidarity with him. In her memoirs she cites a letter she received from him just after her arrest: " 'Now you are indeed my sailor girl,' " he had written; one senses that Berkman's approval was very important to Goldman at that moment.[13]

She had learned, moreover, from Berkman's experience the previous year how to use the press to her advantage. Whereas in 1892 she had shied away from reporters, speaking to them only when relentlessly pursued, in 1893 she appeared to invite them. Awaiting trial in the Tombs in early September, she gave a two-hour interview to the intrepid Nelly Bly of the *New York World*; the article—portraying Goldman, Johann Most, and Justus Schwab, three major personalities in the New York anarchist world—appeared on the front page. Expecting to find a "great raw-boned creature" with murder constantly on her lips, Bly instead found herself face to face with an attractive, self-possessed young woman of about five feet, "not showing her 120 pounds; with a saucy, turned-up nose and very expressive blue-gray eyes that gazed inquiringly at me through shell-rimmed glasses." Emma dressed for the occasion in a modest blue serge Eton suit with a blue muslin shirtwaist and scarf; her light brown hair fell loosely over her forehead and was gathered in a little knot behind. Emphasizing Emma Goldman's girlishness and seriousness of purpose, as well as her "German" cleanliness and love of good books, Bly allowed her to speak at length about herself: her family background, her education, the reasons for her anarchism, and her views on marriage, labor, and religion. She was an anarchist, Goldman solemnly told Bly, because she was an "egotist"; it caused her pain to see others suffer. She did not believe in murder, but in the war of labor against capital—"masses against classes"—which unfortunately would not come soon; in the meantime, "I am satisfied to agitate, to teach, and I only ask justice and freedom of speech." Goldman's depth of conviction and obvious sincerity impressed Bly, who, enchanted, presented her to the *World*'s readers as a "little Joan of Arc." [14]

Goldman's trial began October 4. She was defended, gratis, by A. Oakley Hall, a man who had once been mayor of New York and who hoped, in this much-publicized trial, to expose the corrupt methods of the New York City police. At the trial, Goldman was questioned about her anarchism, her atheism, and her association with Alexander Berkman, as well as about her exact words on August 21. The *World* was evidently pleased enough with the results of the Bly interview to offer Goldman a chance to publish her trial statement. She had become something of a celebrity, although she was sure, she wrote in her memoirs, that "it was the social theories I represented, and not I personally, that was attracting attention." On October 9, a jury (which included no workers) found her guilty of "inciting to riot," although all the testimony agreed that there had been no riot on August 21. On October 18, she was sentenced by the judge to one year in prison. [15]

That very day, Emma Goldman entered Blackwell's Island Penitentiary, the dank, forbidding building located on an island in the

East River (today Roosevelt Island) next to a "lunatic" asylum, an almshouse, and a smallpox hospital. Initially she was placed in charge of the sewing room, where she was responsible for distributing, folding, and packing the cloth, and with keeping track of incoming and outgoing bundles. According to Goldman, the other inmates shunned her at first because she was an "anarchist" and didn't go to church, but became devoted to her when they learned that she had stood up to the head matron and refused to become a slave driver. After two months in the shop, Goldman suffered an attack of rheumatism and was confined to the prison hospital. A month later, when her symptoms subsided, she was appointed orderly in the hospital, in charge of medications and, eventually, of patients as well. She also attended the operations conducted by a visiting physician, Dr. White, with whom she became quite friendly. Here she spent the next seven months. Goldman, who had long been attracted to the study of medicine, enjoyed this work and felt that she was well treated.

Blackwell's Island was close to midtown Manhattan, and Emma evidently did not feel terribly isolated. Some Austrian anarchists sent meals from their restaurant; her devoted grandmother and others, including John Swinton, came to see her. Her autobiography indicates that she read extensively in English. The prison library had novels by George Eliot and Ouida and translations of George Sand, and from the outside she received works by Emerson, Thoreau, Hawthorne, Herbert Spencer, John Stuart Mill, Albert Brisbane, and Walt Whitman. Reading American writers of libertarian sentiment not only improved her English but showed her that her anarchism had American as well as European precursors.

After ten months in prison, Emma Goldman was released on August 17, 1894. A crowd of some 2,800 people packed the Thalia Theater at 46 Bowery Street to welcome her; a thunderous ovation greeted her appearance on the stage. She delivered her speech both in German and in English, with her characteristic panache:

> Friends and comrades, I have come back to you after having served ten months in prison for talking. If the representatives of your Government intend to prosecute women for talking, they will have to begin with their mothers, wives, sisters and sweethearts, for they will never stop women from talking [cheers]. But it was not Emma Goldman who

was prosecuted. It was the thoughts of Emma Goldman, the principles of Anarchy, that were prosecuted; the views held by thousands of brave men and women who have died and who are ready to die as did Santo [Caserio, who assassinated French President Sadi Carnot in June of 1894]. It was the right of free speech that was prosecuted in the Court of General Sessions, and not little Emma Goldman.[16]

Emma now found herself besieged by reporters and swamped with invitations to lecture. She never regretted her time in prison. For one thing, she had gained considerable nursing experience. Despite her lack of formal training, she was able on her release to secure private nursing assignments from the doctor who had been assigned to the prison hospital, as well as referrals from a few others. Prison had been "a school of experience," she said on her release, and had made her "more of an Anarchist than ever." Having "seen the injustice of the law," she was increasingly "determined to use every means in my power to spread my doctrine among the people."[17] Prison had also enhanced Goldman's status as a revolutionist and confirmed her role as a major presence in the world of New York radicalism. If she was denounced as a menace in court and in certain newspapers, she had also succeeded in winning some admiring publicity, including comments on her responsible and gentle demeanor in prison. At the age of twenty-five, she associated as an equal with longtime activists who were generally men twice her age. She had acquired a new self-confidence. Once the protégée of Johann Most and the follower of Alexander Berkman, she would now become an important and admired figure in her own right. As she reflected many years later, 1894 marked a major turning point in her life. In prison she had learned "to see life through my own eyes, and not through those of Sasha, Most or Ed."[18]

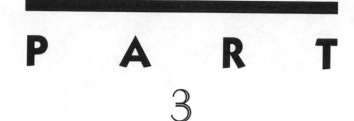

PART
3

ANARCHIST
ACTIVIST

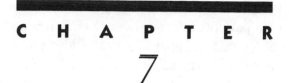

C H A P T E R

7

"THE
SPIRIT
OF
REVOLT"

mma Goldman emerged from prison in August of 1894, the most brutal year of the depression. Unemployment had soared to nearly three million people, with perhaps one in every five wage earners out of work. Efforts to secure aid for the jobless met stiff opposition. Led by a progressive Ohio businessman, Jacob Coxey, an "army" of unemployed men that marched on Washington in May, 1894, was beaten and trampled by police when they demanded work and relief. The July strike of railroad workers at the so-called "model" community built by George Pullman outside Chicago ended disastrously, with federal troops sent in to crush the strike at the cost of some thirty-seven people killed and hundreds wounded.

Following her release, Goldman soon made good her promise to "spread my doctrine among the people" and plunged once again into a busy schedule of meetings and lectures. Political work, however, required a source of income. Enthusiastic about her nursing experience in Blackwell's Island, Emma began to take on private nursing assignments with patients referred by a physician friendly with many anarchists; the doctor at Blackwell's Island also employed her part-time. Within a year, however, she concluded that she would need additional training to make this a sustaining profession. With Ed Brady's encouragement, she decided to go to Vienna in order to study at the Allgemeines Krankenhaus, Vienna's famous general hospital. The United States had the best training for nurses, she informed a reporter in 1901, but there were no good American schools for midwifery or massage. With Brady's blessing and funded by the generous Modest Stein, whose growing success as a newspaper pen-and-ink artist enabled him to underwrite her expenses, Goldman sailed for London in August of 1895, just one year after her release from prison.

Stopping in England, she lectured in London, Glasgow, Edinburgh, and Maybole, where she caused "quite a sensation," according to a British correspondent for *The Firebrand*, the American anarchist weekly paper then published in Portland, Oregon.[1] Her subjects included "The Condition of the Workers in America," and "Political Justice in England and America," as well as a defense of Alexander Berkman's attempted *attentat*, which, she argued, "showed to all who wish to see the real cause of the people's misery." The unemployed movements of 1893 and the strikes at Homestead, Chicago, and elsewhere proved "that the people of America are tired of leading the lives of dogs" and were willing to fight for their rights. Anarchists, moreover, were no longer regarded as "fools or ruffians"; their ideas were being discussed "in the papers, in the pulpit, and in the mansions of the rich."[2] Goldman's confident manner excited much enthusiasm among her English comrades. And in London she was able to meet Errico Malatesta, the distinguished Italian anarchist; Louise Michel, the fierce sixty-five-year-old militant of the 1871 Paris Commune, whom Goldman would often cite as one of her heroines; and, most important, Peter Kropotkin, who played an important role in English and emigré radical politics and now lived with his family in the small town of Bromley on the outskirts of London.

Probably sometime in September of 1895, Goldman—going under the name of "Mrs. E. Brady"—traveled from that city to Vienna, the ebullient Austro-Hungarian capital. With its fin de siècle blend of political decadence and cultural renaissance, this was the city of

Freud, Wittgenstein, Klimt, and Schiele. Though a foreign student, she had an advantage, she tells us, because she was a native German speaker, unlike the other Russian Jewish students who attempted to slide by on their knowledge of Yiddish. Besides her regular courses at the Allgemeines Krankenhaus, she attended some lectures by Freud.[3] In the evenings, accompanied by a young Austrian anarchist, she haunted the concert halls and theaters, eagerly taking in Wagner, Eleanora Duse, and most of all the work of the new dramatists, whom she had first read about in the pages of the Detroit anarchist paper, *Der arme Teufel*. She also immersed herself in Nietzsche, whose magical language and beautiful vision "carried me to undreamed of heights."[4]

Armed with two diplomas and a suitcase full of books, which she carried on board with her, Goldman returned to New York in November of 1896. She immediately threw herself into an exhausting schedule combining midwifery among poor immigrant women on the Lower East Side, the attempt to maintain some semblance of a private life with Ed Brady, with whom she again shared a flat, and a program of organizing and public speaking. In 1897, she traveled as far west as Detroit and Chicago, lecturing at the Rochester Socialist Forum on "The Aim of Humanity"; at the anarchist Ladies Liberal League in Philadelphia on "Free Love"; at the Single Tax Society on "Anarchist Communism"; at the Boston Workmen's Educational Club on "Must We Become Angels to Live in an Anarchist Society?"; and at a Chicago picnic to protest the arrest of the editors of *The Firebrand* (on charges of obscenity) in Portland. She spoke both in German and in English, and everywhere she addressed packed halls. In the spring of 1898, Goldman arrived on the West Coast.[5] Hers was the first cross-country lecture tour ever undertaken by an anarchist.

With her imperturbable self-assurance and blunt, earnest, "sledgehammer" platform style, Goldman created a sensation. A short, sturdy figure with a determined chin and firm mouth, she conveyed an impression of strength and energy. "The secret of her power," ventured one comrade, "lies in the fact that she is the very embodiment of the doctrine she preaches. Every fibre of her being is electrified by the spirit to which her lips give utterance."[6] "She makes great use of sarcasm," noted another, "lashing most severely what she regards as the evils of modern life." Others applauded her "fire and force," her "humorsome [sic] satire," her "vigorous and determined manner."[7] Not everyone was so uncritically enthusiastic. Joseph Labadie, a longtime Detroit anarchist, found her "a very interesting person indeed, well-read, generous in the extreme," refreshingly frank and doing important work, yet at the same time "naïve as a child."[8] An anarchist in Philadelphia was similarly condescending, finding her "unspoiled by ultra-cultivation" and "not paralyzed by seeing too many sides of the problems that confront us."[9]

But despite the occasional disapproval of her comrades, Goldman by 1898 had become well-known and admired as one of the few anarchist lecturers who could attract nonanarchists to her talks, in part because of the storm of controversy she almost always aroused. By this time the pattern of police interference, arrest—"because you're Emma Goldman"—and sometimes a night or two in jail, had been set. In anticipation of such events, Emma routinely carried a book with her when going to meetings, to read in case she was imprisoned. She became highly skilled at handling assaults by the police (or by local officials, journalists, or even vigilantes) through her witty manipulation of the opposition in the press, on the podium, or in court. Her efforts awakened a growing interest, both in her personally and in anarchist ideas. No wonder, then, that in 1898 she could boast enthusiastically to the anarchist paper *Solidarity*, just resuming publication after a three-year hiatus, of the great numbers of people interested in the philosophy of anarchy. "Even the most conservative clubs and organizations, that only a few years ago would have refused to listen to a professed Anarchist, are now inviting Anarchist lecturers. They have learned," she exulted, "that conservatism is fast losing ground, and that nothing but advanced and radical ideas meet with popular approval."[10]

This perspective was far too sanguine in the spring of 1898, as the United States was about to embark on its first overseas imperialist adventure. Yet it reflected the deepening currents of discontent that would stimulate the growth of the Progressive and socialist movements after the turn of the century. An outspoken voice of this discontent, Goldman herself was winning respect and admiration as "a woman of no small personal force." She felt the time was ripe for a revival of anarchism. By now she had developed the initiative and audacity that characterized her as an activist. Almost immediately after her return from Vienna in November of 1896, for example, she wrote to the Buffalo anarchist Max Metzkow of her plan to "develop a widespread movement for B[erkman], and even if we should not succeed in alleviating B's lot or to free him, we will at least have made propaganda for our ideas." This was very necessary, she insisted briskly, "for at the moment we have damned little of a movement. . . . Don't you believe, my friend, that I want to impose myself, all I want is to spread our ideas everywhere and get the movement going, mainly an English one." She was thinking of "making a tour through the country next month in order to awaken the sleeping brothers a little." Were the "gentlemen comrades in Buffalo still devoted with love and life to their pope Hannes [Most]?" she wondered. Two weeks later, Goldman had "firmly decided to travel on my own and to arrange meetings independently." By renting the halls and publicizing the meetings well, "I am firmly convinced that we will have tremendous success. From the collections we can easily cover the expenses. This is the way I have done it in Pittsburgh, Baltimore and other cities, and always with great success. What do you think about that?"[11]

Emma's letters from this period display her pragmatic outlook and the tough-mindedness that made her a forceful presence in the movement. For example, she acknowledged to Metzkow that any hope for winning a shorter sentence for Berkman was doomed as long as it was in the hands of anarchists. It was necessary, therefore, to secure the support of the unions: in choosing union delegates to introduce resolutions supporting Berkman's case, it was important, she advised Metzkow, "that the delegate who submits a resolution is not known as an anarchist or socialist, otherwise people would be prejudiced toward him."[12] On another occasion, in a controversy involving the editor of the Buffalo *Arbeiter Zeitung*, Goldman urged that Metzkow "and the others concerned with the newspaper should be resolute enough to fire this man. In my opinion, propaganda is the most important thing, and whoever stands in its way *must go*. You are probably surprised that I speak so categorically," she added, "but I know from bitter experience that considerations for *one person* destroyed the German movement in this country."[13] Her letters to Metzkow usually included some urgent appeal for funds, delivered with great forcefulness.

As these letters show, Goldman had conceived the independent style that characterized her political work for the next twenty years as early as 1896. She continued through the nineties to speak in

German and in English, primarily to working-class immigrant audiences—at demonstrations, protest meetings, picnics, lectures arranged by radical union locals, chapters of the Workmen's Circle, and anarchist groups around the country. But while most radical agitators and organizers were affiliated with a union, a political party, a particular organization or group, Goldman thought of herself as a "free-lance," working for groups "only temporarily," and indeed, working "for them, not with them. Whatever value my activities had in America was due to my free-lancing and independent position." Although Jewish immigrants were beginning to swell the urban working class, and Yiddish-speaking anarchists now outnumbered the old German emigré revolutionists, Goldman as late as 1906 addressed Jewish audiences in German, insisting that she did not speak "jargon." Not until 1908 did she begin lecturing in Yiddish.[14]

After two successful cross-country lecture tours, in 1897–1898 and 1899, Goldman returned to Europe in November of 1899. She was financed this time by two wealthy, free-thinking Ohio businessmen, one of whom had bankrolled the anarchist paper *Der arme Teufel*. Goldman eagerly accepted their offer to help her realize her dream of becoming a doctor by supporting her medical studies in Zurich. It is doubtful, however, that she ever really intended to enroll in medical school. Instead, "the indefatigable Emma" lectured in England, attracting larger audiences, according to the anarchist paper *Freedom*, than any other anarchist lecturer apart from Peter Kropotkin himself.

Goldman never liked the English, but she did discover, in London, Hippolyte Havel, a bohemian anarchist journalist and agitator of mixed Czech and gypsy origins. The two had a brief affair and an enduring friendship. Havel had already served several jail sentences for his fiery anarchist speeches (he was rescued from his last incarceration in a prison psychopathic ward by Krafft-Ebbing, who certified that Havel was sane even if he disbelieved in government). Deported from Vienna, he eventually ended up in London, where he supported himself by doing menial household labor. A small, excitable man, Havel was by turns witty and morose, charming and buffoonish, amusing and jealous, given to outbursts of vituperative anger that were exacerbated by his heavy drinking.

According to her autobiography, Goldman persuaded Havel to give up his job in a London boarding house, and together they roamed the streets and slums of the city. In late January or early February of 1900, they left for Paris. The purpose of the visit to Paris was to help organize an International Anarchist Congress scheduled for September of 1900: a Congress regarded with mixed feelings by many anarchists in the United States, who were uncertain that the benefits would be worth the expense. The organizers of the Congress proposed to provide a forum for contacts between anarchists from different countries, to establish an international correspondence bureau, and to publicize anarchist ideas. Goldman enthusiastically favored the plan, emphasizing in particular its publicity value. An international Congress would attract favorable attention in the press, she pointed out, while local propaganda meetings were noted only by small anarchist periodicals reaching a tiny audience. At the last moment, however, the socialist municipal authorities of Paris, anxious about the Exposition being held at that time, prohibited the Congress from meeting. This suppression angered Goldman, but she retorted that by banning the meetings, the authorities were "doing more to provoke interest in the ideas they are so anxious to kill than the ablest man in our movement."[15] The delegates met clandestinely on the outskirts of the city. Most gave reports on the state of the anarchist movement in their respective countries. The practical-minded Goldman's was characteristically titled, "A Report on the Ways and Means to Arrange Successful Propaganda Tours through the States."[16]

The achievements of the Congress were limited, due partly to the intensive surveillance by French police to which the anarchists were subjected and partly to the constant danger from agents provocateurs. The spate of sensational terrorist acts between 1892 and 1894 in France had not been forgotten by the Paris police; not until the Amsterdam Anarchist Congress of 1907, to which Goldman was once again a delegate, were anarchists able to hold an open international meeting and effectively publicize their views. She did, however, also attend in 1900 a clandestine Neo-Malthusian Congress. Here she met the leading European advocates of contraception, who supplied her with literature and contraceptives to bring back to the United States for her future work.

By November of 1900, after nearly ten months in Paris, Emma's money ran out; her benefactors in America had stopped sending funds on learning that she was not in fact studying medicine. With her usual practical ingenuity, she set herself up as a cook to some anarchist comrades visiting Paris and acted as a guide to a few American tourists to earn additional money and extend her visit. Late in November, however, pursued by detectives, shocked to learn of the failure of Berkman's escape plan, and without funds, Emma decided it was time to leave. On December 7, 1900, Goldman, accompanied by Havel, arrived once again in New York.

By the time Emma Goldman returned from Europe, she had formulated the politics that guided her actions for the next twenty years. She did not attempt to organize her ideas in a systematic way, but developed them in her lectures, in pamphlets, in articles published in both the anarchist and the commercial press, and even in interviews, which contained some of her best insights. Goldman's political thought, as it emerged in the late nineties, blended Kropotkin's theory of communist anarchism with the individualism of Stirner, Nietzsche, and Ibsen and a strong emphasis on woman's emancipation and sexual freedom, drawn from Chernyshevsky, Freud, the British sex radicals, and the American free love tradition. Less interested in theory than in practice, she used these ideas to criticize contemporary society and to propose methods of change.

The essential basis of her politics was opposition to the state. Translated into strategy, this meant opposition to centralized authority, to large organizations, to legal compulsion such as the draft, and to any form of censorship or coercion. While all anarchists opposed dictatorship and repressive government authority, they also resisted more liberal forms of the state. Goldman for a long time did not make distinctions between states: all were equally unjust. She opposed not only undemocratic forms of government, but also parliamentary democracy, on the grounds that it subordinated the individual or minority to the will of the majority and required individuals to delegate decision-making power to a representative. On this point Goldman was adamant, actively urging people not to vote, participate in electoral campaigns, or hold any government positions. Indeed, she often harshly criticized comrades who occasionally compromised their principles to campaign or vote for socialist or labor candidates. Elections and voting, she often asserted, gave people the illusion of political participation without the reality; electing radicals to political office merely created a new class of bureaucrats within the radical movement. The ballot was "simply a means for the transference of the rights of the people to the control of rulers."[17] In her view, the struggle must not be fought by electoral politics. "Correct ideas must precede correct action," she affirmed in 1901. "Education and agitation are the means. Whenever the people shall have arrived at a knowledge of the true principles governing harmonious social relations, they will put them into practice, without the ballot box."[18]

Instead of parliamentary "political action," the anarchists advocated extraparliamentary "direct action"—demonstrations in the streets, strikes at the workplace, the assertion of individual will in everyday life. Instead of mass organizations or political parties, she urged action by small, autonomous groups and by individuals seizing initiative to oppose oppressive laws and to create alternative institutions such as radical schools, theaters, libraries, and cooperatives. She actively defended trade unions, urging them to become more revolutionary in their demands, and spoke often in support of striking workers. "Direct action against the authority in the shop, direct action against the authority of the law, direct action against the invasive, meddlesome authority of our moral code, is the logical consistent method of Anarchism," she wrote later.[19]

In addition to opposing the state, Goldman as a communist anarchist also opposed capitalism: a position she shared with the Marxist (or parliamentary) socialists and which sharply differentiated her from the individualist anarchists who imagined an ideal society composed of small property owners. However, while parliamentary socialists argued for nationalization of the means of production, the anarchists argued for "socialization"—that is, the transfer of private property, not to the state, but to the individuals who actually worked or used it. Goldman, therefore, opposed socialist and Populist demands for state social welfare programs and for nationalization of major industries such as railroads, utilities, and banks, on the grounds that this would only increase the power of the government.

A third major strand of Goldman's politics, and that of most of her anarchist contemporaries, was an antipathy to religion that at times bordered on obsession. Goldman frequently lectured on atheism and the failure of Christianity, a religion she thought "admirably adapted to the training of slaves," and insisted on the evils, not simply of the church, but of religious belief itself.[20] Delighting in provocative attacks on religion that scandalized not only middle-class Americans but also most immigrant workers, for whom church or synagogue still remained a center of community life, Goldman nevertheless was inspired by a deep ethical and moral passion that led some of her contemporaries to see her as an essentially religious figure, bearing witness to the evils of her time. In her autobiography she quotes, with evident pride, the rabbi who proclaimed her "the most religious person I know."[21] For the Jewish immigrants in the movement, to be an anarchist meant not only work in the unions, building cooperatives, educating oneself and others; it meant applying anarchist principles in everyday life: "living like a human being," treating others with respect, refusing to dominate others or be dominated oneself.[22] On this point, Goldman once remarked, "I don't care if a man's theory for tomorrow is correct, I care if his spirit of today is correct." She defined this spirit as not trying "to enrich ourselves at the expense of others," not seeking government protection or holding government positions, not miseducating children in the public schools, catering to public opinion, or bowing to existing standards of morality. "It seems to me that *these* are the new forms of life, and that they will take the place of the old, not by preaching or voting, but by living them."[23]

If the central thrust of Goldman's politics was critical—"the spirit of revolt, in whatever form, against everything that hinders human growth"—she also took care to emphasize that anarchism was not just "kicking against everything—especially private property." Anarchism was indeed committed to the "tearing down of existing institutions which hold the human race in bondage."[24] It was also committed to building a free society in which the potential of every individual could reach its fullest expression. Goldman accepted Kropotkin's view that human beings were "naturally" social and that there was no inherent conflict between "the individual and the social instincts." Without the domination of powerful institutions of authority, and of "man-made laws," people would be free to follow the dictates of "natural law," which Goldman defined as "that factor in man which asserts itself freely and spontaneously without any external force, in harmony with the requirements of nature." The removal of artificial forms of authority would result, not in chaos, but in the emergence of "natural" forms of social cooperation and mutual aid.[25]

Like most anarchists, Goldman refused to prescribe the anarchist society of the future, affirming only that "its economic arrangements must consist of voluntary productive and distributive associations, gradually developing into free communism. . . ."[26] In contrast with present-day society, in which man was robbed "not merely of the products of his labor, but of the power of free initiative, of originality, and the interest in, or desire for, the things he is making," the anarchist society would leave the individual free to do meaningful work. The average worker would resemble the artist: "one to whom the making of a table, the building of a house, or the tilling of the soil, is what the painting is to the artist and the discovery to the scientist—the result of inspiration, of intense longing, and deep interest in work as a creative force."[27]

While many radicals shared this view of work, Goldman went beyond most of her immigrant comrades in arguing that sex was also a source of creative energy and that love was the only "inspiring, elevating basis for a new race, a new world." What most distinguished Goldman's anarchism from that of her European contemporaries was her insistence on making sexuality a central concern of her politics. For the Jewish immigrant anarchists, "free love" was more a religious than a sexual question; it meant opposition to religious and legal marriage, but implied no necessary challenge to monogamy or stress on eroticism. Goldman, too, opposed legal and religious marriage, which she regarded as another form of prostitution. She believed only in "the marriage of affection." "If two people care for each other," she insisted, "they have a right to live together as long as that love exists. When it is dead, what base immorality for them still to keep together."[28] Yet Goldman, drawing on the ideas of Freud and of the American free love tradition, also went on to define "the sex question" as "the very basis of the weal or woe of the race" and to urge frank public discussions to overcome the prevailing "conspiracy of silence."[29] In matter-of-fact talks in the late nineties on "Marriage," "The New Woman," "Free Love," and "Sex Problems," she explained that "the sex act is simply the execution of certain natural functions of the human body, as natural, as healthy and as necessary when exercised temperately, as the functions of the stomach, the brain, the muscles, etc."[30] Each individual should be the sole determinant of his or her sexual behavior, and it was nobody's business if a woman was a monogamist or a "varietist"; indeed, most men were varietists, why not women? Later, in lectures on "Sex, the Great

Element of Creative Art," she stressed the power of the sexual impulse over all aspects of life and argued that sexual repression not only harmed health but inhibited intellectual and artistic creativity as well.[31] Beginning in 1895 with her defense of Oscar Wilde during his trial, Goldman extended the basic anarchist idea of "noninvasion" to a defense of homosexuality. In what may have been her most audacious lecture, "Vice" (later she would draw on the work of Edward Carpenter to discuss "The Intermediate Sex"), she insisted that sex was an absolutely private affair into which state, church, or other people had no right to intrude. She argued that any act entered into voluntarily by two people was not vice. "What is usually hastily condemned as vice by thoughtless individuals, such as homosexuality, masturbation, etc.," she advised, "should be considered from a scientific viewpoint, and not in a moralizing way."[32]

For Emma, "the sex question" was also emphatically a woman's question, since women suffered most from repressive sexual values. Kropotkin had neglected to mention the specific problems of women, and a distinct strain of misogyny stamped the thought of Proudhon and Bakunin. For Goldman, the liberation of women could not be postponed until after the revolution or subsumed under larger political struggles. Free women were essential for the success of the radical movement. The sexual liberation of women was, moreover, integral to their emancipation as fully developed human beings. "I demand the independence of woman," she announced in 1897; "her right to support herself; to live for herself; to love whomever she pleases, or as many as she pleases. I demand freedom for both sexes, freedom of action, freedom in love and freedom in motherhood."[33]

Still, Goldman did not call herself a feminist and took care to differentiate her politics from those of the largely middle-class, American-born members of that movement. Her main argument with the feminists concerned the vote, which she opposed on principle for women and for men. "Now the women were only whipped by the men," she argued, "but if they got the ballot they would be whipped by the Government the same as their husbands."[34] In addition, Goldman criticized the suffragists for ignoring the problems of working women and for either "aping" men or considering women morally superior to men, thereby deepening antagonism between the sexes. She argued that women holding political power would be more militaristic, repressive, and puritanical than men. She especially attacked the mainstream feminists for their tendency to uphold conservative sexual attitudes and to focus on the dangers rather than the pleasures of sex. For such views and for her often critical attitude toward women generally, she was sometimes called "a man's woman," she tells us in her memoirs.[35] And indeed, as one of a very few prominent women in a predominantly male movement, Emma did not easily identify with other women or see herself as part of a community of women. Her closest coworkers in the movement were men, and she remained aloof from all other groups of organized women (suffragists, trade union women, women's club members) in part because her views were far more radical than theirs, but also because she disliked all-women gatherings and groups.[36] Her relationships with individual women tended to be uneasy; she often resented the conventional wives of her male comrades (who sometimes did not hide their dislike or jealousy of her) and was competitive with other prominent women anarchists such as Chicago activist Lucy Parsons (one of "those damn widows," as Emma called the wives of the Haymarket victims) and Voltairine de Cleyre, the most prominent American-born member of the movement; her closest friendships, as she grew older, were with younger women whose admiration and devotion overcame her sense of rivalry.

A second divergence between Goldman's politics and the politics of others in the movement centered around the tensions between collectivism and individualism in anarchist thought. Most Jewish immigrant anarchists were powerfully attracted by the communitarian aspects of Kropotkin's vision. Goldman, too, at times, emphasized the theme of community. In "The Aim of Humanity," for example, she proclaimed that society was based on interdependence, affirming that "the happiness of each is based on the happiness of all" and urging her listeners to "become useful men and women and give what we have of ability and talent to educate and to help others."[37] But more and more she stressed the primacy of the individual, lacing her lectures with references to Stirner, Nietzsche, and Ibsen and announcing early in 1901, "I really work very little with the masses. Not that I am not in sympathy with concerted action, but I believe our ends are reached more quickly by educating the individual."[38] Goldman always remained ambivalent about communal living arrangements and regarded anarchist colonies—embraced with enthusiasm by some immigrant comrades—with Stirnerian suspicion, fearing that they did not allow enough individual privacy and that shared ideas did not necessarily foster social compatibility. She wanted "collective work but individual lives."[39]

Goldman's individualism deepened over the years. By 1909 she was lecturing on "Minorities versus Majorities"—an attack on American habits of conformity aimed against the socialists, whom Goldman felt flattered the masses with demagogic praise to garner votes and boost themselves into power. Arguing for a vanguard of "intelligent minorities" and superior individuals to set an example for the mass, she came close in this essay to blaming the workers for their own exploitation. "That the mass bleeds, that it is being robbed and exploited, I know as well as our vote-baiters. But I insist that not the handful of parasites, but the mass itself is responsible for this horrible state of affairs. It clings to its masters, loves the whip, and is the first to cry Crucify! the moment a protesting voice is raised against the sacredness of capitalistic authority or any other decayed institution."[40]

Increasingly, Goldman differed from her mentor, Peter Kropotkin —indeed from most Kropotkinite anarchists—who argued that pioneering individuals derived their inspiration from the masses, rather than the reverse. If he and others had contributed to the liberation of exploited mankind, Kropotkin wrote, "it is because our ideas have been more or less the expression of the ideas that are germinating in the very depths of the masses of the people. . . . no truthful social action is possible but the science which bases its conclusions, and the action which bases its acts, upon the thoughts and the aspirations of the masses."[41] Repudiating this idea, Goldman argued instead for an aristocracy of spirit—regarding anarchists as the true aristocrats —that would lead the masses through example. Though she insisted on the difference between bourgeois "rugged individualism" and her own anarchist individualism, the distinction tends to blur in her recurring references to "the ignorant mass" and "the poor, stupid, free American citizen."[42] As Richard Drinnon has observed, Goldman never resolved the tension in her thought—shared by other anarchists as well—between the populist faith of Kropotkin and the individualism of Stirner, Nietzsche, Ibsen, and Emerson.[43] Her sympathies remained with the poor and oppressed, she hated the arrogance of wealth and power, but she most admired the independent, innovative individual with the strength to resist social convention. She believed radical social change would come about "only through the zeal, courage, the non-compromising determination of intelligent minorities, and not through the mass."[44]

Still, Emma Goldman's ideas were not startlingly extreme within the context of the international anarchist movement. For all her equivocation about violence, she never indulged in paeans to bombs and explosives as did earlier anarchists. She always insisted that education, not dynamite, would lead the way to revolution. She never went as far as anarchist women like de Cleyre, who opposed the nuclear family altogether and denounced, not just legal marriage, but any long-term commitment between two people as inherently enslaving emotionally. Goldman's lectures on subjects such as "Charity," "Patriotism," "A Criticism of Ethics," and "The Basis of Morality" accorded at many points with the views of liberal reformers and anti-imperialists, who also decried militarism and exposed the economic origins of crime.

Had anyone called Goldman a moralist, she would have been deeply offended, for she always regarded herself, and was regarded by her critics, as an enemy of all "morality." Yet anarchism itself had a strongly moralistic element, as historian George Woodcock has pointed out.[45] Goldman opposed not morality but conservative nineteenth-century moral values, offering instead a radical moral vision that accounted both for her unpopularity and her appeal. Although she allowed that "the main evil today is an economic one," Goldman refused to accord economics a determining role in her social theory. Character, she insisted, had nothing to do with social class.[46] In her eagerness to criticize what she regarded as the fatalism and economism of her Marxist contemporaries—and even of other anarchists —she sometimes went to extremes, insisting that individual moral character was the most important determinant of material life. "The men who consider economic conditions the cause of all the evils in society are absolutely wrong," she proclaimed in 1901. "They say man is on a low level because of oppressive conditions. Upset everything, set him free and things will adjust themselves. They will do nothing of the kind. I don't deny that economic conditions are important, but they are not a cause. They are a result—a result of lack of responsibility in the individual man. Man has given up his birthright because he didn't understand himself, his responsibility, his power."[47] Anarchism in general rejected a Marxist, materialist interpretation of society, insisting instead on the primacy of consciousness in shaping the conditions of life. Goldman went even further than many anarchists in her stress on the determining role of ideas and in her faith in the political potential of art. Gradually she moved away from lectures on politics and economics to talks on literature and art (her reasons were also tactical: "to hammer away at the economic conditions of society did not prove to be a success").[48] The key to the anarchist revolution was a revolution in morality, the "transvaluation of all values," a conquest of the "phantoms" that have held people captive. As she wrote many years later, "man's true liberation, individual and collective," would come only with his emancipation from authority and from the belief in its necessity.[49] As Alexander Berkman insisted, "it is ideas that maintain conditions," and therefore changes "must *first* take place in the ideas and opinions of the people."[50]

By the end of the nineties, ideas and opinions were changing. This depression-wracked decade had stirred powerful voices of protest, with the great strikes at Homestead and Pullman, armies of the unemployed marching on Washington to demand relief, a Populist party arising out of the South and West to voice the interests of impoverished farmers, and social settlements such as Jane Addams's Hull House blossoming in the middle of the Chicago slums. Even within the churches, liberal voices of a Social Gospel criticized the harshness of prevailing conditions and urged more humane treatment of the poor. But the conservatism of the Gilded Age remained strong. With the lifting of the depression in 1897, confidence returned to the business community, which soon welcomed "a splendid little war" to suppress revolutionary movements in Cuba and the Philippines while acquiring new markets and natural resources. The American Federation of Labor sought to consolidate a strong, conservative labor movement within the structures of corporate capitalism. The women's movement languished as numerous state suffrage referenda failed. If growing numbers of women went to college, worked in offices, and became social workers and physicians, most were destined for marriage and childbearing and the dreariest of jobs on farms, in factories, or in the mansions of the wealthy. In the South, lynchings multiplied and de facto segregation of the races was rapidly hardening into formal Jim Crow legislation, while in the Northeast and West, hostilities toward the rising flood of immigrants

—indeed, toward all Jews, Catholics, Asians, and blacks—reemerged whenever the economy took a downward turn.

In this setting, Emma Goldman intensified her challenge, as Alix Kates Shulman notes, by proclaiming her ideas in dangerous places —attacking patriotism before soldiers, mocking religion to clergymen, deriding the ballot to suffragists, publicly declaring her sympathy for terrorists such as Angiolillo, assassin of the Spanish Prime Minister Cánovas del Castillo—and by practicing free love and smoking in public "up to forty cigarettes a day."[51] If she was becoming a popular figure on the radical lecture circuit, "that terrible name" was also becoming "synonymous with everything vile and criminal."[52] No wonder, then, that in 1898 the *San Francisco Call* spoke for many in denouncing Goldman as "a despicable creature," a "snake," "unfit to live in a civilized country." Not a few people would have applauded the proposal that she "be hanged by the neck until dead and considerably longer."[53]

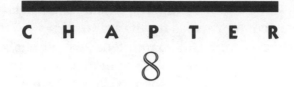

C H A P T E R

8

CZOLGOSZ

Nineteen hundred and one opened on a promising note. Goldman's ideas struck a responsive chord in growing numbers of people. If some were attracted by the sensational publicity surrounding her, others found that she spoke to their real interests and anxieties. Invitations to lecture poured in from such diverse quarters as the Scandinavian Painters' Union in Chicago, which heard a lecture on "Cooperation as a Factor in the Industrial Struggle," and the prestigious Manhattan Liberal Club in New York, which turned out in large numbers for the lecture on "Vice." *Lucifer* and *Free Society*—successor to *The Firebrand*, and now published in Chicago by the family of Abraham Isaak—covered her talks at length; Goldman was by this time well-known to all readers, for she regularly participated in the various controversies aired in these papers. Should anarchists lecture for pay? No, she thought. Could an anarchist also be a lawyer? Or participate in an election campaign? She thought certainly not and denounced those who did as scurrilous and immoral.[1]

While grotesque caricatures and harsh attacks still appeared in the commercial press, she also received some very favorable coverage. In January of 1901, for example, a long, sympathetic interview in the *New York Sun* headed "Woman Anarchist Says She Opposes Violence" faithfully reported Goldman's family background, her great faith in America, and her views on Russian, French, and American women. It also discussed various misconceptions about anarchism. Insisting that she never advocated violence and would think any man an "utter fool" who told her he was planning an assassination, Goldman nonetheless admitted that she would never condemn the man who resorted to violence. "I look behind him for the conditions that made him possible, and my horror is swallowed up in pity," she explained. She was pleased to observe that "the wealthy and educated class in America is at last getting a glimmering idea that anarchy isn't bomb-throwing—that it is philosophy."[2]

This admiring interview—which Goldman herself liked—nevertheless inspired her angry recantation in *Free Society* early in February, where she insisted that "I have never opposed force or propaganda by deed, either publicly or privately." In a tone of high irritation, she added that she was "on the side of every rebel, whether his act has been beneficial or detrimental to our cause; for I do not judge an act by its result, but by its cause; and the cause of each and every rebellious act has been organized despotism, robbery and exploitation on the part of society, and the innate sense of justice and a rebellious spirit on the part of the individual." Violence was not a phase of anarchy, and indeed anarchy absolutely opposed violence; yet organized force—that is, government—left no other method of propaganda than acts of violence.[3]

Such confusing statements, over eight years after the attempted *attentat* at Homestead, suggest Goldman's continuing struggle to reconcile her loyalty to Berkman with her belief that education, not explosives, was the correct anarchist method of action. Equating terrorism as a political tactic with political violence as a spontaneous mass protest against unbearable conditions, she blurred their quite different significance. While she instinctively sympathized with all protesters, she tried to explain their acts both as spontaneous, inevitable reactions to oppression and as deliberate acts of heroic will: to glorify terrorists while deploring terrorism. It was hardly surprising that even her close associates were uncertain of her views.

Goldman spent a strenuous winter and spring nursing and lecturing, stopping in Chicago for several weeks at the home of the Isaak family to work with local comrades. Emma had felt especially close to Abe and Mary Isaak ever since she met them in San Francisco in 1898. Russian Mennonite immigrants who had settled on the West Coast, they had become anarchists; in 1895, together with some American-born comrades, they began publishing *The Firebrand*. Later they founded *Free Society*, which they published first in San Francisco and later in Chicago. The Isaaks outspokenly defended sexual freedom in their papers, for which they had been sharply criticized by their East Coast and European comrades, including Kropotkin. Emma, however, had welcomed their position, for she had been chastised for similar views. Feeling isolated in her own immediate ranks on account of her emphasis on sex, she had been delighted to discover that the Isaaks "felt and lived as I did."[4]

In July, Goldman went to Rochester for a six-week holiday with her family, which now included a new generation—the American-born children of her sisters. One wonders, perhaps, if the presence of these American descendants of Taube and Abraham may have prompted in Emma thoughts of her own deepening commitment to America. She had by this time lived in the United States for nearly eleven years, longer than she had lived anywhere else. Her English was now fluent—the careful English of a well-educated foreigner. It betrayed her European origins only in its precision and slight burring, most noticeable when she became angry or excited. (To some, her slight accent sounded more like that of the native upper class than the foreign-born.)[5] She had not yet begun to think of herself completely as an American—she was "Russian, Russian through and through," she assured a reporter—but for several years now she had been seeking out English-speaking audiences and expressing her great faith in the possibilities for anarchism in America. Compared to Europeans, Americans, she thought, had great perseverence and "finer innate ideas of freedom." "It takes a long time to make an Englishman or American think, but when he gets started he will not stop. He isn't fickle. When he gives his heart to a cause," she observed, "he is capable of sticking to it."[6] Goldman also thought that American women were bound to help the anarchist movement, particularly those of the middle class, since they already had considerable freedom. In America Goldman had found a milieu far more hospitable to her ideals than any she had known before—certainly more than St. Petersburg, with its virulent anti-Semitism. True, as she would later joke, "one had to go to prison from time to time." Yet she and Berkman had "our own publication, our own platform, our own life. . . . we could at all times speak out or write what we damned pleased."[7] She had discovered in Emerson, Thoreau, and Walt Whitman an American anti-authoritarian tradition congenial to her own anarchist vision, while her contacts with John Swinton had further convinced her that Americans, too, "once aroused, were as capable of idealism and sacrifice as my Russian heroes and heroines."[8]

If such optimistic thoughts about America ever occurred to the thirty-two-year-old Goldman as she relaxed with her nieces and nephews in the rooftop garden of her sister Helene's house in Rochester, they were destined to be short-lived. After a six-week idyll, she once again headed west. She was in St. Louis lecturing and, on the side, soliciting orders for a new "novelty album" that Ed Brady was trying to market, when she heard the news that the President of the United States had been shot. Headlines announced the following day: "Assassin is Leon Czolgosz who says he is an Anarchist and Follower of Emma Goldman."

On Friday, September 6, at four o'clock in the afternoon, a young man named Leon Czolgosz had walked into the Temple of Music at the Pan-American Exposition in Buffalo, New York, and shot President William McKinley as he greeted visitors.

The assassin Leon Czolgosz was the twenty-nine-year-old son of Polish immigrant parents. He had grown up in Detroit, moved several times with his family, and eventually landed in Cleveland, where he found work in the Newburg wire mills on the outskirts of the city. Here he was drawn first to socialism, then to anarchism. He had attended Emma Goldman's lecture "Modern Phases of Anarchy," which she delivered at the Franklin Liberal Club in Cleveland early in May. Later, Goldman remembered a young man with "a most sensitive face" who had asked her, during the intermission, to recommend some reading.[9] In early July, calling himself Nieman, he had appeared at the Isaak home in Chicago just as she was leaving for Rochester. He had accompanied her on the elevated train to the railway station. Here she had given him over to the care of Hippolyte Havel, who had moved to Chicago shortly after his arrival in the United States. Nieman's strange behavior, however, aroused mistrust. After consulting with Cleveland anarchist Emil Schilling, whom Nieman had also visited, Abe Isaak became convinced that the man was a spy—not an unreasonable suspicion at a time when agents provocateurs infested anarchist groups—and printed a warning in the September 1, 1901, issue of *Free Society*. "The attention of the comrades is called to another spy," Isaak wrote. "He is well-dressed, of medium height, rather narrow-shouldered, blond, and about twenty-five years of age." His demeanor was of "the usual sort, pretending to be greatly interested in the cause, asking for names, or soliciting aid for acts of contemplated violence." He had appeared already in Chicago and Cleveland; should he appear elsewhere, "the comrades are warned in advance, and can act accordingly."[10] Five days later the President was shot; within two weeks, he was dead.

Immediately after the shooting, anarchists in Buffalo, Pittsburgh, New York, and other major cities were arrested and held for questioning. In Chicago, twelve anarchists were held without bail, including Abraham Isaak and Hippolyte Havel. The Isaak home was ransacked. Anarchist meetings everywhere were broken up, the participants clubbed, beaten, arrested, driven out of their homes and communities. A Pittsburgh anarchist was nearly lynched; an anarchist in Kansas City was dragged through the streets by an angry crowd, pelted with stones, and threatened with lynching; others were chased by vigilantes, even tarred and feathered. In New York, a mob nearly demolished the offices of the *Freie Arbeiter Stimme*, the Yiddish anarchist paper. And Johann Most, for having had the misfortune to reprint in the *Freiheit* one day before the shooting a fifty-year-old essay defending the assassination of kings, was arrested, tried, and sentenced to a year in prison.[11]

Of all the anarchists, however, Emma Goldman was the most wanted, for the newspapers displayed an alleged "confession" quoting Leon Czolgosz as saying that Emma Goldman had "set me on fire," and that after hearing her lecture, he had resolved "to do something heroic for the cause I loved."[12] In Buffalo, where Czolgosz had immediately been incarcerated, the chief of police and the district attorney were especially eager to track down Goldman for what promised to be a spectacular murder trial. For three days, however, her whereabouts remained unknown, despite the efforts of police and reporters in Rochester, Buffalo, and elsewhere who subjected Goldman's family and friends, including ten-year-old Stella Cominsky, to intensive questioning. Then, on September 10, she was arrested at the Chicago apartment of Mr. and Mrs. C. J. Norris, prosperous American-born friends who had no known associations with anarchism.

Why had Goldman gone immediately to Chicago? In her autobiography—recalling the event thirty years later—she wrote that upon seeing in the newspapers a photograph of Czolgosz, whom she recognized as Nieman, and learning that her Chicago comrades were being held without bail, she felt that it was "plainly my duty to surrender myself." Besides, she knew that "there was neither reason nor the least proof to connect me with the shooting."[13] Yet Goldman must have known that reasons and proof were irrelevant, and it is not clear in what sense she felt that she had a "duty" to return to Chicago and to what must have seemed like certain death. Perhaps she recalled the example of Albert Parsons, one of the Haymarket anarchists, who had dramatically surrendered himself in court as the trial opened in order to share the fate of his comrades. Perhaps at that moment she even wanted to share the fate of her Haymarket heroes, as the autobiography implies.[14]

In any event, Goldman was indeed arrested and was locked up at the Harrison Street Police Station under the surveillance of an extra detachment of guards. She had tried unsuccessfully, by disguising herself as a Swedish maid, to delay the arrest until the arrival of a reporter from the *Chicago Tribune*, which reportedly offered her five thousand dollars for an interview. The reporters who flocked around her at the station seem to have admired her in spite of themselves. They describe a defiant Goldman, with the slight accent that lent "fascination" to her speech and looking more like a student than an anarchist—she was dressed in a white shirtwaist of fine material, a dark blue cheviot skirt, patent leather boots, and a straw hat encircled by a dotted veil—holding court in the middle of a room, calmly answering the questions hurled at her. "Am I accountable because some crack-brained person put a wrong construction on my words?" the *New York Times* quoted her as saying.

Leon Czolgosz, I am convinced, planned the deed unaided and entirely alone. There is no Anarchist ring which would help him. There may be Anarchists who would murder, but there are also men in every walk of life who sometimes feel the impulse to kill. I do not know surely, but I think Czolgosz was one of those downtrodden men who see all the misery which the rich inflict upon the poor, who think of it, who brood over it, and then, in despair, resolve to strike a great blow, as they think, for the good of their fellow-men. But that is not Anarchy. Czolgosz . . . may have been inspired by me, but if he was, he took the wrong way of showing it.

Anarchism, stated Goldman, "did not teach men to do the act for which Czolgosz is under arrest. We work against the system, and education is our watchword."[15]

Despite sensational headlines, the persistent efforts of police to uncover a grand anarchist plot against the President, and the determined attempts of the Buffalo authorities to wring a statement of Goldman's complicity from Czolgosz, the plan to extradite Goldman to Buffalo soon collapsed. On September 11, one day after her arrest, the Buffalo district attorney announced his belief that sufficient evidence existed to issue requisition papers for Goldman, to bring her to Buffalo, and to try her for conspiracy to assassinate the President. But the next day, September 12, he was forced to admit that he had no evidence against her and that unless "something of importance" turned up, no requisition papers would be issued.[16] Mayor Carter Harrison of Chicago, for his part, affirmed on the day after Goldman's arrest that she was "a woman of decidedly great ability, and even if she were connected with a deed of that sort, I think she is too smart to get caught at it."[17] But in fact Harrison doubted that a plot existed, and he admitted that the only evidence against her in Chicago was that she was wanted in Buffalo.

Nonetheless, Goldman, along with the other Chicago anarchists, was kept locked up without bail until September 18, when bail was fixed at twenty thousand dollars for her and fifteen thousand dollars for all the others together. Reporters lingered at the jail—the anarchists had been transferred to Cook County Jail, where the Haymarket men had been held—and reported her activities with a mixture of admiration and horror. Albert Parsons must have been much on her mind during these tense days, for she often sang his favorite song, "Annie Laurie."[18]

On September 24, after a brief, perfunctory trial, the unfortunate Leon Czolgosz was convicted of assassinating the President. Those who subsequently studied the record of his trial confirmed Emma Goldman's judgment that it was a travesty of justice.[19] Most of the jurors had formed an opinion of Czolgosz's guilt prior to the trial; the lawyers assigned to defend him made maudlin apologies for their role; the "alienists" assigned to determine sanity or insanity made little effort to study his life. In fact, Czolgosz had a long history of peculiar behavior, was regarded by his father and stepmother as demented, and from his youth had been isolated, timid, and frightened of everything. His stepmother believed that he had been insane, at least at the moment of the shooting, and also thought that he lacked the intelligence to read and understand Goldman's works.[20] This diagnosis was essentially confirmed by the doctors who examined the trial records after Czolgosz's death and concluded that he had been "a diseased man, a man who had been suffering from some form of mental disease for years."[21] He was certainly not medically responsible, they wrote, and it was questionable whether he was legally responsible for McKinley's death.

The same day that Leon Czolgosz was convicted, Emma Goldman was released from jail. (The other Chicago anarchists had been freed one day earlier.) Newspapers that had proclaimed her complicity in front-page headlines now buried the news of her release in small, back-page items. In retrospect, she attributed her release to the good will of the Chicago police chief, who had become convinced of her innocence; he was also in the midst of a feud within the department and did not wish his subordinates to get credit for rescuing the country from anarchy. Immediately upon her release, Goldman tried to mobilize support for Czolgosz from other anarchists, but she met with absolute refusal except from the Spanish, Italian, and French comrades. Most of the Jewish and American anarchists refused any public expression of support, insisting that Czolgosz was not an anarchist, maintaining that he had harmed the movement, and generally concurring in the view that he was mentally ill.

During the weeks following the assassination, Goldman grew increasingly enraged at the failure of other anarchists to come publicly to Czolgosz's defense. The more he was vilified in the commercial press, the more strongly she defended him—her earlier tirades against him notwithstanding—and the loftier grew her praise. In an essay, "The Tragedy at Buffalo," which she published in the October 6 issue of *Free Society,* just one month after the assassination, Goldman insisted that men like Czolgosz were motivated by a greater sensitivity than others, a deeper sympathy for suffering, "a love so strong that it shrinks before no consequence, a love so broad that it can never be wrapped up in one object, as long as thousands perish, a love so all-absorbing that it can neither calculate, reason, investigate, but only dare, dare at all costs." His was a "soul in pain, a soul that could find no abode in this cruel world of ours, a soul 'impractical,' inexpedient, lacking in caution . . . but daring just the same, and I cannot help but bow in reverenced silence before the power of such a soul, that has broken the narrow walls of its prison, and taken a daring leap into the unknown."[22] Goldman insisted that anarchists must analyze the psychology of such an act, and she denounced the "shallow multitude" and the "rabble" incapable of understanding its meaning. When, two days later, *Lucifer* quoted her as saying at a lecture that she deplored the assassination and believed that "if the people want to do away with assassins, they must do away with the conditions which produce murderers," she replied angrily that she had said no such thing.[23] Czolgosz, she had firmly concluded, was "a man with the beautiful soul of a child and the energy of a giant," a man "so pitiful in his loneliness and yet so sublime in his silence and superiority over his enemies." Goldman then let loose a scathing attack against "the majority of anarchists," who had "utterly failed to comprehend the depth of that soul" and who had "joined the thoughtless rabble in its superficial denunciation of Leon Czolgosz," bowing "before respectability by sacrificing their ideas to its altar."[24] Whatever her earlier reservations about Czolgosz may have been, she now idealized him. In her 1911 essay, "The Psychology of Political Violence," she essentially restated and extended the views of 1901, insisting again that "it is their supersensitiveness to the wrong and injustice surrounding them" that compelled men like Angiolillo, Bresci, Berkman, and Czolgosz to "pay the toll of our social crimes." * To understand the motives inspiring an act of political violence, one must "feel intensely the indignity of our social wrongs;

* Angiolillo assassinated the Spanish Prime Minister Cánovas del Castillo in 1897 as a protest against tortures inflicted on political prisoners; Bresci, an Italian immigrant anarchist living in Paterson, New Jersey, shot the Italian king, Umberto, in 1900 in protest against the shooting of hunger demonstrators in Milan.

1 0 8

one's very being must throb with the pain, the sorrow, the despair millions of people are daily made to endure." The "untuned ear" hears nothing but "discord" in such acts of violent protest, "but those who feel the agonized cry understand its harmony; they hear in it the fulfillment of the most compelling moment of human nature."[25]

From a reasoned plea for psychological understanding, Goldman had moved swiftly toward romantic glorification. Despite the general condemnation of Czolgosz and even while her own life was in danger, she defended him publicly in the weeks immediately following the McKinley assassination, not simply as a misguided or desperate or sick young man but, increasingly, as a hero. Goldman in fact idealized Czolgosz for the remainder of her life, and by this attitude toward him—as toward other terrorists and assassins, whom she also praised—she gave tacit approval to his action. The public perception of her as a defender of terrorism was thus not entirely without foundation.

In her impassioned defense of Leon Czolgosz, Emma Goldman stood virtually alone, at least among the Yiddish- and English-speaking members of the movement. Now even more than in 1892, after Berkman's *attentat*, she found herself truly isolated from her closest comrades and, indeed, from Berkman himself; he wrote to her from prison that while he agreed that intolerable conditions had pushed Czolgosz to violent protest, his act had been motivated by individual rather than social necessity and therefore was not a genuinely political act of terrorism.[26] Nevertheless, Goldman wanted her comrades to participate in public meetings proclaiming sympathy, if not support, for a man she had come to regard as a martyr. Many were willing to defend Goldman, to protest the hate campaign against her and her treatment in prison; they were anxious for her safety. But most anarchists by 1901 had long since repudiated any belief in individual propaganda of the deed and felt, with good reason, that whatever Czolgosz's motives, the assassination had harmed the cause. If some anarchists continued to feel a romantic admiration for the daring of assassins, most had come to share the view of Kropotkin that masses, not individuals, make the social revolution, and that "propaganda of the deed" meant mass resistance to state oppression, collective action against tyranny, the spontaneous response of the people during a revolution—not individual acts of violence.[27] In the prevailing atmosphere of anti-anarchist hysteria, they were unwilling to engage in public demonstrations of sympathy for a man whose action most of them deplored.

The world of 1901 was not that of 1881; the America of William McKinley differed enormously from czarist Russia; an isolated assassin in Buffalo, New York, did not resemble the committed political terrorists of St. Petersburg and differed significantly even from Alexander Berkman, who—however misguided his attempted assassination of Frick—had been steeped in a revolutionary tradition in which terrorism had historical precedent and rationale. Czolgosz's vague statements that he "did it for the people" and the political context of imperialism and exploitation did not explain why he chose assassination as a means of protest; they failed to define his act as rational.[28] But Goldman would not accept such distinctions or differences of opinion, and she accused those who stated them of betrayal and cowardice.

The intensity of her commitment to Czolgosz suggests that, despite Czolgosz's insistence that he had acted entirely on his own and the complete absence of any evidence connecting her with the assassination, Goldman seems to have felt in some way responsible for what had happened. Anyone in her position might have wondered if she had not, inadvertently, encouraged such an act. Czolgosz had, after all, sought her out, and she, in the midst of a busy schedule, had treated him offhandedly. Perhaps she considered herself partly culpable for not recognizing the depth of his difficulty, blamed herself for his subsequent action, and felt she owed him her allegiance. She felt that other anarchists, by the same token, should share in the responsibility for Czolgosz's act; in her autobiography she singles out Abe Isaak, suggesting that the spy notice he had placed in *Free Society* might have inspired Czolgosz to demonstrate his "sincerity" by committing a "heroic" act.[29]

Then, too, the assassination certainly awakened bitter memories of 1892 and unresolved doubts about the justification for Berkman's act, for which he was still in prison. The ironies linking these two events were not lost on Goldman. Leon Czolgosz had succeeded where Berkman had failed, but instead of being eulogized as a hero, he had been denounced as a villain and unceremoniously executed. Emma may well have seen in the fate of Czolgosz a frightening reminder of what might have happened to Berkman, had he been successful. To fight for Czolgosz was in a sense to fight for Berkman. In addition, while she had not been arrested in 1892 for an attempted assassination in which she had been an active accomplice, she had now been in danger of losing her life for an act with which she had been completely uninvolved.

If she associated Czolgosz with Berkman, moreover, on an even deeper level she, herself, clearly identified with him. In the pathetic Leon Czolgosz, Goldman seemed to see a terrifying image of her own deepest fears of rejection and abandonment, as well as—less consciously, perhaps—her own anger and violent fantasies. For the rest of her life she was haunted by the memory of Leon Czolgosz and regarded October 29, the day of his execution, as a day of mourning. Long afterward, on that date she inscribed a photograph of herself (for an admirer) with Czolgosz's name, adding, "Just 25 years ago the State of New York killed a helpless human being." [30] The day of his death each year brought back painful memories of the man whose fate might have been her own. "I don't feel very cheerful today," she confided to a friend in 1932. "Czolgosz' death came near to causing mine. Perhaps it would have been for the best if it had. I would have been sanctified and canonized by the comrades. However, it is not the memory of the close shave I had in 1901 which makes me sad. It is the memory of the treatment that poor boy received at the hands of the comrades. Never had anyone been so denied and forsaken." [31]

Feeling forsaken and denied herself, deeply hurt by the refusal of other anarchists to support her defense of Czolgosz, criticized by her closest comrades, who feared for her life and urged her to flee the country, Goldman lashed out furiously at everyone around her— including Alexander Berkman, who drew very different conclusions from the events of 1901. It is from this date that their political thought began to diverge most strikingly. By 1901 he had come to the conclusion that terrorist acts, to be politically effective, had to be popularly understood. While the assassination of McKinley was indeed understandable as an expression of desperation and personal revolt, it was, in Berkman's view, politically inappropriate in the current American context and, indeed, more likely to confuse than to inspire. Unlike the situation in Russia, he wrote Goldman in December of 1901, "the real despotism of republican institutions is far deeper, more insidious, because it rests on the popular delusion of self-government and independence." The real battleground, he concluded, was economic; the battle must be waged in that arena.[32]

Berkman never repudiated terrorism or his action in 1892, but by 1901 he was moving away from his youthful notions of propaganda of the deed and toward a stronger commitment to agitation within the labor movement. Emma Goldman, however, refused to relinquish her romantic defense of the assassin and repudiated instead the "ignorant mass" and the "rabble" incapable of comprehending him. She reacted to Berkman's differing view—despite his warm praise for her courage in standing up to the persecution to which she was subjected—with hysterical anger and disbelief. As Berkman put it in his memoir, "my friend, in her hour of bitterness, confounds my appreciative disagreement with the denunciation of stupidity and inertia."[33] On this occasion, disagreement was betrayal, "a cruel senseless farce," as she wrote in her autobiography. "I felt as if I had lost Sasha. . . ."[34] Soon after receiving Berkman's letter, she ceased all correspondence with him.

By the end of 1901, Goldman had essentially withdrawn from all contact with others in the movement. Furious at those comrades who had "betrayed" Leon Czolgosz, she was determined never to return. Subject to continuing popular hostility, unable to rent a room in New York under her own name, she decided bitterly to adopt "the most ordinary, commonplace name I could think of." "Red Emma" became "Miss Smith" and left revolutionary agitation for a grim round of drudgery as a private nurse in the tenements of the Lower East Side.

PART

4

"MOTHER EARTH" AND "MOMMY"

C H A P T E R
9

TOWARD
A
NEW
ANARCHIST
COMMUNITY

n the aftermath of the execution of Leon Czolgosz, Emma Goldman, now Miss E. G. Smith, fell into a deep depression. Once
again, as nine years earlier, she had become a pariah, condemned as the murderer of President McKinley in newspapers across
the country, if not in court. Weary, fatigued, indifferent to all except
the immediate details of her life, she felt "spiritually dead," as if her
identity had vanished with her name. Disgusted with her anarchist
comrades, who now "filled me with loathing,"[1] she shunned all public events where she might be recognized. She remained, as she tells
it, in seclusion, securing private nursing assignments and living in a
series of apartments with her brother Moishe ("Morris"), now a
twenty-two-year-old medical student, and one of his friends—"Dan"
in the autobiography—with whom she had a brief, romantic affair.
For the most part, life seemed bleak and futile. Her voice, so distinc-

tive in its ardor and irritability, vanished from the pages of *Free Society* and *Lucifer*.

Goldman's personal crisis coincided with the general crisis in the anarchist movement that followed in the wake of the McKinley assassination. Three states—New York, New Jersey, and Wisconsin—passed anti-anarchist laws imposing harsh penalties on advocates of "criminal anarchy" or members of organizations that defended anarchist views. In 1903, Congress enacted national legislation that excluded anarchists or those belonging to organizations upholding anarchist beliefs from the country: the first law to make entry conditional upon acceptable political convictions.[2] Although rarely enforced at first, this legislation set a dangerous precedent for later repressive actions against the Left. The shock of the assassination and the continuing persecution of anarchists inspired many long-time activists to leave the movement, which was further weakened over the next few years by the deaths of some of its most dedicated members, including Justus Schwab, Kate Austen, Ed Brady, Moses Harman, and Abe Isaak. Johann Most died, old and embittered, in 1906.

Still, Goldman's retreat did not last long. By the summer of 1902, she was beginning to yearn again for public activity. She resumed her correspondence with Berkman. She eagerly accepted an invitation from a young British anarchist, William McQueen, to speak to the striking silkworkers in Paterson, New Jersey. The night before she was scheduled to appear (June 18), she dreamed that she was addressing the strikers: suddenly the "sea of people at my feet" began to rush away, and she remained alone on the platform, silent and waiting, while a strange form advanced toward her, "head thrown back, its large eyes gleaming into mine. My voice struggled in my throat, and with a great effort I cried out: 'Czolgosz! Leon Czolgosz!' "[3] Terrified that this apparition might rise up to rob her of her audience and her voice, she cancelled her appearance. But by November she was ready once again to attempt a short lecture tour on behalf of striking coal miners and the Russian revolutionary movement. The Kishinev pogroms in May of 1903 and the suppression of student demonstrations in St. Petersburg the following August had aroused widespread protests on the Lower East Side; Emma, throwing herself into these efforts, found her energies slowly returning.

Upon resuming her political work, Goldman did not revise her interpretation of the events of 1901, but she did come to recognize how deeply hurt she had been by the public condemnation directed at her. Emma had always prided herself on her ability to stand alone, but she discovered in 1901 that there were limits to her stoicism. "I could not bear being repudiated and shunned," she admitted; "I could not bear defeat." She came painfully to the conclusion, after a period of "tortuous introspection," that it was wrong to have turned her back on the movement when she was most needed, "all because of a handful that had proved to be base and cowardly."[4]

But Goldman's work did now begin to assume new directions. Disgusted with many of her former associates, disillusioned by the spectacle of hatred unleashed by "the masses" toward Leon Czolgosz, and faced with the shattered morale of a severely diminished movement, she began to seek new contacts and connections, particularly among the American-born middle-class liberals and radicals who showed an increasing interest in her work.

Although Goldman attributed this change in attitude to the anti-anarchist legislation of 1902 and 1903, which she thought had assuaged public fears of anarchists, in fact her new prestige owed more to the growing strength of socialism and Progressivism. The Progressives were liberals rather than radicals. Alarmed by the agrarian unrest and labor militance of the nineties, dismayed by the human costs of capitalism, and hoping to counter revolution through moderate reform, they campaigned to patch up the worst abuses of capitalism while consolidating business control over government. They would "clean up" city corruption and ease conditions for the poor through a benevolent spirit of paternalism and "uplift." Investigative journalists and militant social workers—the new heroes and heroines of the Progressive Era—increasingly turned toward the slums, the ghettoes, and the lecture halls of the radicals, willing now to learn about "how the other half lives," as Jacob Riis put it in 1890. Muckraking magazines such as McClure's and Cosmopolitan and the novels of socialist writers like Jack London, Frank Norris, and Upton Sinclair exposed corporate greed and working-class miseries. Sinclair's exposé of vile working conditions in the Chicago meat-packing industry, intended by its author to speak for labor, ironically led to the passage of the first important consumer legislation, the Pure Food and Drug Act. Four years later, Lincoln Steffens's Shame of the Cities would expose in scathing detail the corruption of numerous urban political machines. Settlement houses in the midst of slum neighborhoods in Chicago and New York would instruct a generation of urban reformers who, entering municipal and state government, often worked effectively to upgrade services, housing, health, and education for the poor. The first legislation providing minimum wages and maximum hours in particular industries was enacted during these years.

The militant legacy of the nineties also inspired a host of radical organizations: the Socialist party in 1901, the Women's Trade Union League in 1903, and soon the Industrial Workers of the World. For a time at least, immigrant radicals like Emma Goldman encountered a slightly less hostile atmosphere. Despite patrician President Theodore Roosevelt's hatred of all radicals and labor unions, anti-anarchist legislation was only rarely enforced. The limited prosperity also allayed the fear of foreigners that might well have been expected to accompany the skyrocketing immigration rate—from 450,000 in 1900 to over a million in 1907.

By the end of 1903 Emma Goldman, immigrant and radical, generally shunned only a year before, once again found herself widely invited to lecture, particularly by the middle-class liberals and radicals who gathered in groups such as the Manhattan Liberal Club, the Brooklyn Philosophical Society, and the Sunshine Club. Here she made friends with such people as Theodore Schroeder, libertarian lawyer and mainstay of the Free Speech League; Elizabeth and Alexis Ferm, talented if eccentric educators who later headed an anarchist school; Alice Stone Blackwell, translator and lifelong supporter of liberal and radical causes; John Coryell, author of the famous Nick Carter detective stories; the Tolstoyan (pacifist) poet Ernest Crosby; and Bolton Hall and Gilbert Roe, respected Single-Tax lawyers, active in many civil libertarian cases and later in the birth control agitation of 1915 and 1916. Both men donated legal services and money to Goldman over the years, and sometime around 1906 Hall bought her a small farm in Ossining, New York, about thirty miles up the Hudson River from Manhattan, which she used as a retreat on weekends and in the summer.

For Goldman a critical turning point came in the fall of 1903, when John Turner, an English anarchist and head of the powerful Shop Assistants' Union (of clerks and salespeople) was arrested in New York under the provision of the anti-anarchist act of 1903 and held for deportation on Ellis Island. Furious at this treatment of a distinguished comrade (who was locked in a nine-foot-by-six-foot cage), Goldman, acting as "Miss E. G. Smith," helped to organize a Free Speech League to protest the case—and, by extension, the anti-anarchist law—to the Supreme Court. The League engaged Clarence Darrow and his partner Edgar Lee Masters as counsel and organized a series of mass protest meetings that were supported by many nonanarchists as well as members of the movement. Miss E. G. Smith became chief fundraiser and publicist for the case, raising about sixteen hundred of a total of two thousand dollars for Turner's defense and mailing out thousands of leaflets and fliers to mobilize opinion and publicize the case. Although Turner was eventually deported, the League obtained his release in time for him to deliver a number of lectures and managed to stimulate widespread discussion of the case.

The Turner campaign further countered Goldman's feeling of paralysis, drawing her out of her brooding bitterness back into the current of public life. But her recovery proceeded slowly and fitfully, and she continued to suffer from the weariness and fatigue symptomatic of her lingering depression. "I never felt so weighed down, so tired and worn out from and through people," she wrote to Berkman. "I feel as if I were in a swamp and try as much as I may I can not get out. Why can I not emancipate myself from them, why am I cursed with the inability to say no although my whole being rebels against the everlasting yes, which people so easily abuse and misuse? Just say yes, once, and everybody seems to have a mortgage on you. I am like the incurable drunkard, I have the best intentions to be reformed, to get away from people, to take a small place and live alone or only with one friend, I know that I even have energy enough to carry it out, but will I have the strength to keep it up? I fear not, I fear I am forever doomed to remain public property and to have my life worn out through the care for the lives of others. Oh, my friend, I can not say all I feel, but I only know I feel crowded out of my need for elbow space. I am tired, tired, tired." [5]

In this period, for the first time, a martyred tone begins to creep into Goldman's letters. She refers to herself as "doomed to remain public property," imprisoned by her "publicity" and by people who have "acquired too much right to my life for me to shake them off." "Why not retire to a private life with one's friends," she asks Berkman in another letter.

Why, why? Can you always answer all whys? I can not. Not that I have not often longed to do so or that I do not long for it now. I never was so tired of people, I never felt so hedged in, so pressed to the wall by my surroundings, yet I see no way of getting out of this nerve-destroying life of mine. I am tied economically hand and foot. I owe nearly 500£ some of which must be paid. I am worn out from the fierce struggle of the past 3 years in building up a [nursing] practice and I simply have not the energy and courage to drop whatever little ground I have gained here and go in search of a new field. To lead a private life and live in N.Y. is no more possible than for a druncard [sic] to deal in liquors and not to drink. I have lived too long here and people have acquired too much right to my life for me to shake them off. This is just one feeble attempt to give you the reason why I can not retire. Ah your bird was lucky indeed to have you as its cage keeper, I am my own cage keeper. Or rather my publicity is my cage and it is a strong hard and piercing cage at that.[6]

And yet even as her depression lingered, Goldman's complaints are peppered with cheerful discussions of plans and projects. By early 1904 she was full of enthusiasm about new possibilities for the movement. The Turner case, she writes excitedly to Berkman, "has given birth to a general revival, we have been holding splendid meetings in our club. . . ." New York was "still a gold mine for propaganda purposes, especially the Ghetto is simply remarkable," and there was great potential in the "very large intellectual Jewish life on the East Side," where "Literature, the Drama, the Social Life have grown wonderfully. . . ."[7] Representatives of the Russian revolutionary movement were arriving in New York, seeking funds and support. As a gesture of solidarity, Goldman joined a local branch of the Socialist Revolutionary party, even though "it did not agree with our ideas of a non-governmental society."[8] In December of 1904, she acted as hostess and translator for the visiting Catherine Breshkovskaya, longtime activist and a founder of the Socialist Revolutionary party, whom Goldman counted as one of her heroines.

In the summer of 1905, still struggling with ways to earn a living—when private nursing drained too much energy from her work in the movement, Emma had briefly opened an office on East Broadway offering the services of a "Vienna Scalp and Facial Specialist"—she dropped most of her other commitments to become translator, press agent, and manager for the Pavel Orleneff theater troupe, a visiting company of distinguished Russian actors who created a sensation with their performances, in Russian, of Ibsen, Dostoyevsky, and Strindberg. Besides putting her in touch with many prominent theater people in New York, Boston, and Chicago, Goldman's work with Orleneff—an early proponent of "theater for the people"—renewed her enthusiasm about the political potential of the modern drama, which had first been awakened in Vienna in 1895. At least as early as 1904, she had given an occasional lecture on "The Unpleasant Side of George Bernard Shaw" and on "Anarchism and the Modern Drama." Soon she would speak regularly on "The Revolutionary Spirit of the Modern Drama" and "The Drama: The Strongest Disseminator of Radicalism." Her new contacts also set her to thinking about the fruitful possibilities for bringing together the worlds of radical politics and the arts. Since 1896 she had contemplated publishing an anarchist paper, and the demise of *Free Society* at the end of 1904 had left the movement without a national English-language periodical. Now, when Orleneff offered to stage a benefit performance to raise seed money for a magazine, she eagerly welcomed the opportunity to translate her vision into reality: to publish an anarchist monthly magazine that would "voice without fear every unpopular progressive cause," and would "aim for unity between revolutionary effort and artistic expression."[9]

The founding of *Mother Earth* in March of 1906 was another major turning point for Goldman in her struggle to free herself from her depression of the previous five years, for it marked the realization of a long-cherished dream and gave a definite focus to her work. It crystallized her public persona as mother of the movement—"Emma Goldman *is Mother Earth*," acknowledged one friend—and provided the center for a Mother Earth "family," an informal collective of people who assumed major responsibility for the magazine.[10] Indeed, Emma's apartment at 210 East Thirteenth Street now became a kind of clearinghouse and central office for the anarchist movement. In a practical sense, too, the magazine resolved her long-standing dilemma of how to combine wage-earning with political work. In order to support the magazine and, by extension, herself, she would now devote herself full-time to lecturing for pay.

The birth of the magazine also signalled the recovery of the anarchist movement from the devastating repercussions of the McKinley assassination. In working through her personal trauma, Emma Goldman had gradually elaborated a vision of anarchism that laid the foundations for a rebuilding of the movement on a new—and controversial—basis during the prewar decade. From its militant working-class origins in the eighties, the movement would now include middle-class professional people as well: teachers and doctors, pharmacists and journalists, even shopkeepers, salesmen and lawyers. From an emphasis on economic and labor issues, it would accord more importance to social and cultural questions. From an almost exclusively immigrant membership, it would attract native-born sympathizers and supporters, particularly on the West Coast, and often from old and aristocratic families. While foreign-language anarchist groups continued to publish and agitate in Yiddish, Italian, German, or Bohemian, *Mother Earth*—continuing the tradition of *The Firebrand* and *Free Society*—sought to create a self-consciously "American" movement, to bring anarchism out of its immigrant enclaves and into the mainstream of American life. That the publisher, editors, and many of *Mother Earth*'s writers and readers were themselves immigrants underscores the depth of their desire to reconcile their European education and radical values with their commitment to America, and even to teach Americans about their own traditions of dissent. As Goldman put it in 1901, "Americans who insisted on believing that anarchy was foreign revolution are finding out that it is universal philosophy, and that their own Emerson and Thoreau said more sensible anarchical things than many of our professed Anarchists." [11] *Mother Earth*—with a circulation of three to five thousand—served as inspiration and focus for this revitalized "American" anarchist community which, with Emma Goldman as its dominant figure, now entered a decade of creative action.

Mother Earth was from the start a distinctly personal magazine and vehicle for Goldman, although it was edited for the most part by others. Goldman envisioned it partly as an extension of her own voice—another place besides the platform where "I could feel at home." [12] She published many of her lectures here, as well as reports on current struggles and a running commentary on her annual coast-to-coast speaking tours. Activists in towns and cities where she spoke also reported frequently on "Emma Goldman in Portland," or "Emma Goldman in San Francisco." As a journal of political and cultural radicalism, the magazine also invited the contributions of "those who strive for something higher, weary of the commonplace . . . who breathe freely only in limitless space."[13] To this end, *Mother Earth* welcomed the articles, reports, essays, and stories of anarchists all over the country and abroad; their writing gave the magazine a lively, grass-roots immediacy and made it an effective medium of communication for the movement. Berkman published lectures and articles on labor and legal defense for radicals. Voltairine de Cleyre wrote about American history and about sexual slavery. Theodore Schroeder discussed freedom of speech and of the press, while John Coryell argued for freedom in marriage and the family. From Denver, Portland, Schenectady, Los Angeles, Chicago, and Cleveland, local groups sent their reports on strikes, free speech fights, unemployed movements, birth control campaigns, legal defense cases, I.W.W. activities, and efforts to organize cooperatives. They used the magazine to raise funds for anarchist schools and free speech committees. Comrades from abroad sent news of the movement in France, Japan, New Zealand, and Latin America. Two Mexican anarcho-syndicalists—the Flores Magón brothers—reported on the 1910 revolution in Mexico, which Voltairine de Cleyre complemented with some noteworthy articles of her own on the Mexican Revolution from an anarchist viewpoint.

In addition to commentary on current issues, the magazine also published excerpts from the major libertarian writers from Proudhon, Kropotkin, Malatesta, and Elisée Reclus to the French syndicalists Fernand Pelloutier and Emile Pouget. Rudolph Rocker, organizer of Jewish immigrant anarchists in London's East End, sent an occasional article, as did Max Nettlau, a German historian of the movement, and the Wisconsin anarchist C. L. James. There were selections from Thoreau, Walt Whitman, Edwin Markham, Heinrich Heine, William Morris, and Mary Wollstonecraft, as well as frequent passages from Nietzsche. Reviews of translations and books by writers such as Anatole France, Flaubert, Gorky, Tolstoy, Olive Schreiner, Charlotte Perkins Gilman, Theodore Dreiser, and Frank Harris appeared regularly; so did poems by Joaquin Miller, Ben Hecht, Morris Rosenfeld, and Arturo Giovanitti, along with short stories by Sadakichi Hartmann, Floyd Dell, Maxwell Bodenheim, and Gertrude Nafe. Man Ray, Robert Minor, and the French anarchist cartoonist Grandjuan contributed eloquent cover drawings.

As a medium of communication, *Mother Earth* served to stimulate, inspire, connect, and crystallize the views of anarchist groups and individuals across the country. It introduced immigrant readers to American radical traditions and American-born readers to European libertarian thought. It was one of the first of the pre–World War I "little magazines" to voice that note of individual and social rebellion that distinguished the radicalism of the 1910s. And it influenced, as well, liberals outside the anarchist movement who were attracted by Emma Goldman's personal prestige. Readers ranged from Italian immigrant silkworkers and Philadelphia pharmacists to Alfred Stieglitz, Eugene O'Neill, and the painter Robert Henri. Most important, it kept alive a dissenting radical tradition alert to the dangers of centralization, bureaucratization, and censorship—within the Left as well as in society at large—that enriched the radical dialogue of the time.

As a journal of new ideas or a voice of the cultural avant-garde, *Mother Earth* was rather less successful. It remained more a magazine of propaganda and polemics than of original criticism. Its contributors were activists and agitators, not talented writers or critics. None of its political reporting compared to that of a John Reed or a Max Eastman; none of the analysis compared to that of a Randolph Bourne in *Seven Arts*. Despite Goldman's original aim of blending social criticism and the arts, the magazine accorded primary importance to social, political, and economic commentary. Art was distinctly subordinate to revolution. Unlike the situation in France, where avant-garde poets and painters had important ties with anarchism and contributed to anarchist reviews, in the United States radical writers and artists were drawn mainly to socialism, not anarchism. *The Masses*, not *Mother Earth*, reaped their talents. While the *Freie Arbeiter Stimme* actively sought out and promoted promising Yiddish writers, the occasional poems and stories in *Mother Earth* had sometimes appeared elsewhere and were often naïvely propagandistic or crudely sentimental.

The magazine's most serious limitation as a journal of the arts was the relatively conservative aesthetic taste of both publisher and editors and their indifference to experiments in form and style. Although Goldman insisted that the artist need not be consciously revolutionary, and even scolded radicals who failed to realize that "art speaks a language all its own," in practice she was less accepting than in theory, demanding that both artist and writer deal critically with "great social wrongs." Goldman's personal tastes were rooted in nineteenth-century realism. Her favorite writers were Dostoyevsky, Tolstoy, Conrad, Gorky, Turgenev, Walt Whitman, Ibsen, and Hauptmann. She did not like D.H. Lawrence, Joyce, Proust, or later, Hemingway, who was "too deliberate in his cold, matter of fact and labored modernity."[14] (Surprisingly, she also disliked Theodore Dreiser, whom she thought "so terribly detailed," except for *Sister Carrie* and "Girl in the Coffin.")[15] She found Gertrude Stein "decadent" and evinced little interest in such modernist writers of the prewar years as Sherwood Anderson, Amy Lowell, or Ezra Pound, who appeared in *The Little Review*, which was edited by her friend Margaret Anderson.[16] Goldman thought *Susan Lenox: Her Fall and Rise* (1917), a minor novel about prostitution by the muckraking journalist David Graham Phillips, "the greatest American novel" she had ever read, "far superior" to *Sister Carrie*.[17] And she hailed Eugene Walter's 1908 Broadway hit melodrama, *The Easiest Way* (also about prostitution), as "the greatest American drama by an American author I have ever seen," predicting that if he continued in the same vein, Walter would become "the American Ibsen."[18] Curiously, despite their potential for reaching mass audiences, Goldman did not like the movies, insisting that even the best "have never left the slightest impression beyond the moment when they were reeled off."[19]

Both the strengths and the limitations of the magazine were expressed in the tastes and characteristics of the *Mother Earth* "family." The principal members were all long-time movement activists and experienced radical journalists, immigrants and American-born, yet without the sophistication, education, exuberance, or ease of their more affluent counterparts at *The Masses*. Max Baginski, for example, the first editor and a frequent contributor to the magazine, brought years of experience as a radical journalist, first in his native Silesia—where he had spent over two years in prison for his anarchist articles—and later in Chicago, where he had edited the *Arbeiter Zeitung*. Baginski had a passion for literature—his articles on fiction and drama, especially on the playwright Gerhardt Hauptmann, whom he knew personally, were among his best. However, his inability to write easily in English (Goldman translated his articles from the German) and his ties to the old German-speaking anarchist movement—Most was one of Baginski's great heroes—limited his effectiveness as an editor of an English-language magazine. He remained European in his outlook, pessimistic about America just at the moment when American radicalism would achieve its greatest strength.

Baginski was, however, an important intellectual influence on Goldman, as well as one of her closest friends. She had met him briefly in Philadelphia in the summer of 1893, shortly after he had come to America and just before she went to prison. Four years later, they renewed their acquaintance in Chicago and quickly developed an "intellectual kinship" that also found its "emotional expression."[20] Though their relationship was evidently more of the intellect than the senses, Emma hints in her memoirs at a brief romantic involvement, suggesting that her hopes for something more intimate were frustrated by Baginski's involvement with another woman, who subsequently became his wife. Emma recalled her rendezvous with Baginski in the nineties as feasts of reading and literary talk. He first made clear to her the importance of Nietzsche, and her own later writing on the drama owed much to Baginski's articles on theater.[21] He was also a calming personal influence. Evidently a quiet man who hated sectarian polemics and, as Emma put it, "withdrew into his shell at the least disharmony," he was consistently kind, tender, and tactful, "really the only being in NY who has a soothing effect on me like a mother's touch to a sick child."[22] Baginski often traveled with Goldman on her early lecture tours, and they remained close friends for many years.

Another important "family" member was Hippolyte Havel, who had left Chicago to return to New York. According to Ben Reitman, Havel "thought in German, spoke in English, and drank in all languages." A polemicist of some wit and talent, his many contributions ranged from reviews of new translations of Dostoyevsky to articles on trade unions. Famous in Greenwich Village for his eccentric bohemianism, and a close friend of Emma's for years—"Havel is really the one I spend most of the time with," she confided to a friend around 1909—he never really adjusted to American life. Emma felt that America had changed him and that, "like many foreigners," he should never have come to this country.[23]

A third member of the "family" was Harry Kelly, a self-educated former printer, activist in the International Typographical Union, and long-time anarchist from St. Louis.[24] He had helped publish a short-lived anarchist paper in Boston—*The Rebel*—in 1895, and had later lived and worked in England, where he cultivated a friendship with Peter Kropotkin and wrote for *Freedom*. After his return from England in 1904, Kelly earned his living as a salesman of printing equipment, devoting all his spare time to the movement. Kelly brought to the magazine his union experience, knowledge of the British anarchist movement, and concern with building ties between anarchists and labor. Affable, straightforward, generous, and practical, he had no pretensions to being a writer, although he had contributed to the anarchist press for years. His many articles included a plea for a more "impersonal" thrust to anarchism, a meditation on the origins of his own anarchist commitment, and extended polemics against Marxism. Kelly was a great admirer of Goldman, whom he first met in Boston in 1895, but the two remained comrades rather than close friends.

Leonard Abbott, another American anarchist, also joined the "family" almost at its inception. Abbott was a professional journalist who served on the editorial boards of the socialist paper *The Comrade* and of *Current Literature* (later called *Current Opinion*). His articles in *Mother Earth* included graceful portraits—as, for example, his tribute to Voltairine de Cleyre, "Priestess of Pity and Vengeance"—book reviews, and reports on the free speech movement of 1909–10, the anarchist Ferrer Association and School, and the birth control movement, in all of which he was a principal organizer and mainstay.

The son of a well-to-do New England family, born and brought up in Liverpool, Abbott came to anarchism from the socialist movement, which had attracted him as a young man. In England he attended lectures by the leading socialists of the time, met Edward Carpenter and Kropotkin, and corresponded with William Morris. On his arrival in America in 1897, he rejected his family's plans for him to have a university education and business career and chose instead to become a journalist. Active as well in Socialist party politics—a member of the executive committee of the party, he helped found the Inter-Collegiate Socialist Society and was on the first executive board of the Rand School—Abbott had always been attracted to the libertarian vision of unorthodox socialists like Morris and Carpenter. His meeting with Emma Goldman in the winter of 1903 and his contacts with the anarchists in New York turned him increasingly in their direction. Indeed, Abbott indicated later in his life that as a result of Goldman's and Berkman's influence, "my entire life was shaped along new lines."[25]

Abbott may also have been attracted to anarchism by Goldman's sexual radicalism and defense of homosexuality; although married, he was evidently a man of strong homosexual leanings who, from about 1906 to 1910, "played with the idea that I was myself homosexual."[26] The ambivalence that characterized Abbott's sexuality also colored his politics. Despite his long association with the anarchists, he wavered between socialism and anarchism. He admired Goldman enormously—another comrade thought he was "hypnotized" by her, and he himself, in a tribute, admitted that she had "an almost hypnotic influence over her associates."[27] Yet unlike Goldman, he was a confirmed pacifist who hated violence, whether verbal or physical. He thought Goldman "really quite a warlike person" and believed that "she did not shrink from using violence to accomplish her aims."[28] As with Kelly, Goldman's relationship with Leonard Abbott was more that of mutually respectful comrades than that of close friends.

Apart from Goldman and Berkman, the *Mother Earth* contributor of greatest intellectual power and originality was Voltairine de Cleyre. Living in Philadelphia, de Cleyre did not belong to the "family," but she wrote some of the most significant pieces in the magazine. Several of her best essays—"Anarchism and American Traditions," "Sex Slavery," "Those Who Marry Do Ill"—as well as stories, poems, and articles on the Mexican Revolution first appeared here. A few years older than Goldman, de Cleyre had hoped to make a career as a writer and had written for the anarchist and free thought press long before her association with *Mother Earth*. However, the difficulty of earning a living wage as a single woman (she tutored Jewish immigrants in English), complicated by chronic ill health and spells of paralyzing self-doubt and depression, prevented her from pursuing her literary aspirations as she had hoped. For the last six years of her life, *Mother Earth* became an important outlet for her work. And she contributed significantly to the success of the magazine, through her writing and her assistance as editor and proofreader.

A close friend of Berkman, with whom she had corresponded throughout his prison term, de Cleyre always had a tense relationship with Goldman. Apart from their politics, the two women had little in common. The daughter of a French socialist father and a Yankee mother descended from New York abolitionists, de Cleyre grew up in rural Michigan. She was educated in a convent school in Ontario, Canada—an experience that nourished a lifelong hatred for the church and, ultimately, for all forms of authority. She became an antireligious freethinker and embraced anarchism after the Haymarket affair. At first she called herself an individualist anarchist, defending the rights of private property and deploring all violence, but she gradually moved to the left and approached the views of the immigrant Kropotkinite anarchists among whom she worked. Although her thinking remained, in the words of her biographer, Paul Avrich, "a romantic, backward-looking vision of an idealized rural past inhabited by sturdy artisans and homesteaders who lived in harmony with nature, joined by ties of voluntary cooperation," she nonetheless supported the I.W.W., defended Czolgosz, and championed the Mexican Revolution. De Cleyre called herself "an Anarchist simply, without economic labels attached," and urged unity among anarchists with different economic views.[29]

De Cleyre and Goldman first met in 1893, when de Cleyre defended Goldman after her arrest in Philadelphia for "inciting to riot." They corresponded, and de Cleyre visited Goldman at Blackwell's Island. However, tensions arose almost immediately. As personalities they differed strikingly. De Cleyre was reserved, ascetic, and shunned notoriety. Emma thought Voltairine was jealous of her, but in fact de Cleyre never liked Goldman, considering her too flamboyant, self-indulgent, and greedy for the limelight.[30] Emma, for her part, praised de Cleyre highly to those who were skeptical of her achievements, but tended to criticize her to her admirers, pointing out the limited scope of her agitation. "She has great ability and great influence, but she is tied down in Philadelphia," Emma typically told a reporter in 1901. "So her field of work is not what it ought to be."[31] In an ostensible tribute to de Cleyre, Emma in fact belittled her, emphasizing her failures and defeats.[32] Apart from the clash of personality, the immediate causes of the falling out between Goldman and de Cleyre are unclear; in her memoirs, Goldman claims that Voltairine had been hurt because Emma, while in Blackwell's Island, had refused to receive a visit from de Cleyre's current lover, a follower of Johann Most. Goldman, in turn, felt that "Voltairine had shown herself too narrow ever again to enable me to be free and at ease with her. My hope of a close friendship with her was destroyed."[33] Still, the two women were often brought together through their shared loyalty to Alexander Berkman—the most important member by far of the *Mother Earth* "family"—who walked out of the Allegheny County Workhouse on May 18, 1906, a free man for the first time in fourteen years.

Berkman's first meeting with Goldman at the Detroit train station, as he described it in his *Prison Memoirs*, was charged with emotion. As he descended from the train to the platform, his gaze fell "on a woman leaning against a pillar. She looks intently at me." Berkman recognized "the Girl," whose appearance had changed little. Disturbed by the excited voices and quick motions of other friends who were present, he was surprised that she did not rush forward like the others, but at the same time pleased at her self-possession. He walked slowly toward her, "but she does not move. She seems rooted to the spot, her hand grasping the pillar, a look of awe and terror in her face. Suddenly she throws her arms around me. Her lips move, but no sound reaches my ear."[34]

Berkman had gone into prison a youth of twenty-one, full of romantic certainties, naïve, rigid and intolerant in his convictions, desperately eager to join that sublime company of revolutionary Nihilists he so passionately admired. Berkman in 1892 still translated all American events into a Russian idiom. His revolutionary sympathies, according to his own descriptions, had been abstract, disembodied. He had imagined "the People" in his "Greek mythology moods" as a "mighty Atlas, supporting on his shoulders the weight of the world."[35] During fourteen years in prison, with long stretches of solitary confinement, Berkman had managed to educate and Americanize himself. The privileged bourgeois student who had had little contact with workers moved toward sympathy with real working-class individuals. "Boston Red," "Horsethief," "Wild Bill," Johnny Davis —all of whom he would portray with insight and tenderness in his memoirs—showed him concretely what it meant to be poor and powerless. From an abstract hatred of authority, he moved to an understanding of the specific ways in which the exercise of arbitrary power could destroy the best in men, and the ways in which shreds of dignity and decency often survived, against all reason and logic, in the most downtrodden. Far from weakening his hatred for law and

130

property, prison had deepened it. But whereas Berkman in 1892 had seen capitalists and politicians as beasts—the ideological opposites of the inherently noble and heroic workers—he had, without losing any awareness of class antagonisms, come to a more complex appreciation of both the humanity of the former and the mixed capacities of the latter.

Perhaps the most telling expression of Berkman's evolution was his lack of bitterness toward the workers who repudiated his beliefs. Initially shocked and disgusted by the failure of fellow prisoners to understand the motives for his *attentat*—in his memoirs he can hardly contain his contempt for the Homestead striker Jack Tinsford, whom he met in prison and who regarded Berkman suspiciously as an outsider who must have had some "business misunderstanding" with Frick—Berkman came to see this failure of understanding as a problem anarchists must seriously confront.[36] While he never repudiated his action of 1892, he did increasingly reject terrorism—except under very exceptional circumstances—precisely because such acts were so often misunderstood. He gradually gave up his romantic obsession with motives to consider the political impact of terrorist tactics. If American workers were unable to grasp the revolutionary meaning of an *attentat* against the President, then the tactic itself was at fault, not the workers. Some other way of awakening consciousness must be found. For Berkman this was, increasingly, propaganda directed at labor, and work in the unions.

Emma Goldman, however, had moved in quite a different direction. Inevitably these differences gave rise to painful arguments between them. They disagreed over the direction that anarchist agitation should take: while Berkman wanted to strengthen ties with the workers, Goldman wanted to agitate among the middle class. Berkman emphasized economic issues—labor organizing and agitation for a General Strike. Goldman downplayed the importance of strictly economic campaigns, insisting that the struggle must be waged on many fronts at once. Berkman thought more in terms of collective action; Goldman reserved her greatest enthusiasm for heroic individuals.

The political tensions were compounded by personal and psychological strains. Their first night together, at the Detroit home of Carl Nold (who had served five years in prison on charges of complicity in Berkman's *attentat*), was an anguished one. Despite her joy, "my face burned with shame," Emma later told him, "that I should have been so close to you, a stranger, a perfect stranger."[37] Instead of bringing them closer together, the following months deepened the distances between them. The task of adjusting both to life outside of prison and to a world strikingly different from that of 1892 at first threatened to overwhelm him. The world of immigrant radicalism had grown less fervid, more intellectual and pragmatic. The Lower East Side had become more prosperous. Emma herself appeared worldly and sophisticated. He was chilled by what he felt as "the air of intellectual aloofness, false tolerance and everlasting pessimism" that pervaded the atmosphere at 210 East Thirteenth Street, where he went to live after his release.[38] Perhaps, too, he wanted to think of Emma as "the Girl" she had been fourteen years earlier, but found instead a cosmopolitan, amazingly self-possessed woman of thirty-seven. Perhaps he was not altogether pleased to see that his little "Sailor Girl" had grown up.

After his release, Berkman became deeply depressed, haunted by his memories of the penitentiary and of his fellow prisoners who still remained behind bars. His first encounters with the world were most discouraging. He attempted a lecture tour too soon after his release; the anxiety and stress of that venture brought him to the verge of suicide. A printing shop he had opened in December of 1906 had to be closed the following April, since he could not afford to hire a union pressman. Emma, struggling to encourage and support him through this difficult period, found herself the target of his bitter censure and pent-up rage. He hated being financially dependent and resented being treated as a sick child. She could not find a way to help him without making him feel patronized. "We did not seem to have a single thought in common," she wrote later. "Yet I felt bound to Sasha, bound for ever by the tears and blood of fourteen years."[39]

Through all these difficulties, Emma nourished hopes that their previous romantic relationship might be restored. They did indeed resume their earlier sexual involvement for a time, but Emma realized, she wrote later, that "whatever physical appeal I had for you before you went to prison was dead when you came out."[40] She hoped, nevertheless, to awaken Berkman's passion. Setting out on a four-month lecture tour early in 1907, she flooded him with anxious love letters. "I have such a longing for you, my own, and for our home," she wrote from Detroit. "I never imagined that I would suffer from homesickness, real genuine homesickness. Is it 210 E. 13th do you think? Or the sunshine and love I have left there, my precious Dush[enka]? Do you not think it is disgraceful to be so completely in love at my age?"[41]

In her letters, Emma blamed herself for Berkman's withdrawal from her. The months following his release had been "horrible," she admitted, until the evening late in October when Emma and other comrades were arrested at a meeting commemorating Leon Czolgosz. News of the arrests had momentarily jolted Berkman out of his depression; he felt that at last he had work to do. "Dush, I think at that moment our love was born, not until then," Emma wrote. "Until that evening, Oct. 27th—that date is burned with letters of fire into my mind—we were really strangers. But at that moment when I held on to your arm and looked into your face, I knew some wonderful light had lifted the veil from both of us, so that we could look into each other. Sasha dear, it was then that I became part of you and you of me." Assuring Berkman of her love, Emma anxiously sought reassurances from him. "Tell me, Sasha dear, if you can," she asked, "when was your love for me born, how did that mysterious force take possession of you? You never spoke of it, my precious one," she reproached him gently. "Do you want me Dush? I want you badly. Affectionately, E."[42]

"Dearest precious treasure mine," she wrote from Chicago a few days later. "I developed a terrible headache from [the] anxiety of waiting for a word from you. I know it is foolish to be so uneasy, but you can not imagine how I suffer through our separation and the anxiety about you." Her lectures were tremendously successful, she reported, but they did not ease her yearning "to get back to my darling lover who means life, joy, happiness to me."

> The great E.G. You make me laugh, Dush. I am more of the little sailor today, than I have been 15 years ago. My greatness adds nothing to my life or the wealth of my nature. If I am proud of anything, it is that I have learned to appreciate real true value in human nature, that I have learned the power of love. Everything else means naught to me. 1200 people applauded, waved hats and yelled last night when I was finished. Yet I saw them not, I saw only one face, one soul, one being far away from me and yet so close. I could almost feel his warmth. And my soul cried for that being all night long. Do you know who it is? Can you guess it?

Advising him on a series of practical business details, she urged him to "please, please write me often if it is only a postal, only do not keep me in suspense. Let me nestle close to you and in your strong passionate embrace, let me drink the joy of life, the ecstasy of our love. I am all yours, E."[43]

But Emma's political commitments kept her away from New York for nine months in 1907. Even if Berkman's feelings for her had not always been more comradely than romantic or erotic, her extended absences might well have caused him to seek out other women. Within a short time he became romantically involved with Becky Edolsohn, a respected activist in the New York anarchist movement whose extreme youth (she was about fifteen) prompted Emma's caustic remark that, with regard to women, Berkman "had remained as young and naïve as he had been at twenty-one."[44] If she felt hurt by his rejection, however, Emma nonetheless accepted the other women in his life. Becky Edolsohn soon became part of the *Mother Earth* "family," and even lived for a time at 210 East Thirteenth Street. Reconciling herself to Berkman's sexual withdrawal, Emma turned toward the motherly role in which she felt most comfortable. "I believe my strongest and most compelling feeling for you is that of the mother," she would write him many years later.[45]

Eventually, *Mother Earth* proved the vehicle of Berkman's recovery. Taking over as editor in the spring of 1907, he found in this work a growing source of confidence and commitment to life. Their shared work on the magazine also helped heal some of the personal tensions between Berkman and Goldman, although he always felt impatient to start his own labor-oriented paper, which he finally did in 1915. With Emma away from New York for six to eight months of the year, Berkman assumed the major day-to-day responsibility for the magazine and soon emerged as a greatly respected, admired, even beloved figure in New York radical circles. By the summer of 1910, he was able to begin work on the *Prison Memoirs*, which Goldman's support, both moral and financial, made possible.

Berkman's return to life as a radical activist after fourteen years' imprisonment was greatly aided by the revival of anarchism, both nationally and internationally. Johann Most's death in March of 1906 made way for younger activists such as Berkman and Goldman. In Europe the movement was experiencing a rebirth in the form of anarcho-syndicalism—a kind of revolutionary trade unionism—which developed in France during the 1890s as an alternative to the increasingly sterile terrorist and conspiratorial tactics of the eighties and nineties. After a decade in which intensive police surveillance and persecution made international meetings of anarchists impossible—except such clandestine gatherings as the suppressed Parisian Congress of 1900—a major International Anarchist Congress was held in Amsterdam in August of 1907. It debated issues of current importance, like the relationship of anarchists to the syndicalist unions and the problem of organization within the movement itself. Significantly, the immigrant Emma Goldman represented the American English-speaking anarchists at the Congress, while Max Baginski represented the foreign-language groups.

Apart from being one of the largest gatherings of its kind—some eighty delegates attended, representing groups in the United States, Japan, and Latin America as well as nearly every European country—this was the first open international meeting of anarchists since the London meeting of the Second International in 1896, from which the anarchists had been decisively expelled. Goldman joined here some of the most eminent figures in the movement: Errico Malatesta, the grand old man of Italian anarchism; Rudolph Rocker, a German gentile who edited a Yiddish anarchist paper in London and had become a leading organizer among the impoverished Jews of the East End; Domela Nieuenhuis, the distinguished Dutch anarchist and antimilitarist; and two respected and influential syndicalists, the Swiss Pierre Dunois and Pierre Monatte from France. Seeking a way of bringing the anarchist movement into closer contact with labor, these men, along with Fernand Pelloutier, were instrumental in infusing into the Confédération Générale du Travail—France's largest labor federation—an anarchist opposition to all parliamentary involvement and a commitment to decentralization. The syndicalist unions were at once committed to the pursuit of immediate workers' gains and to ultimate social revolution. In the United States, the Industrial Workers of the World, or I.W.W., formed in 1905 in Chicago, represented the closest American approximation to a syndicalist movement. Although many of the individual members belonged also to the American Socialist party, the I.W.W. as an organization eschewed all political participation, stressed direct action at the workplace, and like the French "syndicats," combined a commitment to

135

immediate improvements in wages and working conditions with a long-range commitment to the overthrow of capitalism. The Wobblies, as they were called, born in the harsh conditions of the mines and timberlands of the West, were fiercely democratic—unlike French syndicalism, which tended to stress the role of a revolutionary elite. The Wobblies scorned the elitism of the more conservative American Federation of Labor—which aimed to organize the most highly skilled workers, the "aristocrats of labor"—and appealed to the least skilled, worst paid, more vulnerable segments of the labor force, especially immigrant labor and migratory workers in the fields, forests, and mines. Although the centralization implicit in the I.W.W. notion of "One Big Union" was uncongenial to many anarchists, and despite the fact that the I.W.W. tended to be apolitical rather than "antipolitical," many individual anarchists joined the I.W.W., where they exercised considerable influence as organizers and agitators, especially within the foreign-language federations.[46]

In part, the Amsterdam Congress was called in order to discuss the relationship between anarchists and the new syndicalist unions. This issue was debated in a lively contest between Malatesta—who, wary of anarchists losing themselves in the syndicalist unions, defended a traditional insurrectional anarchism—and Monatte, who argued that syndicalism was the best arena in which anarchists could translate their ideals into reality and build a mass working-class revolutionary movement. Although Malatesta envisioned anarchism as a movement of small autonomous groups rather than individuals, he rejected the idea that anarchism was exclusively a working-class movement, insisting further that the general strike—a syndicalist tactic—was not the same as an insurrection and that only insurrection could lead to a true revolution: a fact that he felt syndicalism obscured. Ultimately the Congress endorsed resolutions proposed both by Monatte and Malatesta, urging "the comrades in all countries without forgetting that Anarchist action cannot be entirely contained within the limits of the syndicate, to take an active part in the independent movement of the working classes, and to develop inside the Syndicates the ideas of revolt, individual initiative, and solidarity, which are the essence of Anarchism."[47] This compromise resolution ended the discussion without resolving it. As James Joll has noted, however, as far as effective action by anarchists was concerned, Monatte rather than Malatesta was proven right. In France until

1914, and even more in Spain, "anarchism in association with trade unionism was to show itself, for the only time in the history of the anarchist movement, an effective and formidable force in practical politics," at least until the student uprisings of 1968.[48]

In this debate, Emma Goldman sided with Malatesta. Indeed, she went farther than he did in emphasizing "individual autonomy" as the "essential principle" of anarchism. Throughout the Congress, she defended the absolute freedom of the individual, including the right of the individual to commit terrorist acts. Goldman wanted Kropotkin *and* Ibsen, community and individualism. She insisted that there was no conflict between these two ideals, but when pressed, she would almost always advocate the individual over the collective.[49]

Though she defended syndicalism on her return to the United States, her own relationship with labor, including the Wobblies, remained that of an outside supporter. Throughout her years in America she gave energetic support to many I.W.W. campaigns, doing fund-raising and publicity for the Lawrence, Massachusetts, strike of 1912 and the Paterson strike of 1913, joining the San Diego free speech fight of 1912, and supporting the legal defense cases of many accused Wobblies. She was remembered by many people as one of the I.W.W.'s ardent supporters, "greatly admired and respected by the working people in America," as one Wobbly put it. "She was a powerful organizer—her word meant a lot toward unionism."[50] And yet Goldman never joined the I.W.W. These alliances were always temporary. She was too individualistic—and too successful, perhaps, as a freelance lecturer—to feel the need of a larger affiliation or backing. She worried that anarchists who became active in the unions would cease to be anarchists: a fear she later felt was confirmed by the experience of the French anarcho-syndicalists.[51] And she was too committed to the struggle for woman's emancipation, especially in the realm of sexuality, to feel comfortable with a predominantly male union that focused its principal energies on campaigns in the workplace.

But despite her defense of individualism, Goldman's failure to raise women's issues at the Congress in Amsterdam suggested the limits of her own individualistic position. Apart from a passing allusion to "sexual subordination," Emma made no references to sexual politics at any time during the official debates of the Congress. Acting as an individual woman in a setting dominated by men, even so powerful a figure as Emma Goldman evidently felt constrained not to introduce women's concerns and accepted a definition of the major issues that largely excluded women. Her insistence on the importance of a psychological dimension in anarchism—"nothing would prove more disastrous to our ideas, were we unable to unite the external, the physical, and the internal, the psychological motives of rebellion against the existing conditions"—was perhaps a veiled expression of her feminism, insofar as she regarded psychological constraints as the most difficult obstacles to the true liberation of women.[52] Yet apart from that oblique reference, the issues of women and of sex—to which Goldman devoted so much attention at home—were not addressed.

Goldman's silence on this issue was especially poignant in the summer of 1907. As she approached forty, she was becoming increasingly aware of the difficulty of being an independent woman. Despite her own successes, she felt her life painfully incomplete. Hailed by her admirers as a "daughter of the dream," she could not fill the "inner void" that continued to plague her quieter moments and that led her to seek relief in constant activity and travel.[53] She had been speaking partly for herself when she began lecturing, in 1904, on "The Tragedy of Woman's Emancipation," and lamented that "emptiness in woman's soul that will not let her drink from the fountain of life." She had no such inner barriers to love, she thought, and yet she, too, suffered from loneliness and discontent. Woman's most vital right, she often affirmed, was "the right to love and be loved," yet where was that love in her own life?[54] In the spring of 1908, as anarchism once again leaped into the headlines of the Chicago newspapers, Emma Goldman unexpectedly found an answer.

CHAPTER

10

"THE
SUBLIME
MADNESS
OF
SEX"

E ver since Haymarket, Emma Goldman had felt a special sense
of connection to militant, industrial Chicago, the spiritual
home of anarchism in America. Her feeling of connection
was powerfully reaffirmed in 1901, after the McKinley assassination,
when she found herself imprisoned in the city that had taken the
lives of the Haymarket men, "in the same jail, even under the guard-
ianship of the very man who had kept watch in their silent hours."[1]
Then, in the spring of 1908, this most American of cities gained even
more significance for her when she encountered there a flamboyant
young physician-activist and former hobo named Benjamin Lewis
Reitman. Reitman offered her the use of his storefront "hobo hall"
when no one else would rent her space, and then he offered himself
as well. She responded eagerly to his advances. What evidently began
for him as a casual seduction—standard procedure on his part—

soon became the education that he felt justified his entire existence. For Goldman, it became "the Great Grand Passion" of her life.[2]

At the time of his meeting with Emma Goldman, Ben L. Reitman was twenty-nine years old, nearly ten years younger than Goldman. Born in St. Paul, Minnesota, in 1879 to Jewish immigrant parents, he grew up in the predominantly black and Irish tenderloin district on the South Side of Chicago. "There was no time in my whole memory," he later wrote, "when I did not know social outcasts, drunkards, pimps and whores, beggars and crooks." As a young boy, Reitman played in the Chicago railroad yards, thrilled by the hobos with their exciting stories of riding the rails from city to city. Fascinated by their tales, he ran away from home at the age of eleven and became a hobo himself, spending nights in the hobo "jungles" of the Midwest and West, panhandling or begging or working odd jobs to survive. He developed a liking for the unemployed men and women, the adventurers and wanderers, the rebels and petty crooks, who made up the world of the hobos. Attracted by the kindness of the railroad chapel ministers, he eventually became a Baptist. As a child in a neighborhood where he and his brother were the only Jewish boys, he had suffered keenly from the epithet "Sheeny Ben" and came to resent his Jewish background. As an adult, Reitman regarded himself with pride as a religious man, a follower of Jesus, and a good Christian.[3]

After tramping all over the United States and working his way to Europe aboard a British steamship, Reitman returned to Chicago sometime around 1897. He was hired as a laboratory boy by Dr. Maximilian Herzog, an eminent pathologist and bacteriologist. Impressed by Reitman's intelligence and apparent interest in medical research, Herzog encouraged him to enter medical school. Despite his erratic schooling, Reitman managed to pass the entrance examinations to the College of Physicians and Surgeons of Chicago (later called the University of Illinois College of Medicine), and graduated with an M.D. degree in 1904. In the same year, he also began his lifelong career as a teacher. He taught pathology and bacteriology at the Chicago Veterinary College and the Chicago College of Dental Surgery; hygiene and public health at the American College of Medicine and Surgery; and hygiene at the Chicago Nurses' School and the Chicago College of Medicine and Surgery.

Reitman's new professional identity did not bring stability. He was seized periodically with an urge to roam and wander—the legacy, perhaps, of his hobo days and, he thought, of a thousand generations of wandering Jews. From time to time, he would close down his medical office and take to the rails. After receiving his medical degree, he tramped through Europe, helped treat the injured following the 1906 earthquake in San Francisco, explored the American Southwest, and served as doctor to a railroad construction gang in Mexico. Returning home from one of these expeditions, he stopped off in St. Louis, where he learned about the Brotherhood Welfare Association. Better known as the Hobo College, this group worked to secure medical assistance, food, and housing for the unemployed and disabled, pressuring social agencies to improve their meager services. Reitman organized a Chicago branch of the Hobo College and through it became actively involved in the movement to organize the unemployed. His arrest while leading a big parade of unemployed workers in Chicago in 1907 and his subsequent trial and acquittal won him considerable publicity and respect from local labor leaders and radicals.

Throughout his life Reitman practiced medicine among the hobos, prostitutes, pimps, and underworld characters with whom he had grown up. Through this work he became interested in public health issues, particularly in the treatment of venereal disease. In the twenties he would become an active campaigner for venereal disease prevention and help to establish the first venereal disease clinic at the Cook County Jail. Later he chaired the famous Dill Pickle Club, a radical bohemian discussion group in Chicago, and also published many articles and two books: *The Second Oldest Profession* (1931), a study of pimps, and *Sister of the Road: The Autobiography of Box-Car Bertha* (1937). In different ways, all these efforts expressed "the dominant idea" of his life—"to rid the world of poverty." "I am a propagandist by nature, a teacher by inclination, a religious man by tradition," he later said. "I always had the soul of a philanthropist, the mind and heart of a humanitarian but the methods of a soapboxer."[4]

Much of this, however, came later. At the time Goldman met him, Reitman was still a struggling young doctor who, for all his intelligence and adventurousness, lacked discipline and decision and was unable really to commit himself to his profession, to social activism, or to a relationship with a woman—other than his mother, to whom he was passionately, and in Emma's opinion abnormally, devoted. Married at the age of twenty-two and the father of one daughter, he had separated from his wife after a year, dedicating himself to the indiscriminate and obsessive pursuit of women. In an unpublished autobiography, "Following the Monkey," Reitman suggested that this behavior had precedents in his family, for he described himself as "a member of the third generation of family deserters."[5] His peddler grandfather had abandoned his grandmother, his peddler father had left his mother, and he in turn would be unfaithful to most of the women in his life, including Emma Goldman.

Tall and handsome—with a thick, black, drooping moustache, dimpled chin, and wavy black hair continually falling over mischievous eyes—Reitman hid his insecurities behind a loud buffoonish manner full of swagger and bravado. Acquaintances recalled his flamboyant dress—big Garibaldi hat, flowing silk tie, snake-tipped cane—and loud, penetrating voice. His humor tended toward the vulgar and ribald; at least in Emma's circle, Reitman loved to provoke and shock with sexual allusions and crude jokes. There was about him always the air of the poseur or charlatan, as if he could not quite convince himself that "Sheeny Ben" who had run errands for the whores as a child had really become a physician. Despite occasional tantrums and outbursts of anger, he approached the world with a cheerful, childlike optimism and the expectation that somehow everything would turn out for the best without too much effort on his part.

Emma Goldman arrived in Chicago at a tense moment. The son of the Chicago police chief had recently shot and killed a young Russian Jewish immigrant suspected of intent to assassinate the chief. This incident had once again stirred up the anti-anarchist paranoia of the Chicago police. Although the alleged would-be assassin had had no known connection with the movement, the police raided anarchist headquarters and threatened to prosecute any hall owners who rented space to anarchists for meetings or lectures. Emma Goldman faced a boycott until Ben Reitman contacted her and offered her the use of his "hobo hall." His courage impressed her. The hall was then declared "unsafe" by fire officials. The anarchists decided on a ruse, advertising a concert and "social" but omitting any mention of Goldman, who would appear as a "surprise" guest to deliver her lecture. On the appointed evening, just as she was about to speak, the police arrived and arrested various people, including Goldman and Ben Reitman, the only man outside the small group of local comrades who knew that Goldman would be present. Following her arrest, Goldman was soon released and went to the home of a local comrade, Dr. Becky Yampolsky, where she expected that Reitman would join her. But he did not surface until the next morning. Where had he been? Who had betrayed her presence at the meeting?

These questions remained unanswered as she found herself irresistibly drawn to this man, so unlike her previous lovers. Surrounded until now by serious immigrant radicals and a few native-born, middle-class liberals, Goldman was charmed by this brave, brash, breezy American—"naïve and unsophisticated as a child," she confided to a friend—whose companions in life had ranged from tramps and derelicts to distinguished doctors.[6] The spark of their attraction ignited quickly. She was thrilled by this character out of the pages of Dostoyevsky and Gorky.[7] He fulfilled her romantic fantasies of the noble outcast; moved her with his stories of the open road and the underworld; attracted her with his good looks and his flirtatiousness. Reitman's medical degree must also have heightened his attractiveness, for this immigrant daughter—whose favorite brother had become a physician and who had once aspired to medicine herself—would often refer to her companion as "The Doctor," as if for the mere pleasure of the title. Reitman, for his part, was powerfully drawn to this "striking and distinguished looking person," impressed by her self-assurance, her knowledge of books and of politics, and the romantic drama of her life.[8] For all his impulsiveness, he seems to have been looking for some alternative to his chaotic, disorderly, drifting life. Emma Goldman's strength gave direction and discipline to his own grandiose fantasies of saving the world—or at least of rescuing all the hobos from their "homeless womanless jobless lives."[9] He was filled with admiration, flattered by her attention, excited by her notoriety, aroused by her passion. He needed someone to inspire and organize his life; she needed someone to help her and cheer her, to work for her by day and make love to her at night. Both in a way had found the realization of their dreams—but also of their nightmares.

As Emma would later put it—perhaps speaking for both of them—"how cruel of fate that one who can give such bliss shall also give such agony."[10]

The hints of agony were apparent from the very beginning. Their affair began in a flurry of misgivings on her part. Goldman's arrest had prompted widespread indignation and moved several prominent Chicagoans to write angry letters to the newspapers, opposing the arbitrary police actions and declaring sympathy for her. Emma herself wrote a statement of protest that appeared in the Chicago *Inter-Ocean*. Her lectures were filled to overflowing. A local Free Speech League was formed to prevent further attempts at police censorship. Late in March, at the height of the controversy, Goldman and Reitman became lovers. But Emma discovered that her new lover, whose behavior had previously aroused her suspicion, appeared to be on friendly terms with her great enemies, the police. One night during dinner with friends at a restaurant, he went over to a nearby table and, in a familiar, genial manner, greeted several policemen—including one Captain Schuettler, who had not disguised his hatred for Goldman during her incarceration at the Cook County Jail following the McKinley assassination in 1901. Shocked, disgusted, and ashamed, Goldman left in a cold rage, departing the next morning for lecture engagements in New Ulm and Minneapolis without saying goodbye. She already cared a great deal for him, she told Ben later in a letter. "But my work, my principles, will never permit me to do anything that would make me blush before myself. At least that's what I boasted of all my life. But I can boast of it no more since last night. I do not remember ever to have had such a sense of shame, of disgust, as I did last night, when you went over to *that table*. . . . I must remain strong," she insisted, "even if it should break my heart, for I would rather never never see you again than to go through last night's experience. . . ."[11]

But away from Ben her anger subsided, and she found herself again consumed with longing for this unlikely stranger. They had been lovers only a short time, but she already felt that blend of yearning, doubt, and revulsion that would plague her throughout the years of their affair. She wanted to invite him to join her, but could not calm her suspicions. Finally, according to the autobiography, she let a dream decide the issue. "I dreamed that Ben was bending over me," she wrote, "his face close to mine, his hands on

144

my chest. Flames were shooting from his finger-tips and slowly enveloping my body. I made no attempt to escape them. I strained towards them, craving to be consumed by their fire."[12] The next morning, she wired Ben to come. A brief, ecstatic visit, during which Ben explained that his work with the hobos had brought him into close contact with the police, reassured her for the moment. But then, as she proceeded alone to Winnipeg, she continued to worry. Now her fears assumed a new shape. She had always championed freedom and harmony in love. Was Ben Reitman capable of such a love, any more than Ed Brady had been? Would he let her love him "in my own way, to come and go as I *must* . . ."? Would he respect the claims of her public life—the fact that she was, as she put it, "public property"?[13] He had asked to join her on her lecture tour, to accompany her to the West Coast. Did he really want to be with her or was this only a passing impulse? Would she make him happy or only bring him misery? As she waited anxiously for his reply, she could not help but be struck by a certain ludicrousness in the situation. "Not that you are undeserving of affection, indeed you are, dearie," she wrote to her "beautiful tramp sweetheart" on April 1. "Only it seems so foolishly strange, that anybody should get such hold of my affection just now, with the entire force of police both in America and here [Canada] after me, and the repeated outbreaks against Anarchy. Don't you think it foolish to be infatuated at such a moment, when one needs as much fighting spirit as one can muster up?" But already he had helped her, she noted, "to keep bitterness out of my soul," and she was overjoyed when he decided to join her on her lecture tour.[14] Pushing aside all fears and doubts, she now welcomed the man who would dominate her sexual and emotional life for nearly ten years.

At last Emma Goldman felt that she had found a man who would "love the woman in me and yet who would also be able to share my work. I had never had anyone who could do both."[15] Life on the road for a radical agitator was hard—long, lonely train rides, late-night arrivals and departures at deserted railroad stations across the country, uncomfortable hotel rooms or the cramped homes of comrades where she was not always entirely welcome, endless arrangements for scheduling and publicity, and the ever-present danger of arrest and imprisonment. To such a life a traveling companion was a most welcome addition. And here was a man—a former hobo, a

"Doctor," an adventurer and showman like herself—who not only assuaged the loneliness but lightened her melancholy with his "cheerful bohemianism," and who eagerly assumed a multitude of tasks, performing them with zest and energy. At first, it is true, Reitman had not thought much about her work. He was too absorbed, as he put it, with being taken under her wing. But when they arrived in San Francisco in April, he found himself in the midst of another exciting controversy. The St. Francis Hotel refused to accept them. They were shadowed by detectives. A battalion of some seventy-five policemen lined the streets near Walton's Pavilion, where Goldman was scheduled to lecture, in an attempt to frighten people away; then the police filled the auditorium, in a further effort at intimidation. Without thinking much about it, Reitman found himself defending Goldman's right to speak and becoming involved in the actual work of agitation. He began making himself useful and drifted into the role of her "manager"—arranging meetings, hiring halls, advertising her lectures, and selling anarchist literature. He also generally chaired her lectures. This meant warming up the audience before she appeared by proclaiming in his booming voice the anarchist literature for sale—exhorting the audience to "take a chance" and "invest a nickel" before the "big show" began—and sometimes joking with his listeners in a manner both amusing and irritating.[16] He and Emma were, as one observer put it, an "odd combination, but how Ben could handle a crowd, getting it angry first, then joshing it to tameness!"[17] The pattern they established in 1908 continued for the next ten years: six or eight months in the winter and spring together on the road, then four to six months living apart—Reitman in Chicago, Goldman in New York—with frequent visits back and forth. While before she had had to supervise all tasks and depend upon busy, sometimes unreliable or timid comrades in each city, now she had an aggressive, enthusiastic manager whose energy matched her own. If Emma cringed at Reitman's excessive penchant for publicity —announcing her presence to all and sundry on trains when she wished to travel in privacy, or "running to the newspapers," as she put it—she nevertheless appreciated his effectiveness. After the spring of 1908, attendance at her lectures soared.

Most important to Goldman, however, was the discovery of a lover who "satisfied my deepest yearning."[18] At last, at the age of nearly thirty-nine, Emma Goldman was awakened to "the sublime madness of sex."[19] Ben Reitman, as she wrote him in her letters, "opened up the prison gates of my womanhood," released "all the passion that was fettered and unsatisfied in me for so many years. . . ."[20] Over and over she rejoiced in "the greatest most exquisite ecstasies" she had discovered in his arms, and in "the miracle" of his "sublime" embrace, which lifted her "right out of everything into a new and beautiful World."[21] His lovemaking overwhelmed her with ecstasy and showed her "the acme of beauty"—perhaps for the first time in her life.[22] She felt that she had at last found "my mate in the true sense of the word."[23] Her fidelity, she would tell him, was neither possession nor monogamy, but simply "aesthetic exaltation."[24] "You fill me," she would exult, "fill every nerve and atom, you intoxicate me, you are the great passion of my life."[25]

Goldman left an extraordinary record of this tumultuous affair in a flood of astonishing letters filled with erotic intensity. Although she abbreviated some words of the lover's language that Ben spelled out fully—t-b for treasure-box, m for mountains ("Mount Blanc and Jura"), W for Willie—she named her physical desires with an explicitness and passion that astounded even her.

"I want my sweetheart, Willie boy," Emma wrote in a typical letter of 1910. "I want to give him the t-b, she is simply starved and will swallow him alive when she gets hold of him."[26] "Good night, Hobo dear," she ended another letter, "come hold me let me nestle up, let me put my face to W and drink myself to sleep."[27] The same year she wrote Ben that "the day seems unbearable if I do not talk to you. I would prefer to do something else to you, to run a red hot velvety t[ongue] over W and the bushes, so Hobo would go mad with joy and ecstasy. . . . Oh, for one s—— at that beautiful head of his, for one drink from that fountain of life. How I would press my lips to the fountain and drink every drop."[28] If Ben came to her, she would "devour you, yes I would put my teeth into your flesh and make you groan like a wounded animal. You are an animal and you have awakened the beast in me."[29] "The t-b is full of red wine," she wrote on another occasion, "and waits for W—— to drink it all."[30] When she was anticipating a visit to Reitman after some weeks of separation, she warned him not to "try W—— too much, cause when I come to NY, ten times won't be enough. I is hungry and thirsty."[31] "I wish you were here," she told him, "to hold me in your arms, to fondle the m and kiss the T-B leisurely until she yields her jewels. She never can, you know, when you come but for the moment."[32] If only he were with her, "I could love you as wildly as I pleased, as wildly as you make me when you drink the tb dew and pluck the petal of the M rose and give me W juice. The thought of it is maddening. Absolutely maddening."[33] If Ben would come and "minister to the great needs of the m—— and T-B, I will feel inspired and conquer every difficulty."[34] "Come warm me darling," she wrote him,

pour your precious life essence into mine and let me forget, that I have neither home nor country. If I have you, I have the World. What more do I want? . . . If only I can wrap around that body of yours, if only I can drink *from the fountain of life*. My, but I will drink every drop of W. juice. Darling lover sweet heart, champion f—— just 4 days more and then and then! The thought of it dazzles me. It is so sublime. I sometimes dread it, yet it has such charm, such intoxicating charm. . . . It is moonlight now and I am planning the most wondrous orgy of our life. If I think of it much longer, some thing will happen to the t-b. And I'd rather not if she is to be starved. But my imagination works havoc with me. Every nerve is tense, my t—— is hot and burning with the desire to run it up and down up and down W. My m—— scream in delight and my brain is on fire. I want to f—— you. . . . Ben Reitman, you are my precious treasure, my joy, my life's ecstasy. I wait for you in love and passion. Come. Mommy.[35]

The signature "Mommy" at the close of so impassioned a letter suggests another dimension of this love affair. Both Reitman and Goldman imagined their intensely erotic relationship in terms of a mother-child paradigm. Emma, nearly ten years older than Ben, imagined him as her child, her "baby hobo" whom she would educate, instruct, protect, and rescue by bringing him into her idealistic anarchist world. Ben, for his part, looked up to Emma as guide and teacher, respecting her advice even when he rejected it and admiring her culture, education, and fame. Yet in certain respects the game of "Mommy" and "baby" they played together was an elaborate screen for the fact that Emma too wanted to play the child, to be taken care of herself. "Because I love you so," she would tell Ben, "I crave your care. I actually want you to take care of me." "I have always given in my life," she would say. "Surely I am entitled to take, am I not?"[36] Her constant rhetoric of thirst and hunger suggests not only the oral sexuality so important to both Emma and Ben, but also perhaps the needs left unsatisfied by the cold emotional climate of her childhood—needs for nurturing and love and comfort. Reitman, perhaps because of the caretaking role he played toward his own mother—paying her rent, entertaining her, assuming responsibility for her welfare—seems to have understood more than any other man in her life that the formidable Emma Goldman wanted to be taken on his lap and held, reassured, and caressed. He grasped, at some level, that this "Mother Earth" wanted to be mothered herself.

Hobo dearest. What a baby boy you are, so naïve, so very much a child. I really ought not to get angry with you. If only you had not awakened the woman in me, the savage primitive woman, who craves the man's love and care above everything else in the World. I have a great deep mother instinct for you, baby mine, that instinct has been the great redeeming feature in our relation. . . . But my maternal love for you is only one part of my being, the other 99 parts consists of the woman, the intense, passionate, savage woman, whom you have given life as no one else ever has. I think therein lies the key to our misery and also to our great bliss, rare as it may be. I love you with a madness that knows no bounds, no excuses, no rivals, no patience, no logic. I want your love, your passion, your devotion, your care. I want to be the centre of your thoughts, your life, your every breath. Anything that takes you away from me even for a moment drives me insane and makes my life an absolute hell. Because I love you so, I crave your care. I actually want you to take care of me. No one ever has, you know. I have always taken care and provided for others. I never wanted anyone to take care of me. But with you I long for it, oh so much. . . . I have been thinking that there is something deeper in a woman's clinging to the man she loves. It is the soothing feeling of safety, of having some human being who delights in making you happy, in finding nothing too hard in his effort for you. I never missed it, never cared for it, never imagined I would need it until you came into my life, until you awakened that side of my nature, that side of my psychology. You see, my precious, you have given life to a force, that you do not know how to handle, how to meet, hence the conflicts, hence the lack of harmony and peace. And until you will know how to deal with this tremendous force, I fear we will never have harmony.[37]

The "tremendous force" of Goldman's desire often led her to states of almost unbearable anxiety in the early years of their affair. She who had always proclaimed the glorious, liberating powers of sex now found herself in the grip of a passion more binding than anything she had known before. "Of what avail is reason, intelligence, saneness, freedom, etc. etc.," she would ask, "if I am absolutely and completely bound in my love to you?"[38] Her longing for Reitman was so intense—"so terribly painful"—that it frightened her at times, making her feel that theirs was "a diseased love" that might "offer itself for pathological study."[39] She who had always disclaimed possessiveness in love now wanted her lover entirely at her command. A frantic sense of urgency, a note of desperation, sounds through her letters to Reitman in the summer of 1910 as he was about to sail to Europe alone, his travel expenses paid by her.

Hobo! Hobo! Hobo! What have you done to me? Why have you crept into my bones and blood? Hobo you drive me mad with longing. Never, never since I know you have I wanted you so much, never has life seemed so impossible without you. I cannot let you remain in Chicago, do you hear Hobo, I must have you here. I don't see how I will ever let you go to Europe. Why I could not endure the separation, certainly not if I am to work. Why did I ever make myself dependent on you to that extent, on you of all men in my life. One so fickle, so irresponsible, so moody, so cruel. A thousand things you have done should have killed my love, long ago. Instead my love has grown deeper, stronger, more elemental, until it has become light and air and food to me. Oh Ben, mean, cruel Ben. I am in agony. I do not want you to know how much I love you, how much I need you, how much I long for you. Yet I must shout it out, scream it out, call it out so that you should hear me and come to me. You are mine, all mine. I gave you life, I gave you purpose, I gave you everything. I need you more than anyone else. Do you understand it, do you fathom this tremendous flame that is consuming me? Hobo I am raving. I am feverish. I am ill with anxiety. I don't think you love me. Maybe while I suffer you are with someone else. Oh I shall yet commit violence. I must stop. I must pull myself together. It will be Hell to wait for an answer to this letter.[40]

During the first three years of their relationship, Emma held on tightly to her beloved Hobo through daily letters, visits, and extended periods of touring. Her moods were exquisitely dependent upon Reitman. When he was loving and attentive, she felt inspired, hopeful, and full of energy—"as if I could conquer the World, so many plans come to me, if Hobo loves me and is kind and thoughtful."[41] Ben's expressions of passion, in life or in letters, left her radiant. "My darling, my Hobo, life and all," she wrote late in November of 1910. "Your beautiful letter was a most wonderful morning greeting, like the rising of the Sun, bathing me in warmth and love. Dearest lover, I am so grateful to the stars for your love. I want it more than all else in the world. It is not often you can give it to me, dear, then I am cold and lonely. But when you pour your love, as you did last week and in your dear letter, I am like a flower kissed by the Sun, everything begins to bloom, m——, t-b, my whole being. Dear Hobo, not only three years, but the rest of my life, I want to be with you, in love, in work, in everything."[42]

When Ben was cold, harsh, neglectful, impatient, Emma was reduced to despair. "Hobo mine, I am a failure in my love life, nor yet much of a success in anything else," she would tell him. "But with all that I love you."[43] When they were apart, his silence was "simply unendurable." "I wanted so much to hear from you today, then the ice crust around my soul might have melted," she wrote on one occasion. "But nothing came and the sun is again obscured."[44] If his letters were too cool or too brief, she felt equally wretched. When Reitman, on "the unfortunate day of my birth" (her forty-first), sent her "a poor, puny little scrap of paper, a wretched crumb, while I was famished for your love," she grew despondent. "Talk about a fool, no, there is none to equal EG, not another woman in the World. . . . Hobo, my own, I am so torn by my love for you. I have no pride, no strength, no ambition left. I want you, I want to hold you close to me, I want to touch your body, I want, I want! I am mad, absolutely mad and miserable. Write me. Mommy."[45]

Yet if Goldman was often depressed—"the most forlorn human derelict, stranded"—she was also given to dramatizing and display, in love as in politics. "Emma was always agonizing about something or other, one could hardly make out just what it was all about," recalled Lucy Parsons years later.[46] At times Emma's intimate love letters ring with the rhythms of the lecture platform. Affirmations of passion shift abruptly to matter-of-fact discussions of meetings and schedules. Confessions of torment alternate with cheerful proposals for printing and publicity. Emma herself often engineered the separations of which she complained so bitterly, refusing Reitman's invitations to visit and expressing reluctance to spend too much time with him.[47] If reality approached the mundane, she would invent scenes and complications, applying to love the same tenacious energy that she gave to her politics. To be genuine, love must be tragic. The purple prose of the letters sometimes sounds as if it were lifted straight out of the most sentimental nineteenth-century fiction, complete with desert wanderers, flashes of lightning, wild, reckless storms, mighty specters, and sacred love shrines. Like so much of Goldman's writing, the letters are often double-edged, full of discrepancies between conscious and unconscious intent, between overt and covert meanings. Praise masks criticism, tributes conceal attacks, assurances of love bristle with hostility. Displays of suffering seem designed to inflict guilt.

It was almost as if Goldman, who had felt deeply unloved and unwanted as a child, could not as an adult believe that she really deserved to be loved or that anyone could possibly love her; she therefore tried to get what she longed for by making everyone around her dependent upon her, and by mesmerizing, browbeating, or ordering them into submission. "I will have your love," she once threatened, "if I have to drink it through your blood, if I have to suck it out of W——, if I have to tear it out of you! it's mine! it's mine! it's mine!"[48] Imperious and dominating, used to issuing commands—"My god, what a military man she would have been," exclaimed one admirer—she wanted Ben also to obey her orders.[49] Playing the martyred mother was a form of manipulation, one way of asserting power over Ben.

If Emma was "mad, absolutely mad, and miserable" when apart from Ben, she made it clear to him that she was often equally miserable when they were together. "When you go away, you leave me weak and nerveless," she would complain. "Yet, when you stay, you cause me tortures of hell."[50] Her letters are laced with accusations and criticism. She continually reminded him of how boyish and petulant he was, and what tremendous burdens he placed on her shoulders. She never tired of cataloguing his faults, lecturing, scolding, preaching, beseeching, pleading, insisting, and exhorting him in an endless series of sermons and complaints. He was cruel, callous, and heartless, she would tell him; he said harsh things to her, complained to her; he failed to sympathize with her in her difficulties or support her in her struggles; he was self-absorbed, infantile, churlish; he was never around when he was most needed; he offended her friends, was inconsiderate, rude, vulgar, tactless; he neglected her, ordered her about, shouted at her; he was dishonest with women and careless with money; he preferred hobos, tramps, and derelicts to her friends. "Ben is wonderful with the dregs of society, more wonderful than with us people," she once said in disgust.[51] Reitman's insecurities and lack of self-confidence, exacerbated by the disparity of experience and prestige between them, provoked her not to support but to attack. While she was tormented by doubts about Ben's love for her and demanded continual reassurance, she held up his doubts and jealousies to scorn and ridicule. Even her constantly proclaimed declarations of great love teemed with reproaches. "Do you have my love?" she would scoff in response to one of his oft-repeated queries. "How pathetic that you still ask this question, or that you doubt it. Do you not know in your own heart, dear, that only a great deep, all-consuming love, can put up and endure, what I have these two years?"[52]

Her litany of complaint certainly had considerable justification. Reitman was expert at creating anxieties and doubts. Vacillating and self-indulgent, given to unpredictable whims and impulses, he tortured her with uncertainty. At moments of crisis, he would suddenly back out, leaving her feeling stranded. She never knew when he might be seized with an obsession for another woman, an attack of wanderlust, a sudden burst of loyalty to his mother, or simply a desire to nurse his soul, tabulate his ideas, and get acquainted with himself, as he put it.[53] In a life already filled with risks, Reitman multiplied the dangers, emotionally and also politically. His loose threats of political violence failed to provoke more serious consequences only because few people, including the police, took him seriously; and perhaps also because he was, as he once remarked, "American," not a "foreigner" like Goldman.[54] He embarrassed Emma in front of her comrades; he humiliated her before her women friends, insulting them with "fuck talk," and even trying to seduce them.[55] He lied to her. His connections with the police were never wholly clarified. At the start of their relationship, he even stole money from people at her lectures and filched funds from the receipts to send home to his mother.

Their worlds, as Emma quickly realized, were separated by a deep cultural abyss. Reitman felt awkward, uncertain, and ill at ease in Emma's circle of intellectual radicals. Until he met her he had rarely associated with Jews, despite his own Jewish origins, and he never really felt comfortable with the Jewish immigrants who predominated in the anarchist movement. He felt much more at home with "Americans."[56] She, for her part, had little interest in his world of hobos, tramps, and prostitutes. When Ben was in New York, she would urge him to avoid the Bowery; when he stayed in Chicago, she hoped his "old haunts will not call you." It was not "moralism," she explained, "that makes me hate those places so, but the fact that those who, through no fault of their own, are cursed to spend their lives in those places, have lost all hold upon themselves and all that is vital in life."[57] Despite her theoretical defense of the "victims of society," she personally regarded them with a certain disdain.

The fact that Reitman was not an intellectual, not really a radical, certainly not an anarchist, created an even greater barrier between them. "He had profound sympathy for society's derelicts, he understood them, and he was their generous friend," she allows in the autobiography, "but he had no real social consciousness or grasp of the great human struggle."[58] For all his vaguely religious humanitarianism and his feeling for social outcasts, he lacked the intense hatred for organized government and for the police, the intransigent spirit of opposition that inspired the anarchists. He had always felt that he had received a "fair deal" from the courts and the police.[59] Reitman had entered the movement because of his attraction to Goldman and the glamour of her life. As he unselfconsciously admitted in "Following the Monkey," whether "Emma Goldman had been a Socialist, a Theosophist, a Buddhist, a pure food crank, or a single taxer, I should have joined her party with the same zeal and enthusiasm that I brought to the anarchist movement." The crowd, he confessed, had always thrilled him; he loved "being in a critical situation or meeting critical situations with the mob. I like to stand before a howling audience."[60] Goldman, who understood very early in their relationship that Reitman loved the excitement of her life without having any deep feeling for anarchism, at first thought she could educate him, "make him over." She set about this task "with the patience of a Job," as Reitman put it bemusedly, supplying him with books and reading to him by the hour.[61] While eventually she relaxed her strenuous efforts, she never wholly abandoned her attempt to "regenerate" him through love, to liberate the noble character she was convinced lay beneath the "edges and hard crust."[62] Her love, she believed, could strengthen and inspire Reitman to reform himself, to discipline and organize his life and free himself from his lethargy, his love of the hobos, and his addiction to other women.

From Emma's point of view, Ben's compulsive infidelity was their most serious problem. She discovered his sexual promiscuity less than four months after they met. That first summer she learned that he had "outraged her sacred shrine" almost from the start of their affair.[63] He had suffered from this "disease for women," as she called it, for years. It was a compulsion, he told her, an obsession over which he had little control, but which gave him little pleasure. As a long-time champion of "free love," Goldman had always attacked conventional notions of monogamy and fidelity. She lived her own life as a free woman, loving men outside of marriage, and indeed outside of any conventional relationship. In theory, it did not matter "whether love last but one brief span of time or for eternity. . . ."[64] Still, to her free love was not indiscriminate sex, nor Reitman's casual encounters, nor sex divorced from love. Indeed, when she first met Ben, she was eager to assure him that her feeling for him was love, not "mere sex."[65] A belief in free love, however, always meant the renunciation of jealousy. Here was the source of Emma's dilemma: if she truly believed in freedom, she should allow her lover to act as he wished—or in this case, as he must. Intellectually she believed in such freedom; emotionally, however, she was deeply pained by Reitman's behavior. She could not reconcile herself to it. If he loved her, he should be able to control himself and overcome his "sex morbidity," which she recognized as an addiction "like drink, drugs, gambling etc."[66] If her love was strong enough, she should be able to inspire strength and fortitude in him, enabling him to transcend his weakness and resist temptation. She rationalized her feelings, at times claiming that her objections were really to his indiscriminate taste in the women he seduced or to his dishonesty with them. "I feel like you, dear, 'your body is your own,' " she wrote. "Yet, I haven't it in my heart to be satisfied or happy with the fact, that the body which means beauty, musik [sic], ecstasy, all the maddening joys, should be in the arms of each and every woman, common, coarse, mediocre, ugly. Oh, Ben, Ben, you would go mad, if you knew the same of Mommy's body." Or, she would argue, if he would only be honest with these women, explaining to them that "I want you for a sex embrace and no more," then she could endure it.[67] She dreaded nothing, she wrote loftily years later, "so much as vulgarity in love or sex life. And it was that and not any feeling of jealousy that hurt so frightfully during the years with Ben."[68]

In truth, each time he was "possessed by his pathological craving," her "soul and body" went through "a thousand purgatories."[69] She was jealous, hurt, and furious with Ben for abandoning and humiliating her, and also angry with herself for feeling so jealous. She felt torn between her commitment to absolute individual freedom and her intense feelings of betrayal and rejection. Her confident pronouncement that "all lovers do well to leave the doors of their love wide open. When love can come and go without fear of meeting a watch-dog, jealousy will rarely take root . . ." was simply not adequate to the problems raised by Reitman's behavior.[70]

Emma's typical response to his infidelities is vividly conveyed in a poignant series of letters written to him after one particularly painful episode in Boston in December of 1909. Ben had openly pursued a woman who resisted his advances while Emma, according to her own description, "followed him like a dog." Immediately after this incident, Emma fired off a long scolding lecture to Ben, haranguing him for his cruelty and self-absorption, his coldness, his love that "takes and takes and when it can take no more, it thrusts love aside, in a manner so cold, so brutal, so inhuman, as if love had never existed."[71] Insisting that she did not blame or condemn him, she proceeded to berate him at length, accusing him of having destroyed her faith in her work, in his love, and in the power of her love "to teach you, to make you see the beauty, the force, the greatness of love." She would "never again endure what I have endured last Thursday. Never again."[72] The next day, after receiving a pleading letter from Ben begging her forgiveness, she responded with eight pages of her own, denying that she was angry even as she proceeded to become enraged. He had forgotten her existence as he stood for an hour and a half in the rain, "trying to get the woman of your obsession. She spoiled your mood, you wrote. Yes, I know, she did not yield, that always spoils your moods. I could name any amount of instances when some fool obsession blotted out my image. The consciousness of it, the fear of it, made me cling to you even more, made me humiliate myself, made me follow you like a dog. Well, the outcome was inevitable. If love goes into the dust, it deserves to be spat upon. If it crouches on its knees, it deserves to be kicked, if it can not let go, it must be brutally thrust aside. My love was given what it deserved. So why should I be angry with you, dear?" He had killed the spirit of her work: it would never again amount to anything, can "never again give me the joy, the ecstasy, the peace and glory of our first year."[73] If they ever did work together again, it would be purely a business arrangement.

A few days later, however, Goldman's resolution began to weaken as she found herself torn between "my mad love for you, my sickening craving for your look, your voice, your touch, your embrace, and horror, cold, dread horror of that day, of your cold cruel merciless indifference and fickle mood."[74] A few days more and her anger dissipated further as she pleaded with Ben for help:

> Don't you know how affected children become when you lock them into a dark room? On that terrible day in Boston, all the light and warmth were shut out of my life. I was in impenetrable darkness, with a thousand evil spirits clutching at my being. I have not yet been able to shake the horror out of my bones. At night when I fall asleep after hours of struggle, the terrible phantom pursues me, sits on my chest and chokes me, and I wake up with a scream, all trembling from horror. It was the most awful experience of my life, Ben dear, it's hard to shake off the effects. But you will help me, dear, won't you? You will love me, as only you can love at times, you will be kind and tender, as you have been on our first trip, won't you Hobo mine? That will help me find my way back to you. I want so to come back to you. Life is so very terrible without you, so very terrible.[75]

Two days later, the crisis was over—from being "the poorest, most dejected creature on Earth," she felt "regenerated, reborn, new. What has performed the miracle? Why love, only love. . . . If I have your love, I have all that life can give, *I want nothing else.*"[76] Love alone had compelled her to return to him, against all the claims of reason. And yet: "Oh Ben, my lover, I love you too much, ever to be really happy. I will always want more than you will be able to give, therefore I shall always be bitterly disappointed, it is inevitable and I must bow to the Inevitable."[77]

It was an impossible project, this battle to change the character of a man who would not change and to get from him what he could not give. "You are like Anarchism to me," she told Ben. "The more I struggle for it the further it grows away from me. The more I struggle for your love your devotion, the further away it seems from me. Yet struggle I must. For like liberty, you are the highest Goal to me, the most precious treasure." The elusiveness of Reitman had attracted her to him, just as the elusiveness of anarchism was part of its appeal. But if in the realm of politics the struggle for an ideal was creative and inspiring, in love it was not so simple or so certain. Emma herself brooded endlessly over the reasons for her continuing fascination with Reitman "in spite of all the pain and hurt you cause me."[78] At first she was willing to "pay the price" for the moments of bliss Reitman gave her; but as these became fewer and fewer, it was perhaps the voluptuousness of the struggle itself, the sadomasochistic pleasures of martyrdom, the excitement of scenes, fights, and reconciliations that sustained her.

One solution to her torment—for Emma also to have other lovers —was a possibility both of them considered in their letters. But although Ben actually encouraged her, she found herself unable to respond sexually to other men so long as she was with him. She found that she was monogamous in spite of herself. Fear of being hurt, fear of hurting others, dislike of being the "medium of a moment's pleasure" in a man's life, a certain pleasure in displaying her suffering, and feelings of physical revulsion from other men—all bound her to her unfaithful lover. As she once wrote to Reitman, "unfortunately, every nerve in me recoils the moment real intimacy is to take place. A friend of mine came in from the country yesterday. I invited him to the flat to stay overnight. I was alone in the flat. I like the man, yet when I went to bed, my whole body convulsed at the thought of an embrace. Yet I could have had the man. He was waiting for me to call him. Now, I do not tell you that to prove my virtue. I merely say I feel unhappy that I am tied, absolutely tied by my love for you." My soul "hungers for your love," she told him, "but it will have none other than yours."[79]

Clearly Emma felt herself to be the subordinate, suffering partner in this relationship, bound by her erotic dependence on Reitman. But Ben, for his part, had some deeply felt complaints as well. Emma was gloomy, wearying, depressing, he would tell her. She wore him out with her constant complaints about the magazine office, the bills, her great misery. She accused him of cowardice when he was only thinking of her safety. He had come to New York to be the

158

business manager of *Mother Earth* and run the office. But she and Berkman scowled at all his plans, discouraged his ambitions, made him feel like a "whipped cur."[80] He wanted less bitterness, more love and joy in anarchist propaganda; he was sure that the bitterness had kept the movement from growing as fast as it might. And Ben did not feel he had had a chance to "expand" as he would have liked; he had not "given my best as I wanted to."[81]

Indeed, both in their work and in their private life, Ben eventually began to feel suffocated and overwhelmed by Emma. "You are such a powerful creature," he wrote plaintively, "it is difficult to be a simple lover to you."[82] As Emma herself admitted, moreover, she was "insatiable" in her need for constant attention, reassurances, and demonstrations of love. Nothing Reitman did was ever enough. Her pleasure in love, as in work, was always fleeting. No matter how intense, the memory of it seemed rapidly to drain out of her, leaving her once again feeling famished, thirsty, empty. Ben often felt bewildered by his demanding lover and fled in self-defense to the arms of other women, to Chicago, to the tramps and hobos with whom he felt at home—or, most often, to his mother.

But Ben's primary complaint was Emma's unwillingness to make him a "home," to live with him and bear his children. While the initial excitement of the lecture tours sustained him for several years, his longing for domestic life began to assert itself with increased urgency. Perhaps because he had never known a stable home as a child, he found himself, in his mid-thirties, full of longing for a family life. Although he had one child, who lived with her mother, Reitman wanted another. Emma, of course, had confronted the issue of children long before she met Reitman. Ed Brady, too, had wanted to have children, but she had decided while still in her twenties that she would remain childless. Now, in her forties, she was no more attracted to the prospect of child rearing than she had been twenty years earlier. When Ben broached the matter, she was at first skeptical, chiding him for neglecting the child he already had.[83] She did not categorically refuse to have children, however; she tended, rather, to evade the subject, using it as grounds for reproaching him by telling him that she might want to have children if he loved her more—but then suggesting that if he did, she might not want to share the ecstasy of his love.[84] While the issue loomed increasingly large for Ben, Emma seems to have dismissed it, even though Ben's

159

longing for a home and family was an increasing source of his unhappiness in the relationship.

During the summer of 1911, the eighteenth-century feminist Mary Wollstonecraft was much on Goldman's mind. In preparation for her fall lectures, she read a new biography that depicted the author of *A Vindication of the Rights of Woman* as a romantic heroine. In the story of Wollstonecraft's unhappy love affair with the American adventurer Gilbert Imlay—and her two suicide attempts—Goldman saw a frightening parallel to her own affair with Reitman. When she had first read about Wollstonecraft's life, she reported to Ben, she had been repelled by her "weak and humiliating love life with Imlay. . . . Mary Wollstonecraft, the most daring woman of her time, the slave of her passion for Imlay. How could anyone forgive such weakness?" But now, "EG, the Wollstonecraft of the 20th century, even like her great sister, is weak and dependent, clinging to the man no matter how worthless and faithless he is. What an irony of fate."[85]

The ironies, in truth, were many. Publicly proclaiming the necessity of freedom in love, privately Emma took a certain pleasure in her erotic dependence on Reitman, even while fighting against it. She felt reassured by the thought that even the great Mary Wollstonecraft had been a slave to sexual passion, as if their shared erotic bondage were a mark of their sisterhood. Portraying herself in her letters as "weak and dependent," she nonetheless remained in many respects the dominant partner in the relationship, socially, financially, and intellectually. Despite the intensity of her pleasure with Reitman, Emma was deeply unhappy so much of the time—with and without Ben—that she decided to effect a change. Gradually she began to loosen the frantic hold over Reitman she had tried to maintain and to recast and redefine the relationship. In her letters, she increasingly insisted on his role as her manager and downplayed his importance as her lover, as if to remind him of his subordinate place in her life. Certainly she was trying to persuade herself as much as Ben. Her desire for him remained as strong as ever. But she no longer gave way to the fantasies of wild desperation or the frenzied soliloquies of earlier years. She no longer grew hysterical with rage over his infidelities. There is a brisker, more detached, sometimes even a brusque tone in some of the later letters, a growing weariness with the dramas and scenes of their first years. She no longer felt confi-

160

dent in the power of her love to transform her incorrigible lover. Perhaps she felt that she had finally to protect herself against the disappointment she considered "inevitable."

From Wollstonecraft's experience she drew a lesson: perhaps if Mary had had a "work companion in Imlay, she would not have attempted to drown herself nor would her life [have] been wrecked through that one great passion."[86] (In fact, Wollstonecraft recovered completely from the Imlay affair, going on to a happier relationship with William Godwin, the first British philosopher of anarchism.) The solution, then, was work. "Activity, propaganda. That is my salvation," she wrote Reitman. "That is the only force which reconciles me to my mad passion for you."[87]

In a sense, Goldman had never lost herself as totally as she feared. She may have felt herself a slave of love—"as helpless as a shipwrecked crew on the foaming ocean"; nevertheless, the years she spent with Reitman were the most productive and creative of her American career.[88]

P A R T
5

CELEBRITY

C H A P T E R

II

"MORE OF
A PUBLIC
THAN
A PRIVATE
PERSON"

rom the spring of 1908 until the summer of 1917, Goldman spent nearly half of every year on the road, racing from one train station to the next, from the home of one comrade to that of another, from one hotel room to the next, always in a flurry of meetings, lectures, demonstrations, free speech fights, dinners, debates, and "socials." She lectured on "The Intermediate Sex" in Portland, on "Woman's Inhumanity to Man" in St. Louis, "The Psychology of War" in Rochester, "Syndicalism" in San Francisco. Keeping up "a perpetual mad run"—"more of a public than a private person even in your own room," as her admirer Theodore Dreiser once put it—she maintained a level of activity that astonished even herself.[1]

By all accounts, Goldman's propaganda tours were a great success. Her friends and admirers extended far beyond the anarchist movement. The attendance at her lectures steadily increased. In May of 1908 in Los Angeles, a hall seating 350 people was packed every night for two weeks, with hundreds standing. Six hundred people heard her one night in Indianapolis, and 1,500 on another night in Winnipeg. In San Francisco in January of 1909, she spoke nightly for two weeks to 2,000 people. In Los Angeles that same month, her lectures averaged from 200 to 600 people nightly. With the outbreak of the war in August 1914, the numbers increased even further. The birth control lectures of 1915 and 1916 drew large crowds, and the antiwar meetings of 1916 and 1917 still larger ones. The reports of spies sent to cover these lectures for the Justice Department always indicated that they were "packed." At a meeting in Detroit in September 1917, for example, Goldman reported an attendance of 1,500 people, with over 2,000 turned away at the door. Perhaps the largest turnout ever was an anticonscription meeting in May of 1917 in New York City, which according to Goldman's estimate attracted 8,000 people![2]

Lecturing on an average of three to five times a week throughout the year except during the summer months, Goldman spoke to an impressive number of people. During her 1910 speaking tour, between January and June she spoke in 37 cities in over 25 states, lecturing 120 times to a total audience of 40,000 people. In 1915, according to Reitman, she gave 321 lectures. Later she estimated that she had spoken to between 50,000 and 75,000 people every year.[3]

Her popularity was in part a result of her notoriety—people wanted to see this "exponent of free love and bombs," the "murderer of McKinley"—and in part because of Reitman's high-powered advertising techniques. Particularly in New York, the Left in general gained new impetus from the arrival of radical exiles after the collapse of the 1905 revolution in Russia, and from the rising tide of East European immigrants responsive to the appeal of socialism and trade unionism. The growing strength of the unions, including the I.W.W., the mounting influence of the Socialist party, and the increased visibility of women in politics meant that Goldman was no longer so isolated in her outspoken social protests. But if a more favorable political climate and artful publicity created a positive setting for Goldman's work, surely the key to her success was the extraordinary excitement she generated as a platform speaker. Many who heard Goldman lecture said that she had changed their lives. "Life takes on an intenser quality when she is present," exclaimed

166

Margaret Anderson; "there is something cosmic in the air, a feeling of worlds in the making."[4] The passion of her convictions gripped and inspired her listeners. "You felt her emotion," recalled Ahrne Thorne, former editor of the Yiddish anarchist paper *Freie Arbeiter Stimme*.[5] Tributes from a spectrum of people including artists, writers, workers, and prostitutes consistently testify to Goldman's powerful impact. She held before our eyes "the ideal of freedom," wrote Floyd Dell, a novelist and critic, taunting us with our cowardice for "having acquiesced so tamely in the brutal artifice of present-day society."[6] As Sadakichi Hartmann summed it up, "whether her teachings have any economic value I can not say, but I know she educated MANY."[7] "There were thousands of men and women all over the country who loved her," wrote Hutchins Hapgood. She "performed a distinct service—that of removing despair from those who would otherwise be hopeless. Those who would otherwise regard themselves as outcasts, after hearing Emma, often felt a new hope and thought better about themselves."[8]

Goldman was aware of her almost magical power. When truly inspired, she seemed to enter a kind of trancelike state. Her autobiography describes this sensation, which she evidently first experienced on her first lecture tour in Rochester in 1890. "I began to speak," she writes. "Words I had never heard myself utter before came pouring forth, faster and faster. . . . The audience had vanished, the hall itself had disappeared; I was conscious only of my own words, of my ecstatic song." On this occasion she had a revelation. "I could sway people with words! Strange and magic words that welled up from within me, from some unfamiliar depth. I wept with the joy of knowing."[9] Goldman had always been extremely sensitive to the force of language and of voices. Her autobiography is full of her father's loud, harsh voice; her mother's vivid storytelling; the musical Russian of her first husband; Berkman's "powerful voice" ringing out at Sachs Cafe the day they met; the pungent language and pleasing voice of Johann Most; the "soft, deep, and ingratiating" voice of Ben Reitman, which formed one of her first impressions of him. Johann Most's speeches convinced her, she wrote in 1910, that "the spoken word hurled forth among the masses with such wonderful eloquence, such enthusiasm and fire, could never be erased from the human soul." People had only to hear his voice "to throw off their old beliefs and see the truth and beauty of Anarchism." Her one great longing had been "to speak with the tongue of John Most, —that I, too, might thus reach the masses."[10] If she could only speak well enough, long enough, loud enough, she, too, could change the world.

Although Goldman was often described as a firebrand, she was considerably quieter, less rhetorical, and less flamboyant than most of her male contemporaries. She would stand simply before her audience—"small, stocky, strong and earnest," as the socialist painter John Sloan described her—her penetrating blue eyes gazing steadily at her listeners as she addressed them briskly in her low, melodious voice, which sounded to Reitman like "the angel Gabriel."[11] Roger Baldwin called her "a great speaker—passionate, intellectual and witty." "Her English was impressive," he recalled, speaking of the first lecture he attended. "She had hardly any accent and her flow of words was as eloquent as her plain good sense. I was quite overcome by the range and depth of her speech. I had expected fireworks, denunciation and anger. I got reason, sense and sympathy."[12] In a similar vein, a Detroit newspaper admired "her clearness of expression, her pleasing voice, and the total absence of the vehemence generally associated in the public mind with people who talk on anarchy."[13] The painter Robert Henri found her "a woman of remarkable address, convincing presence. I never heard so good a lecture. This is a very great woman." He subsequently also described her, as Baldwin did, as "a cool, logical and brilliant speaker, appealing to the reason and understanding of her audience."[14]

Others recalled her in different terms. Sadakichi Hartmann praised "the magnetism of her sledgehammer style," and a judge who convicted her acknowledged her "magnetic power" even as he sentenced her to prison.[15] Wobbly leader Elizabeth Gurley Flynn also recalled being surprised at "the force, eloquence and fire that poured from this mild-mannered, motherly sort of woman," and Hutchins Hapgood remembered that when truly inspired, Goldman was capable of making a speech that was "a pure poem of feeling, springing spontaneously into form."[16] Others described her as "a spellbinder," surely "the finest orator—man or woman—living."[17] Even government agents sent to spy on her sometimes found themselves admiring her against their will. Wrote one such agent in alarm, in the fall of 1917, "she is doing tremendous damage. She is womanly, a remarkable orator, tremendously sincere, and carries conviction. If she is allowed to continue here she cannot help but have great influence." [18]

Margaret Anderson effectively captured Emma Goldman as she appeared in action at a luncheon meeting of the Chicago Press Club in November of 1914:

> Picture a large club dining-room filled with about five hundred hard-faced men ("oh! those faces!" Miss Goldman said afterward; "how they seared me!"); imagine their cynical indifference as she began to speak amid all the clattering of dishes and the rushing of waitresses; and then imagine the stillness that gradually descended upon them as she poured out her magnificent denouncement. Her subject was "The Relationship of Anarchism to Literature," and she talked to those men about making their lives and work free and true and beautiful in a way that would pull the heart out of anything but a veteran newspaper man. "You are mental prostitutes!" she hurled at them. "You sell yourselves and your work to your editors or your publishers. There is no such thing as a free man among you. You say what you're told to say— whether it's the truth or not; you must not have an opinion of your own; you dare not have any ideas; you'd die of indigestion if you had. It is men like you who are responsible for public crimes such as the hanging of my five Anarchist comrades in this city twenty-seven years ago." She berated them for an hour, she told them what her Anarchism means—how it can contribute to the living of a rich life; "You call it a dream, gentlemen; well, I plead guilty. But when we can't dream any longer we die. That's what is the matter with you. You've lost your dreams!" She sat down under an applause that burst out like bullets. [19]

Goldman's tone varied with the occasion, the subject, and the audience. She could be brusque and abrupt or warm and motherly. She might carry an audience of young women from the Lower East Side of New York with her "like a mother hen followed by a brood of chicks," as the cartoonist Art Young once observed. [20] Or she might rip into an audience, taunting them with their lack of independent thinking, their hypocrisy, complacency, and cowardice. She especially loved to "roast" the police who were ever present at her lectures and sometimes lashed them, Harry Kelly recalled, "until I felt sorry for them and wondered how they stood it." [21] Although she looked solemn—even grim—on the platform, Goldman was witty in a style that tended toward the sarcastic. The few available transcripts of her talks note frequent interruptions for laughter, not so much in the prepared text of her lectures as in her opening, off-the-cuff remarks or spontaneous jests and asides. Yet she could also be deadly serious, relying on the simple, straightforward presentation of facts to move and arouse her audience. At all times she was definite, with "an air of absolute finality." "There was nothing tentative about anything she said," recalled Eva Langbord, whose anarchist parents in Toronto were close friends of Goldman in the twenties and thirties; "everything was positive, determined and hit its target!"[22]

At the start of her career Goldman had read her lectures, but she soon began to memorize her text and to speak extemporaneously, referring to notes only to quote facts, statistics, or lines from plays. She spoke very rapidly; indeed, the speed of her delivery was often an issue in trials, which depended upon the accuracy of police stenographers' transcripts. Emma used to joke about her speed with detectives and reporters, promising that if any of them could manage to take down her every word, she would give him a kiss.[23] She also often spoke "long"—too long, according to some; and very occasionally she spoke "rotten," even in her own view, especially when the audience was unenthusiastic or the surroundings uncongenial. It was "utterly impossible to speak well in a dismal hall to empty benches," and while hostile audiences could be wooed, mocked, shouted down, or won over, dull audiences could reduce Goldman to despair.[24]

Goldman spoke in a simple, blunt style characterized by the rhythmical repetition of short phrases or words. She usually greeted her audience as "friends" and repeated this direct address frequently throughout her talks. Her argument was built on a pattern of denial and affirmation, a series of questions followed by an answer. "How are you going to create a wide-awake public opinion?" she asked, in a 1917 speech on amnesty for conscientious objectors. "You cannot get halls. . . . you cannot reach the people at a dinner like this. . . . You have not the pulpit, you have not the press, you have nothing. How are you going to reach the people? How are you going to create an intelligent public opinion? It seems to me that an organized amnesty movement should make it its purpose to send its emissaries into every hamlet and village and town of the United States to appeal to the workers, to appeal to the women, to appeal to all thinking men and women. . . ."[25]

Her language was scathing, pungent, full of startling reversals and

TOP LEFT Taube Goldman. "The grande dame par excellence." (*International Institute of Social History*)

TOP RIGHT Abraham Goldman. "As long as I could think back, I remembered his saying he had not wanted me." (*International Institute of Social History*)

ABOVE Alexander Berkman in 1892. "An obsessed fanatic to whom nothing but his ideal and faith existed." (*International Institute of Social History*)

RIGHT Helene Hochstein. "The one who meant more to me than even my mother." (*Courtesy of the Hochstein Music School*)

RIGHT   Emma Goldman in the 1890s. *(International Institute of Social History)*

BELOW LEFT   Edward Brady. "The most scholarly man I had ever met." *(International Institute of Social History)*

BELOW RIGHT   Hippolyte Havel. "A veritable encyclopedia." *(International Institute of Social History)*

OPPOSITE   Emma Goldman in Chicago, 1906. *(Chicago Historical Society, DN3882)*

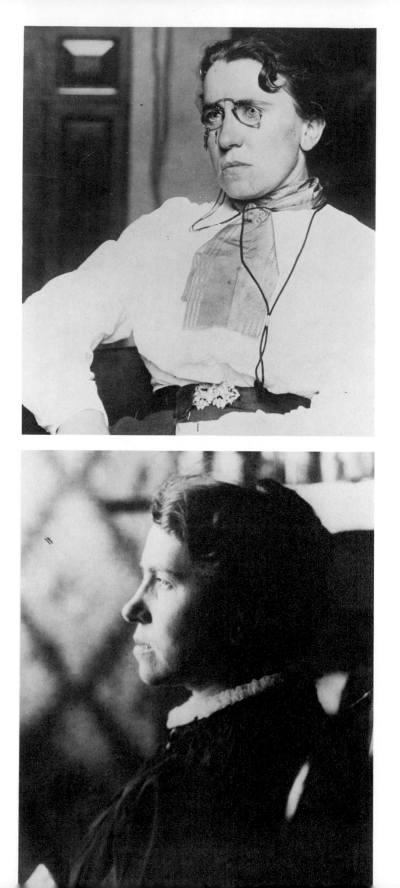

OPPOSITE ABOVE   Emma Goldman. "I had long realized that I was woven of many skeins, conflicting in shade and texture." (*National Archives, 165-WW-164-5*)

OPPOSITE BELOW   Emma Goldman. "I feel so lonely, so hungry for an affection that would assert itself in real life." (*National Archives, 165-WW-163F-5*)

RIGHT   Ben L. Reitman. "This living embodiment of the types I had only known through books." (*International Institute of Social History*)

BELOW LEFT   Ben L. Reitman, ca. 1906. "My Great Grand Passion." (*Photograph courtesy of Paul Avrich*)

BELOW RIGHT   Ben L. Reitman. "How cruel of fate that one who can give such bliss shall also give such agony." (*International Institute of Social History*)

LEFT *San Diego Union*, May 15, 1912.

BELOW LEFT *Mother Earth*, June 1912.

BELOW RIGHT *San Diego Union*, May 18, 1912.

ABOVE San Diego, May 21, 1913.
Crowd at the city police station and
jail after the arrival of Emma Gold-
man and Ben Reitman. (*Historical
Collection, Title Insurance and Trust,
San Diego, California*)

LEFT *San Diego Union*, May 21,
1913.

BELOW San Diego, May 21, 1913.
Mob outside the city police station
and jail, where Emma Goldman and
Ben Reitman are in custody. (*Histori-
cal Collection, Title Insurance and
Trust, San Diego, California*)

RIGHT   Alexander Berkman and
Eleanor Fitzgerald on Mount Tamal-
pais, ca. 1916. *(International Institute
of Social History)*

BELOW   Emma Goldman and
Alexander Berkman, 1917. *(National
Archives, 165-WW-163F-9)*

surprising formulations. What did love, she would ask, "the strongest and deepest element in all life," have to do with "that poor little State and Church-begotten weed, marriage?"[26] "What does the history of parliamentarism show?" she asked. "Nothing but failure and defeat, not even a single reform to ameliorate the economic and social stress of the people."[27] "Prisons, a social protection? What monstrous mind ever conceived such an idea?"[28] America was "the stronghold of the Puritanic eunuchs."[29] School was "for the child what the prison is for the convict and barracks for the soldier. . . ."[30] Christianity was "most admirably adapted to the training of slaves. . . ."; indeed, "never could society have degenerated to its present appalling stage, if not for the assistance of Christianity."[31] Was there anything "more terrible, more criminal," asked Goldman, "than our glorified sacred function of motherhood?"[32] Her extravagant speech, slight accent, and occasionally awkward constructions and jarring metaphors— modern women reminded her of "artificially grown plants of the female sex"—simply added to the original effect.[33]

But for all their hyperbole, Goldman's appeals were concrete, connecting the abstract ideas of anarchism with the everyday experience of her listeners. "Emma Goldman does not bore her audiences with fancy pictures of the cooperative commonwealth," wrote one anarchist, praising her talks as examples of good propaganda methods. "On the contrary, she bends every energy to the demonstration of a fact . . . that this is not a question of the possibility of a revolution at some future date, as yet entirely uncertain, but of the present system having ALREADY BROKEN DOWN HOPELESSLY, since there are vast masses whom it cannot provide with the barest of life's necessaries. Hearing this, people ponder. They go away worried, harassed by an essentially revolutionary idea."[34] Fifty years after the event, one listener still recalled Goldman insisting that "everyone is an anarchist at heart, all the people walking down Second Avenue are anarchists, only they don't know it."[35]

The high point of an evening with Goldman was the question-and-answer session that followed the prepared lecture. This was the moment everyone seemed to await most eagerly. Sometimes Goldman would ask for questions from the floor, write them down, arrange them in some order, and then answer them all at once.[36] On other occasions, bombarded by questions from her audience, she would toss back answers "as fast as the questions came," in the "true 'Red

Emma' style—caustic and biting."[37] Her "repartee and wit," wrote Reitman, "together with her enormous collateral reading made it easy for her to meet most queries. She always responded intelligently, simply and to the point." She was patient with her questioners, but had no fear of hurting their feelings, either.[38] Indeed, she was "very sharp with all her answers," recalled another observer, "and was able to cut down her critics with a phrase or a word."[39] Reitman recalled that "in this fire and counterfire of questions and answers she seemed to be in her element."[40] And Goldman herself liked these verbal confrontations; she excelled at sarcastic rejoinders and crushing retorts: "the more opposition I encountered, the more I was in my element and the more caustic I became with my opponents," she boasted.[41] Eva Langbord vividly described the excitement of these encounters. "I remember how frightened and anxious I felt after the one hour lecture when the questions and heckling began," Langbord recalled. "But I soon overcame that when I saw her handle those sessions. She was at her best then and she was masterful, even brilliant, in these sessions. . . . I'm quite sure people came more for the question period bravura performance than the actual lecture."[42]

A general discussion usually followed the question period. People lingered, reluctant to stop talking, arguing and debating even as they left the hall. Often a small group would accompany Goldman to a cafe or restaurant for dinner (she never ate before a lecture, usually shutting herself in a room alone for an hour to gather her thoughts and go over her notes—perhaps also to steel herself against the stage fright that she suffered at the start of every lecture throughout her life). Or a group would go with her to the home where she was staying, to continue the discussion informally late into the night (sometimes until four or five in the morning), with Goldman seated in a chair holding forth to a circle of admiring listeners crowded around her on the floor. Though she usually stayed up late and got up early, capable of getting by comfortably on six hours of sleep, after such nights, recalled Reitman, she would sleep late, have coffee in bed at ten, and not get up until noon.[43]

On tour with Reitman, she rarely felt homesick or missed New York. In the midst of a series of lectures, she was all business: tense, brusque, brisk, a "machine," as one man put it. With her terrific powers of concentration, she would think of nothing but the work ahead. On occasion, she could be extremely insensitive to those around her, demanding that all dedicate themselves totally to her needs. One admirer recalled the "commanding voice and presence —never asking, always commanding things to be done. . . . it was rather like a royal command."[44] Others remembered dismal private dinners after meetings, with Emma "tired and morose, occupied with her mail, disgusted with something about her meal . . . [and] Ben . . . eating like a hungry animal. . . ."[45] As another admirer put it, "Emma was theatrical: she loved the stage and she loved admiration. But when she subsided with no audience, she was heavy."[46] And yet, with people she really liked, another off-stage, after-hours persona emerged, one that could be "gay, communicative, tender" in marked contrast to the public demeanor that one friend thought "serious as the deep Russian soul itself."[47] For all her seriousness, Emma loved parties, good food (she was an excellent cook), fine wines, music, dancing, the theater, lively conversation, and a spirit of gaiety that she at times found lacking in her comrades. The tours were intensely social undertakings: a small party of friends often accompanied Emma on short trips for lectures in nearby towns, and hordes of visitors usually descended upon her wherever she was staying. Not only did she meet everyone in the movement all over the country; she also had access on these tours to some of the most interesting members of the literary, theatrical, journalistic, and political worlds. In San Francisco, Jack and Charmian London invited her to visit at their Glen Ellen home; in St. Louis, the future Pulitzer prize–winning playwright Zoë Akins entertained her with amusing stories of her escapes from her respectable family; the publisher of the liberal *St. Louis Mirror*, William Marion Reedy, a great admirer, took her to lunch and arranged lectures for "society"; Judge Ben Lindsey in Denver, famous for his enlightened views, invited her to his home and chaired one of her meetings on birth control.

Certainly Goldman found these tours inspiring and energizing, but they were also hard work and often filled with strain. She was a professional, and despite the emphasis on spontaneity in her presentation, the lecture tours were carefully planned. Long before she met Reitman, Goldman had developed a keen sense of public relations and the power of the mass media. Her lectures were preceded by extensive advertising and publicity, sometimes in the commercial as well as the radical press. Even after Reitman became her manager, Goldman continued to pay attention to the details of each lecture:

173

her correspondence is full of discussions of the location and nature of halls to be rented, the pricing of tickets, the hours and days of the meetings, promotion and advertising. Typically she would recruit members of local anarchist groups to do some of the advance work; her presence in a town often revived the flagging energies of these groups and became the catalyst for organizing new ones.

Though commercial newspapers often refused to carry announcements of Goldman's lectures, publicity was usually not difficult to generate. Her letter to a comrade in Minneapolis gives typically complete instructions about preparations for her arrival:

> First, get a few people to help you with the factory district between 5–6 tomorrow, and noon Saturday, as many important factories and locomotive shops as there are. Secondly, cover the University thoroughly, if you have not done so already. It might also be a good idea to have two people near the bridge between Minneapolis and St. Paul, so many people come and go there, Saturday evening especially. . . . Fourth, have some cards taken to the Industrial Workers headquarters. As to the most important part, the Press! Will you go yourself Saturday morning between 8:30 and 10 to every afternoon paper, ask to see the City Editor and tell him of my lectures, or anything you like. Tell him in the afternoon meeting I will speak on the McNamaras in a new light, also about the strike in Lawrence Massachusetts and the Coal strike in England.* Make it as interesting as you can and get them to announce the meetings. The same process must be followed Saturday evening with the morning papers. If the afternoon papers do give us a notice, well and good. If not, you will have to put a small ad among [the] City brevities, if there is such a column, or under 'Church notices,' something that will not cost much, about $2 each the highest. Just announcing the 2 Sunday lectures. I am sorry to cause you so much work, but I am sure you will forgive me. . . . P.S. Please be careful not to get into the hands of the police [while] distributing the cards. . . .[48]

Securing halls for lecture engagements was another, more difficult matter. Unlike the Wobbly agitators, who held free outdoor meetings to recruit itinerant workers or those between jobs in remote locations (timber workers, for example), Emma Goldman hated street speaking. At least in America, she believed it inconsequential. "Where

---

* The McNamara brothers were trade unionists tried and convicted in the October 1910 bombing of the *Los Angeles Times* building.

there are parks set aside for that purpose it is different," she once wrote Ben. "But people in the streets are too restless to listen."[49] Goldman did, of course, often end up speaking at outdoor demonstrations and mass meetings. But she much preferred to speak indoors, in some kind of hall or auditorium. She was not above occasionally scolding the local organizers of her lectures for "being incapable of learning that Anarchism and dirty halls in squalid sections of the city are not synonymous." Even for the survival of *Mother Earth*, she once announced indignantly, she could not "speak in dingy little halls, dark and gloomy, with the dust and smoke making it impossible to breathe."[50] Reitman noted that she had spoken in the Eagles' Hall, the Owls' Hall, the Elks' Hall, the Odd Fellows' Hall, the Masons' Hall, and indeed in every kind of fraternal hall except those of the Knights of Columbus! She spoke at Carnegie Hall in New York, the Fine Arts Theater in Chicago, the Jewish Consumptive Sanitarium in Edgewater, Colorado, and the City Hall of Sioux City, Iowa; she also spoke in churches, college auditoriums, Wobbly and socialist halls, and occasionally in barns, vacant lots, back yards, the back rooms of saloons, and underground mine shafts.[51]

If Emma loved the excitement and variety of life on tour, the strain and anxiety at times reduced her almost to despair and caused her to doubt her suitability for public life. Touring for Goldman was in some ways a grim business. She never knew when police or local officials would attempt to interfere with her lectures, and the heavy police presence at her talks always created the potential for violence. Although she handled emergencies with superb aplomb—on more than one occasion she prevented violent outbreaks by her coolheadedness—she always felt responsible for the audience and frequently complained of the strain under which she worked. She was "so damnably sensitive to all kinds of impressions," she often told friends, that "every little thing burns my flesh and tears my nerves to pieces," making life "hell every hour of my existence."[52] "Fate or the devil must have entered into some sort of a conspiracy, when I was thrust into the public arena," she lamented to Hutchins Hapgood in February of 1911. "I realize more and more how deficient I am for that. And yet I am not much fit for a private life. Truth is, I am pretty much of an abortion, Hutchie boy. I find life hard to endure under all circumstances." She longed to escape, to "bask in love and flowers and mad forgetfulness," yet even then she probably would not be contented for long. "Just fancy wishing for such things," she remarked, "yet standing in ugly dirty halls facing dull people with your soul inside out for everyone to stick a dirty thumb into it. . . ."[53] "The Joys of an Agitator," as she described them in the running commentary on her lecture tours in *Mother Earth*, were often ambiguous. Her world, she once announced to Reitman, was "a World of war, bitter relentless war, everlasting strife and battle until death."[54] "Fun" consisted of putting "oneself up against a world of stupidity, mental laziness, and moral cowardice. If there is anything the world hates, it is to be conscious of itself, to be brought face to face with its own decrepit hypocritical rotten self. But the funniest of all things is to witness the frantic efforts of this world to shout and howl down the voice that cries in the wilderness. It's truly a farce comedy."[55]

Goldman had plenty of opportunity to witness this "farce comedy" during two decades of cross-country lecture tours. Despite the liberalism of the Progressive Era and the growing grass-roots strength of radicalism in the decade before World War I, Emma Goldman could never be sure of her reception. In times of general prosperity she was less likely to be harassed than during periods of recession or depression, with high levels of unemployment and heightened social tensions. On the West Coast—where the I.W.W. was waging its own vigorous free speech fights between 1909 and 1912—Goldman encountered opposition from police and local businessmen on account of her support for the Wobblies. In towns of the Pacific Northwest such as Seattle, Everett, and Bellingham, Washington—all centers of Wobbly strength—she and Reitman were continually harassed, frequently arrested, and often attacked in the press.

The police used a variety of techniques to silence Goldman. They intimidated hall owners; declared halls "unsafe" just prior to a lecture; locked audiences out or speakers in; arrested her and her listeners in the middle of a meeting; and sometimes resorted to outright physical violence, swinging clubs and sticks against the unarmed crowd. Sometimes they simply lined the streets outside the hall and then occupied it themselves in order to frighten and intimidate the audience.

Of course, Goldman was only one of many radicals in America who were subjected to such persecution and police brutality. But the antagonism toward her was of a peculiarly intense, vicious, and personal nature. Her blend of sexual and political radicalism, the aura of violence surrounding her, seemed to mobilize the deepest anxieties of conservatives. The legend of her complicity in the McKinley assassination still lingered. "For God's sake deport this miserable wench!" demanded one angry correspondent to the Justice Department in 1908; "she is a curse to this country. And if all this is permitted under the name of 'free speech' *then* it's high time we had some new laws doing away with unlimited *unqualified* free speech!!!!! Are all our Presidents and great men to be assassinated one by one by these miserable foreigners while Congress does NOTHING?"[56] Determined to take action, the New Haven police chief tried to prevent Goldman from speaking, as "an undesirable person, and one whom the good and respectable people of this City do not care to have speak on any subject." The chief was convinced that Goldman was "the cause of the murder of President McKinley" and that immediately following the assassination, Congress had enacted legislation "making it a crime for anyone to speak against the government in a derogatory manner. . . ."[57] (Goldman did speak in New Haven, on the lawn of the liberal Reverend Eliot White, who had been angered by the chief's arbitrary action.)

Goldman's image as a terrorist also persisted. In January of 1909, she and Reitman were arrested in San Francisco and charged with "conspiracy and riot, making unlawful threats to use force and violence and disturbing the public peace." As usual, Goldman turned this incident into a small triumph for anarchism. Held in jail for four days before being released on sixteen thousand dollars bail each, she and Reitman were tried in police court—the charges having been changed to "unlawful assemblage, denouncing as unnecessary, all organized government, and preaching anarchist doctrines"—and acquitted.[58] The victory left Goldman exultant. After the acquittal, she addressed an audience of 1,500 people. "The police were there in full force," she reported gleefully to a friend, "but they must have felt like whipped dogs. I am not vain, as you probably know, but I spoke last night in letters of fire, raising the audience to the highest pitch of enthusiasm." She had been exhausted, "in a worn and desperate state, but my experience here has put new blood into my system. I no longer feel tired," she exclaimed. "I am full of the fighting spirit. . . . I am so happy with our victory, I wish you were here so I could embrace you. Hurrah for truth!"[59]

A short time later, however, her exuberance had vanished. Constant rain had spoiled her remaining meetings; the lecture tour had been a failure. "Every little gleam of hope is covered with a black sky of disappointment and despair, so that life seems a perfect mockery to me, at times," she lamented to friends. She had continued the tour like a gambler—knowing he is losing, but "driven on by an irresistible force until he has lost his last shirt."[60] And then, Emma was chagrined to learn early in 1909, her citizenship was cancelled. A law passed by Congress in 1906 had provided for the cancellation of citizenship obtained fraudulently or illegally. By harassing the family and friends of Jacob Kersner in Rochester, federal officials extorted information that purported to show that Goldman's former husband had not met the five-year residency requirement when he had applied for United States citizenship in 1884. His citizenship was thereby declared null. Kersner was never contacted with regard to these proceedings, nor was Goldman; all information was gathered at second or third hand. The acknowledged purpose of the case was to denaturalize Emma Goldman. Since the authorities decided not to make her a party to the suit, she had no chance to contest it. Although her sister Helene had informed her that "two suspicious-looking individuals had been snooping about" in Rochester gathering information on Kersner, Goldman learned of his denaturalization, and by extension her own, only when the cancellation had been completed. The withdrawal of citizenship meant that she could no longer leave the country and be assured of reentry. She felt herself now "a prisoner in America," but there were other, more ominous implications as well.[61] Increasingly, radicalism would be regarded by Congress, not as a response to conditions in America, but as the alien import of foreigners who could be denied entry or deported at will. Procedural safeguards for the rights of all noncitizens were gradually cut back.[62]

Consistent with this inauspicious beginning, 1909 set a new record for free speech violations and free speech fights. In June, Goldman's appearances were stopped almost continually in New York, Connecticut, and New Jersey: eleven meetings in all suppressed by the police. Typically, Emma used these incidents for publicity and for mobilizing liberals who believed in free speech, although not necessarily in anarchism. She responded to all efforts to stop her lectures with vigorous free speech fights: going to court (often with the aid of an attorney) to defend her right to speak; writing articles in the press; organizing local free speech leagues to combat future attempts at police censorship. She recruited some of her most valued supporters during these fights. After one such incident in New Jersey, for example, Alden Freeman, son of the treasurer of Standard Oil and scion of a distinguished and wealthy New England family, became so incensed at the arbitrary action of the New York police that he invited Goldman to speak on his estate in the affluent suburban community of East Orange, New Jersey. Goldman held forth in his large barn and "roasted" the police before hundreds of cheering listeners.[63] Freeman later became a generous financial supporter of Goldman and of various anarchist projects. Sometimes members of the audience were the target of assault. In San Francisco in 1908, for example, a private William Buwalda stationed at the Presidio Army base had attended Goldman's lecture at the Walton Pavillion and liked it so much that he came up afterward to shake her hand— whereupon he was courtmartialed and sentenced to five years' military imprisonment![64]

By the middle of 1910, the tide seemed to be turning. Goldman's free speech fights—and the efforts of a National Free Speech Committee, which she helped to organize along with Leonard Abbott, Theodore Schroeder, and a libertarian doctor, E.B. Foote—began to yield results. Press coverage grew more favorable and police actions less frequent. By May of 1911, Reitman in *Mother Earth* could praise the fairness and accuracy of press reports of her lectures and observe that the lectures were now rarely stopped.[65]

This was, however, a truce rather than a triumph. Arriving in San Diego in May of 1912, Goldman and Reitman found themselves in the middle of a fierce fight led by the Free Speech League—a local coalition of Wobblies, socialists, liberals, and trade unionists— against a conservative city administration that had closed off an area in the central downtown business district long used as a kind of Hyde Park by soapbox orators of all kinds.[66] I.W.W. organizers, particularly, used street speaking as a major organizing strategy to recruit workers who were difficult to reach while on the job. Ordinances like that passed in San Diego were directly aimed against the union, which had waged a series of free speech fights since 1909 in places such as Spokane and Fresno in order to defend their right to organize. When the San Diego ordinance against free speech first went into effect in February, members of the League had challenged it, using tactics of civil disobedience. Within a week, 150 people were in jail. As illegal street meetings continued in the prohibited district, the jails were soon packed. The I.W.W. called on members from all over to join the fight for free speech in San Diego, and many responded to the call.

The response of the police and city officials was savage. Leading private citizens organized into vigilante bands, inflicted beatings and tortures, and forcibly removed Wobblies and their sympathizers from the city with warnings never to return—all with the full knowledge of the police. Early in May, a young Wobbly was killed by the police. A week later, on May 14, Goldman and Reitman arrived on the scene, after having organized a funeral procession for the murdered Wobbly in Los Angeles. Jeered and hooted at by a hostile mob at the train station, the two barely made it to their hotel, the U.S. Grant. Later, with the certain connivance of the police chief and the hotel manager, Ben Reitman was kidnapped from the hotel, driven out of town by a group of vigilantes, forced to undress, kicked, and beaten. The vigilantes burned the letters I.W.W. on his buttocks with a lighted cigar, poured tar over his head, and rubbed sagebrush on his body; one man tried to push a cane into his rectum, another twisted his testicles. After forcing him to kiss the American flag and to sing "The Star-Spangled Banner," they made him run a gauntlet while they kicked and beat him. Then they returned his clothes and left him. Eventually Reitman flagged down a sympathetic passer-by who took him to a nearby station; here he caught the train for Los Angeles, where Goldman awaited him.[67]

The publicity stirred up by the events in San Diego, including the barbarous treatment of Reitman, generated considerable sympathy for the victims and led to a special investigation by a commissioner appointed by California's Progressive governor, Hiram Johnson. But no state or federal action was ever taken to stop or punish the San Diego vigilantes, who continued their outrages for several months. The disputed downtown district remained off-limits to speakers, and the free speech struggle was gradually abandoned. The Wobblies after San Diego decided to give up their general strategy of free speech fights, which they had been pursuing since 1909, in order to concentrate on organizing workers at the workplace. San Diego had never been an important labor center, and they questioned what had been gained by their bloody, costly fight in that city.[68]

For Ben Reitman personally, the events of May 14, 1912, were profoundly traumatic. Not only was he frightened by the physical brutality to which he had been subjected, but he was also tormented for a long time afterward by a painful feeling that he had behaved like a coward. Goldman's efforts at reassurance seemed almost calculated to exacerbate his anxieties. "I hope Hobo dear that if you ever face another S.D. you may not have to herald your action as cowardly," she wrote him briskly, "or at least if you feel it to be such, that you will keep it to yourself." It was painful "to the woman who loves a man, especially the woman who has all her life faced persecution to hear that man shout from the house tops, he is a coward. It's a million more times painful than to have the rest of the World say so."[69] He had failed to resist his attackers, she explained to him, because of the element of surprise, which had caught him off guard. "I am confident that under similar circumstances you would not submit again," she added.[70] It is not clear, of course, given the force arrayed against him, what else Reitman could have done without incurring even more severe injury; the treatment meted out to him was typical of that inflicted on hundreds of Wobblies, who were no more able to resist than he was. While Reitman suffered several months of depression and extreme self-doubt following this incident, Goldman seems quickly to have put it behind her.

She was, moreover, determined to come back and speak, and return she did. In 1913, when Goldman and Reitman arrived in town once again, they were met at the train station by the police chief— who, claiming to fear for their safety, escorted them directly to jail. And indeed, a menacing lynch crowd did gather outside the jail, shouting for Reitman in ominous tones. The two anarchists left the next morning without attempting to press the issue. Finally in 1915, this time without Reitman, Goldman did succeed in speaking, thanks to the combined efforts of the San Diego Free Speech League and a group called the Open Forum. The three indoor lectures—on Ibsen, Nietzsche, and birth control—proceeded without interference.

While the Wobblies considered San Diego a decisive defeat, Emma Goldman always called it a victory, since "the Vigilante conspiracy had been broken" and the repressive methods of the police and vigilantes widely publicized.[71] That the Wobblies had chosen to abandon the fight, that the downtown street speakers and meetings were effectively suppressed, was to her ultimately less significant than the fight for free speech itself. Her own eventual success in speaking, even if indoors in an auditorium in respectable middle-class surroundings, constituted a victory of principle. Perhaps in this case she was too quick to equate her personal success with that of the struggle as a whole. Almost certainly she was too ready to equate widespread publicity with political victory. The vigilantes might have ceased their more flagrant outrages, but no state or federal action was ever taken against them.

For Goldman, events such as the San Diego struggle were all part of "the ups and downs of an anarchist agitator." This was the drama at which she excelled. "The worse the ordeal, the cooler I become," she once told a reporter.[72] But apart from the strain of crises like that at San Diego, there was another, less visible burden associated with public life. Goldman had to contend not only with the hostility of conservatives, but also with the inflated expectations and sometimes the disappointment of admirers, who often projected onto her their own needs, wishes, and fantasies. Almeda Sperry, for example, a young, literate, working-class radical from an industrial suburb of Pittsburgh, had wanted to meet Goldman "to see if it were possible for anyone to be consistent with his philosophy. I must say that you are the only one I have ever met whom I believe has no treachery in his makeup. You are on the square." Sperry quite openly admitted her wish that she had a mother like Emma—"you are my mother," she once told Goldman.[73] But after they had corresponded for a time and Goldman had invited Sperry to visit her at the "farm" in Ossining, the younger woman fell in love with her and began sending her letters filled with erotic fantasies that sometimes became quite bizarre. That Sperry's sexual feelings toward Goldman were ever reciprocated seems unlikely. Goldman seems to have remained somewhat detached, finding Sperry "the most interesting of American women I have met," as she told a friend, "an odd and abnormal type" whose letters were a "great human document" worthy of publication.[74]

At some point, perhaps after Sperry had sailed off into particularly violent or suicidal erotic flights—"If I had only had courage enough to kill myself when you reached the climax then—I would have known happiness, for then at that moment I would have had complete possession of you"—Goldman evidently rebuked her, provoking a poignant apology from Sperry.[75] "I feel that you are right in all you say and that I have done you an irreparable injury," she wrote Emma. "It may be true that some day I may lose those tendencies but I do not know that I have any desire to lose them as they are natural and not acquired. For the life of me I do not understand why people look askance at those tendencies which, by the way, have been directed toward but two women. However I will never offend you again unless you entertain thoughts of return and you are too nearly normal for that."[76] Although the correspondence continued for a time, Emma eventually returned the letters to Sperry and the relationship ended—not before Sperry had begun to suspect that Emma was "just studying me" as a "peculiar product of our civilization. Her cause is first."[77] As Sperry learned, there were limits even to Emma Goldman's openness and tolerance. Despite Goldman's theoretical defense of homosexuality, her own feelings on the subject were ambivalent. "For a woman of your knowledge," Sperry told her, "you are strangely innocent."[78]

Goldman's status as a celebrity sometimes led to confusion between followership and friendship on the part of other of her admirers. For all her warmth, Goldman was actually quite careful in her confidences, trusting only a very few of her closest associates with her most intimate thoughts. At times her supporters and confidants were disappointed to learn that their relationships with her were rather more political and less personal than they had imagined. Agnes Inglis, daughter of a wealthy and conservative family in Ann Arbor, Michigan, was a case in point. Inglis was employed as a social worker when she first read Goldman's pamphlet, "What I Believe," in 1908, an experience that changed her life. She began attending Goldman's lectures in 1910, met her personally in 1914, and in 1915 began to secure halls in Ann Arbor and in Detroit for Goldman's lectures. After this they corresponded often, at first about movement issues: fund-raising, letter-writing campaigns, petitions, distribution of literature, the organizing of meetings. Inglis had great admiration for Goldman, who "enriched my whole life and started it going in those channels that keep life eternally enriched." Emma was "perhaps the most courageous and remarkable woman I ever met. . . . She has the gift of humor and sincerity and honesty—and she has such strength!"[79]

Inglis became a generous contributor to Goldman's many projects, and increasingly, Emma began to rely on her, at first for funds and work. Gradually, she began also to write more personally to Inglis, and by about 1916, Agnes had become a trusted confidante. In her letters Emma repeatedly expressed her gratitude to Agnes for her support and her friendship. "I think of you so much and with deep love," Emma would write. "I feel rich beyond words to have you among my friends."[80] Later Emma would describe Inglis as "one of my dearest and most considerate friends," a woman "who combined her active interest in the social struggle with a broad humanity in personal relations."[81]

In fact, while Emma was quite dependent upon Inglis for funds and support and deeply grateful for her help, Inglis was not really an intimate friend. As Emma's demands upon her increased, Inglis came to feel somewhat restive under Goldman's "compelling nature," chagrined to learn that "so much of the personal relationship was based on my activity for her work and on money that I gave so willingly, but that I was not rolling in as I now learn I was supposed to be. . . ."[82] While Emma had helped free her from the Presbyterian conservatism of her family, Inglis felt she had traded one religion for another, that the movement "became more of a religion and it was more exacting than the church by far."[83] Inglis grew increasingly critical of what she saw as Goldman's egoism, her tendency to build the movement around herself, to identify "her Cause" with "the Cause."[84] Expressing her ambivalent feelings about Goldman in letters to many anarchists—which she eventually assembled for the Labadie Collection of anarchism at the University of Michigan— Inglis after many years made her peace with Goldman and summed up the feelings of many who worked closely with her. "Emma was an irritant and an inspiration to many," she wrote. "I cannot think of her as beloved, but surely as an inspirer to courage."[85]

Some of Goldman's admirers, however, were more accepting than Inglis. Leon Malmed, a young anarchist in Albany, not only worshipped Goldman; like Sperry, he also fell in love with her and in time became quite close to her. Twelve years younger than Goldman, Malmed had emigrated from Russia to New York, where he worked as a cigar maker, eventually moving to Albany and opening a delicatessen. Active in the Albany anarchist group, he met Emma in 1906 and became a devoted supporter, arranging her meetings, donating funds to *Mother Earth,* and opening his home to her when she visited Albany. Unhappily married, Malmed focused all his dreams on Goldman, seeing in her the embodiment of idealism and freedom, which he felt slowly ebbing from his own conventional life. Emma quite willingly played the role of savior to Malmed, telling him that she was "proud to have been the force which has awakened you and pulled you out of the sordidness of your surroundings"; on another occasion, she advised him to "imagine I am your Jesus, pray to me."[86] Yet Malmed, torn between his sense of obligation to his family and his desire to flee, could not make a decision, vacillating for years until finally he left Albany to accompany Goldman on her 1915 cross-country lecture tour. The Albany anarchists were inclined to blame Emma for breaking up the Malmed home, and sympathized with Millie Malmed, who hated Emma. But Leon Malmed, rebuffed by Emma in his desire for a more intimate relationship, eventually returned home to Albany and resumed his marriage. He remained devoted to Emma, however (eventually consummating the relationship in a brief, unhappy affair in the twenties), and she in turn depended heavily on his support.[87] Malmed's son, in fact, recalled with distaste the heavy financial demands she made on his father— who, though "fairly successful" in his business affairs, was far from affluent. According to Daniel Malmed, Emma was "always after him [Leon]," and many of her letters were "demand letters." "Every letter we have she demands—she demands money, she demands good coverage, she demands you get out and sell her books, she demanded all these things. . . ."[88] Emma was not above occasionally trying to evoke a sense of guilt in her comrades ("Are you so absorbed in your store that you have no interest in the struggle I am making?" she would ask).[89] Still, Malmed's devotion to Emma Goldman never flagged. She remained the touchstone of his life, while he was, for her, "a true knight of old, serving without thought of reward."[90]

Despite her gratitude toward admirers such as Agnes Inglis and Leon Malmed, Emma recognized the limits of these relationships. Later in her life, she looked back with some bitterness on her years of touring, which she felt had prevented her from "developing intimacies with anyone worth while." "I never had much personal life anyhow," she would say sadly.[91] And yet, as Emma herself sometimes acknowledged, it was not only the demands of her work, but something within herself that also complicated her friendships—an ambivalent feeling about close relationships, a fear of becoming emotionally dependent, a perpetual discontent that only the intense response of audiences to her public persona and the intensely sexual presence of Ben Reitman could temporarily assuage. Capable of great sensitivity and delicacy in her dealings with others, Emma could also treat people in high-handed, condescending ways. "I think E.G. could have accomplished as much if she hadn't made folks feel she thought they were dumb," complained Inglis.[92] Goldman could, as well, be sharp and abrupt in a manner that many people found intimidating, and she had a "genius for hurting people," which Berkman often criticized.[93] When other anarchists reproached her for being too dominating, Goldman would occasionally retort that "in this life of ours there are only two ways in order to maintain one's identity, and that is to ride over people or be ridden over."[94] Given her harsh view of human relationships, it is not surprising that she avoided intimacy. Perhaps public life offered some relief from the pressures of intimacy; perhaps she kept up an exhausting pace of activity partly in order to distance herself from the emotional demands of friendship and love.

Whatever the difficulties of her public existence, Goldman was never seriously tempted to withdraw from it, not even when the personal cost proved high. By now her public life had become an integral part of her identity, essential to her sense of well-being and self-worth. She was quite conscious of herself as "E.G. the public character." She and Berkman were "public people" who had to live their lives accordingly.[95] Whatever her doubts about her suitability for public life—and she had many—she nonetheless felt unalterably committed. And while she was often at odds with other members of the anarchist movement—"I have not the support of the Anarchists at large, I don't want it, as I could not be myself," she would say— Goldman saw herself as a kind of higher embodiment of anarchism.[96] She also identified with a tradition of heroic radical women—from Mary Wollstonecraft to Catherine Breshkovskaya—seeing her own disappointments and frustrations as the inevitable price paid by all pathfinders and pioneers. In this context, the overbearing ego and demanding personality that made for difficulties in her personal life were perhaps essential to the success of her public existence. Perhaps no one without her tremendous self-confidence and sense of mission could have withstood the assaults she encountered in thirty years as an anarchist agitator. In so small and vulnerable a movement, she felt driven to demand the utmost from herself and entitled to demand the same from those around her.

But however complex her motives and however great the costs of such a life, Emma Goldman clearly derived great satisfaction and fulfillment from her work, even though she saw it at times as "an escape from the emotional dissatisfaction deeply hidden in my inner life."[97] Inclined to think of her own existence as a tragedy—indeed, of all great lives as tragic—she nonetheless pursued it with energy, enthusiasm, audacity, and flair. By about 1912—the year of the San Diego free speech fight—Goldman had, moreover, growing reasons for optimism. The cautious liberalism and sober leftism of the Progressive years was spawning an exuberant "new radicalism" strongly tinged by libertarian ideas. A new generation of American youth and a new type of American—the "young intellectual"—began to show up at Goldman's lectures. Sensitive to the change, she began to assess strategies for addressing this potential new audience for anarchist ideas. Despite the continuing "ups and downs" she encountered on her tours, she felt full of hope about the possibilities for radicalism, for anarchism, and for herself.

12

ANARCHISM, FEMINISM, AND THE INTELLECTUALS

L ooking back upon it now," wrote Mabel Dodge, "it seems as though everywhere, in that year of 1913, barriers went down and people reached each other who had never been in touch before; there were all sorts of new ways to communicate, as well as new communications. . . . It was as if men said to other men, 'Look, here is a new way to see things . . . and a new way of saying things. Also new things to say.' "[1] In an international context of resurgent radicalism, with revolutions bursting forth in Russia, China, and Mexico, this explosion of intellectual ferment and experiment, a sweeping assault against all the orthodoxies of the nineteenth century, constituted that renaissance which historian Henry May has termed the "innocent rebellion" in honor of its high optimism and certainty, soon to be shattered with the outbreak of the Great War.[2] Blending political and cultural protest, the "new radicals" of the pre–

World War I years combined socialist ideas with a celebration of freedom in the arts, in education, and in sexual life. The intellectuals who led the revolt were just beginning to emerge in America as a visible and self-conscious social group in the first decades of the twentieth century. Their rebellion began in Chicago and shifted to New York, where it reached its most distinctive expression in Greenwich Village. Against a national background of sober Protestant uplift, personified by the professorial President Woodrow Wilson, Greenwich Village blossomed into a genuine community in which young reformers, bohemians, and artists, many of them women, sought to invent and also to live the forms of the future.

The rebellion drew inspiration from a multitude of sources, European and American. An authorized complete translation of Nietzsche's work first appeared in 1909 and was embraced for its attack on conventional values; Freud's visit that year to Clark University in Worcester, Massachusetts, stimulated a flood of interest in psychoanalysis (Goldman attended one of Freud's Clark lectures); Constance Garnett's translations of Dostoyevsky in 1912 heightened the already powerful attraction of Russian literature for Americans, and indeed fostered a veritable "cult of Russia." All these European idol-breakers became allies for young Americans in their attack on the "gloomy sages" of Victorian, Anglophile, and bourgeois gentility, as did American writers like Walt Whitman, favorite poet of the young bohemians. The celebration of expression and spontaneity over "puritanism" and respectability, of youth over age, of life over thought; a spirit of experiment and daring; and, above all, an exuberant optimism—these were the hallmarks of the prewar rebellion.

The young intellectuals also looked to the increasingly militant working class for another kind of inspiration. The "direct action" tactics of the Wobblies especially excited their romantic admiration. In the class struggle of the workers, they saw the economic expression of their own revolt against middle-class values. The great strikes led by the Wobblies at the woolen mills of Lawrence, Massachusetts, early in 1912 and the next year in the silk mills of Paterson, New Jersey, galvanized the imagination of young writers, journalists, artists, and activists. They flocked in droves to the scene of the action, wrote sympathetic reports, testified in Congress on behalf of the strikers, raised strike funds, led children's crusades, and even staged a huge Paterson Pageant, in Madison Square Garden in the summer of 1913, in which the silkworkers themselves reenacted the events of the strike before an audience of thousands.

One important element of this increasing labor militancy and heightened intellectual revolt was the restlessness of women, which journalist Hutchins Hapgood saw as the very center of the prewar rebellion. As strikers, journalists, editors, lawyers, suffragists, labor organizers, and social workers, women stepped into the limelight during the prewar years, more vocal and visible than ever before. The numbers of women in the workforce had doubled, from four million in 1890 to nearly eight million by 1910. In the winter of 1909–10, the great strike of women shirtwaist makers in New York—the "Uprising of the Twenty Thousand"—had dramatically demonstrated the new militancy of women and given life to the International Ladies Garment Workers' Union. The Wobbly-led strikes at Lawrence and Paterson were to a great extent dependent upon women. And the suffrage movement—organized into the National American Women's Suffrage Association—which had secured the vote in four states by 1910, now entered a period of vigorous action and won ratification of the Nineteenth Amendment in 1920.[3]

In this heady atmosphere of prewar radicalism and feminism, Emma Goldman began to feel as if the world were finally catching up with her. The anarchists, too, began to acquire a measure of prestige among the avant-garde. True, most of the radical intellectuals joined the Socialist party, which by 1912 had become the unifying center of the American Left. Few young American radicals actually joined anarchist groups—these remained largely an immigrant stronghold. But many young American radicals and bohemians read Kropotkin and Stirner, subscribed to *Mother Earth* or *Liberty*, attended anarchist-led demonstrations, and in general carried libertarian, anti-authoritarian, direct-action ideals into other forms of political work. They were excited by the militant left wing of the Socialist party and drawn to the syndicalism of the Wobblies over the moderate bread-and-butter socialism of a Morris Hillquit, which seemed tame by comparison. Indeed, the attraction of anarchism was such that socialists like Max Eastman, the brash editor of *The Masses*, considered it highly dangerous to the socialist cause and actively fought it at every turn.

The intellectuals and bohemians inevitably "discovered" Emma

Goldman just as she was beginning to "discover" the revolutionary potential of the intellectuals. The intellectuals, she told a reporter in 1914, were proletarians, too. Indeed, "the danger to present-day society is greater from these intellectual proletarians than from the unemployed, because they have tasted the good things of life and know what they are missing."[4] The intellectuals had themselves become proletarianized, and as salaried employees selling their labor for a wage, were in a similar, if not worse, position than the factory hand: worse because they were "so steeped in middle-class traditions and conventions, so tied and gagged by them, that they dare not move a step." Goldman urged the "intellectual proletarians" to come down off their pedestals and realize that they, too, were workers. Holding up the example of the Russian intelligentsia of the 1870s, which dedicated itself to liberating the masses, Goldman urged American intellectuals to do the same. Only then could they hope to produce a real culture. The intellectuals needed the "bold indifference and courage of the revolutionary workers." They must go among the people, "not to lift them up but themselves to be lifted up, to be instructed, and in return to give themselves wholly to the people." Only through the cooperation of the intellectual proletarians and the revolutionary proletarians, she concluded, will we in America "establish a real unity and by means of it wage a successful war against present society."[5]

Mother Earth in 1906 represented one effort to reach out to the intellectual community. *Anarchism and Other Essays,* a collection of her lectures published late in 1910, was another. Although Ben Reitman's adept handling of her 1910 cross-country tour had attracted the largest audiences ever, Goldman insisted that she was disillusioned by the results of "oral propaganda" and hoped, through her book, to "reach the few who really want to learn, rather than the many who come to be amused."[6] She was uniquely qualified for her efforts to radicalize the intellectuals, since she had, as Greenwich Village chronicler Floyd Dell put it, "the heightened sensibilities, the keen sympathies of the middle-class idealist, and the direct contact with the harsh realities of our social and industrial conditions which is the lot of the worker." She capitalized, moreover, on the prestige of Russia, presenting herself in her book, as in her lectures, from a dual perspective: partly as a European educating Americans about European radical traditions—scolding Americans for their inferiority to Europeans, holding up examples of European sophistication in the arts, in labor organization, in revolutionary movements—and partly as an American appealing to American radical traditions and symbols. Although her arguments would have been familiar to those who attended her lectures or read her magazine, *Anarchism and Other Essays* represented Goldman's most systematic effort to organize her thoughts into a unified whole; as she put it, to gather together "the mental and soul struggles of twenty-one years."[7]

Since Goldman always emphasized that anarchism was a "broadening" ideal, her essays touched a wide range of issues. "Anarchism: What it Really Stands For" stressed the importance of resistance and revolt and defined a Kropotkinite vision that aimed at "the freest possible expression of all the latent powers of the individual" in a society based on "the free grouping of individuals for the purpose of producing real social wealth." The most controversial essay, "Minorities versus Majorities," criticized American habits of conformity and praised the "intelligent minorities" and dissenting individuals who set an inspiring example for "the mass." "The Psychology of Political Violence," relying heavily on long quotations from French and British anarchist writers, denied connections between anarchism and violence, insisting that violent societies themselves generated violent resistance, but also lauding the anarchist assassins of the nineties for their heroism. Another essay urged the ultimate abolition of prisons and called for more humane treatment of prisoners, including pay for convict labor and an end to the definite sentence, insisting that social and economic deprivation, not inherited criminal tendencies, are "the most poisonous germs of crime." "Patriotism" unmasked the connections between capitalism and militarism, denouncing the myth that saw arms buildups as a means to preserve peace. "The experience of every-day life fully proves that the armed individual is invariably anxious to try his strength," she wrote. "The same is historically true of governments." The purpose of large military establishments, she argued, was not to counter foreign danger, but "to meet the internal enemy," the masses, or to distract attention from domestic social conflict. Goldman urged not only a spirit of internationalism to replace the narrowness of nationalism, but also "a propaganda of education for the soldier" to enlighten him as to the nature of American imperialism. "Francisco Ferrer: The Modern School" focused on the Spanish founder of secular "modern schools" in Spain, who was executed in October of 1909 for his alleged participation in an antimilitarist uprising in Barcelona; it further traced the history of libertarian educational experiments in Europe. Education of yet another kind was her subject in "The Drama: A Powerful Disseminator of Radical Thought," a brief, perceptive introduction to the social drama of France, Germany, Russia, and Scandinavia.[8]

At the heart of *Anarchism and Other Essays*, however, was Goldman's effort to address problems of women and of sexuality, which had been one of her major concerns since the nineties and which she recognized as central to the prewar cultural rebellion. Like the rest of the essays in this collection, those entitled "Marriage and Love," "Woman Suffrage," "The Hypocrisy of Puritanism," "The Traffic in Women," and "The Tragedy of Woman's Emancipation" offered many arguments already familiar to Goldman's audience. Some had already appeared in *Mother Earth*. "Emancipation," Goldman insisted in "The Tragedy of Woman's Emancipation," "should make it possible for woman to be human in the truest sense. Everything within her that craves assertion and activity should reach its fullest expression; all artificial barriers should be broken, and the road toward greater freedom cleared of every trace of centuries of submission and slavery."[9] In opposition to suffragists, who looked to the vote to empower women, and socialists, who hoped that the abolition of capitalism would strengthen traditional institutions of marriage, family, and motherhood—or at least strengthen woman's power within them—Goldman took a far more critical stand, insisting on the ways in which women were victimized by all these institutions: imprisoned in the home, thwarted by motherhood, made dull and dependent by marriage, deluded by the notion that voting conferred any real power. As always, she especially stressed the repressiveness of marriage, both as "an economic arrangement, an insurance pact," and as "a safety valve against the pernicious sex-awakening of woman." Was anything more outrageous, she would ask, "than the idea that the healthy, grown woman, full of life and passion, must deny nature's demand, must subdue her most intense craving, undermine her health and break her spirit, must stunt her vision, abstain from the depth and glory of sex experience until a 'good' man comes along to take her unto himself as a wife? That is precisely what marriage means."[10]

Even work and economic independence, extolled by feminists

such as Charlotte Perkins Gilman in her pathbreaking *Woman and Economics* (1898) as the key to woman's emancipation, offered no real solution, since the jobs presently available to most women were so dismal and ill-paid. "How much independence is gained" for the great masses of working women, she would say, "if the narrowness and lack of freedom of the home is exchanged for the narrowness and lack of freedom of the factory, sweat-shop, department store or office?"[11] For Goldman, the lack of opportunity and low wages that were the lot of most women were directly responsible for the high incidence of prostitution. While the Progressive reformers sought to abolish the practice by closing brothels and imposing penalties on prostitutes, she argued for far more sweeping changes. "Nowhere is woman treated according to the merit of her work, but rather as a sex," wrote Goldman. "It is therefore almost inevitable that she should pay for her right to exist, to keep a position in whatever line, with sex favors. Thus it is merely a question of degree whether she sells herself to one man, in or out of marriage, or to many men. Whether our reformers admit it or not, the economic and social inferiority of woman is responsible for prostitution." Only the "complete transvaluation of all values—especially the moral ones—coupled with the abolition of industrial slavery" would bring about its disappearance.[12]

The most distinctive aspect of Goldman's thinking about women at this time was the stress she now laid on the subjective, psychological aspects of women's emancipation. Although this psychological dimension had always been implicit in her politics, she had stated it most clearly for the first time in 1904, when she began to deliver her lecture "The Tragedy of Woman's Emancipation"—later published in the first issue of *Mother Earth* in 1906. Here she criticized modern feminists for concerning themselves merely with the "external tyrannies," such as denial of the vote or lack of a job, while the "internal tyrants, far more harmful to life and growth—ethical and social conventions—were left to take care of themselves." Not until women could overcome the fear of public opinion, the voices of the "busybodies, moral detectives, jailers of the human spirit, what will they say," and insist on their own unrestricted freedom could they call themselves truly free.[13] In making this argument, Goldman specifically addressed the middle-class, professional, "emancipated" woman who had already achieved economic independence, but failed to find satisfaction in her personal life. As she put it to a reporter in 1909, "the revolutionary process of changing her external conditions is comparatively easy; what is difficult and necessary is the inner change of thought and desire."[14] Both her own experiences and her observations of other women—many of whom confided their problems to her and sought her advice—persuaded her that women must learn "to accept themselves, and to value themselves as beings possessing a worth at least equal to that of the other sex. . . ." Only when a woman "stands for something in her own life, and is no longer a mere echo or a slave" could she make any meaningful contribution "to the race, to the country, to her children. . . . She must be an individual before she can do anything for anybody else."[15] The solution, argued Goldman, was for women to begin with their "inner regeneration," to cut loose from the weight of prejudices, traditions, and customs. True emancipation, she urged, began not at the polls or in court, but in woman's soul.[16]

In her eagerness to expose the limits of current conceptions of emancipation, Goldman at times came close to blaming women for their own subordination. Some of her contemporaries even detected an antifeminist strain in her thought. If motherhood was woman's "most glorious privilege," the woman as mother was often "the greatest deterrent influence" in the life of her children, treating them as her own possession and robbing her offspring of any independence.[17] It was really "woman's inhumanity to man" that had created the kind of men who oppressed women: as mothers, women inspired in their sons the possessiveness and arrogance that created male tyrants; as lovers, women idolized in men the very traits that helped to enslave them—strength, egotism, and exaggerated vanity.[18] Goldman in fact tended to view single, professional, "emancipated" women just as their critics defined them—as cold, humorless, man-hating, miserable, and lonely—instead of as women who often enjoyed their independence, freedom, and relationships with each other. "Rather would I have the love songs of romantic ages, rather Don Juan and Madam Venus," she admitted, "rather an elopement by ladder and rope on a moonlight night, followed by the father's curse, mother's moans and the moral comments of neighbors, than correctness and propriety measured by yardsticks." She preferred "our grandmothers," who had "more blood in their veins, far more humor and wit, and certainly a greater amount of naturalness, kind-heartedness, and simplicity, than the majority of our emancipated professional women who fill the colleges, halls of learning and various offices."[19]

In considering Goldman's arguments about women, we should recall that as a young woman in her twenties and early thirties, she had felt confident of her ability to overcome any discrimination based on sex. Her own success in establishing her independence led her to judge less successful women rather harshly and to underestimate the obstacles confronting them. "I believe I owe my success to my being a woman," she told a reporter confidently in 1901. "The audience in this country will grant a woman a hearing because she is a woman. Then she must hold them. She must talk to them, not as a woman, but as a comrade. . . . I have never been made to feel before any American man that my sex impressed him before my argument."[20] Goldman strongly criticized those "strong-minded women" who wanted "to topple men off their pedestal in order to take it. I am contented to share it."[21] Nor did she like the suffragists who "rave against men and exalt women." Repudiating the idea, current among feminists at that time, of women's moral superiority to men, Goldman criticized her own sex as freely as she did the other. "The question of sex," she insisted, "has no place in a great movement toward truth, save as women accomplish certain forms of work better than men, and vice versa. When men find a woman does not abuse them and howl for her rights and theirs too; when she meets them on logical grounds, is rational and fair and able, they welcome her generously. I have always found it so. . . ."[22]

As she grew older, however, Goldman became more sensitive to the problems women faced and more sympathetic to the difficulties of overcoming them. Recognizing the extent to which she, too, suffered the doubts, conflicts, and loneliness of other "emancipated" women, she grew less inclined to blame and condemn. As she became more dependent upon her women friends, she grew more willing to see herself as part of a community of women and even to call herself a feminist, although she remained critical of the suffragists' generally middle-class bias. Joking with Stella Ballantine about her "conversion" shortly after Congress passed the suffrage amendment in 1919, Goldman warned her niece not to think "it is the vote which has charmed me, or any of the silly Feminist stuff. I flatter myself," she wrote, "to have been more interested in the fate of woman and by far from a broader and deeper point of view than those who label

196

themselves Feminists and have no interest whatever in the general social question." Emma had always been on the side of the "under-dog, whether that be man, woman or child, as an individual, as a sex, or a class," she added. "My quarrel with the Feminists wasn't that they were too free or demanded too much. It was that they are not free enough and that most of them see their slavery apart from the rest of the human family. Finally, also because the Feminists foolishly believe that having a man's role, or professions, makes them free." Toward the end of her life, Goldman still expressed her impatience with women less liberated than she, but she also saw herself as part of a transitional generation of "modern women . . . still rooted in the old soil, though our visions are of the future and our desire is to be free and independent."[23]

But if Goldman grew more sympathetic to the dilemmas of the "modern woman," her strategies for change remained focused on the individual. Much of the time, she seemed to regard liberation as "simply an act of personal will."[24] Holding up to American women the example of her Russian revolutionary heroines, she emphasized that these women "had become man's equal, not through the ballot," but by their "will to be and to do." Woman's freedom, she insisted, "must come from and through herself. First by asserting herself as a personality, and not as a sex commodity. Second by refusing the right to anyone over her body; by refusing to bear children, unless she wants them; by refusing to be a servant to God, the State, society, the husband, the family, etc., by making her life simpler, but deeper and richer."[25] How the individual woman was to overcome institutionalized barriers to freedom and independence—low-paying jobs, lack of education, professional discrimination, absence of contraception and of child-care—remained unclear.

Implicitly, however, Goldman suggested that by identifying with her example, women—and also men—might achieve the liberation they sought. *Anarchism and Other Essays* quite openly attempted to promote a heroic Goldman legend by calling attention to the personality of the author. It featured Hippolyte Havel's long biographical tribute, comparing her to Mary Wollstonecraft and Louise Michel; a photograph of Goldman as the frontispiece; and her tacit identification of herself, in "Minorities versus Majorities," with all the great pathfinders, dissenters, and martyrs of the past. Certainly reviews of the book, highly favorable for the most part in both the commercial and the radical press, responded to this emphasis on personality, commenting as frequently on the character of the author—her idealism, courage, "the often very fascinating style" of her prose—as on her ideas.[26]

Goldman's deliberate self-mythologizing, the martyred stance, the messianic tone that now often entered her writings and was evident in the running narrative of her lecture tours, was not simply an expression of vanity. It also expressed her political faith in the power of the individual to motivate change in the masses. Cognizant of her own need for inspiring role models, she recognized a similar need among her readers. As she understood quite well, young people who vigorously repudiated the outworn values of their parents often found it difficult to embrace new ones with confidence. "In most cases they balance in the air . . . unable to throw off the weight of tradition," she wrote.[27] To these people, Goldman offered herself as a model of strength and certainty. For her, personality was inextricable from politics. "After all," she would say, "it is more important to do propaganda with one's personality than with words."[28] The way one lived one's life every day was an individual's most important political statement.

The woman who perhaps understood this aspect of Emma Goldman's politics most clearly was Margaret Anderson, whose *Little Review* was one of the important "little magazines" of the prewar cultural rebellion. The brilliant young daughter of a conservative Indianapolis family, Anderson had run off to Chicago, joined the literary avant-garde, and in April of 1914 began publishing *The Little Review*. Shortly afterward, in the winter of 1914, Anderson and Goldman met in Chicago and quickly became great friends. More passionate about art than about politics, Anderson was drawn to anarchism because, "like all great things, [it] is an announcement." Socialism, on the other hand, was "an explanation, and falls, consequently, into the realm of secondary things."[29] Despite her genteel, society-girl appearance, Anderson was fiercely unconventional, battling for new writers such as Joyce, Pound, and Amy Lowell [the *Review* was taken to court for publishing *Ulysses* in 1917], living openly with her female lovers, and for a time, championing both Emma Goldman and anarchism in her magazine. Anderson, then in her twenties, was excited by the boldness of Goldman's attack on convention, her skill as a fighter, the sense she conveyed of living "in the great style."[30] To her, as to many other young women, Goldman became a heroine. She filled the *Review* with paeans to "the most challenging spirit in America" and to anarchism (which cost her one of her backers), organized lectures for Goldman in the elegant Chicago Fine Arts Building, wrote tributes in *Mother Earth*, and introduced Emma to the Chicago literary avant-garde. Goldman, in turn, responded gratefully to the younger woman's adulation, and even hinted at feelings deeper than affection when she noted "the stirrings as result of my friendship with Margaret—expressive of my previous theoretic interest in sex variation."[31]

Anderson was given to rapidly changing enthusiasms, and her attraction to anarchism eventually waned. She grew impatient with the anarchists' insistence on realism in the arts and their hostility to modernism. In her own memoirs, *My Thirty Years' War*, published in 1931, Anderson presented a slightly ironic portrait of "the great martyred leader" who spoke "only in platitudes" and was excessively sentimental about people.[32] Goldman, however, continued to cherish her memories of Margaret Anderson, observing in her autobiography that while she regretted Anderson's lack of social consciousness, her young friend had "strengthened my faith in the possibilities of my adopted country."[33]

For all of Goldman's impact on young women, women were by no means her only admirers. The journalist Hutchins Hapgood in New York was also fascinated by Goldman and became her most important link to the Greenwich Village radicals. Indeed, outside of her immediate *Mother Earth* circle, Hapgood was perhaps her most intimate friend. In flight like so many of his generation from the constrictions of his upper-class background, the Harvard-educated Hapgood was immediately attracted by the vigor and passion of Goldman's personality and by the rebellious ethic of her world. They had met in 1909 in Chicago, where Hapgood had previously become acquainted with many anarchists and had written a sympathetic portrait in *An Anarchist Woman*. By 1911, he had become Goldman's confidant—Hapgood was famous as a listener—and lingered often and long at the *Mother Earth* headquarters and at the Hotel Brevoort's basement café with Goldman and her cohorts. Hapgood liked to call himself a "philosophical anarchist," to differentiate himself from the "direct actionists" like Goldman and Berkman. Attracted by the anarchist emphasis on individualism and self-expression, he demurred at its militant aspect. He actively sympathized with the labor movement, about which he wrote a number of articles and books; he insisted, however, that Goldman's ideas on the subject did not interest him, since they were "too simple and too orthodox as a faithful expression of the traditional revolution of the workingclass."[34] Emma, in turn, regarded this "literary rebel and social iconoclast" with mixed feelings of affection and bemused skepticism, grateful for his enthusiastic articles (he glowingly reviewed *Anarchism and Other Essays* for *Bookman*; he also wrote an admiring introduction to Berkman's *Prison Memoirs of an Anarchist*, published in 1912) but aware that he cultivated her and other radicals for copy. Hapgood had the added advantage of being the only one of her friends who liked Ben Reitman, and to whom she could thus confide her anguish about their relationship.[35]

Through Hapgood, Goldman came to know Mabel Dodge, a wealthy young woman who ran what Lincoln Steffens considered "the only successful salon in America," where "Socialists, Trade-Unionists, Anarchists, Suffragists, Poets, Relations, Lawyers, Murderers, 'Old Friends,' Psychoanalysts, I.W.W.'s, Single Taxers, Birth Controllers, Newspapermen, Artists, Modern-Artists, Clubwomen, Woman's-place-is-in-the-home Women, Clergymen, and just plain men all met . . . and, stammering in an unaccustomed freedom a kind of speech called Free, exchanged a variousness in vocabulary called, in euphemistic optimism, Opinions!"[36] This experiment began sometime in the winter of 1912, when the adventurous, thirty-three-year-old Dodge began inviting the "Heads" of everything to "Evenings" of conversation at her 23 Fifth Avenue apartment. In part because of Dodge's unobtrusive social skill, the "Evenings" blossomed into one of the important meeting places for radicals and intellectuals and the most renowned of the prewar avant-garde "happenings."

Goldman met Dodge when Hapgood brought her to dinner one night at 210 East Thirteenth Street. Nervous because she "knew" that Goldman "believed in killing people if necessary," Dodge approached the place with dread. "These people were not intellectual anarchists," she worried. "They lived under the constant espionage of the police." But she soon felt reassured by the "warm, jolly atmosphere, with a homely supper on the table and Emma herself like a homely, motherly sort of person giving everyone generous platefuls of beefsteak . . . and fried potatoes." Goldman appeared to Dodge not wild or frightening but "rather like a severe but warm-hearted school-teacher, and I am sure that was essentially what she was: a teacher . . ."—a prosaic assessment, made by others as well, which did not please Goldman. Whatever her initial misgivings, Dodge came to admire the moral power of Goldman and Berkman; she wanted their approval. "They were the kind that counted," she would later write. "They had authority. Their judgment was somehow true. One did not want their scorn."[37]

Subsequently Dodge invited Goldman, Berkman, and Hippolyte Havel to her "Evenings," which they attended on several occasions. One of the most famous of the "Evenings" involved a "Conversation" between the advocates of Political Action—led by socialist William English Walling—and those of Direct Action, including Big Bill Haywood, Berkman, and Emma Goldman. The Evening, attended by the likes of Amos Pinchot and Walter Lippman, was not a success. Haywood, Dodge recalled, "so impassioned a speaker out in the rain before a thousand strikers, talked as though he were wading blindfolded in sand." And Goldman, too, "was not at all to the point. She was more than ever like a severe schoolteacher in a scolding mood."[38]

If Mabel Dodge's salon introduced immigrant radicals to the largely American-born, generally middle-class Greenwich Villagers, a less ephemeral institution, the Ferrer Center and School, also helped to bring these groups together. The Ferrer Center in fact provided an important point of contact between anarchists and intellectuals, for it was an anarchist project in which literary intellectuals could take part. In October of 1910, the Ferrer Center opened on St. Mark's Place. Dedicated to the memory of the libertarian Spanish educator Francisco Ferrer, it became a lively community gathering place, a combined meeting hall, theater, café, and free university where eminent radicals and intellectuals lectured and offered classes and where visitors might hear concerts, participate in discussion groups, watch experimental theater, or linger over endless cups of tea. Courses were offered in subjects such as English, philosophy, the history of the Left, and painting—the art classes of Robert Henri and George Bellows were extremely popular—and Clarence Darrow, Lincoln Steffens, Margaret Sanger, Will Durant, Hutchins Hapgood, and the French syndicalist André Tridon all might be found lecturing for a night or a week. In October of 1911, the Center—now at 104 East Twelfth Street—opened a libertarian day school for children; this subsequently moved uptown to East 107th Street in Harlem and, in 1915, out to Stelton, New Jersey, where the Modern School, as it was called, became the centerpiece of a new anarchist colony.

Although the institution was not exclusively anarchist, most supporters and participants at both the Center and the School were sympathetic to the politics of anarchism and syndicalism, while also attaching great importance to notions of individual inner liberation. For a long time this was the only progressive school in America that deliberately sought working-class pupils and attempted to fuse cultural and educational radicalism with a spirit of militant class consciousness. It was also one of the few institutions in which working-class Jewish immigrants and middle-class Americans—who provided most of the Ferrer teachers and principals—associated on terms of remarkable equality and mutual respect.[39]

Goldman played a critical role in the early stages of the Ferrer Center and School. She publicized it on her 1910 lecture tour and recruited financial backers such as Alden Freeman and Gilbert Roe and teachers such as Robert Henri and Bayard Boyeson, son of an eminent Norwegian scholar at Columbia University and himself a young professor fired from his post on account of his radicalism. After the Center was established, however, Goldman withdrew, playing a relatively minor role in its day-to-day operations and limiting her participation primarily to ceremonial occasions, fund-raising, and publicity.

Among the radical intellectuals associated with the Ferrer School, with Mabel Dodge's salon, and with the Greenwich Village bohemia, reactions to Emma Goldman were predictably mixed. Some, like the young Eugene O'Neill and the painter Robert Henri, idolized her. Henri in particular found in his contact with her "the catalyst that helped him translate his abstract belief in philosophical anarchism into a deeply felt personal creed."[40] Henri's student, the socialist painter John Sloan, admired Goldman as a "wonderful character," though he was less enchanted by her ideas.[41] Like Mabel Dodge, Louise Bryant, and the young Margaret Sanger, many women and radicals and feminists of Greenwich Village admired Goldman greatly and looked to her as a role model. But there were other, more skeptical voices. Will Durant, who also taught at the Ferrer School, thought Goldman "the most authoritarian of all the libertarians I have known" and found her rather frightening.[42] And Max Eastman never liked her, though he admired her courage. She could not understand method or "purposive thinking," he insisted, and he found her force and eloquence less impressive than "her impermeability to humor and logic." Her "whole life wisdom," he claimed, "consisted of comparing reality with an absolute ideal, and breaking her neck, and if need be all necks, in some obviously desperate leap for the ideal."[43] By 1914, according to Margaret Anderson, Goldman's ideas were generally accepted by "thinking people" as a matter of course, and though "the ignorant public still shudders at her name, the 'intellectuals'—especially those of the Greenwich Village radical type—dismiss her casually as a sort of good Christian—one not to be taken too seriously."[44]

Still, these intellectuals, mostly "Americans," turned up at her lectures in growing numbers. Pleased by their attendance, Goldman decided to devote more time to addresses on literature and the drama. These lectures, she argued, were more effective in raising the political consciousness of middle-class professional people than were conventional propaganda talks about economics. While workers, "who learned the great truths of the social travail in the school of life," did not urgently need to learn about the theater, the intellectuals, who "are only now beginning to buck up against life and who are by training and habit utterly unfitted for the shock," could learn from the modern drama "their relation to the people, to the social unrest permeating the atmosphere."[45] The theater was a particularly effective means of educating the intellectuals because "it reflects all life and embraces every ramification of society. The Modern Drama showing how each and all are in the throes of the tremendous changes going on, makes it clear that they must either become part of the process or be left behind."[46] In the fall of 1913, Reitman acknowledged in *Mother Earth* that he and Goldman were speaking less about economics and more about literature.[47] By this time Goldman was giving regular "courses" on the drama. In the winter of 1914, she hired a young stenographer to transcribe a series of her lectures, which she revised for publication as a book, *The Social Significance of the Modern Drama.*

In her lectures, as in her book, Goldman organized her discussions of individual plays by nationality, focusing specifically on Germany

(Hauptmann, Wedekind, Sudermann); Scandinavia (Strindberg, Ibsen); Ireland (Lenox Robinson); Russia (Tolstoy, Gorky, Chekhov, Andreyev); France (Maeterlinck, Brieux, Rostand), and England (Galsworthy, Shaw, Githa Sotherby). (She lectured as well on the Jewish, American, and Italian drama, although these were omitted from the book.) Each lecture consisted essentially of a plot summary, illustrated with extensive quotations from the text, followed by some commentary about the author, with the "moral lesson" or "revolutionary message" appended at the end. Thus, in exposing sex as woman's primary commodity in the marketplace, Shaw's *Mrs. Warren's Profession* also exposed "the sorest and most damnable spot in our social fabric. . . ."[48] (Goldman did not like Shaw, finally considering him "a puritan through and through, much as he might rave against puritanism.")[49] Similarly, Wedekind's *Spring's Awakening* showed "the shams of morality in reference to sex"; Ibsen's *Ghosts* dramatized the destructive power of conventional social lies about "duty" and "sacrifice"; and Hauptmann's *Lonely Lives* illuminated the loneliness and isolation of "the dreamer, the creative artist, the iconoclast in whatever line." Andreyev's *King Hunger* prophesied the revolt of the poor, and Githa Sotherby's *Rutherford and Son* exposed "the chasm between the old and the young, the tragic struggle of parents against their children, the one frantically holding on, the other recklessly letting go."[50]

With her flair for the dramatic and her natural feeling for the psychological conflicts of the characters, Goldman could be perceptive and lucid, as in her analysis of Strindberg's *Miss Julie*, which commented astutely on the divided nature of both the aristocratic Julie and the servant Jean and related the conflicts between the characters to the inner contradictions experienced by the author. But often, where there was ambiguity or ambivalence, she tended to impose a simple moral conclusion, "to push an attitude into the place of an argument," as Margaret Anderson put it. As one critic wrote in *The Little Review*, her analysis was weakened by "the intrusion of dogma and platitude into the discussion, the wearying insistence upon 'the moral' of each play, the uncritical acquiescence in the veracity of each dramatic picture of life. . . ."[51] Eager to defend Strindberg against charges of misogyny and pathology, for example, she asserted that his often extremely hostile portraits of women were true and accurate. Unlike the sentimentalists who idealized women,

Goldman insisted, Strindberg loved women and did not wish to flatter them falsely. In *The Father*—a bitter portrait of a destructive wife who schemes with her female allies to drive the husband-father mad and dominate the child—Strindberg showed the destructiveness of motherhood. The "revolutionary message" of the play for Goldman was that true motherhood meant granting the child freedom. She also endorsed Strindberg's savage portrayal of the wife in *Comrades* as a lifelike portrait of the average "emancipated" woman. Pretending to be emancipated, she is often, claimed Goldman, "a cold-blooded exploiter of the work and ideas of the man. . . ."[52]

If this was crude as criticism, Goldman's drama lectures and book nevertheless provided a lively introduction to the European theater of revolt, set in a social rather than a literary context, at a moment when most American theater consisted of light melodrama. The novelist Henry Miller was certainly not the only person to use Goldman's essays as a guide for study; her book sent him scurrying off to explore the experimental little theaters of New York, and turned his reading in wholly new directions. As he would later put it, Goldman "opened up the whole world of European culture for me and gave a new impetus to my life, as well as direction."[53] *The International Socialist Review* praised Goldman's book as "an eloquent and stimulating introduction to a study which no socialist of whatever school can afford to miss." Though Goldman was not the first to treat these playwrights, as Van Wyck Brooks observed, other critics such as Huncker discussed them "as authors only," while Goldman saw them as social analysts. Criticizing both conservative and radical thought that imagined art divorced from society, Goldman insisted upon their interrelationship, arguing that "any mode of creative work, which with true perception portrays social wrongs earnestly and boldly, may be a greater menace to our social fabric and a more powerful inspiration than the wildest harangue of the soapbox orator."[54]

Among anarchists, however, Goldman's literary interests and her fascination with the intellectuals aroused considerable criticism. Harry Kelly worried that the English-speaking movement was becoming too middle-class, too concerned with cultural rather than economic issues, too isolated from labor. It had become "a movement for individual self-expression rather than collective revolution." The European anarchists fought the capitalists; the Americans fought Comstock. "Instead of participating in the trade unions, organizing the unemployed or indulging in soap-box oratory, we rent comfortable halls and charge ten cents admission. Added to that," he continued, "are, in many cases, ten cents carfare and Anarchism has become a luxury. Instead of inspiring the workers with revolutionary ideas, we teach them speculative theories of liberty."[55] Voltairine de Cleyre complained about the tendency of anarchist propagandists to cultivate "respectable audiences, respectable neighborhoods, respectable people." She felt that anarchists should work with the workers, not with the bourgeoisie; with "the poor, the ignorant, the brutal, the disinherited, the men and women who do the hard and brutalizing work of the world."[56] Alexander Berkman also continually lamented the failure of anarchists to attract a larger following among the workers. Just presenting "lectures for outside and chance audiences," he insisted, did not build a movement.[57] And even some radicals outside the anarchist movement, notably Elizabeth Gurley Flynn, felt disappointed that Goldman had turned into a "lecturer" for the entertainment of wealthy liberals.[58]

For her part, Emma Goldman insisted that "I am tired of the old story, 'we do not reach the workers.' We do reach them." Indeed, "you reach more workers at a large meeting than you do in unions," she argued. Still, stung by these criticisms, she defended her agitation among the middle class, insisting that the movement had made so little progress precisely because it had been limited to the workers, who immediately lost their ideals once they grew affluent.[59] Goldman may have been thinking particularly of the Yiddish-speaking anarchists with whom she had long been at odds. Critical of these "timid" radicals who lived all their lives on the Lower East Side and never associated with "Americans," Goldman had always argued for the necessity of building an American, English-speaking movement of national scope. If the American comrades were few in number, she acknowledged, those few "know at least what Anarchism means. They do not sell their Anarchism in real estate, or in playing domino in restaurants. They live Anarchism and thereby they are having a moral influence, of greater [and] more lasting value, than 10 years publication of a F[reie] Ar[beiter] S[timme]."[60] Anarchism, she argued, "builds not on classes, but on men and women." Besides, "the pioneers of every new thought rarely come from the ranks of the workers," but rather from "the so-called respectable classes." Not material poverty but "spiritual hunger and unrest" were, in her view, the most powerful incentives to radicalism.[61]

The arguments were strong on both sides. Goldman was far more imaginative than her critics in her insistence on a cultural agenda for anarchism. Clearly her sense of the movement as a coalition of workers and intellectuals, of activists and artists, was more exciting and creative than the narrower visions of her detractors. At their best, her meetings became the occasion for freewheeling dialogues between workers and intellectuals: places where "doctors, lawyers, and judges rubbed elbows with procurers and dive-keepers, while good moral ladies sat side by side with the Alice Smiths, and . . . the so-called cultured gentlemen were compelled to listen to the strong, revolutionary language of the I.W.W.'s, Anarchists, and other free elements."[62] Moreover, Goldman grasped sexual politics—the importance for women of challenging Comstock as well as capitalism—in a way that eluded many others in the movement. Many of the "intellectual proletarians" whom she wished to reach through her lectures on literature were precisely those "emancipated" women—teachers, stenographers, journalists, artists—whose freedom she felt was so incomplete.

But it was also true that Goldman's critics saw more clearly than she the need for a larger working-class base of support, if anarchism were not to remain a small community of like-minded intellectual workers and professionals. Her attraction to the intellectuals, her infatuation with "Americans" at a time when most of the working class was of immigrant origin, and her disdain for "the ordinary man" tended to widen the distance between anarchists and workers. Although Goldman did help to organize anarchist groups in the cities she visited—in particular a series of Social Science clubs in cities such as Minneapolis, Seattle, Los Angeles, and Rochester—she had no organizational agenda beyond the small local group. Although she often addressed Wobbly audiences and women's groups such as the Women's Trade Union League, she remained outside these organizations and sought followers among professional people and wealthy liberals. In doing so, Goldman in fact encouraged her admirers to distinguish between her and other anarchists, facilitating a cult of personality around herself. She was not the "popular" kind of anarchist, she assured the playwright Israel Zangwill.[63] And Margaret

Anderson also stressed that Goldman did not belong "with the rank and file of Anarchists," because "cults and 'isms' are too restrictive for her."[64] Emma did not compromise her beliefs, but she too easily equated the large audiences and the excitement she generated among these people with the spread of anarchism, when in fact the people who flocked to her lectures, did not, for the most part, join the movement or become anarchists.[65]

The arguments persisted between those like Alexander Berkman, who thought of anarchism as the left wing of the labor movement, and those like Goldman, who regarded it more as a movement of cultural, social, and sexual radicalism. For a time, however, these controversies subsided as the movement in New York flourished and a new issue—birth control—emerged into the political arena in the spring of 1914. Despite the recession and severe unemployment of the previous winter and the deepening tensions in Europe, there continued a sense of exhilaration and optimism on the Left. Radicalism was gaining adherents, the revolution could not be far off, and Goldman, gratified by the enthusiastic audiences at her winter lectures in and around New York, now plunged into yet another campaign that would have important consequences for both her public and personal life.

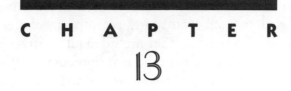

"A
GREAT
INNER
CONFLICT"

From her earliest days in the movement, Emma Goldman had insisted on "freedom in love and freedom in motherhood" as an essential strand of anarchism. Her observations of poor immigrant women on the Lower East Side whom she had nursed in the nineties had persuaded her that the right of woman to control her own body was essential both to woman's freedom and to the emancipation of the workers. From the neo-Malthusians she met in Paris in 1900, she had even learned of actual contraceptive methods being made available by the advanced birth control movements in countries such as Holland. On her return to America, however, she did not attempt to lecture on the subject or initiate similar programs. "I did not discuss methods," she wrote in her memoirs, " because the question of limiting offspring represented in my estimation only one aspect of the social struggle and I did not care to risk arrest for it."[1] Although growing numbers of women were in fact practicing some form of birth control, the 1873 Comstock Law remained in effect, making it illegal to mail, transport, or import "obscene, lewd, or lascivious articles," a heading that included all contraceptive devices and information.[2] But Goldman did not immediately decide to challenge it. To her, birth control always remained a somewhat abstract issue, perhaps partly because her infertility removed the dilemma of contraception from her own experience. She always made her priorities clear. The issue of birth control was important, "first because it is tabooed and the people who advocate it are persecuted," and only secondly because "it represents the immediate question of life and death to masses of people."[3]

For Margaret Sanger, on the other hand, the issue of birth control was personally and passionately felt. The daughter of a working-class Catholic family in upstate New York, Sanger was influenced by her unconventional socialist father and by the sufferings of her mother, who had died of tuberculosis complicated by cervical cancer after giving birth to eleven children when Margaret was only sixteen. Margaret, who had begun reading medical books during her mother's illness, was later tormented by the feeling that she could have saved her mother if only she had had a greater knowledge of medicine. Shortly after her mother died, she began her training as a nurse. Later, working with poor families on the Lower East Side, her grief over the death of her own young mother fused with a sense of the sufferings of all mothers—which she associated with uncontrollable childbearing—and filled her with a determination to "do something to change the destiny of mothers whose miseries were as vast as the sky."[4]

When she was in her early thirties and the mother of three children, Sanger found the impetus for action in the radical and feminist world of New York, where she and her architect husband William Sanger, himself a socialist, moved in 1911. At the Sangers' uptown apartment, a gathering place for liberals and radicals of all shades, and downtown at Mabel Dodge's, Margaret met all the leading figures of the New York Left, including Wobbly leader Big Bill Haywood and Emma Goldman. She worked for a time with the Socialist party, lecturing widely on health and sex for community groups. Later, attracted by the more militant tactics of the I.W.W., she did support work for the strikers at Lawrence and at Paterson. After spending a year in Paris studying European contraceptive methods,

Sanger returned to the United States and, in the spring of 1914, began publishing a magazine, *The Woman Rebel*, which echoed the militant rhetoric of the I.W.W. and of Emma Goldman in its general call for revolution and its social and sexual radicalism.

The Woman Rebel advocated the prevention of conception and used the term "birth control," coined by Sanger, for the first time in the June 1914 issue. It contained, however, no specific contraceptive information. Still, Sanger immediately ran into difficulties with the postal authorities. Right from the start, Goldman offered her support. She vigorously promoted *The Woman Rebel* on her 1914 lecture tour, recruited agents in various cities to take charge of local distribution, and wrote the younger woman enthusiastic letters of encouragement. *The Woman Rebel*, Emma reported, was the number one best-seller on her lecture tour—it was going "like hotcakes," better than any of her own literature—and she urged Sanger to make a lecture tour herself; she was sure she would have great success.[5]

In August of 1914, Margaret Sanger was arrested and indicted under the Comstock Law. At this point she decided to write a pamphlet, "Family Limitation," with detailed instructions on contraceptive methods: a deliberately provocative act. An anarchist Wobbly friend of Goldman and of Sanger, William Shatov, printed one hundred thousand copies, which were mailed out, principally through I.W.W. locals, to radicals all over the country. Sanger, fearing almost certain conviction for the pamphlet, if not the magazine, decided to return to Europe. While she was away, William Sanger was also arrested—on January 10, 1915—for selling a copy of "Family Limitation" to a Comstock agent. Now Goldman felt that she must "either stop lecturing on the subject or do it practical justice. . . . Even if I were not vitally interested in the matter, the conviction of William Sanger and his condemnation to prison would have impelled me to take up the question."[6] In the spring of 1915, she began to offer specific contraceptive information in her lectures. Instead of general lectures on "The Mother's Strike" or "The Birth Strike," she spoke, in Yiddish and in English, on "The Limitation of Offspring" and "Birth Control." She and Reitman also distributed Sanger's pamphlet, "Family Limitation," as well as another pamphlet, written by Reitman, "How and Why the Poor Should Not Have Many Children," which gave information on the use of condoms, pessaries, and douches.

At first during her winter lectures in New York and later on her coast-to-coast tour, Goldman and Reitman encountered no opposition. In fact, the Sanger cases had helped to stimulate a grass-roots birth control movement around the country, centered in Socialist party and I.W.W. locals.[7] With attitudes toward sex becoming more liberal, growing numbers of women entering the workforce, and a resurgence of organized feminism, the laws against contraception appeared increasingly anachronistic and ripe for challenge. The Sanger cases struck a responsive chord in many feminists and women radicals, who saw birth control as part of a larger movement for social revolution. So, too, did Emma Goldman's exhilarating 1915 cross-country lecture tour, which further dramatized the issue and prepared the way for Margaret Sanger, who undertook her own coast-to-coast speaking tour the following year.

Fully aware that she was risking arrest, Goldman was still surprised when she was in fact arrested while lecturing in New York on February 11, 1916; she had already delivered this very birth control lecture many times in that city without interference. Moreover, when she and Reitman had, previously, been fined one hundred dollars in Portland for circulating "literature of an illegal character," their sentence had been overturned on appeal. In the New York incident, Goldman was charged with violating Section 1142 of the New York Penal Code, which made it a misdemeanor for anyone to "sell, lend or give away" or to advertise, loan, or distribute "any recipe, drug or medicine for the prevention of conception."[8] Shortly afterward, on April 27, Reitman too was arrested on similar charges.

As Goldman geared up for a massive publicity campaign to attract attention to her case, friction was building between her and Margaret Sanger, whose case had been dismissed in February. (Her husband, however, had been sentenced to thirty days in jail and fined one hundred fifty dollars.) Complaints and recriminations flew back and forth between the Sangers and Goldman, in letters and in *Mother Earth*. Goldman, as a seasoned agitator, could dispense judgments and directives with high-handed insensitivity, provoking complaints from William Sanger about "anarchist judges" and hurt feelings from Margaret, who was increasingly inclined to turn her back on Goldman, acting as if birth control were her own personal crusade and denying her debts to the radicals as she herself grew increasingly conservative.[9]

As Sanger, lecturing across the country, refused to speak on Goldman's behalf, Goldman mounted a vigorous protest campaign without Sanger's support. On March 1, a mass meeting in Carnegie Hall heard John Reed, Bolton Hall, Theodore Schroeder, and Goldman discuss all aspects of birth control; on April 19, some two hundred people—including writers, artists, anarchists, socialists, doctors, and poets—attended a pretrial banquet for Goldman at the Hotel Brevoort, where Rose Pastor Stokes, wife of millionaire socialist J.B. Phelps Stokes, took direct action herself and handed out birth control leaflets; she was not arrested. On April 20, Goldman was tried at the Court of Special Sessions in New York's Criminal Court Building. People flocked to court "as if to a play, with Emma Goldman in the leading role," commented the *New York Times*.[10] Of the five hundred people eager to attend, only two hundred gained admittance.

Using the trial as a political forum, Goldman argued the case for birth control on several grounds. She had earlier outlined these in an essay, "The Social Aspects of Birth Control," featured in a special "birth control" issue of *Mother Earth*. First, birth control was necessary for scientific reasons, to halt the drastic increase in defective children: "an overworked and underfed vitality cannot reproduce healthy progeny." Second, there was "the mental awakening of woman," who will "no longer be a party to the crime of bringing hapless children into the world only to be ground into dust by the wheel of capitalism and to be torn into shreds in trenches and battlefields." Woman, after all, risked her health and sacrificed her youth for the reproduction of the race. "Surely she ought to be in a position to decide how many children she should bring into the world, whether they should be brought into the world by the man she loves and because she wants the child, or should be born in hatred and loathing." Indeed, women had been practicing birth control since time immemorial in any case, often driven to attempt drastic abortions with tragic results. And not only women, but also many men—especially working-class men—now supported birth control and saw that large families were "a millstone around their necks." "A worker with a large brood dare not join a revolutionary organization; he dare not go on strike; he dare not express an opinion." Finally, "a change in the relation of the sexes" had led men to expect more of women than simply the breeding of children. Men were coming to realize that the emancipation of woman was necessary to their own progress, and that condemning woman to continual childbearing made her into an enemy of the man, rather than an ally. Birth control was, Goldman concluded, "a pressing, imperative necessity" and part of "the larger social war; not a war for military conquest, not for material supremacy, but a war for a seat at the table of life on the part of the people, the masses who create and who build the world and who have nothing in return. I look upon Birth Control as only one phase of that vast movement, and if I, through my agitation,—through my education, I should rather say,—can indicate a way towards the betterment of that human race, towards a finer quality, children who should have a joyous and glorious childhood, and women who shall have a healthy motherhood, if that is a crime, your Honor, I am glad and proud to be a Criminal." At this point the audience burst into applause. She had committed no offense, Goldman added matter-of-factly; "I have simply given to the poorer women in my audiences information that any wealthy woman can obtain secretly from her physician, who does not fear prosecution. I have offered them advice as to how to escape the burden of large families without resorting to illegal operations."[11] Observed Leonard Abbott from the audience, "the judges seemed to be in a quandary. Their three heads came together for a long conference."[12] Finally the presiding judge presented Goldman with the choice of fifteen days in the workhouse or payment of a hundred-dollar fine. Without hesitation, she chose the workhouse.

"Our Lady of Sorrows," as Reitman called her, entered the Queens County Jail on April 20, upon sentencing. After the exhausting activity of the previous months, she found prison almost relaxing. She felt happy "to have had the opportunity to be here," she wrote her Denver friend Ellen Kennan, and to come back into touch with the victims of society, to observe the viciousness of the system directly. She was moved by the flood of support she received. "It's embarassing to receive so much love for so little," she told Kennan. "After all, it is so little what I have done compared with the Grand Heroic Deeds of a Louise Michel or Breshkovsky and so many others. I only hope some day I too may be able to do an heroic deed but so far it is such a bagatelle, why make so much of it?"[13] On her release fifteen days later, May 4, she felt distressed. Moving from the "smaller prison" to "the larger prison called life" made little difference, except that "while in Queens County Jail I knew I had no liberty and outside of it, I, like many others, delude myself by the thing which it is not. I don't know whether you will understand the feeling since you have never had the experience," she wrote a friend, "but I felt more miserable yesterday and today than on the day I was sentenced and in fact the two weeks while I was in prison. However there is no time to contemplate one's feelings."[14]

Indeed there was not. Within a month Goldman was scheduled to depart on her annual cross-country tour. May was filled with birth control meetings, demonstrations, protests, rallies. Goldman continued to lecture on "Free or Forced Motherhood (The Need for Birth Control)," but she was careful now to limit herself to giving "oral information and . . . not to distribute these circulars." She did not wish to risk jail again. In truth, she felt that birth control was "a very important issue, but it is not the only issue I care to engage myself in."[15] Goldman had never seen herself as a pioneer in the movement; she always credited the free-love radicals, Moses and Lillian Harman, Ida Craddock, E. C. Walker, as the real pioneers. She saw herself rather as a gadfly, someone who would sting others into action. This aim achieved, she was ready to go on to other issues. She felt satisfied, she wrote in the December 1916 *Mother Earth*, "that this issue was advanced by at least ten years through the publicity given to it by our arrests and trials."[16] As Reitman said, "we were not the pioneers of the birth control movement, but we have done a great deal toward popularizing the question, and as far as I know, E.G. was the first and the last to give actual methods from the platform."[17]

Ben Reitman, in fact, had played a particularly important role in the birth control campaign of 1915 and 1916—not simply as Emma Goldman's manager, but as a campaigner in his own right. As a physician he could address with some authority the medical aspects of birth control, and he had spoken publicly himself and distributed contraceptive pamphlets with enthusiasm. He had, moreover, suffered more onerous consequences than Goldman. Tried in April on the same charges of distributing illegal pamphlets, he was sentenced to sixty days in the workhouse. In December of 1916 he was arrested in Cleveland once again on the same charges; tried in January of 1917, he was fined one thousand dollars and sentenced to six months in prison, which he served from April to September of 1918.

Reitman's involvement in this campaign and his growing self-confidence had deepened tensions between himself and Emma that had been building for the past several years and which came to a head in the summer of 1916. Though he still relished the excitement of the lecture tours, Reitman had never relinquished his longing for a wife and family and "home" of his own. As early as 1911, he had begun complaining to Emma that all they did together was work, that hotel rooms on tour and Emma's crowded apartment in New York did not really constitute a "home." Number 210 East Thirteenth Street, at the edge of the Fourteenth Street theater district and not far from the Bowery, was more a public institution than a private residence—"the home of lost dogs," Hutchins Hapgood called it, referring to the bereft characters Emma was perpetually taking in. Ben, still torn between Chicago and New York—and in any case always feeling like an outsider in Emma's world—wanted something more decisively his own.

Emma initially resisted Ben's pleas. She felt little attraction to the idea of a home together and saw no reason for lovers to act conventionally: "begin housekeeping and such nonsense."[18] She met Ben's proposals with a variety of objections. But finally he wore down her resistance. Sometime during their 1913 tour, he persuaded her to find a place where they could move in together on a more permanent basis. When she arrived back in New York in August (while Ben stayed in Chicago), she immediately began hunting for a house. By September 13, she had found a promising brownstone at 74 East 119th Street in Harlem. Desperately short of money, faced with numerous bills and debts, uncertain how they could manage this new burden, Goldman nevertheless felt cheerful. "I never felt more hopeful & confident in my life," she told Ben.[19] Within a week she had decided to take the house. It was "a dream," she reported—four floors, including a large basement that could be used for the office and bookshop, a long parlor that could seat one hundred people, a "magnificent dining room," and rooms so arranged on the first and second floors that they afforded considerable privacy to the residents, who would include Emma's niece Stella and nephew Saxe, Alexander Berkman, and a housekeeper, Rhoda Smith ("Smithy").[20]

If this grand establishment—so incontestably Emma's—was sure to exacerbate the problems of 210 East Thirteenth Street, Ben was also prepared to introduce further difficulties: he wanted his mother, now in ill health, to come and live with them. Although willing to try the experiment, Emma felt concerned about the prospect, joking one day that Ben was a better son than lover, then worrying the next that his mother might not like the house or that she might feel excluded —"shoved away," as Emma put it.[21] If at any time, she told Ben, his mother felt she would "rather be away with you in her own little Apt., be perfectly at liberty to tell me so." Emma hoped fervently that "all will be well and harmonious at our new house." She looked forward to having "a real house and not a miserable tenement apartment" to come back to from her tours, but she approached the moving day, October 1, with growing apprehension.[22] Reassurances from Ben (who was still in Chicago as of September 21) seemed only to deepen her anxieties. "Hobo lover, you are so wonderful in your letters, so poetic, so tender, so fragrant, why can I not be satisfied with that? Oh Hobo I am such a hungry lover. Perhaps I am getting old," she wrote sadly. "I want your mother to be comfortable," she assured him, "but I have fear in my heart. You see, dearie, I know the Psychology of mothers, and your mother is so very much the mother. Will she be able to fit in[to] her new life, with her son's sweetheart ever present? That's the question before me. If she should not it would cause friction and if there is anything I want most to avoid [it] is to stand between you and your mother in the position of a daughter-in-law. Indeed, indeed, I could not endure that."[23]

The experiment was not a success. Within a month, tensions had become explosive. With everything under one roof—home, office, bookshop—and so many strong personalities to boot, the situation was worse than ever. Rather than bringing Emma and Ben closer together, the experiment of living together seemed to drive a deeper wedge between them. Surrounded constantly by Emma's friends and admirers, Ben felt unappreciated, excluded, subordinate. He worried about his financial dependence. He quarreled not only with Emma, but with Havel, Baginski, and especially with Berkman, of whom he was particularly jealous and resentful. Sensitive to the scorn of Goldman's comrades and self-conscious about his lack of education and culture, the insecure Reitman retreated into self-pity and self-doubt. Ben received little reassurance from Emma, who tended to blend her protestations of passion with attacks on his character and capabilities. He felt overwhelmed at times by his dominating lover. "I am only a small fish and you are a whale," he would tell her.[24]

Further, Reitman bitterly realized that despite his hard work for the movement, he continued to remain an outsider. Everyone in the *Mother Earth* group had his disciple, he later recalled, "and *all* were disciples of Emma. I was the outstanding exception." [25] After six years in the movement, he had remained Emma's "janitor and office boy." "I am 35 years old," he complained, "and I haven't a thing and I am only the jester, joker or clown. I don't amount to a damn in the movement and I know it. No one takes me serious [*sic*]. The best thing they say about me is that I sell literature. You are a power, Berkman is a force, and Reitman is a joke. I will be forgotten in 3 months. There is nothing to me." [26] Within a month, Reitman decided to move into an apartment of his own, taking his mother with him. Soon they both returned to Chicago.

Emma, however, blamed all their problems on Ben's mother, who, she insisted, "has stood like a spectre between us since . . . you forced her down my throat when I knew it would be a failure. . . ." His growing devotion to his mother had, in Emma's view, caused his estrangement from her. "Please please Hobo darling don't be superficial and say it's jealousy on my part. It is nothing of the sort." It was rather that his obsession with his mother had become increasingly dominant, eliminating everything else in his life. But "back of your obsession for your mother is a deeper subtler reason," she added. It was "the decline of sex, of your physical passion, Hobo dear. In proportion as you have declined in that the child in you has awakened and it is the child in you which is centered around your mother . . . the child which craves the utter abandon, the care and presence of the mother." If Emma had given him that, she continued, he would not have grown away from her; but she would not want to even if she could have, "because the old time motherhood to me is the most terrible thing imposed upon woman, it has made her so unspeakably helpless and dependent, so self-centered and unsocial as to fill me with absolute horror." No, Ben had been wrong to conclude anything from this situation. "Oh Hobo, how superficially you judge. The only time we have lived together was on the road and that has not been a failure." [27]

In truth, Emma was more than a little jealous of the bond between Ben and his mother, infantile as she thought it was. She argued that, although she could not devote herself to him as his mother had done, she had "been able to do what she has not, imbue you with an ideal, with a desire to do big things. And if I have been critical at times it was because I did not want you to waste yourself," but wanted him to do "deep and thorough work. I have succeeded in that so I need not complain."[28]

While Ben nursed his wounds in Chicago, trying to decide what to do with his life, Emma in New York had begun to reconcile herself to Ben's withdrawal and even to the possibility of a permanent separation. Without her manager, she had nonetheless been busy and productive throughout the winter. She felt independent, in a good humor, and not especially anxious for Reitman to return to New York. Nor was she eager to try living with him alone in a flat, as he suggested. If, as he insisted, there was "a special bond" between him and his mother, wrote Emma, then he should live with her. And if Ben wanted security or domesticity, he should look elsewhere. "My life must of necessity remain insecure always and what is more," she announced, "I do not wish it otherwise. Security means stagnation. I hope I shall never get to that."[29]

Within a short time, Ben announced to her that he was cured of "home and business" and eager once again to join her on the road. The 1914 lecture tour the beginning of the birth control campaign —was highly successful, both on the personal and the political levels. But an event in the summer of 1914 suddenly brought into sharper focus the political differences between Goldman and Reitman: differences that would once again widen the gap between them. On July 4, 1914, a tremendous explosion destroyed an apartment on Lexington Avenue between 103rd and 104th streets, in a thickly populated immigrant district of Harlem. Three men and one woman were killed in the top-floor apartment where the blast had occurred. The explosion had its origins in the events of the previous spring, when the vehemently anti-union Colorado Fuel and Iron Company, owned by Rockefeller, retaliated against striking miners on April 20, 1914, by setting fire to a tent colony of evicted strikers' families. Thirteen children and a number of unarmed women and men were killed by flames, smoke, and machine-gun fire. This outrage, known as the Ludlow massacre, aroused massive public protest against the company's actions. (Emma, arriving in Denver shortly afterward, was pained to learn that her presence was not wanted either by labor leaders or by her own comrades.) In New York there were demonstrations, mass meetings, and a "silent parade" organized by Upton

Sinclair and his wife in front of the Rockefeller offices. The anarchists, including Berkman, organized protests at Rockefeller's Tarrytown residence. Some of the young protesters evidently decided to blow up the Rockefeller residence in retaliation for Ludlow—a plan that miscarried when the bomb exploded prematurely.

Goldman, who was on the West Coast at the time, had neither knowledge of nor connection with this plan. Historian Paul Avrich has argued, on the basis of testimony from surviving participants and their associates, that Alexander Berkman was directly involved in the plot to blow up the Rockefeller estate and may even have been the chief strategist.[30] Berkman himself never acknowledged complicity, but he did organize a public funeral for the bomb's victims, where he eulogized them as heroic martyrs and pioneers of the social revolution. The July 1914 issue of *Mother Earth* was filled with paeans to violent action. "Anarchists have taught people that violence is justified, aye necessary," proclaimed Berkman, "in the defensive and offensive struggle of labor against capital. . . . The power of economic solidarity of labor will ultimately knock the last master off the back of the last slave, and meanwhile—while labor gathers this power, its success will be hastened, its courage strengthened by tempering oppression with dynamite."[31] Berkman had always affirmed that under the right circumstances he might consider violence necessary, and if so, he would not advocate it to others, but would execute it himself. Avrich suggests that for Berkman, Ludlow, "with its Pinkertons and militia and killing of workers, was a repetition of Homestead, and Rockefeller another Frick. Although twenty-two years had since elapsed, all the indignation came rushing back, and all the determination to retaliate."[32] Still, it is difficult to believe that the older, more experienced Berkman—having lived through the disastrous consequences of Homestead—would have masterminded a bomb plot that risked the lives of young, inexperienced comrades while he himself remained in the background.

In any event, Goldman in her autobiography eventually claimed that she had been "aghast" at the irresponsibility of comrades making bombs in a crowded tenement and—recalling her own similar experiments with Sasha in 1892—had decided that "I could never again participate in or approve of methods that jeopardized innocent lives," even though she would always sympathize with those who chose violent protest.[33] At the time, however, Goldman came close to defending terrorism; certainly she had consistently defended the terrorists driven to engage in such acts by outrage against the Ludlow massacre. At first she insisted in letters to Ben that she did not approve of "the Lexington business" because "it is impardonable to endanger the lives of innocent people. . . ." The editorials in *Mother Earth* were stupid and bombastic, she felt, but since she was not on the scene in New York, she could not "as a free person coerce or force a man who acts as editor to write what I want when I am miles away."[34] But when Reitman expressed his strong disapproval both of the terrorist plan and of Berkman's eulogies, Goldman replied impatiently, "I absolutely must insist that my position *is not against violence* and never will be unless I become weakminded. When I said the Lexington affair was to be regretted, I only meant that the place was ill and stupidly chosen. But not for one moment did I mean to imply that I am opposed to the thing itself. Furthermore, even if I did not approve of the purpose, I should still be on the side of the actionist because I hold that if society makes no provision for the individual, society must take the consequences."[35] Like Berkman, she eulogized the bomb victims as "the conscious and brave spokesmen" of the oppressed.

Ben Reitman did not agree. He was alarmed by the fact that he, too, was indirectly implicated, through the magazine, as a supporter of the Lexington Avenue terrorists. The use of bombs and explosives damaged the anarchist movement, he complained. "I won't support such stupid work and it is unfair of Sasha or anyone else to involve us. I can well imagine what will happen with the unemployed and others this winter, and Sasha *must* not make *Mother Earth* an organ of such propaganda. Not without giving us a chance to secede." Reitman said that he wanted their work to *count*, and "such murderous silly things ought not to be continued (or countenanced)."[36] A few days later, he insisted that he was arriving at the pacifist position of a Tolstoy or a Ferrer. "I don't want to be a part of any group that shows the Master Class what bombs can do. To me, these guys are terrorists and . . . I want a chance to prove that our ideas are correct and will help the World. Violence never proved any truth. As far as I can see, I and my class are not invaded and crushed—(Yes I remember Ludlow), we have a chance to live and work and prove the value of ideas. Now why the hell should I take my stand with a lot of temperamental boys and men—to whom violence is a matter of sex and emotion. . . . If I am opposed to violence on top can I condone violence at the bottom?" Reitman insisted again that he loved Emma and wanted to work with her. "But I want to be honest. I don't want to have to stand for things I don't believe in." Ben felt sure, he told her, that "violence a la Lexington Avenue can not help the working class or [help] any propaganda—to know, to understand, to teach quietly, to love, to be helpful, that is all that is worth-while." He was sure that one reason for the slow growth of anarchism in America was the "lack of love" and the gloominess of the anarchists who were always "scolding, condemning, complaining, attacking Institutions and parties and systems and people." He wanted to work "quietly and sweetly and honestly" and to emphasize love in their propaganda.[37]

Meanwhile, there were practical dilemmas to consider. Returning home to New York in mid-September at the close of the 1914 tour, Goldman found the business affairs of *Mother Earth* in disarray and the house full of "leeches." She and Berkman were heavily in debt, with the large 119th Street house consuming a disproportionate amount of income from her lectures and Berkman's. Emma was indignant with Sasha for his carelessness in dispersing their meager resources to various political causes, while turning the house into a "free-for-all lodging-and-feeding-place."[38] Some action was necessary. She would undertake a second lecture tour in the fall to try to earn enough money to pay off their considerable debts. She would also find more modest living quarters. Berkman was moving in with his lover, Eleanor Fitzgerald ("Fitzi"), whom Reitman had recruited from Wisconsin to act as secretary for *Mother Earth*. Berkman's former lover, Becky Edelsohn, would join them; "life is certainly strange but I have no time to philosophize now," Emma commented dryly to Ben.[39] That meant that there were two fewer people to worry about. By mid-September Emma had found a two-room flat at 20 East 125th Street in Harlem. The front room would serve as an office; the back room, looking out onto a yard, would be Emma's living quarters—all available for the modest rent of twenty dollars a month. She was "tired [of] feeding leeches and I am tired of living with people. I know you will smile, say I am a social animal etc. etc.," she wrote Ben. "But just now I feel an urgent need of having a nook for myself." She felt that the move to a small flat was a move toward peace and away from people. "I am so tired of lectures, meetings and the mad chase," she wrote to Ben on October 1, the last night in the old house. "I want rest, I want time to read and think and love."[40]

Ben, in Chicago, left everything to Emma. "You are really the boss in this case," he told her, "everyone is dependent upon you and you must decide. I shall love you and work with you whatever you do." he assured her. "But I am not going to worry and I hope you won't. Just work things out the best you can and let it go at that."[41] Though Emma was not averse to making decisions, she resented Ben's absence from New York at this time and his unwillingness to assume any responsibility for choices that affected both of them. While she worked desperately to put the *Mother Earth* affairs back on a sound financial footing, Ben was relaxing in Chicago in "a beautiful state of mind . . . nursing my soul and tabulating my ideas and experiences."[42] Ben's love, Emma complained, expressed itself only in joy; he did not want to share her pain, only her pleasures. Still she wanted him, had to stick with him, "out of necessity you know. Hobo, my hobo, I could not for the life of me say why I love you but I do. . . ."[43]

This time the move had the desired effect. By December of 1914, Emma was contemplating the future with an unusual sense of calm. She felt tired, but also at peace with herself—perhaps, she thought, because in her new small quarters there was no one around to jar her nerves or sap the life out of her, as she put it. "I have many plans," she exclaimed to Reitman on December 25; "I have a perfect obsession for work. I feel more eager to proclaim my faith than ever before. . . ."[44] The next year was, in fact, their most successful ever, with their large lectures drawing enthusiastic audiences across the country, a growing demand for anarchist literature, the continuing excitement of the birth control campaign, and the tenth anniversary of *Mother Earth*, certainly a triumph for its publisher.

Reitman shared Emma's exhilaration, but his frustration with the movement nonetheless continued to mount. He loved the adventure of life on the road, but disliked working in the *Mother Earth* office, which he found dull, boring, and routine. "While I had worked hard with excitement for breakfast, police for dinner and riot for supper, I was taking part in a different way. I was becoming a drudge in the battle."[45] In truth, his commitment to anarchism had always been tentative at best. With the Lexington Avenue affair and the growing

likelihood of American intervention in the war, which made all opposition or resistance dangerous, Reitman grew even more uncomfortable. The impending danger drew Goldman and Berkman closer
together and left Ben feeling increasingly excluded from Goldman's
intimate life. He became even more critical of the anarchists, and
also of Goldman—"You are so constituted that ONLY THOSE who
serve you body and soul can you love," he would later tell her angrily.[46]

Reitman's dissatisfaction with their personal life increased as well.
The most immediate cause of his unhappiness remained his growing
desire for a wife and children. In the summer of 1916, while they
were on the West Coast, Ben had finally confessed to Emma his
involvement with Anna Martindale, a young Englishwoman and suf-
fragist he had met in New York (sometime in the winter of 1913 or
1914, according to his memoir). They had carried on a "strange romance," he wrote, since "all this time I was living and working with
Emma Goldman." Emma had by now more or less resigned herself
to Reitman's erotic escapades, which he often flaunted. But this affair was serious. As he later wrote in his memoir, crossing out one
explanation and replacing it with another: "~~and if ever I did I think I
can say that I fell desperately in love with her~~ and for the first time
in my life I wanted to marry a woman, and have a home and children." At this time he "began to dream of a home with my mother,
my wife and baby, and a steady practice. I had visions of myself
teaching in a medical college, of being a reformer to the outcasts,
and an active worker in the church."[47]

In February of 1917, Ben Reitman and Anna Martindale were
married in New York. In March or April, they moved back to Chicago. Reitman would occasionally return for brief periods to New
York to chair Emma's Sunday night meetings. He still contributed
articles to *Mother Earth*. He and Emma continued to correspond,
and she mobilized support for his birth control trials. But, as she
painfully understood, their love affair was now over. The winter of
1916–1917 was especially difficult. She was going through "a great
inner conflict which has left me pretty bruised," she confided to
Agnes Inglis. "But I am not allowing this to interfere in my work. I
never have, least of all now, when one needs all one's energies."[48]
From early in her relationship with Ben, Goldman had found in work
some consolation for the anguish she felt in love. "Activity, propa-

ganda. That is my salvation," she had written Reitman in 1911. "That is the only force which reconciles me to my mad passion for you."[49] And so Goldman now turned, with ever more concentration and determination, to her work, even as the approaching war heightened political tensions. She sought comfort from her women friends— Agnes Inglis, now one of her closest confidantes; her Denver friend Ellen Kennan; her niece Stella Cominsky Ballantine. There were also the ever-faithful Max Baginski, and Leon Malmed, up in Albany. Ultimately she took consolation in the thought that "the struggle to maintain my own individuality and freedom was always more important to me than the wildest love affair. . . . I am so constituted that I can't bear being at the beck and call of what is commonly called love."[50]

As Emma Goldman resigned herself to the loss of Ben and bravely continued with her life, Reitman began a quite different existence as physician, reformer, and family man. He always considered his years with Emma Goldman as the most valuable of his life and Emma herself his greatest teacher. But he turned now toward more conventional satisfactions, a less exhausting kind of love, and Chicago, "the one place where I could rest." In his autobiography he frankly acknowledged these reasons for his final separation from Emma Goldman. "I had been seduced by the ordinary man's desire for a home, a wife and a child."[51]

CHAPTER

14

"THE QUESTION OF CAPITALIST WARS"

Between the summer of 1916 and the spring of 1917, as Emma Goldman struggled to come to terms with the loss of Ben Reitman, the mood of the country darkened. The war in Europe, which all concerned had believed would end quickly, was dragging into its third year: a grim, savage round of trenches, barbed wire, artillery, machine guns, mud, boredom, death. John Reed, the *Metropolitan*'s correspondent at the front, was so disgusted by the spectacle, as he said, of both sides slaughtering each other to preserve their commercial empires in Asia and Africa that he could hardly write his reports for the magazine. In the United States, "Preparedness"—the campaign for building the nation's military strength, which Theodore Roosevelt had enthusiastically spearheaded in 1915—became a reality in 1916. In the summer of 1916, Congress doubled the regular army and provided for the strengthening of the navy. In the fall, the presidential campaign focused on the concern for peace. Soon after the election, however, Woodrow Wilson, the candidate who had thus far "kept us out of war," moved inexorably toward intervention on behalf of the Allied powers. American papers highlighted the dramatic news of German submarines torpedoing Allied ships, while the comparable violations committed by England—the slow starvation of the civilian population of Germany and Austro-Hungary, which the Allied blockade was gradually effecting—drew far less publicity and protest. By late 1916, American prosperity was coming to depend heavily on an Allied victory to ensure repayment of war loans and credits for the purchase of munitions and supplies, which by April of 1917 would exceed two billion dollars. The resumption of unrestricted submarine warfare by Germany in late January of 1917; the discovery in February of the so-called Zimmerman telegram, which hinted at the possible involvement of Mexico in an attack on the United States; and the February Revolution in Russia, which ended the czarist regime—all provided occasion and legitimacy for American intervention. Indeed, the collapse of the Romanov dynasty and the coming to power of a moderate provisional government committed to constitutional parliamentary rule seemed to enhance the claim that this was a war of democracy against Prussian militarism and autocracy, rather than a fight among rival imperial powers. By April 6, the United States was at war.

The April declaration of war touched off an unprecedented campaign to stifle criticism of the government and whip up chauvinistic enthusiasm. George Creel's hastily organized Committee on Public Information, charged with selling the war to an initially reluctant public, labeled all dissent as subversion and promoted a narrow, intolerant version of patriotism. The war served as the occasion for legislation that severely restricted the civil liberties not only of pacifists and critics of the war, but also of leftists and foreigners, who were often equated. The Selective Service Law of May 1917, in which the *New York Times* saw "a long and sorely needed means of disciplining a certain insolent foreign element in this nation," ordered all men of eligible age to register for the military draft.[1] The Espionage Act of June 1917 decreed stiff fines and prison terms of up to twenty years for anyone who obstructed the draft or encouraged "disloyalty." The even more draconian Sedition Law of May 1918 threatened similar penalties for discouraging recruiting, obstructing the sale of government bonds, or speaking, printing, writing, or publishing "any disloyal, profane, scurrilous, or abusive language" about the American form of government, constitution, flag, or uniform. Any interference with production deemed essential to the conduct of the war was made liable to similiar penalties. The war, in short, constituted an opportunity for the prosecution of labor activists, dissidents, and radicals—especially the anarchists, Wobblies, and left-wing socialists—who had gained considerable strength during the previous decade.[2]

In this campaign against the Left, immigrant radicals became special targets. Although anarchists and Wobblies composed only a small minority of all immigrants, they were highly visible and vulnerable to the ultimate weapon of deportation. Throughout the war and after, foreign-born radicals were given the stiffest fines and the harshest prison sentences. Moreover, deportation, formerly used only for those convicted of criminal acts, now came to be seen as a means of expelling all foreign-born radicals from the country. The hostility to immigrants became centered with particular virulence on Americans of German descent: German music, language classes, and books were banned in many states; German-Americans were harassed and hounded. The publication in 1916 of Madison Grant's racist diatribe, *The Passing of the Great Race*, was symptomatic of the growing acceptability of racism generally and of a new nativism—closely intertwined with antiradical sentiment—that was evident as well in the passage, early in 1917, of two laws for which immigration restrictionists had long been pressing. One was a literacy test, which would effectively limit entry of the poorer, less educated "new immigrants" from southern and eastern Europe. The other expanded the provisions of the 1903 anti-anarchist law, empowering the government to deny entry not only to individuals who made specific statements opposing government and advocating violent revolution, but also to those who simply belonged to any organization espousing such beliefs—a much broader and looser category. Moreover, a noncitizen who was found defending such doctrines after entering the country could be deported, no matter how long he or she had resided in America. (Previous legislation had limited liability to three years after entry.)

Events in Russia contributed to the assault on dissidents. If czarist Russia was an embarrassment as an ally and democratic Russia enhanced the Allied claims to righteousness, the Bolshevik Revolution in October of 1917 once again changed the alignment of sympathies. By suing for a separate peace with Germany, the Bolsheviks came to be perceived as enemies of the Allies, and antiwar liberals and radicals in the United States were accused of being either German spies, Bolshevik agents, or both.

In this climate of hostility, few centers of opposition survived. With the declaration of war in April, most groups that had opposed war or worked for a negotiated peace abruptly tempered their opposition. The Women's Peace Party, for example, defending the right of dissent, nonetheless felt constrained to state publicly that once war and conscription had become law, common sense as well as loyalty and "the habit of obedience to law" counseled an end to antiwar activity. "We have never in the slightest degree urged or suggested resistance to the selective service law nor followed any other policy of obstruction," announced its socialist chairman, Crystal Eastman, who had also been executive secretary of the American Union Against Militarism.[3] Many previously antiwar reformers and intellectuals took a similar position; some, such as John Dewey, suddenly found unsuspected virtues in the administration's decision to intervene. As the young social critic Randolph Bourne bitterly argued in his famous essay, "War and the Intellectuals" (which Goldman reprinted in the June and July 1917 issues of *Mother Earth*), the prospect of losing their newly won influence—of becoming "negligible, irrelevant"—had frightened the intellectuals into submission.[4] Even the Socialist party, which at its April 1917 meeting in St. Louis had voted by an overwhelming majority to oppose the war and conscription, suffered the defection of some of its prominent intellectuals, who supported the war and, in some cases, resigned from the party.

The Socialist party as a whole, however, remained firmly against the war, and many of its leaders, including Eugene Debs and Kate Richards O'Hare, were sent to prison. The National Civil Liberties Bureau, largely staffed by socialists and headed by Goldman's admirer, Roger Baldwin, did significant work on behalf of conscientious objectors. The I.W.W., traditionally both anticapitalist and antimilitarist, was another center of opposition to the war. As an organization, the I.W.W. did not take an official stand against the war; indeed, ninety-five percent of all Wobblies actually registered for the draft. Rather, the union expressed its opposition in the refusal to abide by the no-strike pledge taken by the American Federation of Labor for the war's duration. By early 1917 the I.W.W. was at the height of its influence, with a membership of some one hundred thousand workers. Determined to continue vigorous agitation to improve working conditions, it called strikes in war-related industries such as copper, thus provoking the wrath of government and business already hostile to the Wobbly operation.

Like the Socialists, the anarchists suffered some defections over the issue of war, including Harry Kelly and even Kropotkin himself, who argued that a German victory would be disastrous for the Left. Most anarchists, however, remained firmly opposed—including, of course, Emma Goldman and Alexander Berkman, who were preparing to organize "concerted action." Since the outbreak of hostilities in Europe, Goldman had lectured frequently on "The Speculators in War and Starvation" and "The Promoters of the War Mania." Now she prepared for active resistance. Weary from constant lecturing, she hesitated to embark on another tour. But the national situation was "too awful to contemplate." Action was necessary, and she was determined to "go on no matter what the consequences to the very end." "I never was more sure of myself than I am in the question of Capitalist wars," she wrote to Inglis, "but I am afraid it is going to be a physical test."[5]

Early in May, just before the passage of the Selective Service Act, Goldman and Berkman, along with Leonard Abbott and Eleanor Fitzgerald, decided to organize a No-Conscription League. The aim of the League was to encourage and aid conscientious objectors and to oppose "all wars by capitalist governments." "We believe," stated the platform, "that the militarization of America is an evil that far outweighs, in its anti-social and anti-libertarian effects, any good that may come from America's participation in the war. We will resist conscription by every means in our power, and we will sustain those who, for similar reasons, refuse to be conscripted."[6] In its short life —some six weeks—the League organized three mass meetings to protest conscription, printed and distributed thousands of leaflets protesting the draft, and advised hundreds of young men about their options.

Exhausted, and missing Ben terribly—particularly since she now had to "look after all the details which he so ably took off my shoul-

230

ders"—Emma nevertheless threw herself with her usual gusto into antiwar work. The tremendously enthusiastic response she received, particularly at the "sublime" anticonscription meeting of May 18 at the Harlem River Casino, attended by some eight thousand people, seemed to lift her out of her weariness. Her letters of late May and June breathe a sense of exaltation. "Many are the great meetings I have addressed," she announced elatedly to Inglis, "but with the exception of the great Russian meetings, I have seen no such eagerness and determination in many years. I believe it was that which has inspired me. My friends say I spoke as if possessed by some divine fire. I know one thing. I forgot danger and personal feeling. The great Ideal lured me to the very height."[7] The date May 18—the twelfth anniversary of Berkman's release from prison—and the fact that he and Goldman were together on the platform for the first time in years added to her excitement. These were "great days," she rejoiced to Inglis.[8] The anticonscription meetings (a second took place on June 14, the night before registration day, and a third on June 15) attracted not only thousands of opponents of the war, but also soldiers and patriots who came to heckle and stir up trouble. On these occasions, faced with tense, angry crowds, Goldman was superb. Confronted with this volatile mixture of pacifists, radicals, recruits, hostile soldiers who pelted the stage with light bulbs, and battalions of restless, heavily armed police, she maintained an astonishing composure and showed a keen grasp of crowd psychology that several times averted violence. "The way in which Emma Goldman and Alexander Berkman faced the war fury of 1917," recalled her awed collaborator, Leonard Abbott, "was the most stirring manifestation of sheer physical courage that I have ever seen. They did not seem to know the meaning of fear, either of them, and Emma Goldman's oratory during this period was of the kind that lifted audiences from their seats, either in passionate support or in passionate hostility."[9] But despite the overwhelming response, Goldman and her coworkers decided to cease mass meetings after police at the June 14 demonstration arrested all young men in the audience who could not produce a draft card. Emma sensed, too, that her own arrest was imminent.

On June 15 at about five in the afternoon, a New York federal marshal and about a dozen of his cohorts dashed eagerly up the stairs at 20 East 125th Street, where they found Goldman calmly at work. Announcing that she was under arrest, they then proceeded to ransack the place—refusing Goldman's request to see a search warrant—and later carried off "a wagon load of anarchist records and propaganda" (none of which was ever recovered). Goldman, with her usual self-possession in such situations, demanded a few moments to change into more presentable attire. She disappeared briefly, then returned garbed, according to the *New York Times*, in a gown of "royal purple." Upstairs in the *Blast* office, Berkman, reported the *Times*, "was taken completely by surprise and did not appear nearly as brave or defiant as his woman companion."[10]

As a large crowd gathered in front of the *Mother Earth* and *Blast* offices, the two "big fish" of the anti-conscription movement were hurried off to the Federal Building and then to the Tombs, where they were held on an exorbitant twenty-five thousand dollars bail each.[11] Once again behind bars, Goldman regretted only that since she and Berkman were both imprisoned, neither could help the other. Beyond this, far from feeling depressed, she seemed almost elated. "I have felt so much at peace since the arrest," she confessed to Inglis on her fourth day in jail. "I always have when something heroic confronts me. I wish I could say the same for the little things of life." It would be "a bitter and stiff fight but even if we are convicted it will be our gain. People will see what crimes and injustices are committed in the name of democracy."[12]

Goldman's optimism, however, was ill-founded. After ten days in the Tombs, she and Berkman were released on bail, with their trial scheduled to begin two days later, on June 27, Goldman's forty-eighth birthday. Still thoroughly worn out, she found it difficult even to contemplate an immediate trial, but when their request for an adjournment was denied, there was no alternative but to proceed.

To John Reed, who testified on behalf of the defendants and reported on the trial for the soon-to-be-suppressed *Masses*, the Goldman-Berkman trial was the overture to "the blackest month for free men our generation has known."[13] To Goldman, on the contrary, it was great political theater: a courtroom packed with friends of the prosecution (many friends of the defense were arbitrarily denied admittance); two witty, determined agitators acting as their own lawyers (though they consulted daily with their attorney Harry Weinberger, himself a pacifist who specialized in civil liberties and censorship cases); distinguished journalists like John Reed and Lincoln Steffens as defense witnesses; a stolid male, middle-class jury; and a solemn, pedantic "law and order" judge who admired the talents of the defendants in spite of himself. The charges against the defendants bore only the flimsiest relation to the issue at hand: Goldman and Berkman were accused of misusing funds donated to the No-Conscription League, of accepting German money (a charge routinely leveled against antiwar activists), of advocating violence, not only at the May 18 antidraft meeting, but also earlier, and of "conspiring" to prevent draft registration. Though the outcome seemed certain, the two threw themselves into their defense with their usual energy, often staying up all night to prepare for the following day. Simply seating a jury required three days, during which time Goldman and Berkman subjected potential jurors to a vigorous barrage of questions about their politics. It was clear to everyone that the real crime on trial in the courtroom was the anarchism of the two defendants, which both the judge and the prosecuting attorney repeatedly defined as a philosophy advocating the overthrow of society by violent means. But since the prosecution resorted to technical and peripheral issues, the defendants, too, argued their cases partially on technical grounds.

A position of opposition to war and to the draft that had been publicly affirmed for almost thirty years could not be called a "conspiracy," they insisted. Furthermore, the May 18 anticonscription meeting had been held before the President signed the Selective Service Act. (The meeting began at 8 P.M., and the Act was signed by Wilson at 10:15 P.M.) In addition, they tried to distinguish between registration and conscription, noting that they had offered their support to those who refused to be conscripted, but said nothing about registration: an equivocal argument, as Richard Drinnon has observed, since both clearly opposed compulsory military service.[14]

Ultimately, the stand of Goldman and Berkman on political violence emerged as the central issue in the trial. The prosecution claimed that at the May 18 meeting, Goldman had stated, "we believe in violence and we will use violence."[15] She denied that she had made such a statement, which would indeed have been entirely out of character, and she challenged the veracity of the police stenographers who claimed to have recorded it. She argued that, as a "social student," she tried to explain the causes of violence; to explain was not to judge or to advocate. "To simply condemn the man who has committed an act of political violence, in order to save my own skin,

233

would be just as [un]pardonable as it would be on the part of the physician who is called upon to diagnose a case, to condemn the patient because the patient had tuberculosis or cancer or any other disease."[16] (Berkman put it somewhat differently in his own summing-up: "We all believe in violence and we all disbelieve in violence," he said; "it all depends upon the circumstances.")[17]

Adopting the tone of the earnest preacher in her two-hour-long summation, Goldman asserted that "an act of political violence at the bottom is the culminating result of organized violence on top. It is the result of violence which expresses itself in war, which expresses itself in capital punishment, which expresses itself in courts, which expresses itself in prison, which expresses itself in kicking and hounding people for the only crime they are guilty of: of having been born poor." On a messianic note, she quoted Havelock Ellis to argue that "the political criminal is the hero and the martyr and the saint of the new era." If her vision of anarchism was illegal, she added, so too "every great idea was considered extralegal, illegal, in its time and place."[18]

Goldman affirmed her commitment to education, not assassination, and then went on to raise larger questions posed by the trial itself. She pointed out the contradictions between claiming to fight for democracy abroad and suppressing free speech at home. If America "had entered the war to make the world safe for democracy," she insisted, "she must first make democracy safe in America." They were called unpatriotic, but in fact "the kind of patriotism we represent is the kind of patriotism which loves America with open eyes. . . . we love her beauty, we love her riches, we love her mountains and her forests, and above all we love the people who have produced her wealth and riches, who have created all her beauty, we love the dreamers and the philosophers and the thinkers who are giving America liberty," she affirmed with a Whitmanesque flourish. "But that must not make us blind to the social faults of America. That cannot make us deaf to the discords in America. That cannot compel us to be inarticulate to [sic] the terrible wrongs committed in the name of patriotism and in the name of the country." With free speech and free assembly and free press outraged daily, how could America give democracy to the world? Their real crime, "if crime there be," was to point out the economic and social causes of the present war. "Are we justified," she concluded her summing-up to

234

the jury, "in telling people that we will give them democracy in Europe, when we have no democracy here? . . . shall free speech and free press and free assemblage continue to be the heritage of the American people?"[19]

The jury, to no one's great surprise, did not see it that way, particularly after hearing Judge Mayer's stern warning that this was not "a trial of political principles," not "a trial of free speech," but "an indictment for crime." America, proclaimed Mayer, was "a country of law and order. The law must be obeyed." The jurors must consider that question only and not be diverted into thinking that anyone was on trial "for the expression of opinion."[20] On Monday afternoon, July 9, after thirty-nine minutes of deliberation, the jury announced their verdict: guilty as charged. Judge Mayer imposed the maximum sentence of two years imprisonment, fines of ten thousand dollars each, and possible deportation at the end of the prison sentences. Goldman had anticipated such an outcome several days earlier, yet continued to feel optimistic about the value of the trial: "We have been able to do remarkable work," she wrote to Agnes Inglis, "and if only we are not interrupted in our summing up it will be worth going to jail for the propaganda accomplished and that's the main thing after all."[21] John Reed felt less sanguine. "Who that heard it will ever forget the feeling of despair he experienced when Judge Mayer charged the jury in the Goldman-Berkman trial: 'This is not a question of free speech,' he said, 'for free speech is guaranteed under the Constitution. . . . but free speech does not mean license.' "[22] Margaret Anderson, who attended the trial and lunched daily with the two defendants, came away shaking with "the hideousness and absurdity" of the trial, noting however that it was converting many to anarchism. "One newspaper reporter told me that this trial was making a good Anarchist of him though he had never dreamed of needing to be one before; a university professor who came to all the hearings told me that he had always had a respect for the law until now; one of the biggest lawyers in the city laughed in a kind of fierce derision because, as he said, the prosecution hadn't a leg to stand on; one of the recognized intellectuals of the country remarked that Russia has never had cause for such rebellion as we are now facing; an artist said that he figured there were about a hundred perfectly good new Anarchists made during these ten days because of the court's asininity. . . ."[23]

Goldman received the verdict defiantly. Berkman, noted the *Times*, appeared very much crestfallen at the prospect of yet another long imprisonment. Judge Mayer ordered them to be taken immediately to their respective destinations—the Missouri State Prison and the Atlanta State Penitentiary. He denied them the usual time allowed to make final arrangements, a gratuitous insult that provoked a sarcastic "Thank you, your Honor" from the furious Goldman and an angry report by John Reed in the *Masses*. By 1 A.M. Tuesday morning, July 10, Emma Goldman, accompanied by two United States marshals, was traveling aboard the Baltimore and Ohio Railroad to the place which would be "home" for the next two years. Exhausted, drained, alternately elated and disgusted, disappointed at the lack of response in the I.W.W. or socialist press, she nevertheless felt that the struggle had been worthwhile. She had no regrets.

Judge Mayer, however, did have reservations, which he could not refrain from expressing lengthily in court after the jury had announced the verdict. He regretted in particular that "the extraordinary ability displayed by the defendants has not been utilized in support of law and order." He was sure that "the magnetic power of one of the defendants" might have been of "great service, in reforms legitimately advocated, for the betterment of conditions" in the world. Mayer imposed the maximum sentence "with regret that these abilities were not better used," though with the "profound conviction that I am speaking for organized law, for the kind of liberty that we know and we understand. . . ."[24]

The *New York Times* did not bother with regrets. Praising Judge Mayer for handling the trial "with perfect fairness, dignity and good temper," the *Times* editorialized that the conviction of "these chronic fomenters of disturbance for conspiracy . . . is a public service that honors the jury. . . . Deportation, if any country will consent to receive them, is the proper punishment of such alien demonstrators of anarchy."[25]

Shortly after Goldman arrived at Jefferson City, Harry Weinberger secured a writ of error from Justice Louis Brandeis, which allowed him to appeal the case to the Supreme Court. Weinberger managed to get Goldman and Berkman released from Jefferson City and Atlanta and brought back to the Tombs in New York City. En route to New York, Goldman wired Inglis that "the many tokens of love" she had received made her "feel humble. Have done little to receive so much. Am glad of the two weeks' experience in prison, brought me back to humanities [*sic*] suffering."[26] Getting the prisoners released on bail proved an arduous task. The government was determined to make their release as difficult as possible, imposing excessively high bail and harassing those who helped to raise it.

Within a few days, however, Goldman was released, only to find herself confronted with yet another crisis. In July of 1917, Alexander Berkman was indicted in connection with the explosion, on July 22, 1916, during a San Francisco Preparedness Day parade, of a bomb that killed ten people and wounded forty more. Berkman had been living in San Francisco at the time—he had moved west in the fall of 1915, accompanied by his lover Eleanor Fitzgerald—and was publishing a weekly anarchist labor paper, *The Blast*. At the time of the explosion, Goldman, too, was in San Francisco on her regular tour. The response to the bombing of most labor leaders and radicals was silence. Many radicals still recalled with alarm the grim irony of the *Los Angeles Times* bombing in 1910, when the Left had rallied to the support of the McNamara brothers, two labor union activists accused of the explosion, in the belief that they were the victims of a frame-up. Eventually the McNamaras had confessed, shattering the morale and prestige of those who had so passionately defended them. Like the McNamaras before them, the five people charged with the 1916 Preparedness Day bombing were active militants in the trade union movement. In the general atmosphere of hysteria, the press, the Chamber of Commerce, and city officials had been eager to hang not only the defendants, but any other radicals that they could drag into the case—particularly Alexander Berkman. But Berkman was not indicted until a year after the bombing. In the days immediately following the explosion, he and Goldman had almost singlehandedly initiated defense efforts on behalf of the accused.[27] Berkman had taken the most active role; he had revitalized the International Workers' Defense League (a group formed in San Francisco in 1912 to help radicals in the courts) and later traveled across the country as a League agent, talking to unions about the case. Of the five defendants, two were eventually convicted in a trial characterized by flagrant perjury, prejudice, and falsified evidence. In September of 1916, Warren Billings was sentenced to life imprisonment; the following February, Tom Mooney was sentenced to death by hanging. Only the most strenuous efforts by Berkman, Goldman, and the labor unions and individuals whose support they managed to enlist succeeded in mobilizing pressure from Washington that finally led the governor of California to commute the sentence to life imprisonment.

Now, one year after the San Francisco bombing, authorities on the West Coast were determined to try Alexander Berkman as well. With her Supreme Court case pending, anticonscription work, and *Mother Earth* to maintain, Emma Goldman found herself nonetheless compelled to devote nearly all her efforts to blocking the extradition of Berkman to California, where he would face almost certain conviction. For the next three and a half months, Goldman worked frantically to avoid this outcome, while Berkman remained locked up in the Tombs. She organized a Publicity Committee consisting of union activists, writers, and artists; with their help, she was able to recruit considerable labor and radical support. The United Hebrew Trades, the Amalgamated Clothing Workers, the Furriers, the Bookbinders, and other unions all gave money and assistance, as did the Jewish anarchists in New York, the *Freie Arbeiter Stimme*, and the socialist papers the *New York Call* and the *Jewish Daily Forward*. A delegation of some hundred labor unionists, led by the socialist lawyer Morris Hillquit (who was then a candidate for mayor of New York City) and Harry Weinberger, met in Albany with Governor Whitman. Their protests, along with advice (also mobilized by Goldman) to Whitman from Washington to proceed with extreme caution, persuaded the governor not to extradite Berkman until he had examined the records himself. The records from California, however, never arrived. Eventually, as a result of the strenuous protest campaign, the order for extradition was withdrawn. On November 14, 1917, Berkman was released from the Tombs. Tom Mooney and Warren Billings remained in prison until 1939, when they were pardoned by the newly elected Democratic governor, Culbert L. Olson.

Emma Goldman was relieved when Berkman regained his freedom. "It has been the hardest and most depressing month in a long time," she wrote Inglis late in November. "You will realize what it must have meant to me, when you will bear in mind that my life has never been very rosy, but the anxiety and worry about Berkman, and what seemed the utter hopelessness of getting him out on bail even, added to my own inner struggle, made life a perfect hell." Nevertheless she felt unable to enjoy this victory. "Human beings are certainly very queer and contradictory," she reflected. "We counted the moments until we would get S. free, and yet I have been suffering a terrible reaction, I suppose from the terrific anxiety of the last few months. I know I will get myself together in due time, but for the present I feel very restless."[28] She contemplated going on "a little tour," mainly to visit friends, but doubted that it would be worthwhile, since the Supreme Court would decide her case any day and she might be forced to return to New York and, ultimately, to prison.

Government repression of antiwar dissent was rapidly escalating during the summer and fall of 1917, accompanied by the vigilante actions of groups of professionals and businessmen around the country. The Wobblies in particular were victims of savage vigilante violence. In July, hundreds of Wobbly copper miners from Jerome and Bisbee in southern Arizona were sent out into the desert in cattle cars, without food or water. In the same month, Wobbly organizer Frank Little was lynched in Butte, Montana. Antiwar protesters around the country were jeered, beaten, tarred and feathered, and driven out of towns. Their meetings were banned or broken up, their halls raided and wrecked; their papers were seized and denied second-class mailing privileges by the Post Office Department, which had been empowered by the Espionage Act to suppress all antiwar material. Mass arrests of Wobbly leaders began in September with a series of raids of I.W.W. halls.

Goldman watched these events with mixed feelings. "Deeply moved as I am by the plight of the IWW and the Socialists," she wrote Inglis in October of 1917, "I yet feel that it is inevitable that they too should have to pay the price during the war hysteria. The poor fools remained indifferent so long as the persecution was directed against the anarchists, not only that but they themselves would have nothing to do with us or make as much as a comment when we were driven from pillar to post and our boys thrown into prison. Not one of the IWW papers had anything to say when we were hustled out of town. The Call had 5 lines. They were simply indifferent. When the Blast and later ME were suppressed and the Socialists had a protest meeting we could get no one of them to say a word about our papers. . . . Please don't think I am vindictive, that I rejoice now in the persecution of the S[ocialists] or IWW. I only point out what few people seem to realize, namely this, reaction

239

begins always with the most unpopular and ends with everybody who dares to speak up. I only hope the IWW and S will learn this lesson. Perhaps their trouble will not be in vain. But at the same time I will certainly help them as much as is in my power."[29] By December, every frontline I.W.W. leader was in prison, and during 1918 several thousand more Wobblies were arrested and locked up. At the mass I.W.W. trials of 1918 and 1919, the sentences ranged from a few months to twenty years, plus stiff fines. The organization was reduced to inaction, converted from a labor union to a legal defense committee, and had to devote all its energies to protecting its members in court. The Socialist party was eventually bludgeoned into submission and silence, its papers and magazines suppressed, its leaders in prison. Anarchist groups were spied upon, their publications banned, their meeting places—such as the Ferrer Center— forced to close, their members harassed, the most outspoken among them arrested and, often, held for deportation.

Mother Earth was also a casualty, along with *The Masses*. The August 1917 edition of the magazine, the last full issue to appear, was banned from the mails. For Goldman the demise of the magazine was a deep personal loss. "No one will realize the blow this will strike in my heart," she lamented to Inglis. "For twelve years I have struggled and suffered more than any mother has ever done for her child to maintain *Mother Earth*."[30] Though she still hoped that underground circulation might be possible, this plan proved unworkable. From October of 1917 to May of 1918, Goldman, Stella Ballantine, and Eleanor Fitzgerald published the *Mother Earth Bulletin*, an eight-page summary of news about the resistance to the war and about Russia; but it, too, was declared "unmailable" in May of 1918.

Still, Goldman felt optimistic. The repression of all dissent, she believed, would ultimately benefit the Left by exposing the fraudulence of American claims to democracy and justice. "Nothing better could have happened for the advancement of Revolutionary ideas than that so many political offenders were sent to prison," she would later write. "From now on no one will dare maintain in any public meeting that we have free speech and free press. It will be ridiculed like that other famous boast that everyone can become a millionaire in our country. I used to reply, yes indeed, provided one knows how to steal the first million without being caught. That after all is the line of demarcation between the thief within prison and the one outside it."[31] The future was not without hope.

Indeed, it seemed, the millennium had already arrived in Russia—the fulfillment of decades of revolutionary dreams and sacrifices. The abdication of the czar in February of 1917 was followed by the formation of a moderate Provisional Government determined to prosecute the war against Germany and to transform the autocracy into a constitutional republic. The Provisional Government, headed by Alexander Kerensky, soon found itself threatened on the Right by counterrevolutionary generals loyal to the czar and on the Left by the increasingly powerful Bolsheviks, together with workers, soldiers, and peasants demanding land, bread, and peace with growing urgency. By September the Provisional Government had become virtually paralyzed, unable to bring the war to a successful conclusion, to satisfy the starving, angry populace, or to stifle the growing militance of the powerful Petrograd Soviet, now presided over by Trotsky. On the night of October 25, as both counterrevolutionary and German armies advanced on the capital, the Bolsheviks, acting in the name of the Soviets, quietly assumed power.

For a short time after the February revolution, both Goldman and Berkman had contemplated a return to their native land. Goldman wrote Inglis that the revolution had created an upheaval "among all of us Russians who have watched the evil regime of the Czar." She and Berkman planned to join the exodus of Russian immigrants and exiles who were now returning to their homeland, she informed Inglis on March 31. "The irony of it is," she added prophetically, "that we may now go to Russia and may not come back to America. It is almost certain that we will not be allowed in if we leave the country."[32] By April 17, however, the trip to Russia had been indefinitely postponed. Some of the returning revolutionists had been detained en route by the British, and, noted Emma as if relieved, there was "no sense getting into the clutches of England."[33] Actually, a great many Russian émigrés succeeded in returning home from outposts in Europe or America during the spring and summer of 1917; many of them—including friends of Goldman such as William Shatov—assumed prominent roles in the revolutionary government. That Goldman and Berkman so quickly abandoned their plans to return to Russia suggests the extent to which they now felt themselves committed to America. Deeply excited by the events in Russia as she was, Goldman now saw her role not as a participant but as a publicist who would defend that revolution to Americans, of whom she felt herself to be one.

Caught up in the euphoria of these historic days, Goldman began immediately to lecture about Russia. Early in December, she decided to undertake a short tour, both to publicize events in Russia and to raise money for legal defense for herself, Berkman, and the beleaguered Wobblies. Under constant surveillance by "operatives" of the semiofficial American Protective League—which energetically investigated all suspicions of "disloyalty" for the Justice Department—she traveled in December and January as far west as Detroit and Chicago, lecturing in English and in Yiddish in auditoriums packed with eager young people. Speaking on "The Boylsheviki [sic] Revolution: Its Promise and Fulfillment" and "Women Martyrs of Russia," she seemed now to be running on pure will, straining her resources to the limit in order to spread the news about Russia. Significantly, these lectures also emphasized the revolutionary legacy of America and alluded frequently to the Declaration of Independence—"so little known by the average person"—and to Thomas Jefferson, Patrick Henry, and the nineteenth-century abolitionists as the precursors of a genuine social revolution in this country.

From the start, Goldman understood clearly that the Bolsheviks "were Marxists and therefore governmentalists." She defended them on the grounds that many aspects of their program, such as expropriation and redistribution of land, workers' control of industry, and an end to the war, were consistent with anarchist aims. The Bolsheviks, she argued, had abandoned orthodox Marxist theory about the necessity for a bourgeois, capitalist revolution to precede the transition to socialism. Instead they had come to accept the anarchist view of a direct transition to socialism. Countering charges in the American press that the Bolsheviks were German agents, barbarians, or savages, she portrayed them as libertarians, dedicated revolutionists determined to "place all the natural resources and the wealth of the country in the hands of the people for common holding and common use, because the Russian people are by instinct and tradition communists, and have neither need nor desire for the competitive system." Those Russian revolutionists—Kropotkin, Breshkovskaya—who opposed the Bolsheviks, she explained, had been "lured by the glamour of political liberalism" as represented by Western Europe and had failed to realize "that the line of demarcation between liberalism and autocracy is purely imaginary. . . ." Moreover, these revolutionists would soon come to realize that the Bolsheviks "represent the most fundamental, far-reaching and all-embracing principles of human freedom and of economic well-being."[34]

Goldman's enthusiasm was shared at first by most anarchists in Russia and in America. Although the Russian anarchists—a relatively small but vociferous movement of disparate, often quarreling groups—had long been at odds with the Bolsheviks, the February Revolution had temporarily brought them together. Anarchists had worked closely with Bolsheviks against the Kerensky government, and following the October Revolution, many anarchists actively supported the new regime, with some—the "soviet anarchists"—actually taking official positions within the government. But it was not long before tensions again cropped up, as the Bolsheviks pushed to extend state control over industry and party control of the Soviets. Many Russian anarchists, in contrast with their American counterparts, also protested Russia's Brest-Litovsk peace treaty with Germany, which they regarded as an unwarranted accommodation to German imperialism. By early 1918, the Russian anarchists had essentially moved into the opposition, their press keeping up a steady barrage of criticism. The Bolsheviks retaliated in April of 1918 with the first of a long series of raids on anarchist centers and publishing houses, arresting and imprisoning many militants. The summer of 1918 saw a reversion to terrorism by anarchists and Left Socialist Revolutionaries, who engaged in "expropriations" (of residences and offices) and in assassination attempts against prominent Bolsheviks. By this time, however, the civil war had begun, with the revolution fighting for its life against the combined assaults of White Russian armies and an Allied invasionary force. Although this critical new situation provoked acrimonious debates among the anarchists in Russia, in the end, according to Paul Avrich, a large majority decided to support the regime, with varying degrees of enthusiasm.[35] In America, however, many anarchists—the Yiddish anarchists of the *Freie Arbeiter Stimme*, for example—remained skeptical, if not hostile. In their continuing defense of the Soviet Union, Goldman and Berkman now had to meet growing criticism from within their own ranks.

Emma had not finished checking the proofs for her glowing pamphlet, "The Truth about the Boylsheviki [sic]"—dedicated to the Bolsheviks "in appreciation of their glorious work and their inspiration in awakening Boylshevism [sic] in America"—when she received word from Harry Weinberger that the Supreme Court had, predictably, upheld the Selective Service Law and turned down her appeal and Berkman's. In the days before her sentence was due to begin, she helped organize a Political Prisoners' Amnesty League—headed by the faithful Eleanor Fitzgerald, Leonard Abbott, and a Modern School associate, Prince Hopkins—whose purpose was to aid conscientious objectors, work for the recognition of political prisoners, and press for their amnesty. On February 4, Goldman and Berkman surrendered themselves to authorities at the New York Federal Building. Within a few hours, Berkman was headed for Atlanta and Goldman for Jefferson City, Missouri, where she would spend the next twenty months. En route to the penitentiary, Emma dashed off a quick note of farewell to Agnes Inglis. "Two years imprisonment for having made an uncompromising stand for one's Ideal. Why that is a small price," she announced. She wanted her friend to know that she felt "perfectly at ease and serene. Never did I have such an exalted sense of having remained absolutely true to my Ideal and I can say the same for Berkman. All else is immaterial."[36]

PART
6

PRISONER
AND
DEPORTEE

C H A P T E R

15

"MY ONE GREAT LOVE—MY IDEAL"

Say this to all our friends," Goldman wrote Stella from prison, "no one need worry about me. I am quite alright. I have my one Great Love—my Ideal to sustain me, nothing else matters. There are inconveniences of course, but what do they amount to compared with the great events of our time? In moments of depression I look to Russia. She acts like a ray of sunshine working its way through the black clouds. Tell our friends I think of them all with affection. I know they are interested in my welfare. They can help me best by remaining true to our Ideal and our work. I too shall remain true, no matter what happens."[1]

In early February of 1918, Goldman arrived at the Missouri State Penitentiary in Jefferson City, the state capital, about one hundred miles west of St. Louis on bluffs overlooking the Missouri River. The largest prison in the United States, the institution housed some twenty-three hundred people, of whom approximately one hundred were women. Although Goldman, recalling Blackwell's Island in 1893, thought the prison "a model in many respects," a 1929 report found it "chiefly notable for its grave defects," which included overcrowding, low sanitary standards, bad working conditions in the shops, poor medical services, harsh methods of discipline, and the absence of any kind of educational program.[2] The women prisoners were housed in a new women's department: a long building with a cage of cells—four high and two deep, facing in opposite directions—in the center. Windows were plentiful in the cell-house, but they were filthy, painted over, or nailed shut. Each cell measured seven feet wide, eight feet deep and seven feet high, with solid steel ceilings, cement floors, and steel-barred fronts. Each had a toilet, a sink with running cold water, and a steel bunk fastened to the wall, with two bags of straw: one for a mattress, the other for a pillow. A crude kitchen table, broken-down chair, broom, and dustpan completed the furnishings. Each woman was also given raspy brown muslin prison garb to replace her own, which was taken from her when she entered. Those long, wide dresses, of 1890s vintage, fitted like a circus tent around a center pole; the shoes were cheap and uncomfortable. With the primitive laundry facilities, clothes were never completely clean.[3]

The shop, where prisoners spent nine-hour shifts six days a week, was a long narrow room filled with a double row of antiquated sewing machines. Small windows placed eight feet up near the ceiling, along one side of the room only, provided minimal light and made direct ventilation impossible. Electric lights were required on even the brightest days, and the air was always stifling and foul. After a short breaking-in period, inmates were required, on pain of severe punishment, to make a given number of jackets, overalls, suspenders, or jumpers per day. For Emma the "task" was fifty-four jackets daily, a number she managed to complete after almost nine months in prison.[4] The clothing manufactured by the inmates, for which they were paid nominal wages, was produced under contract for reputable manufacturing companies which then sold the goods at a substantial profit to an unsuspecting public, although some prison industries were now operated for the state rather than for private entrepreneurs.

The dining hall was another source of misery. The large, gloomy, cockroach-infested room was filled with rows of long wooden tables and benches, each seating eight women. Table settings consisted of rusty tin dishes and cast-iron knives and forks (no spoons). The food arrived cold, often rancid or spoiled, and full of bugs. Prisoners frequently suffered from severe malnutrition. The diet rarely varied: breakfast consisted of corn syrup, bread, rank hash, and "a dark liquid by courtesy called coffee." Twice a week, worm-filled oatmeal supplemented the regular menu. Lunch brought a fair beef stew, a vegetable, bread, and water; suppers meant bread and corn syrup, sometimes stewed fruit ("always well seasoned with worms"), and the "so-called coffee." Meals were of course eaten in total silence, since talking was allowed only in strictly limited recreation periods.[5]

The harsh treatment meted out to the prisoners exacerbated their physical discomfort. Kate Richards O'Hare, Goldman's fellow political prisoner, bitterly recalled the routine brutality of guards to prisoners, most of whom were poor and uneducated and many of whom were physically ill, mentally retarded, or emotionally disturbed. "Laughter, love, and kindness are the three most heinous crimes possible to a convict," wrote O'Hare. "In all the fourteen months I spent in prison, I never heard an inmate addressed courteously; never heard one single kind, encouraging, or helpful word from the petty officials with whom we were in constant contact."[6]

Goldman found some consolation in the fact that she could (eventually) send up to three letters a week, receive packages and printed material from the outside (privileges denied to Berkman at Atlanta), and enjoy more visits than had been allowed in her previous prison term. Although the men's wing of the prison had a library, the women could not use it until O'Hare's protests finally secured borrowing privileges. Always enterprising, Emma immediately set about "renovating" her cell by decorating the walls with panels of orange crepe paper and pictures. Since the status of political prisoner was not officially recognized (although the prisoners themselves regarded the "politicals" as "aristocrats"), Goldman, like any other inmate, had to work long hours daily in the prison shop. The routine was grueling, though even here Goldman could extract benefits. "Awakened at 5 AM, rather difficult to get used to, but one can do so much under pressure. Breakfast 6:15, in Shop 6:30. I rather like my work. Poor people and not parasites will wear what I make. Also I am not contributing to the war. Lunch 11:30. 1/2 hour rest in cell. Shop again until 4:30. Nine hours in all. So many workers still striking for nine hours. You see the advantage. Supper until 6 pm. Then recreation in yard, which is the one worth while thing everybody is looking forward to. Friday after work cell cleaning and bathing. Sunday the arrangement differs. It includes later breakfast and church. Don't be shocked. I shall attend it, today anyway. Want the experience, besides my soul needs salvation, don't you think? Altogether there is no need to worry about me. Greater heroes and martyrs than I have paid for their ideals with prison and even death, so why not I? Babushka, L[ouise] M[ichel], Spiridonovna, and a galaxy of others will sustain me. . . ."[7]

Despite Emma's lighthearted tone, the nine hours she spent every day in the fetid shop, bent over a sewing maching under the constant surveillance of a sadistic foreman and a subservient shop matron, exacted a severe mental and physical toll. The work demanded absolute concentration; even looking at visitors or other prisoners was prohibited, as was talking, which was severely punished. The threat of confinement in "the hole" or of losing minimal privileges if one failed to make the daily quota led to chronic anxiety among most inmates. Nearly fifty years old and in good health, although slightly overweight, Goldman generally took the physical strains of prison with cheerful good humor (except for the lack of fresh air, which constantly galled her). But throughout this prison term she suffered severe pain at the back of her head and in her neck and spine. The only remedy was to ask to be excused from the shop or for an additional bath (one per week was regulation); but she found these requests humiliating and painful, "like having a tooth pulled each time," she told Stella. Despite the strain of work in the prison shop, Emma preferred it to the isolation and inactivity of just remaining in her cell. "In fact," she wrote Stella, using a simile reminiscent of her relations with Ben Reitman, "the shop and I are like man and wife who live like cat and dog when they are together, yet long for each other when they are apart. The perversity of human nature."[8] Goldman also suffered from periodic stomach complaints and referred jokingly to the amount of castor oil she was compelled to take. Part of her time in prison, she subsisted mainly on food sent to her from the outside.

Sundays afforded some relief. Soon after her arrival, however, Emma decided not to attend church and was thereupon deprived of the Sunday exercise period outdoors. "It is not only that I do not believe in the Church," she explained to Stella, "it is also because it is so uninteresting. If at least the piano were tuned and the Pianist could play I should even put up with the rest. It is torture as it is now, so I will stay away. When all the windows are open I will get enough light and air for reading while the others are at Church. Just now there seems to be a conspiracy against air. . . ."[9] Sundays, in fact, were the most important day of the week for Goldman—a feast of reading and writing letters. "In the morning I gorge myself by staying in bed until nine," she wrote Stella, "then have breakfast in my cell, read a little, and then begin the acrobatic stunt of concentrating a week's thoughts and emotions on two pages, it is some art believe me. It takes me from 1–3 pm to write you and H[arry] W[einberger]. Sometimes I rewrite both letters twice. Since we have had the epidemic [flu] we had no chapel, so I have not been denied the afternoon exercise, but I only go down when we are allowed in the yard; otherwise I stay in my cell and try to read, amidst the pandemonium of nearly 80 voices. Then in the Eve. when comparative quiet is established, I have supper, sponge bath, prepare my things for the week and read, thus ends the only day I enjoy as far as one can enjoy a day in prison."[10]

Toward the other prisoners, Goldman's attitude was above all maternal. She shared with them the food, clothing, magazines, and newspapers that she received from the outside. She intervened with prison officials on their behalf, entreated friends to write them letters and send gifts, tried to hasten parole for some and find jobs for others. She felt pained by the misery all around her, especially the pathetic helplessness and ignorance of the other women. "They feel their sufferings savagely but they know nothing of the forces and conditions which make them," Goldman wrote Agnes Inglis. "Their enemies are the policeman, the detective, the judge, not the whole cruel inhuman system. Yet none of them are so dense that they could not [join] the fight if only it were shown to them."[11]

Prison also provided Goldman with her first prolonged contact with poor black women, who formed two-thirds of the female population at Jefferson City. Like most immigrant radicals, Goldman had not devoted much attention to the segregation, overwhelming poverty, and mounting violence confronting blacks at the turn of the century. There were no black contributors to *Mother Earth* and no articles dealing with black culture or racism. According to Reitman, few black people attended Goldman's lectures (although the lectures on the West Coast attracted a fair number of Japanese and Chinese.[12] Still, *Mother Earth* periodically registered a protest against the lynchings and race riots of the war years. In her report "The Situation in America," prepared for the 1907 Amsterdam Congress, Goldman compared the persecution of blacks in America to that of the Jews in Russia. Although slavery had been abolished "legally and theoretically," in reality "the negro is as much a slave now as in antebellum days, and even more ostracized socially and exploited economically," in the North as well as in the South.[13] Goldman's comments in her prison letters and later descriptions of her prison years indicate that she liked and respected the black women of Jefferson City. They had more pride and self-respect, she found, and were not as cringing or submissive as the whites; they showed a greater spirit of solidarity with one another. Goldman expressed particular gratitude toward the black women who frequently helped her make the "task" by donating their finished jackets to her. Nonetheless, as she herself admitted when she met Paul Robeson in the twenties in London, she was not fully aware of the depths of racism in America while she had lived there. "I have never realized the cruelty to the Negro quite so much as I have since I met the Robesons," she would later write. "It is too awful to contemplate. What agony of spirit they must endure, because of the brutal discrimination against their race."[14]

Goldman's closest companions in prison were the other "politicals": Gabriella Antolini, a nineteen-year-old Italian immigrant anarchist, and especially Kate Richards O'Hare, the Kansas-born socialist activist and organizer sentenced to five years' imprisonment for an antiwar speech delivered in July of 1917. After the failure of her appeals, O'Hare had arrived at Jefferson City on April 15, 1919, and was placed in a cell adjoining Goldman's. Seven years younger than Emma, Kate O'Hare had grown up in Kansas and Missouri, the daughter of a farmer turned shopkeeper. After a deeply religious adolescence, she had been converted to socialism through her contacts with the labor leader "Mother" Jones and the group associated with the Kansas socialist newspaper *Appeal to Reason*. Along with her husband, Frank O'Hare, she soon became a respected socialist organizer among the farmers of the Great Plains. She was also a writer, the editor of a socialist weekly, the *National Rip-Saw*, the only woman member of the Socialist party executive committee, a candidate for Congress, and the mother of four children.

When the tall, somewhat reserved, and severe-looking O'Hare arrived at Jefferson City, her comrades as well as Goldman's nervously awaited a clash between the outstanding woman socialist—as American as apple pie—and the great "Russian" woman anarchist. Had they met on the outside, admitted Emma, "we should have probably argued furiously and have remained strangers for the rest of our lives."[15] In prison, however, they got along famously, engaging in a friendly, affectionate, often teasing rivalry over who could do most for the other prisoners and who was most popular. Laying to rest the shadows of Bakunin and Marx, they quickly developed a warm friendship and, along with Gabriella Antolini, became as inseparable as "The Trinity," their prison nickname. Theoretical disagreements were relegated to the level of good-humored jokes. "Instead of hurling anarchist texts at me," reported Kate, "Emma raps on the wall of the cell and says, 'Get busy Kate, it's time to feed the monkeys, pass the food down the line.' "[16] Kate admired Emma's gift for mothering, her tenderness and kindness toward the most forsaken and forlorn women. As Kate said, the women had no conception of Emma's teachings and did not know if anarchy was "a breakfast food or a corn cure; but Emma DID things for them. She fought for them when she felt they were being wronged; she fed them when they were hungry, and cared for them when they were ill and cheered them when they were sad."[17] Emma, for her part, admired O'Hare's ability to bring about concrete improvements in the prison regime. Kate complained about the food being cold: the food was brought to the table hot. She complained about the sick and the healthy having to share the same bathwater: showers were installed. She wrote about the gloominess of the place: the walls were whitewashed. Goldman attributed these achievements partly to O'Hare's husband, who had political influence in the state, and also to the fact that Kate was "a Socialist and not one of them dynamite-eating Anarchists."[18]

To Kate, Emma was "a brainy, intellectual woman and a wonderful study in psychology." Most of all, she was "the tender, cosmic mother, the wise understanding woman, the faithful sister, the loyal comrade."[19] To Emma, Kate was a cheerful companion who eased her loneliness and sense of isolation. Emma would make dinners for

Kate from food sent her from the outside; and Kate, who was eventually permitted a typewriter, would take dictation from Emma, whose hit-and-miss typing was no easier to read than her cramped prison scrawl. Each welcomed the intellectual companionship of another "political"; each seemed amused by the quirks of the other. Emma, for example, was highly entertained by Kate's preoccupation with her hair—her insistence on maintaining an elaborate coiffure that required complicated preparations every evening. Kate relished Emma's expressiveness; she described, for example, how Emma, enraged by the pieties of a visiting evangelist whose sermon she had attended by mistake, "just swelled up like the toad in the fable until I was absolutely sure she would literally explode."[20] In her letters, Emma often contrasted Kate's serene, cheery, adaptable manner with her own anguished "Slav-Jewish soul" that "exhausts itself in a vain attempt to bring solace to every tortured spirit. Kate has none of that. She is calm, easygoing, thoroughly efficient." Coming from one who admired intensity and passion, this assessment was not entirely flattering.[21] Still, they were having fine times together, Emma informed Harry Weinberger. "Our main sport is to see who can feed the most fellow prisoners. It's great fun."[22] Kate, comparing herself with Emma, thought that "the girls love me too, but never as they loved Emma Goldman. To them I am the dispenser of chewing gum and peppermint drops, a perambulating spelling book, dictionary and compendium of all known wisdom. I am lawyer, priest and physician . . . but I do not and never can fill Emma's place in their hearts."[23]

While in prison, Goldman considered writing an autobiography. She also contemplated a book on women in prison. After working nine hours in the shop, however, she had little energy or inclination for extended reflection or writing. Besides the distraction of persistent physical pain, Goldman needed to stay involved with the outside world, to maintain her wide network of contacts, and to watch over all matters relating to her imprisonment, release, and possible deportation. Instead of immersing herself in the past, she decided rather to become as engaged as possible in political life on the outside. "The Federal authorities had robbed me of my forum and of *Mother Earth*," she later wrote, "and letters became my platform."[24] Though she did no more than jot down a few reminiscences for a projected memoir, she did write hundreds of letters, most of them in a tiny, compressed, illegible longhand that contrasted strongly with her usual expansive scrawl. The letters are, by and large, not introspective or intimate. They are full of information about the daily facts of prison life, her physical and mental condition, her reactions to current events and the books she was reading, her opinions about the prison regime and other inmates, and her messages to friends. And always there are commands: contact the following people; send letters of thanks to those who had mailed presents; organize antiwar demonstrations; write manifestos; purchase clothing; renew subscriptions; arrange visits; order food; raise money.

Goldman's two principal correspondents while she was in prison were her attorney, Harry Weinberger, with whom she liked to discuss the legal ramifications of her imprisonment and deportation case, and her beloved niece Stella Ballantine, whom she had appointed as her secretary, agent, assistant, and general representative for the term of her incarceration. Stella, now an intense, dark-haired woman of about thirty, made valiant efforts to juggle the demands of her young child, her actor husband, and her exigent aunt, but by the summer of 1918 she was prostrate with exhaustion. Her responsibilities included taking care of Goldman's personal needs in prison, the management of the *Mother Earth* bookshop, and—along with Leonard Abbott, Prince Hopkins, and Eleanor Fitzgerald—work in the Political Prisoners' Amnesty League.

Though she did not correspond with them directly, Emma asked for news about the other members of her large extended family, including her mother, sisters, brothers, and her numerous nieces, nephews, and cousins. Emma had also grown closer to her half sister Lena, who now wrote letters to her and affirmed her affection. Helene, however, suffered a double tragedy during this period that seemed to distance her from Emma. In January of 1917, Helene's husband, Jacob Hochstein, died. Less than two years later, in October of 1918, her son David Hochstein, the talented young violinist who had already embarked on a promising professional career, was killed in the Argonne Forest just a month before the armistice. His body was never found. The loss of her son, following so soon upon the death of her husband, was a devastating blow to Helene.

Though Emma had not been close to David, she was saddened by his death. She felt it ironic that he had died in a war that she had gone to jail for opposing. He had chosen active duty, although as a musician he could have been excused from the army or have served in some musical capacity. Goldman wondered if she could have dissuaded him from enlisting, had she tried to persuade him of her views. But if she was sympathetic at first to Helene's pain and frustrated by her own inability to help, Emma soon became impatient and resentful of her sister's continuing, overwhelming grief. "I don't have to tell you how deeply the tragic end of D has affected me," she wrote Stella coldly in March of 1919, "but after all he is but one of many who were sacrificed." Emma complained that Helene's motherhood had made her "narrow. So much so that she has lost all concern for everybody else. . . . My heart goes out to Helena, but there are greater tragedies than even David's death." Emma felt at a loss about how to communicate with her grieving sister. "If I can muster up spirit, I will write her," she told Stella grudgingly. "When one lives in the universe, it is most difficult to speak the language of one limited part, so now it is hard for me to find the right expression that would soothe. . . ."[25]

Emma was understandably upset that Helene, who had always been like a mother to her, was now distraught with grief over her son to the exclusion of all else. Especially now, when Emma was locked up and hence in a particularly vulnerable and needy situation herself, she could not grasp the depth of her sister's sorrow, and she reacted with childish expressions of irritation, hurt, jealousy, and resentment. When by August of 1919, almost a year after David's death, Helene continued to suffer uncontrollable crying spells and remained in deep mourning, Emma concluded harshly that her sister was "certainly sick" and suffered from "hysteria and melancholia." She felt that Helene should leave home and seek professional psychological help.[26] Helene, in fact, never recovered from her grief over the double loss of her husband and son. She died in Rochester on July 7, 1920, shortly after presiding over the opening of the Hochstein School of Music, established in memory of David Hochstein.

When she was not writing letters, Goldman read avidly. She loved John Reed's *Ten Days That Shook the World*, even forgiving Reed his grudging mention of the part played by the anarchists. She read the letters of Ann Gilchrist to Walt Whitman; Galsworthy's *Saint's Progress*; Freud's "Thoughts on War and Death"; Frank Harris's *Contemporary Portraits*; works by Louise Bryant (on Russia), Romain Rolland, Gorky, and Dreiser; the letters of Catherine Breshkovskaya; and David Graham Phillips's *Susan Lenox*. She devoured a multitude of newspapers and magazines, which she received regularly. Her favorite was *The Nation*, "the best, the most fearless, and above all the most liberal publication in the country," which took a resolutely antiwar stand and gave strong sympathetic coverage to events in Russia.[27] She also liked the socialist New York *Call* and the liberal prolabor *San Francisco Bulletin*, which, she told editor Fremont Older, was "making the rounds among my comrades in the cages."[28] Despite the prowar stand of *The New Republic*, Goldman enjoyed its sympathetic articles on Russia.[29] The socialist *Volks Zeitung*, Goldman also felt, was making a brave fight.[30] She reserved her venom for the prowar radical and liberal press. The *Appeal to Reason*, the prowar socialist paper, Goldman called "a renegade sheet," feeling that it lacked all character and self-respect.[31] Even worse was the Jewish anarchist paper, the "simply awful, sickeningly cringing and stupid" *Freie Arbeiter Stimme*, which had come out against the Russian Revolution.[32] She preferred "our grandmother" the *New York Times*, which was "frankly reactionary," to the *New York Post*, which "makes a pretense of liberalism."[33] Goldman's attitude toward the press reflected her often repeated conviction that during a period of repression, the Left must stand together.

Goldman followed with intense interest the various trials of antiwar resisters. She was exhilarated by the strong stand taken by the editors of *The Masses* during their trial in the spring of 1918, and especially by Max Eastman, whom she had watched vacillate between "worship" and repudiation of Woodrow Wilson. He was a poet, she conceded, so he could afford to contradict himself; but when he maintained his opposition to the war, she was delighted. *The Masses*'s editors were eventually acquitted, much to Goldman's satisfaction. She found Eugene Debs's courtroom speech during his trial tremendously inspiring, comparable to that of her Haymarket hero Albert Parsons. There were also the trials of Rose Pastor Stokes, who had reversed her initial prowar position and was sentenced to ten years' imprisonment (the sentence was later overturned on appeal); Roger Baldwin, for his stand as a conscientious objector (Baldwin went to jail for ten months); the important "Abrams" trial of several young anarchists sentenced to twenty-year jail terms for distributing Yiddish leaflets protesting American intervention in Russia; and the various trials of I.W.W. leaders and militants.

Goldman argued strongly in her letters for amnesty and urged her friends to organize a campaign to compel the government to grant the status of political prisoners, rather than grouping all prisoners together. She felt that it was essential to make a distinction between "common crime and political offense," for the workers would never listen to the social rebel "unless they cease seeing in him a criminal, a villain, a wild beast." The concept of amnesty had important educational value—it would make workers realize that anyone who threatened capitalism was considered an enemy, and that a striker was just as likely to get twenty years in jail as an anarchist who proclaimed the former's right to strike. What really mattered was not so much the attainment of amnesty or recognition by the government of the status of political prisoners, but the campaign itself— "work and publicity are the principal thing." Typically, she also saw in the failure of amnesty a possible political gain. "If amnesty is denied, the merrier," she wrote Stella. "It will serve as the best possible example [of] how little feeling there really is for liberty in our land and that it is one thing to turn out fine phrases and another to act upon them."[34]

Goldman's most excited attention, throughout her imprisonment, was directed toward events in Russia. She eagerly read all the articles in the American liberal and radical press that escaped censorship and whatever issues of the foreign press—such as the Russian anarcho-syndicalist paper *Golos Truda*—that her comrades could get to her. Despite her earlier enthusiasm, by the spring of 1918 Goldman had begun to express concern that the goals and methods of the Bolsheviks were not those of the anarchists. "If our newspaper writers knew even the ABC of anarchism," she wrote Stella indignantly in January of 1919, "they would never call the Bolsheviks that. Talk about centralists, why their programme which appeared in the supplement of *The Nation* should gladden the heart of the most rigid governmentalist."[35] By now she had developed serious reservations about the course of events in the Soviet Union, and she felt much less optimistic than Berkman about the prospects of the revolution. She dreaded the idolization of the state in whatever form. "So when I consider that the same monster is being set up in Russia I grow cold all over," she wrote early in 1919. "Of course it is to be a democracy of the Proletariat, but in the end it will be the same delusion, the same snare, the same commoniser of all that is ideal and beautiful."[36] Still, she argued, the Bolsheviks were attacked and opposed on all sides by the forces of capitalism and reaction, and that, she insisted repeatedly, was reason enough to support them. "As an anarchist I am opposed to the rigid centralization the Boyl. proclaim and as much opposed to the Dictatorship of the Proletariat as to that of the Bourgeoisie," she wrote Weinberger in September of 1918. "But the very fact that they are so attacked and maligned compels me to stand up for them and with them."[37] She emphasized this position a few months later, insisting that she realized the "Boylshevikii [sic] are Socialists and believe implicitly in the State. But now, with the whole World against them, I feel it is up to us, the Anarchists, to stand for them. Plenty of time to thrash out differences when Russia is on her feet again."[38] Goldman was especially incensed by the *Freie Arbeiter Stimme*, whose attacks on the Bolsheviks she found "more outrageous . . . than anything in the *Times*," even though she agreed with their sense that Bolshevism meant "the annihilation of all individual and group initiative."[39] When one of her anarchist comrades, Jake Margolis, a lawyer in Pittsburgh, defended his criticism of Bolshevism, asserting that the Bolsheviks did not represent the Russian people, Goldman responded fiercely. If they did not represent the people, if they had not dared to touch the institution of private property, if they had not proclaimed a new and world-stirring gospel, she argued, there would now be no move afoot by the most powerful capitalist governments to crush them. "Tell him also," she wrote Stella angrily in March of 1919, "I am just as much opposed to any and every dictatorship and any and every concentration of power in the hands of the state as he is. But so long as the Boyl. are besieged on all sides, hated and despised, maligned and misrepresented, and now to be crushed, my place is with them, and so is that of Jake and all the others who have a revolutionary spark left. I can't for the life of me understand how any one can theorize or thrash out differences in the face of such a dreadful calamity as the attempt to crush the Soviet. Now is not the time, that's all there is to it."[40]

Goldman's impatient attitude toward the criticisms of Russia placed her at odds once again with the other members of her movement. In her later accounts of her experience in Russia, Goldman would play down her earlier reservations for dramatic effect, so as to highlight her own shift of opinion. But in fact the seeds of that later disillusionment were clearly present in her prison letters of 1918 and

1919. When she eventually reversed her position toward the Soviet Union, it would not be so much the discovery of a new perspective —the "revaluation of all values," as she claimed—as the reconfirmation of long-held values, derived from both anarchism and America, which she had temporarily relegated to a secondary position.

A poignant sidelight to Goldman's arguments about the Soviet Union was provided by her heroine Catherine Breshkovskaya ("Babushka"), who, after several decades of anticzarist agitation, Siberian imprisonments, and leadership in the Socialist Revolutionary party, was now actively campaigning in the United States *against* the Bolsheviks. In her letters to Stella and others, Goldman brooded over Babushka's apostasy, searching for some explanation for her reversal. Was it old age? Intellectual or spiritual exhaustion? Ignorance of the facts? Emma could not find an answer. In a moving, almost pathetic letter in March of 1918, Goldman pleaded with Babushka to support the Bolsheviks, opening her plea with a tribute to Babushka's importance to her as a heroine. "You were, you are, you will always be to me the beacon illuminating my darkest moments," Emma wrote. "Your great heroic past will inspire me always and give me strength to go on in my work to the very end." For this reason precisely, Goldman felt such pain at Babushka's denunciations of the Bolsheviks. "I am not doubting what you say about the Bolsheviki," she admitted. "As an Anarchist I am naturally opposed to their dictatorship, their centralization, their bureaucracy. You know the terrific struggle since the days of Marx, Engels and Bakunin. The struggle between centralization and federation, the struggle between the omnipotent state and free association. . . . But whatever the faults, the shortcomings, the mistakes of the Bolsheviki, they are flesh of our flesh, blood of our blood. They have with them, if not a majority, surely a large percentage of the Russian people for whom you have given fifty glorious years of your life. They have with them your children, Babushka, whom you have inspired with your fiery spirit. . . . Yes, they are your children, even if they are not all you hoped and wanted them to be. Are you, their mother, going to play them false?" Speaking here as one of those whom Babushka was betraying, Goldman emphasized that Babushka had been her hope and inspiration. "Your great past was our goal when we were younger. Your sweet strong heroic personality drew us on and urged us forward when we became faint of heart, when we despaired. You loomed up in all your wonderful strength, in your boundless love, and we grew strong and no longer doubted." Goldman urged her to "come back to us, Babushka, to your children, who love you and need you and revere you. . . . Come back to your children, Beloved Babushka." She signed her letter, "Your heart-broken child, Emma."[41]

It is curious to find that Goldman, who generally played the role of "Mother Earth" or "Mommy," casts herself in this instance as the beseeching child. In couching a political critique in such sentimental imagery, Goldman may have sought to deflect the seriousness of her criticism; or perhaps she hoped to touch a personal, emotional chord in the heart of the "little grandmother" by appealing to her maternal feelings. Locked in a prison cell, moreover, where she felt lonely and abandoned, Goldman may have felt especially bereft by the reversal of this cherished heroine. In her letters to Stella, she returned again and again to the subject of Babushka, trying to understand the latter's position and to define herself in relationship to it. "Not that I would deny Babushka her right to disagree with the rigid centralistic machine the Boyl. mean to operate," she wrote in February of 1919. "I should have to fight them on that ground myself. But not now. Not at a time when all the capitalistic and imperialistic blood hounds have been let loose against them."[42] There is a special poignancy in Goldman's brooding about Babushka in yet another sense; the arguments Emma made against her in 1918 and 1919 anticipated those which would be made against Goldman after she, too, turned against the Bolsheviks in 1921.

In the summer of 1919, Emma Goldman looked forward to her release with mixed feelings of apprehension, anxiety, and excited anticipation. The experience had "increased my burning faith in my ideal of a future society where prisons and all that go with the institution of government shall be no more." She had succeeded, moreover, in making peace with her memories of Ben Reitman and had recovered some of the emotional equanimity that her tumultuous love affair had continually upset. This serenity had come at the cost, however, of relinquishing her youthful hope of combining political commitment and public life with love. "More and more I come to the conclusion that a personal love is not for one who dedicates himself to an ideal," she wrote to Leon Malmed shortly after her fiftieth birthday. "Somehow it is like serving two Gods . . . no man could be satisfied to give all of himself. And to receive in return only a small part of the woman he loves. And how is she to give all when every nerve of her pulls toward the impersonal, the universal love?" A woman could not expect to have both, Emma concluded, "the man and the universe. And so she must forswear the one for the other. No, there can be no personal life for me."[43] As she put it years later in her autobiography, "occasional snatches of love; nothing permanent in my life except my ideal."[44]

The challenge awaiting Goldman outside of prison, however, was more dramatic than even she anticipated. The year 1919 had been one of extraordinary tension and class conflict. Organized labor, freed from the no-strike pledges of wartime, pressed with a new militance their demands for higher wages, shorter hours, and the right of collective bargaining. The Seattle General Strike in February, the first of hundreds of strikes throughout the year, provoked stiffening resistance on the part of employers and growing fears among conservative businessmen, already alarmed by the revolution in Russia, that the widespread labor conflict presaged an American "revolution." The revolution in Russia was now used to dismiss the grievances of labor; all demands for improved working conditions were attributed to the influence of "Bolsheviks." Throughout 1919, business and government exploited the mass strikes, race conflict, and terrorist incidents to whip up antiradical hysteria. The February strike in Seattle, bomb packages mailed to industrialists and public officials in April, May Day Riots (instigated mainly by businessmen and superpatriots attacking socialist demonstrations), and race riots in a dozen cities during the summer—all were identified as Bolshevik-inspired.

When underpaid Boston policemen went on strike for a union and for higher wages early in September of 1919, they were immediately denounced in the press as "Bolsheviks." Massachusetts Governor Calvin Coolidge was hailed as a national hero for calling in the state militia to break the strike. When, a week and a half later, 365,000 steel workers walked off their jobs in Pittsburgh, Gary, Buffalo, and other steel towns, demanding higher wages, shorter hours, and above all the right to collective bargaining in the most anti-union of all industries, the newspaper headlines featured sensational reports of Bolshevik influence. Meanwhile Elbert H. Gary, chairman of United States Steel, in a manner grimly worthy of his predecessor Henry Clay Frick, proclaimed his intention to resist any and all negotiations with the strikers and to defend the open shop. As news of an impending coal miners' strike filled the newspapers in late September, the administration—particularly the Justice Department and Attorney General Palmer—prepared to act. In this atmosphere of manipulated panic, political distinctions were artfully blurred. Any expression of dissent, any form of labor union activism, was likely to be labeled revolutionary, anarchist, "Bolshevik," "un-American." This postwar Red Scare continued the repression of the war years in broader form, casting an even wider net for possible "subversives" and revolutionaries.

On Saturday, September 27, America's most famous anarchist walked out the gates of the Missouri State Penitentiary. Accompanied by Stella Ballantine, Goldman stopped first in downtown Jefferson City. At the Federal Building she signed an affadavit declaring that she possessed no real estate or wealth, then boarded a train for Chicago. But Goldman, to use her own expression, had merely stepped from a smaller prison into a larger one. As she and her niece sped eastward, the war against the Left was furiously escalating and would soon turn its biggest guns against Goldman herself. Patriots everywhere were clamoring for immediate government action against radicals—particularly against foreign-born radicals, whom they generally held to be the most active instigators of revolution. Hoping for a little rest and time to recover from her imprisonment, Goldman, now a major target of the Red Scare, instead found herself at the center of that shocking and shameful episode in American history dubbed by one of its perpetrators "the deportations delirium."[45]

CHAPTER

16

"CAST
OUT
AND A
STRANGER
EVERYWHERE"

En route to New York from Jefferson City, Emma Goldman made two stops. Although the preceding May she had brusquely ordered Ben not to visit her in prison—she did not wish to reopen the wound—by September she had changed her mind. She wanted now to see him one last time, to test her success in rooting him out of her system, as she put it. Emma and Stella stopped overnight in Chicago, where they met Ben's wife, Anna, and their young child. Reitman, having completed his prison term, had reopened his medical practice in Chicago and had begun work on venereal disease prophylaxis that would eventually yield remarkably successful results. Remembering this visit years later, Emma would write that she knew she would never stop caring for this man who had brought her so much pleasure and grief, but that her obsession for him had given way to a more detached and tender affection. From Chicago, the two women traveled to Rochester. Here Emma for the last time saw her mother—now in her eighties, but independent, vigorous, and outspoken as ever. Her sister Helene, still deep in mourning, pleaded with Emma to be allowed to come and live with her. Fearful for Helene's future, Emma reluctantly invited her sister to New York, hoping that a change of surroundings would soothe her and distract her from her grief. Helene and her daughter Minnie soon joined Emma, and Alexander Berkman, freed October 2 from Atlanta, also moved back to New York with Eleanor Fitzgerald.

Far from being restful, life in New York was "a perfect crazy quilt, one round of confusion and chaos," Emma reported to a friend early in October.[1] She felt "wretched"—exhausted and dazed—but nevertheless set to work establishing headquarters in Stella's crowded Greenwich Village apartment at 36 Grove Street. She and Sasha immediately organized a number of projects—protests against prison conditions, aid to political prisoners, fund-raising for the campaign against deportation. With Stella in a state of exhaustion and collapse and Berkman, once again prey to post-prison nightmares, in poor health, Emma again had to shoulder the major part of the burden. Nursing Sasha and Stella, pleading nightly with Helene not to commit suicide, baby-sitting for Ian, Stella's young son, herself not yet recovered from her own prison experience, and plagued by dental problems, Emma nevertheless plunged into activity to counteract the rapidly escalating Red Scare.

Prior to going to prison, Goldman had been under surveillance by agents of the Justice Department and the American Protective League, who reported her activities to Washington. On her release, she was again followed. One agent, Margaret Scully, even managed to get herself hired as a secretary/stenographer to Goldman and Berkman and proceeded for a short time in late October and early November to send illiterate but revealing reports to Washington. Outspokenly anti-Semitic and xenophobic, Scully (whose real name was Marion Barling) nevertheless liked both Berkman and Goldman. They seemed to trust her, she said, since they left her alone in the apartment with all kinds of papers lying about. "E. is affectionate to us all. Sasha is cordial to me. All is faith and good will at #36," she wrote on October 31.[2] A week later, however, Goldman fired Scully, who had twice failed to appear for work at the agreed-upon time. "You must realize," Goldman explained crisply, "that in the kind of work we are doing, a certain amount of regularity must be kept or we would be swamped with the work which accumulates day by day."[3] Goldman's tone suggests that she may have suspected that Scully was a spy and not the radical she claimed to be. She said that she felt reluctant to employ someone who "knows nothing about the social issues and while feeling with the great social struggles," was far removed from them. "I have not the right to involve you."[4] Scully was relieved, for "as I am fond of Goldie and sorry for Sasha it is well that I am no longer forced to deceive my comrades. After all they are well beaten and I prefer to work where the fire is blazing. Things are dreary and cold at 36 and a discouraged and brow-beaten atmosphere exists."[5]

There was good reason for discouragement. Until the war, deportation had been used against immigrants deemed "undesirable," but had not been regarded as a weapon to be employed against radicals. Beginning with the anti-anarchist law of 1903, however, a body of legislation had been passed that was intended to bar radicals from entering the country, deprive them of the right to naturalization (in 1906, all I.W.W. members were automatically disqualified for citizenship), and ease the requirements for their deportation. A 1907 law had limited vulnerability to deportation to three years after entry; in 1917, that restriction was lifted, and an unnaturalized immigrant could be deported anytime after entry. In October of 1918, Congress authorized the deportation of unnaturalized immigrants simply on grounds of belonging to an organization advocating revolution or sabotage.

Emma Goldman was ordered to appear for a hearing at Ellis Island on October 27 so that immigration officials could determine her status under the 1918 law. Alexander Berkman's hearing had already taken place in Atlanta, following his release from the penitentiary. Berkman had never applied for citizenship and did not propose to fight; his deportation seemed assured. Goldman, likewise, had not applied for citizenship; she nevertheless tried to claim it through her father and her husband. Her father had been naturalized in 1894, but since Emma had been over twenty-one at the time, she was not eligible to make such a claim. Her marriage to Jacob Kersner offered no solid protection, either—Kersner had been denaturalized in 1908. Weinberger, however, proposed to argue that this denaturalization had been conducted illegally, since it was a posthumous proceeding.

It was therefore invalid, and by rights Goldman remained a United States citizen.

In the summer of 1919, while Emma was still in prison, a Mr. Sam Sickles (who had read Kate O'Hare's prison letters in the *New York Call*) offered to adopt her. Weinberger urged Goldman not to accept, saying that "though the [Kersner] thread is weak, it may hold."[6] Emma did not find this assessment reassuring. "What you say about the thread in the K. matter being weak and if the powers that be will break that thread it will look like persecution and not like law, is not very encouraging. The powers that be have invented laws for the underdog who is ignorant enough to believe them. Persecution is their [sic] tactics in all their dealings with the opponents of their system, especially in their dealings with us, so I can not say that I am very hopeful of the outcome."[7] Nonetheless Goldman, after some thought, took Weinberger's advice and turned Sickles down.

In July, she had received another offer. Harry Kelly, her close associate on *Mother Earth*, offered to marry her. After serious consideration, she decided to accept. On August 5, she wrote Weinberger to go ahead with the "H.K. proposition," but to be very careful of complications. It is "extremely distasteful to me," she told Weinberger. "I don't mean H.K. I mean the process. It will certainly put me in a ridiculous light. But nevertheless I am willing to go through with it if it can be done."[8] A week later she reaffirmed her determination, asking Weinberger to tell Kelly, "I accept the offer with thanks."[9]

But the marriage did not take place. Weinberger urged Goldman against it, and she accepted his counsel. He felt that "there is a reasonable doubt in our favor" and that it would be better to depend on this than on Kelly's marriage offer.[10] Goldman clearly recognized the flimsiness of Weinberger's argument. In an atmosphere of hatred and suspicion toward all foreigners, it was highly unlikely that any court would reverse the 1908 denaturalization of Jacob Kersner on the ground that it was conducted illegally. Saxe Commins, Goldman's nephew, wrote in despair to his sister Stella that "the case, between ourselves, looks almost hopeless from the K[ersner] angle. Is there no other defense?" Commins even proposed half-seriously that he marry Emma himself, if he could do so "without being held for the more serious crime of incest."[11]

Despite her doubts about the case Weinberger was proposing to argue, Goldman was determined to fight to the very end. "I am not one to submit easily," she announced to Weinberger. "I have no desire to retreat one single inch without a fight. . . . No matter what the result will be my friends can rest assured that I do not propose to lie down with hands folded, or to be rushed out without a strenuous struggle."[12] She saw the case as international in its implications: a demonstration to the world that the United States practiced the same methods as the Russian czar.

At her October 27 hearing before various immigration officials and the ubiquitous J. Edgar Hoover, Goldman, in one of the most eloquent statements in her career, argued forcefully that the real purpose of the "so-called Anti-Anarchist Law" (the 1918 immigration law) was to suppress labor protest:

> Collective bargaining for the workers is now an admitted right, recognized by the highest officials of the land and accepted by the most reactionary elements. Yet when the steel workers of this country, after a quarter of a century of desperate struggle for the right to bargain collectively, have mustered enough spirit and cohesion to enter into a struggle with the steel barons for that fundamental right, the entire machinery of government, State and Federal, is put into operation to crush that spirit and to undermine the chance of establishing humane conditions in the industry where conditions have been worse than those that existed under the most brutal feudalism. The workers in the steel industry have expressed no particular social philosophy. They are certainly not on strike to "overthrow the government by force or violence," yet the Anti-Anarchist law is used as a means to reach out for these simple, hard-driven and hard-pressed human beings, who have endangered life and limb to build up this devouring monster—the Steel Trust. A reign of terror has been established in the strike region. American Cossacks, known as the State Constabulary, ride over men, women and children; deputies of the Department of Justice break into the strikers' homes. . . . the Immigration authorities, the men of your department, take the strikers off secretly and order them deported by such proceedings as I am being subjected to today, without having committed even the slightest offense against American institutions, save the one that is the greatest crime today—the right of the workers to life, liberty and the pursuit of happiness—a right that was made in America, and not imported by these hated aliens.

If, said Goldman, she was being charged with some crime, then "I protest against the secrecy and third degree methods of this so-called 'trial.' But if I am not charged with any specific offense or act, if . . . this is purely an inquiry into my social and political opinions, then I protest still more vigorously against these proceedings, as utterly tyrannical and diametrically opposed to the fundamental guarantees of a true democracy. Every human being is entitled to hold any opinion that appeals to her or him without making herself or himself liable to persecution." The well-being of the country could only profit "by a free discussion of the new ideas now germinating in the minds of thinking men and women in society. The free expression of the hopes and aspirations of a people is the greatest and only safety in a sane society." The object of deportation and of the anti-anarchist law was the opposite: "to stifle the voice of the people, to muzzle every aspiration of labor. . . . With all the power and intensity of my being," she concluded, "I protest against the conspiracy of imperialist capitalism against the life and the liberty of the American people."[13]

A few days later, defying the injunction issued by Attorney General Palmer, four hundred thousand coal miners walked off the job, while government officials hysterically pledged to fight "reds" and General Leonard Wood urged his hearers at a speech to "Kill Radicalism as you would a rattlesnake!" On November 7, the second anniversary of the Russian Revolution, federal agents raided radical headquarters in eleven cities. They broke up meetings, beat and arrested the participants, ransacked offices, and seized literature. Those who could not prove American citizenship were hauled into police headquarters and held, usually without benefit of counsel, for interrogation and possible deportation. The Palmer raids continued for days (they were repeated on an even larger scale in early January of 1920), particularly aiming at leaders of the nine-thousand-member anarcho-syndicalist Union of Russian Workers. While newspaper headlines proclaimed daily discoveries of "Red Bomb Laboratories" and plots to put bombs into Christmas mail, the attorney general hysterically waved his list of "60,000 reds," and government plans to deport immigrant radicals who could not prove citizenship moved into high gear. At Ellis Island, a House Committee on Immigration began hearings to speed up the deportation process, while "Red Specials" continued to bring trainloads of potential deportees arrested during the continuing raids on radicals in the Midwest and West to the island. Though convicted of no crime, they were treated like felons and waited as prisoners until they were hurriedly screened and ordered deported.

Irate, impatient "patriots" especially demanded the immediate deportation of Goldman and Berkman. A Mr. Thomas Elder, for example, wrote to Attorney General Palmer about "these consummate rascals and arch-enemies of society" and raged that "there is too much pussyfooting going on to suit the real American." He continued: "I, as a descendant of three grandfather ancestors who fought in our Revolution to make this land independent, feel the right to make this request. Why allow these two persons, the very scum of the earth, to openly prate about their privileges, rights, etc. . . . Why not make a special effort to rid America of these two disgusting persons?"[14] Another correspondent complained bitterly of "alien nation-wreckers," insisting that "I am an American. This is my country, I fought for it as a volunteer in this war . . . and I will not cease to fight for it until these aliens who are working night and day to overthrow my government are driven back to the lands they came from."[15] A Mr. J. C. Pinckney summed up the feelings of many toward Goldman and Berkman in late 1919: "Gentlemen—Why are Jew anarchist lawyers (Harry Weinberger) who only studied our laws to defeat the ends of justice, allowed to prevent the deportation of Emma Goldman (who murdered McKinley through Colzgoz [sic]) and Bergman [sic] who tried to murder Frick. Ever man woman and child in this country demand their deportation. Yours, J. C. Pinckney."[16]

Suddenly, late in November, in the midst of the general hysteria, the two most notorious targets of the Red Scare decided to undertake a whirlwind lecture tour. As Goldman wrote in her autobiography, "It seemed preposterous to begin a lecture tour yet I could not refuse. I had a foreboding that it would be my last opportunity to raise my voice against the shame of my adopted land." On November 21, Goldman and Berkman left New York for Detroit, where they delivered three lectures to enormous, enthusiastic crowds, under the watchful eyes of Justice Department agents who reported their every move back to Washington. Goldman and Berkman were "Hailed as Martyrs in Chicago," according to the *New York Times*, which reported that four thousand five hundred radicals paid fifty cents apiece to hear the two anarchists and that five thousand dollars was raised to fight their deportation.

But for Berkman, at least, time had run out. On November 26, immigration authorities ordered his deportation. Three days later Anthony Caminetti, Commissioner of Immigration, wired his decision regarding Goldman: "Application for further time case Emma Goldman denied. Case is closed and alien ordered deported."[17] That day, Assistant Secretary of Labor Louis B. Post—a single-taxer who had defended Goldman in his paper, *The Public*, when she was accused of complicity in the McKinley assassination—signed the order for her deportation under the 1918 Immigration Act. This was not the end, but Emma did not feel hopeful. "I may begin the fight on the grounds of citizenship," she wrote Leon Malmed on November 29 from Chicago, "but frankly I am not going into it with much eagerness. I feel that I ought to go with Berkman when he is deported. It seems so cruel to have stood in the same terrible battle for thirty years and then to have him shoved out alone when he is really too ill for a long journey. Then, too, I haven't much hope of the success of my fight. In fact," she added, "I know that in the end I will have to go. It may only be a question of a few months' stay here. . . ."[18]

Harry Weinberger received orders to produce his two clients at Ellis Island on December 5. Berkman immediately left Chicago for New York; Goldman delivered the rest of her scheduled lectures, then boarded "the fastest American train" to New York, travelling "in state" with two friends. As of noon on December 5, Goldman and Berkman were prisoners at Ellis Island. Emma was placed in a room with Dora Lipkin and Ethel Bernstein—the only other women on the island, who had been arrested during the first of the Palmer raids in New York and were now also awaiting deportation. Berkman did not propose to fight deportation; he did, however, ask that he be allowed to take his "common-law wife," Eleanor Fitzgerald, with him, and that he be permitted to determine his own destination. Both requests were denied.[19] Goldman, dispirited, nevertheless planned to challenge the government on the issue of her citizenship.

On December 8, before Judge Julius M. Mayer—the same man who had tried (and admired) her and Berkman in 1917—Harry Weinberger presented the case for Goldman's citizenship. He had no real evidence for his allegation that Emma's former husband, Jacob

Kersner, had died before his denaturalization; he argued only that "there was no proof that he was alive; there was some proof that he was dead."[20] But government investigators had discovered evidence certifying that Kersner had indeed been alive at the time, and they speedily threw out all of Weinberger's claims.

Harry Weinberger's handling of Goldman's deportation case was a disaster. Had he really wanted to save her from deportation, he would certainly have advised her to accept Harry Kelly's offer of marriage the previous July. Weinberger seems to have become increasingly preoccupied with proving the fraudulence of Kersner's denaturalization, rather than with saving Goldman from deportation. Perhaps he was unconsciously swayed by Goldman's own lack of enthusiasm for the fight and by her conviction, voiced in late October, that there was no hope of winning.

After the collapse of the Kersner case, Weinberger filed a writ of habeas corpus for both Berkman and Goldman, which Judge Mayer promptly dismissed. Next Weinberger filed a brief with the United States Supreme Court appealing Mayer's action. Three days later, on December 12, the Supreme Court rejected the appeal filed on behalf of Berkman, but granted Goldman a one-week stay of deportation without bail so that Weinberger could submit the arguments for her case.

Emma decided, however, not to pursue her case. As soon as she heard the news about Berkman, she withdrew her appeal. If Alexander Berkman was to be deported, then she, too, would go. This time they would pay the price together. "Rather than give our enemies a chance to defeat me," she announced defiantly to Leon Malmed, "I have decided to tell them to go to hell. I sent a demand to send me to Soviet Russia." Leaving would be painful, she added. "But I go in the consciousness that I have done my work well or our enemies would not hate me so much. What else does one want in life? . . . I go too feeling that AB and I have the love of thousands. . . ."[21]

Her decision once made, Emma worked frantically to get supplies, money, food, and clothing—for herself and Berkman, but also for the hundreds of other deportees, many of whom had been arrested and brought to New York by train with only the clothes on their backs. Goldman's deportation to the Soviet Union was now certain: only the date and exact destination remained unknown. In the midst of hurried preparations, a trip to the dentist, and farewell visits, Emma also composed manifestos protesting the deportation and sent letters to her friends, bidding them a sad goodbye and urging them to continue the work of agitation. From her cell on Ellis Island, her last home in the United States, she wrote a long, affectionate letter to Ben Reitman, assuring him—and perhaps trying to reassure herself—that while departing from America was terribly painful, she felt "proud to have been chosen by the enemies of truth and justice. Their mad rush in getting us out of the country is the greatest proof to me that I have served the cause of humanity, that I have never wavered or compromised. I really feel proud of my achievement." Urging Ben to "push my *Essays* and prison pamphlets" and "to keep my memory alive," she also wanted to tell him what he had meant to her.

I was glad to have been in Chicago and to see you again, dearest Hobo. I never realized quite so well how far apart we have travelled. But it is alright, nothing you have done since you left me, or will yet do can take away the 10 wonderful years with you. If it is true that the power of endurance is the greatest test of love, Hobo mine, I have loved you much. But I have been rewarded not only in pain—but in real joy—in ecstasy—in all that makes life full & rich & sparkling. I really owe much to you. During our years together, I have done my best and most valuable work. My two books, the continuance of ME during all the years. I owe them to you. Your devotion, your untiring work, your tremendous energy. If I owe also much heartache—much soul-tearing misery to you, what of it. Nothing great in life can be achieved without pain. I am glad to have paid the price. I only hope I too have given you something worth whatever price you have paid for your love. I shall feel proud & glad.[22]

To Eleanor Fitzgerald, Emma wrote of her sadness that so many things had interfered with their friendship, "and so now I shall go away without the chance of getting truly close to you, dearest girl." She admitted to Fitzi that "just now, I feel as if my insides were pulled out of me. I feel terribly empty. Yet I am not exactly unhappy. I am really glad I can go with S. For leaving him to face the journey alone would have been even a greater wrench." (These must have been painful words for Fitzi, who wanted to accompany Sasha herself.) Despite the anguish of parting from friends and family, Emma was "thinking of the future and the work I want to do for America much more than for Russia. Is it because I am forced out of here that I long passionately to do much for this country? What I really wanted to tell you most is this," Goldman continued. "I want you to keep up our work—through our literature anyway. . . . I am sure there will be a demand for it, if it is brought to the attention of the people. Now is the psychologic moment. . . . Good night, dearest Fitzi," she concluded, "I love you very much. I hope some day to be called upon to prove my love. Meanwhile, I want you to believe in it. I know you love me, a little anyway. I hope some day we two can be close enough to each other and under less stress and strain, so you can love me more. I want your friendship and your love very much. I embrace and kiss you tenderly, your E. G." She appended a final affecting admission that the one thing she really dreaded in her life was loneliness, even though "I ought to be used to it by this time."[23]

Early in the morning of Sunday, December 21, Emma Goldman, Alexander Berkman, and the two hundred and forty-seven other immigrant radicals locked up on Ellis Island were suddenly awakened from sleep and hurried out in the freezing darkness onto barges that carried them to the S.S. *Buford*, a battered old army transport that had carried troops during the Spanish-American War. Accompanied by two hundred and fifty guards carrying revolvers, they sailed at dawn, on a ship with sealed orders, into the wintry Atlantic toward an unknown destination. The sailing was witnessed by the Commissioner of Immigration, Anthony Caminetti; Chief William J. Flynn of the Justice Department's Bureau of Investigation; and various other federal agents and officials. "The goal of the Federal agents," reported the *New York Times*, "was the capture of the leaders, the 'intellectuals' of agitation, and on the *Buford*, in the opinion of Chief Flynn, went the brains of the radical movement."[24] Soon after their departure, the *Times* celebrated "the sweet sorrow of parting at last with two of the most pernicious of anarchists, Emma Goldman and Alexander Berkman, for a generation among the most virulent and dangerous preachers and practicers of the doctrines of destruction."[25]

For Goldman, the scene grotesquely reversed the traditional images of America and Russia: "Czarist" America was now sending her back to "free" revolutionary Russia. Thirty-three years earlier, she had sailed into New York Harbor, haunted by visions of Russian officers beating Lithuanian peasants, of public hangings and pogroms and political prisoners sealed for life in the Peter and Paul Fortress. Had she remained in Russia, as Havel noted, "she would have probably sooner or later shared the fate of thousands buried in the snows of Siberia." In America, however, she had hardly found the ideal freedom of which she had dreamed; rather, the constant, strenuous struggle for freedom had itself become the most deeply felt value of her life. Inspired by the examples of Perovskaya and Breshkovskaya, of Bakunin and Kropotkin, of Louise Michel and Mary Wollstonecraft, she had carried the words of the great revolutionists throughout America. Her own radical vision, broader and more encompassing than that of almost anyone else on the Left, had shocked, inspired, and educated thousands, both inside and outside the anarchist movement. And she had made herself a powerful symbol of that "spirit of revolt" which she defined as the essence of anarchism. If she had been, as she liked to boast, the most hated woman in America, she had also been loved, admired, and respected. She had, moreover, come to feel that she was an American "spiritually rather than by the grace of a mere scrap of paper."[26] She had come to love "the other America"—not that of Frick and Carnegie and Rockefeller, but the America of the rebels and radicals, the dreamers and dissenters and poets, of Emerson and Thoreau, John Brown, Walt Whitman, and Eugene Debs.[27] She had expected harassment, persecution, and imprisonment. But for all her denunciations of American tyranny, she had not expected this: deportation for "mere opinion's sake."[28] Czarist Russia exiled people for revolutionary ideas—but not free America!

Aboard the *Buford,* Goldman's thoughts clung to the land that she was leaving, and she busied herself with plans for her return. She was seized with a terrible anxiety and restlessness. Everything seemed vague and confused. She felt as though she had lived years since the day she and Alexander Berkman, only two weeks earlier, had surrendered at Ellis Island. Nothing seemed real. It was all a dream. She would awaken back on Grove Street in New York and find Stella and Saxe and the child Ian and Fitzi and all the other beloved faces around her. She was an American like any other. She was "Emma Goldman, the anarchist," and "would not be forced."

She could never work within the confines of a state, Bolshevik or otherwise. She would go to Russia and organize the Russian Friends of American Freedom. She would go to Mexico and publish an anarchist paper. She would marry an American citizen and come back proudly to her old haunts. Now more than ever, she knew where she belonged.[29] As she sailed out of New York Harbor on that icy December morning, Emma Goldman left behind the only place in the world where she had almost felt at home. Except for one three-month visit, she would never return.

EPILOGUE

The legacy of Emma Goldman's thirty years of activism in America has always been controversial. In several areas, however, her achievement is indisputable. More than anyone else, she sought to integrate a commitment to collective social revolution with a concern for the inner psychological liberation of the individual. She was almost alone among immigrant radicals in resisting a narrowly economic interpretation of social injustice and in stressing cultural, psychological, and sexual issues. At a time when most of the Left, anarchist and socialist, argued that the emancipation of women would occur automatically with the defeat of capitalism, Goldman insisted—as feminists had long argued—that women's issues must be addressed now, not postponed to a hypothetical future. At a time when many radicals looked forward to the strengthening of traditional institutions of marriage and motherhood after the revolution, Goldman insisted that these institutions were part of the structure that imprisoned women and must be radically revised. Along with Voltairine de Cleyre, she gave a feminist dimension to anarchism and a libertarian dimension to the concept of women's emancipation. If she romanticized the issue of sexual liberation— ignoring, for example, the ways in which "free love" was often used by men to rationalize the sexual exploitation of women—she went much further than most radicals in her understanding of the politics of sex.

Goldman also grasped the sexuality of politics and used her own erotic and demonic legend as a weapon to attack the taboos and pieties of nineteenth-century Victorianism. Her public persona, with its aura of sex and violence, was one of her most powerful creations. The fear and hatred she aroused among conservatives suggests the depths of the popular imagination that she touched. The widespread admiration and emulation she also excited was evidence of her ability to project an image of strength and freedom. "She was everything my mother always wanted to be" is a refrain often heard today from the daughters of anarchist mothers. "Emma lived their fantasies," was how one perceptive associate of Goldman's explained her appeal to women.[1]

That the reality of Emma Goldman's private life—especially her life with Ben Reitman—was rather different from her legend does not diminish her achievement. Instead it deepens our understanding of the psychological tensions and conflicts facing women at a moment of rapid historical change. That so independent and strong a woman as Goldman—and so ardent a champion of free love— should find herself caught in a relationship of deep erotic dependence suggests the continuing power of those unconscious "internal tyrants" that Emma herself so eloquently denounced. If, on the one hand, Goldman was able to give herself, in letters and in life, to an intensely sexual relationship with a man considerably younger than herself—a love affair that entailed real risks and dangers, both emotional and political—she was honest enough to recognize that this was not the "free love" she extolled from the lecture platform. If she resisted exploring in her lectures and essays the disturbing implications of her own experience, continuing to insist on the liberating, emancipating aspects of sexuality, privately she was willing to acknowledge the complexity she suppressed in public. "Sex is like a double-edged sword," she wrote later in her life to Stella Ballantine;

278

"it releases our spirit and it binds it with a thousand threads, it raises us to sublime heights and thrusts us into the lowest depths. What people will do to each other in their intimate relations," she admitted frankly, "they never could or would do to their friends. . . ."[2]

Rather than contradicting the pattern of her public life, however, Goldman's private life illuminates its psychological dynamic. Although she was inclined to emphasize the conflicting demands of the public and private, in fact a similar tension informed both realms. At the center of Goldman's erotic and angry correspondence with Ben Reitman is her simultaneous drive for self-affirmation and for martyrdom, the longing for acceptance and the attraction to persecution, the love of battle that informed her political life as well. Moreover, as *Nation* editor Freda Kirchwey acutely put it in a review of *Living My Life* (a review that pleased Goldman), "Her collective emotions moved her as only private feelings move most of us." For Goldman, "the excitement of a mass-meeting was akin to the thrill of an embrace."[3]

The rhetoric of domination and dependence that informs Goldman's dialogue with Ben Reitman emerges also in her other writings. This champion of freedom often spoke of herself, paradoxically, as driven, doomed, fated, bound, tied, obsessed, enslaved—whether to Reitman, to the anarchist movement, to the "public," to the state, to *Mother Earth*, or to "some irresistible force within me that will not let me rest."[4] If this language was partly self-dramatizing, it also expressed a profound sense of inner bondage that may explain, in part, both her attraction to an ideology of total freedom such as anarchism and her great sensitivity to domination in all its guises. It was perhaps Goldman's sense of a powerful "inner discipline . . . more binding than all the laws put together" that helped to make her so trenchant and determined a social critic.[5]

In part, of course, Goldman's conflicts had their sources in her own personal history: the intense feelings of being unloved that she suffered as a child; the early deprivations and punishments that left a deep legacy of anger and seem to have intensified both her adult need for love and her sense of martyrdom. Growing up as an unwanted daughter, Goldman seemed to feel that some ultimate justification for her life lay forever out of reach.

If these conflicts were especially intense in Emma Goldman, they were not unique. Goldman acted out in a highly dramatic fashion the contradictory values experienced by many women at this moment of transition from the Victorian to the modern eras: the conflict between masochistic nineteenth-century values of self-sacrifice, submission, and dependence associated with the ideal of "true womanhood" (or its European equivalents) and the modern values of assertion, self-expression, and independence associated with the "new woman" of the early twentieth century. Emma herself acknowledged this conflict when she remarked ruefully to Berkman that women such as she were "still rooted in the old soil, though our visions are of the future and our desire is to be free and independent."[6]

Goldman's outspokenness on sexual issues and her unconventional love life shocked many of her own comrades as well as those outside the movement. If these reservations reflected the conservatism even of many anarchists, there were other, more serious criticisms as well. However effective she was as an agitator and speaker, however successful in creating an anarchist community (or "family," as she liked to call it), Goldman failed to build a powerful anarchist movement in America. She failed to create strong ties between the immigrant and American groups; when she and Berkman were deported, there was nothing else to hold these elements together. She failed to exercise a decisive influence within the I.W.W. or within any of the feminist organizations of her time. Her love affair with America—symbolized most vividly by her passion for Ben Reitman —led her away from the immigrants and the children of immigrants who constituted most of the industrial working class and who remained at the center of anarchism in the United States. Her desire to radicalize "Americans" drew her inevitably toward the middle class, who often hailed her more as a voice for individual liberation than for social revolution. Excited by the large audiences that turned out for her lectures and bought her literature, she seriously misjudged the impact of her own work. Retrospectively, "there is not a single group in America to which you may lay claim," wrote Van Valkenburgh, for a long time one of Emma's "disciples." "Yours was a personal following, and when the gates were closed behind you none were prepared to pick up the work where you had been forced to drop it."[7]

Clearly the weakness of anarchism in America owed more to the organizational and theoretical limitations of the movement, the greater effectiveness of the Socialist party and trade unionism as vehicles of change, and the government persecution of anarchists than to the personal liabilities of Emma Goldman. Goldman's legacy is indeed a personal one—but it is the important legacy of a life dedicated to free speech, free labor, free thought, free love; a life lived in the grip of a powerful libertarian passion and—not least important—revealed to us in frank and voluminous memoirs and letters. It is the legacy, moreover, of an immigrant who became an American without losing any of her radical commitment. If revolutionary anarchism in America was primarly a European import, brought by immigrants who largely remained within ethnic communities, Goldman was one of the few who, in the words of Hippolyte Havel, "succeeded in preserving their European education and culture while at the same time assimilating themselves with American life."[8] She brought anarchism out of its foreign-language immigrant enclaves into the English-speaking American mainstream. Goldman did not, of course, convert many Americans to anarchy, but her own politics of protest often moved them in more liberal directions and showed by example the meaning of an anarchist life. She was the catalyst for little theater groups, radical libraries, anarchist schools, and birth control clinics. Perhaps had she joined the I.W.W.—as Van Valkenburgh hinted—or some other union or feminist organization, she might have exercised a more lasting influence.[9] Perhaps had she formed closer bonds with other women who shared her dilemmas—as Blanche Cook has suggested—she might have felt less alone in her struggle.[10] As it was, she chose to go her own way, to "bow to nothing except my idea of right."[11] She never made peace either with the world or with herself. She remained restless, disconsolate, discontented, her life a kind of warfare against all the jailers of the human spirit, including the "internal tyrants" of her own mind. She could not vanquish these tyrants, but neither did they vanquish her. In fighting her battles, in living out the contradictions of her own time, she also illuminates ours.

N O T E S

Introduction

1. Margaret Anderson, *My Thirty Years' War* (London: Alfred A. Knopf, 1930), pp. 54–55.

2. *New York Times*, 10 July 1917.

3. Emma Goldman (EG), "Anarchism: What It Really Stands For," in Goldman, *Anarchism and Other Essays* (New York: Mother Earth Publishing Association, 1910), p. 56.

4. Alexander Berkman, "Diary," 30 January 1930, XXI, Alexander Berkman Archive, International Institute of Social History, Amsterdam.

5. Daniel Malmed to author, 18 September 1980.

6. E.G., *Living My Life* (1931; reprint ed., ed. Richard Drinnon and Anna Maria Drinnon, New York: New American Library, 1977), p. 686.

7. EG to "Bob" [Low], 11 October 1935, [XVII], Emma Goldman Archive, International Institute of Social History, Amsterdam.

8. Ahrne Thorne, interview, 19 May 1983.

9. Agnes Smedley to EG, "Sunday," [Berlin], in Richard Drinnon and Anna Maria Drinnon, eds., *Nowhere at Home: Letters from Exile of Emma Goldman and Alexander Berkman* (New York: Schocken Books, 1975), p. 135.

Chapter 1

"MY LONE AND WOEFUL CHILDHOOD"

1. Emma Goldman (EG) to John Haynes Holmes, n.d., EG Papers, New York Public Library.

2. *New York Sun*, 2 May 1909.

3. EG, *Living My Life*, p. 69.

4. EG to Frank Heiner, 24 July 1934, XIV, EG Archive, International Institute of Social History, Amsterdam; EG, "Was My Life Worth Living?" in Alix Kates Shulman, ed., *Red Emma Speaks: Selected Writings and Speeches by Emma Goldman* (New York: Random House, 1972), p. 394.

5. Freda Goldman, Death Certificate #14395, 6 March 1914, City of

Rochester, Monroe County, New York State Department of Health. Samuel Yog, husband of Abraham's sister Lena, signed this certificate; Abraham's will also lists Freda Goldman as his mother.

6. Ibid; interview with Miriam Commins Berman, 3 October 1979, Rochester, N.Y.

7. Interview with Miriam Berman, 3 October 1979.

8. EG, *Living My Life*, p. 144.

9. Abraham Goldman, Death Certificate #1892, 14 January 1909, City of Rochester, Monroe County, New York State Department of Health. This certificate states that Abraham was fifty-five years old at the time of his death, which would have made his year of birth 1854; if this is accurate, he would have been fifteen years old at the time of Emma's birth. A more plausible figure is that given in the 1900 census, which lists January 1845 as his date of birth. The *Letter from the Attorney General* (Senate Document No. 153, Investigation Activities of the Department of Justice, 1919) gives Shavl, County of Kovno, as Abraham's birthplace. This information was presumably elicited from informants in Rochester in 1908, when Emma Goldman was denaturalized.

10. EG, *Living My Life*, pp. 59–60, 209–10, 447.

11. Ibid., p. 447.

12. Ibid., p. 59. Abraham Goldman's will gives further evidence that he strongly favored his sons. To his youngest son, the doctor, he gave "my gold watch and chain and fur overcoat and wearing apparel and the sum of one thousand dollars in cash"; to his oldest son he gave "one thousand dollars in trust"; to his daughter Emma, he left "the sum of three hundred dollars in cash" (Abraham Goldman, Last Will and Testament, 20 December 1908, City of Rochester, Monroe County, N.Y.).

13. Therese Goldman, Death Certificate #43562, 24 July 1923, City of Rochester, Monroe County, New York State Department of Health. Taube used the names Toby, Tobey, and Therese in Rochester. Evidence regarding her age is conflicting. Her death certificate lists a birthdate of March 1837. The census of 1900 gives February 1845 as her date of birth. Emma wrote in her memoirs that her mother was one year older than her father (*Living My Life*, p. 447). During her husband's lifetime, Taube may have indicated that she was approximately the same age as he, but after his death admitted her real age (i.e., eight years older).

14. *New York Sun*, 6 January 1901. Goldman recommended this interview with herself to Theodore Schroeder, a libertarian lawyer, as a reliable source of information about her life. See EG to "Dear Friend," 14 July, no year, Joseph Ishill Collection, Houghton Library, Harvard University, Cambridge, Mass.; interview with Miriam Berman, 3 October 1979.

15. Interview with Miriam Berman, 3 October 1979.

16. *New York Sun*, 2 May 1909.

17. EG to Stella Ballantine, 14 June 1936, EG Papers, New York Public Library.

18. Interview with Miriam Berman, 3 October 1979; Helene Hochstein, Death Certificate #9425, 7 February 1920 (I have retained Helene's spelling, which appeared in all sources except Goldman's letters and memoir); Zodikow is the German transliteration of the Russian, which appears on Helene Hochstein's death certificate. Later, the family also spelled the name Zodikoff. Lena Commins, Death Certificate #66705, 19 November 1950, City of Rochester, Monroe County, New York State Department of Health.

19. Interview with Miriam Berman, 3 October 1979; Miriam Berman to author, 27 October 1979.

20. EG, *Living My Life*, p. 447.

21. Ibid., p. 696.

22. *New York Sun*, 2 May 1909.

23. EG, *Living My Life*, p. 27.

24. Ibid., p. 696.

25. Ibid., p. 11.

26. *New York World*, 17 September 1893.

27. EG, *Living My Life*, p. 13.

28. Frank Harris, "Emma Goldman, the Famous Anarchist," in *Contemporary Portraits*, 4th ser. (London: Grants Richards, 1924), p. 227. Goldman told Theodore Dreiser that "some of the things about my childhood I myself wrote down for him, therefore they are authentic" (EG to Dreiser, 7 January 1929, VIII, EG Archive).

29. EG, *Living My Life*, p. 448.

30. EG to Ben Reitman, 28 August 1909, Supp. II, f. 102, Ben Reitman Papers, University of Illinois at Chicago.

31. EG to Reitman, 4 September 1913, Supp. II, f. 116, Reitman Papers.

32. Helene Hochstein, Death Certificate. Emma called her Helena.

33. EG, *Living My Life*, p. 11.

34. Lena Commins, Death Certificate; Louis Sheaffer, *O'Neill, Son and Playwright* (Boston: Little, Brown, 1968), p. 54; interview with Miriam Berman, 3 October 1979; interview with Ian Ballantine and Betty Ballantine, 29 September 1979.

35. EG to Alexander Berkman, 14 August 1934, XIII, EG Archive.

36. EG, *Living My Life*, p. 448; interview with Miriam Berman, 3 October 1979.

37. EG to Stella Ballantine, 5 September 1919, XVI9, EG Archive.

38. EG, "Outline for Autobiography" (typescript), IVA, EG Archive.

39. See Albert C. Cain, Irene Fast, and Mary E. Erickson, "Children's Disturbed Reactions to the Death of a Sibling," *American Journal of Orthopsychiatry* 34 (July 1964): 741–52. Parental responses may have a deter-

mining impact on the reactions of surviving siblings. "Beyond immediate blaming reactions, in some cases one or both parents continued to maintain explicit or unconscious attitudes of blame toward a surviving child, with constant hostility and guilt inducement toward the child and minimal love for him. The child was never conceded the possibility of 'making it up' " (p. 745). It seems plausible that a man like Abraham, who placed such high hopes in his sons, might have been especially embittered by the death of his eldest son, and inclined to vent his bitterness on his eldest surviving daughter.

40. EG, *Living My Life*, p. 211; EG to Mildred Mesirow, 13 January 1935, XVII, EG Archive; Saxe Commins to EG, 24 December 1934, XVIIA, EG Archive.

41. EG to Frank Heiner, 24 October 1934, XIV, EG Archive.

42. EG to Frank Heiner, 27 March 1935, XIV, EG Archive.

43. Similarly, the poet Leon Mandelstamm wrote that although his native town belonged to the province of Vilna, "spiritually and intellectually it was distinguished by its Kurland culture, and I am therefore accustomed to consider myself a Kurlander." Quoted in Israel Zinberg, *A History of Jewish Literature*, vol. 11 (Cincinnati: Hebrew Union College Press), pp. 96–97.

44. Harris, "Emma Goldman," p. 227.

45. EG, *Living My Life*, p. 21.

46. Ibid., p. 28.

47. Harris, "Emma Goldman," p. 225.

48. According to Adrienne Rich, "The woman who has felt 'unmothered' may seek mothers all her life—may even seek them in men. . . . But the 'motherless' woman may also react by denying her own vulnerability, denying that she has felt any loss or absence of mothering. She may spend her life proving her strength in the 'mothering' of others. . . . In a sense she is giving to others what she herself has lacked; but this will always mean that she needs the neediness of others in order to go on feeling her own strength. She may feel uneasy with equals—particularly women." See Rich, *Of Woman Born: Motherhood as Experience and Institution* (New York: W. W. Norton, 1976), pp. 242–43. Similarly, Otto Fenichel has described individuals who act as "nursing mothers" in all their object relationships. They are always generous and shower everybody with help and presents. "Their attitude has the significance of a magical gesture: 'As I shower you with love, I want to be showered.' " See Fenichel, *The Psychoanalytic Theory of Neurosis* (New York: W. W. Norton, 1945), p. 489.

49. EG to Agnes Inglis, 18 August, no year, Labadie Collection, University of Michigan, Ann Arbor; EG to Reitman, 14 or 15 December 1909, Supp. II, f. 102, and 4 January 1911, Supp. II, f. 109, Reitman Papers. Related to her feeling of emotional starvation was Emma's frequent sensa-

tion of being choked, strangled, or unable to breathe. Emotional stress often triggered this reaction. Visiting Rochester, she would complain that family members "simply choke me with their atmosphere." In close quarters with strangers, she felt stifled, unable to breathe. See EG to Reitman, 28 August 1909, II, f. 102, Reitman Papers; EG to Ellen Kennan, 6 September 1919, XXVII, EG Archive.

50. EG to Reitman, April 4, 2 A.M., II, f. 138, Reitman Papers.

51. EG, *Living My Life*, pp. 66–69.

52. Ibid., p. 59; *Rochester Post Express*, 28 October 1919. It is possible that Abraham's "fainting spells" were epileptic seizures and that he sought the baths at Königsberg in hopes of a cure.

53. EG, *Living My Life*, p. 116.

54. Ibid., p. 118.

55. Ibid., pp. 59–60.

56. Harris, "Emma Goldman," p. 228.

Chapter 2

"THE DISTANT SPECTER OF REVOLUTION"

1. *New York Sun*, 6 January 1901; *New York World*, 24 September 1893; *Pittsburgh Leader*, 27 February 1898; Hippolyte Havel, "Emma Goldman," in EG, *Anarchism and Other Essays*, p. 13; EG, *Living My Life*, p. 15.

2. EG, "Outline for Autobiography" IVA, EG Archive.

3. EG, *Living My Life*, p. 183.

4. Ibid., pp. 22–23.

5. Ibid., p. 23.

6. Ibid., pp. 27–28.

7. Harris, "Emma Goldman," p. 228; Havel, "Emma Goldman," pp. 9–10; *New York Sun*, 6 January 1901.

8. EG, *Living My Life*, p. 362.

9. Richard Stites, *The Women's Liberation Movement in Russia: Feminism, Nihilism and Bolshevism, 1860–1930* (Princeton: Princeton University Press, 1978), p. 153; see also Amy Knight, "The 'Fritschi': A Study of Female Radicals in the Russian Populist Movement," *Canadian-American Slavic Studies* 9, no. 1 (Spring 1975): 1–17.

10. Barbara Alpern Engel and Clifford N. Rosenthal, eds. and trans., *Five Sisters: Women Against the Czar* (New York: Alfred A. Knopf, 1975), p. 69.

11. EG, *Living My Life*, p. 370.

12. Stites, *Women's Liberation Movement*, p. 157.

13. EG, *Living My Life*, p. 11.

14. Steamship Register #1572, S. S. *Geilert* from Hamburg to New York, arriving 29 December 1885, U.S. National Archives. Helene and Emma Binovitz are listed as second-class passengers.

15. EG, *Living My Life*, pp. 11–12.

Chapter 3

"A GREAT IDEAL, A BURNING FAITH"

1. EG, *Living My Life*, p. 23; *New York Daily Tribune*, 11 October 1893; *Rochester Post Express*, 28 October 1919. I have retained the spelling "Kersner" used on all citizenship documents.

2. Goldman recalled that she had been married in February 1887. Lena believed the marriage had taken place at her home in November 1886, two months after their parents had arrived from Russia. Since the religious ceremony was not accompanied by a civil one, there is no official record. See Lena's comment in the *Rochester Post Express*, 28 October 1919.

3. *New York Daily Tribune*, 11 October 1893.

4. EG, *Living My Life*, p. 23.

5. Quoted in Philip Foner, *History of the Labor Movement in the United States*, vol. 2 (New York: International Publishers, 1965), p. 11.

6. Henry David, *The History of the Haymarket Affair* (New York: Farrar & Rinehart, 1963). For a new appraisal, see Paul Avrich, *The Haymarket Tragedy* (Princeton, N.J.: Princeton University Press, 1984).

7. *New York Sun*, 6 January 1901; Havel, "Emma Goldman," pp. 17–18; Harris, "Emma Goldman," pp. 229–30.

8. EG, *Living My Life*, p. 10.

9. Shulman, *Red Emma Speaks*, p. 55.

10. EG to Frank Heiner, 20 September 1935, XIV, EG Archive.

11. EG, *Living My Life*, p. 9.

12. *New York Sun*, 6 January 1901.

13. EG to Berkman, 19 August 1927, in Drinnon and Drinnon, *Nowhere at Home*, p. 100; EG to Frank Heiner, 16 October 1934, XIV, EG Archive.

14. David, *Haymarket Affair*, pp. 480, 531.

15. EG, *Living My Life*, p. 209.

16. *Rochester Democrat and Chronicle*, 26 July 1923; *Rochester Evening Journal and Post Express*, 26 July 1923; *New York Times*, 26 July 1923; Therese Goldman, Death Certificate.

17. *Rochester Post Express*, 14 January 1909; Abraham Goldman, Last

Will and Testament. Abraham died 14 January 1909, of "atrophic cirrhosis of liver" and "exhaustion" (Death Certificate).

18. See Grace N. Knaut, *An Unfinished Symphony: The Story of David Hochstein* (Rochester, N.Y.: Hochstein Music School, 1980). The Hochstein Music School, which opened in 1920 in memory of David Hochstein, was originally located at 421 Joseph Avenue, the home of Helene and Jacob Hochstein, and was dedicated to providing a musical education to the talented but poor. See also David Hochstein's obituary, *New York Times*, 28 January 1919; *World War Service Record of Rochester and Monroe County, New York*, vol. 1 (City of Rochester, 1924); "Who Was David Hochstein?," *Rochester Times Union*, 23 April 1976. Hochstein studied in New York, St. Petersburg, and Vienna; won the highest state prize and scholarship granted to a musician by the Austrian government; made his debut in Vienna in 1911; and performed widely in England and the United States, where he played as soloist with the New York Philharmonic. He was evidently the model for the hero of the novel *One of Ours* by Willa Cather, who had met him shortly before he went to fight in France.

19. Born in 1892, Commins grew up in Rochester and studied dentistry —a profession he hated. In his late thirties, he left dentistry to work as an editor, first at Horace Liveright, then at Random House in 1933. He eventually became editor-in-chief and for many years directed the Modern Library Series. Although relations between Commins and his aunt grew strained in the mid-1930s, they were close while he was young. He lived with Emma for a time in New York, and helped with and wrote for *Mother Earth*. He also did some editorial work on her autobiography. He died on July 17, 1958, at the age of sixty-six. See his obituary, *New York Times*, 18 July 1958; and Dorothy Berliner Commins, *What Is an Editor?* (Chicago: University of Chicago Press, 1978).

20. EG to Reitman, 28 August 1909, II, f. 102, Reitman Papers; EG to Frank Heiner, 27 March 1935, XIV, EG Archive.

21. Nikolai Chernyshevsky, *What Is to Be Done?* trans. Benjamin R. Tucker (New York: Vintage Books, 1961), p. 69.

Chapter 4

EDUCATION OF AN ANARCHIST

1. EG, *Living My Life*, p. 3.
2. Ronald Sanders, *The Downtown Jews* (New York: Harper & Row, 1969), pp. 66–67.

3. *New York Sun*, 6 January 1901.

4. EG to Frank Harris, 7 August 1925, XVIIB, EG Archive.

5. Martin Miller, *Kropotkin* (Chicago: Chicago University Press, 1976), p. 197.

6. Peter Kropotkin, "Anarchism: Its Philosophy and Ideal," in Roger Baldwin, ed., *Kropotkin's Revolutionary Pamphlets* (New York: Benjamin Blom, 1970).

7. EG to Reitman, 12 August 1910, II, f. 105, Reitman Papers.

8. See Paul Robinson, *The Modernization of Sex* (New York: Harper & Row, 1976).

9. See Hal Sears, *The Sex Radicals: Free Love in High Victorian America* (Lawrence: Regents Press of Kansas, 1977); also Linda Gordon, *Woman's Body, Woman's Right: A Social History of Birth Control in America* (New York: Penguin Books, 1977), pp. 96–115. James C. Mohr, *Abortion in America: The Origins and Evolution of National Policy, 1800–1900* (New York: Oxford University Press, 1978), pp. 196–97.

10. See John Carroll, *Break-out from the Crystal Palace. The Anarcho-Psychological Critique: Stirner, Nietzsche, Dostoyevsky* (London/Boston: Routledge & Kegan Paul, 1974). Marx thought Stirner so serious a threat to socialism that he devoted two-thirds of *The German Ideology* to attacking the idealist, "religious" basis of his thought.

11. George Woodcock and Ivan Avakomovic, *The Anarchist Prince: A Biographical Study of Kropotkin* (London: Boardman, 1950), p. 281.

12. EG, *Living My Life*, p. 194. See also EG to Ellen Kennan, 6 September 1919, XXVII, EG Archive.

13. "Tucker himself had the mind of a shopkeeper though he was able with his pen," wrote Goldman in 1934. "And his followers were not better, mere adding machines, no depths, no passions, no intencities [*sic*]. Just sawdust" (EG to Frank Heiner, 27 March 1935, XIV, EG Archive).

14. See William O. Reichert, *Partisans of Freedom: A Study in American Anarchism* (Bowling Green, Ohio: Bowling Green University, Popular Press, 1976), pp. 371–82; EG, "Johann Most," *American Mercury* 8 (June 1926): 158–66; Frederick W. Mitchell, "Johann Most and *Freiheit*," *Lucifer*, 12 December 1902; David, *Haymarket Affair*, pp. 83–106.

15. Johann Most, *The Social Monster* (New York: John Muller, 1890).

16. EG, "Johann Most" (typescript), EG, XVI6, EG Archive.

17. Margaret Sanger, *An Autobiography* (1938; reprint ed. New York: Dover, 1971), p. 72.

18. "I am paying since years [back] for Most's violent harangues. All our trouble is due to that. He has done anarchism no end of harm . . ." (EG to Reitman, 23 August 1910, II, f. 90, Reitman Papers).

19. EG, *Living My Life*, p. 74; interview with Sam Dolgoff and Esther Dolgoff, 13 May 1983.

20. EG, *Living My Life*, p. 72.

21. Paul Avrich, "Introduction," in Alexander Berkman, *What Is Communist Anarchism?* (1929; reprint ed. New York: Dover, 1972), pp. vi–vii; Frank Venturi, *Roots of Revolution*, trans. Francis Haskell (New York: Grosset & Dunlap, 1966), pp. 356, 472. Venturi describes Natanson as "one of the best known of all Populist and Socialist Revolutionaries" and "a man of great energy and initiative and rare organizing ability." He died in Berne in 1919.

22. Alexander Berkman, *Prison Memoirs of an Anarchist* (1912; reprint ed. Pittsburgh, Pa.: Frontier Press, 1970), p. 8.

23. Ibid., pp. 18–19; Richard Drinnon, *Rebel in Paradise: A Biography of Emma Goldman* (Chicago: University of Chicago Press, 1961), pp. 39–41.

24. Berkman, *Prison Memoirs*, pp. 20–23.

25. EG, *Living My Life*, pp. 5–6, 46.

26. Berkman, *Prison Memoirs*, p. 10.

27. Ibid., p. 76.

28. Venturi, *Roots of Revolution*, pp. 364–67. Bakunin and Nechaev described the revolutionary as "a lost man" for whom "everything that allows the triumph of the revolution is moral, and everything that stands in its way is immoral. . . . Hard with himself, he must be hard toward others. All the tender feelings of family life, of friendship, love, gratitude and even honour must be stifled in him by a single cold passion for the revolutionary cause. For him there is only one pleasure, one consolation, one reward, and one satisfaction—the success of the revolution." Venturi notes that Mark Natanson, Berkman's uncle, strongly opposed Nechaev's ideas and was one of his main adversaries (p. 562). Vera Zasulich, too, points out that among the young revolutionaries in St. Petersburg, the precepts of the *Catechism* "provoked both laughter and anger—so little did they correspond to what actually happened." See Engel, *Five Sisters*, p. 75.

29. EG to Berkman, 6 February 1929, XIIIB, EG Archive.

30. Berkman, *Prison Memoirs*, p. 145.

31. EG, *Living My Life*, p. 32.

32. Berkman, *Prison Memoirs*, p. 76; *New York Times*, 27 February 1958.

33. EG, *Living My Life*, p. 45.

34. EG, "Manuscript Outline," IVA, EG Archive.

35. EG, *Living My Life*, p. 120.

36. EG to Henry Alsberg, 20 March 1930, XIX, EG Archive.

37. EG, *Living My Life*, pp. 54–56.

38. See Louis Levine, *The Women's Garment Workers Union* (New York: B. W. Huebsch, 1924), pp. 48–55.

39. *New York Sun*, 6 January 1901.

Chapter 5

ATTENTAT: "THE CONSCIOUSNESS OF GUILT"

1. Henry David, "Upheaval at Homestead," in Daniel Aaron, ed., *America in Crisis* (New York: Alfred A. Knopf, 1952), p. 162; also Leon Wolff, *Lockout: The Story of the Homestead Strike of 1892* (New York: Harper & Row, 1965).
2. David, "Upheaval at Homestead," p. 162.
3. EG, *Living My Life*, pp. 84–85; Berkman, *Prison Memoirs*, p. 9.
4. Berkman, *Prison Memoirs*, p. 10, 76.
5. Ibid., p. 14.
6. Berkman's resolve to commit a suicidal act of political protest may have been heightened by more private passions as well. According to the memoirs of both Berkman and Goldman, Berkman struggled against the temptation to commit suicide at critical moments throughout his life. Fantasies about death pervade the early part of his *Prison Memoirs*, from gruesome images of a hooded executioner slicing off the head of his beloved Uncle Maxim, to fantasies and plans for his own death by dynamite, shooting, hanging, and bleeding. Throughout, Berkman questions his own right to live and debates the merits of life over death. His memoirs suggest that the origins of this attraction to suicide lay partly in an unresolved family conflict. The first chapter, "The Call of Homestead," juxtaposes a description of the strike and the development of his assassination plans with flashbacks to his earlier life in Russia—highlighting the illness and death of his mother, who had become sick at a time when Berkman's relations with her were extremely tense. "Vaguely I feel guilty of mother's illness," he wrote (p. 17). She died when he was longing for a reconciliation but felt too angry to approach her. The deathbed scene, inserted into the narrative of his trip to Homestead, suggests the legacy of guilt the young Berkman had carried with him to America:

> Tenderly I wrap my arms around the weak, emaciated body, and an overpowering longing seizes me to touch her hand with my lips and on my knees beg her forgiveness. I feel so near to her, my heart is overflowing with compassion and love. But I dare not kiss her—we have become estranged. Affectionately I hold her in my arms for just the shadow of a second, dreading lest she suspect the storm of emotion raging within me. Caressingly I turn her to the wall, and as I slowly withdraw, I feel as if some mysterious, yet definite something has at the very instant left her body. (P. 22)

The death of his mother ended forever the possibility of reconciliation—except, in fantasy, through his own death. This early trauma may help to account not only for Berkman's attraction to suicide, but also to a suicidal political act such as the *attentat*, an act which would demonstrate to the people "the depth of a love that will give its own life for their cause. To give a young life, full of health and vitality, to give all, without a thought of self . . . could anyone fail to understand such a love?" (p. 63). In light of Berkman's isolation from the workers at Homestead, the almost mystical aura with which he endowed their struggle, and his glorification of death, we can surmise a multiplicity of motives, personal as well as political, unconscious as well as conscious, behind this one overdetermined act.

7. *New York Times*, 20 September, 1892; on Lingg's suicide see David, *Haymarket Affair*, pp. 254–56.

8. Ibid.; Drinnon, *Rebel*, pp. 19–52, Paul Kennedy, *Emma Goldman: A Life of Anarchy* (Toronto: Canadian Broadcasting Company, 1983), p. 7; Wolff, *Lockout*, pp. 172–75; PMA, pp. 42, 73.

9. *New York Times*, 20 September 1892.

10. Emma recalled that those who defended Berkman included Saverio Merlino, Dyer D. Lum, Joseph Barondess, T. H. Garside, William C. Owen and John Edelman. See EG, "Manuscript Outline," IVA, EG Archive.

11. EG to Max Nettlau, 24 January 1932, XVII, EG Archive.

12. Max Nomad, *Apostles of Revolution* (Boston: Little, Brown, 1939), p. 245, quoted in Terry Perlin, "Anarchist-Communism in America, 1890–1914" (Ph.D. dissertation, Brandeis University, 1970), p. 106.

13. EG to Max Nettlau, 24 January 1932, XVII, EG Archive.

14. *New York Daily Tribune*, 7 October 1893.

15. Havel, "Emma Goldman," p. 22; Harris, "Emma Goldman," p. 281.

16. Berkman, *Prison Memoirs*, pp. 4, 88–90, 125–26, 344.

17. Alexander Berkman, "Diary," 22 May 1930, XXI, Berkman Archive; see also EG to Berkman, 6 February 1919, XIIIB, EG Archive.

18. EG, *Living My Life*, p. 88.

19. EG to Max Nettlau, 24 January 1932, VII, EG Archive.

20. EG to Arthur Ross, 13 January 1929, V, EG Archive; quoted in Drinnon, *Rebel*, p. 82.

21. Ben Reitman, "Following the Monkey," p. 298, Reitman Papers.

22. EG to Max Nettlau, 24 January 1932, VII, EG Archive.

23. Berkman, *Prison Memoirs*, pp. 143–44. Responding to Berkman's charge in her own memoirs, Goldman wrote that "comrades visiting me expressed the opinion that Sasha had 'failed.' " Their doubts had made her "frantic," and she had written asking him "to send word that would stop the horrible rumors about him." (*Living My Life*, p. 103). Thus not she but the "comrades" had spoken of "failure."

24. EG to Max Metzkow, 8 October 1892, Ishill Collection.

25. Berkman, *Prison Memoirs*, pp. 158–60.

26. Ibid., pp. 144–45.

27. EG to Max Metzkow, 8 October 1892, Ishill Collection.

28. Berkman, *Prison Memoirs*, p. 310.

29. EG, *Living My Life*, p, 101.

30. EG to Theodore Dreiser, 15 December 1929, XIXA-G, EG Archive.

31. EG, *Living My Life*, p. 272.

32. EG to Arthur Leonard Ross, 13 January 1929, V, EG Archive; quoted in Drinnon, *Rebel*, p. 82.

33. EG to Berkman, 19 September 1927, XIX, Berkman Archive.

34. EG, *Living My Life*, p. 393.

Chapter 6

"THE STRENGTH TO STAND ALONE"

1. EG, *Living My Life*, pp. 118–19.

2. Ibid., p. 119.

3. Ibid., p. 183.

4. Ibid., pp. 58–61.

5. Ibid., p. 61.

6. Ibid., pp. 61, 340.

7. Ibid., pp. 194–95.

8. *New York Times*, 19 August 1893.

9. *Rochester Daily Union and Advertiser*, 22 August 1893.

10. *New York Tribune*, 7 October 1893; see also Drinnon, *Rebel*, pp. 58–61. Philip Foner notes that while Samuel Gompers and other AFL officials had at first relied on committees to secure aid for the unemployed, they soon realized the necessity for mass demonstrations to back up their resolutions and petitions. See Foner, *Labor Movement*, vol. 2, pp. 236–39.

11. Voltairine de Cleyre, "In Defence of Emma Goldman and the Right of Expropriation," in Alexander Berkman, ed., *Selected Works of Voltairine de Cleyre* (New York: Mother Earth Publishing Association, 1914), pp. 205–19; EG, *Living My Life*, pp. 122–23.

12. *New York Times*, 24 August 1893.

13. EG, *Living My Life*, p. 127.

14. *New York World*, 17 September 1893.

15. *New York Tribune*, 7 October 1893; Drinnon, *Rebel*, pp. 58–61.

16. *New York World*, 20 August 1894.
17. *New York World*, 18 August 1894.
18. EG, *Living My Life*, p. 148.

Chapter 7

"THE SPIRIT OF REVOLT"

1. *The Firebrand*, 1 December 1895.
2. *The Firebrand*, 17 November 1895.
3. Goldman recalled privately that Freud had spoken on "inversion" and that "it was Freud who gave me my first understanding of homosexuality" (EG to Berkman, 20 February 1929, in Drinnon and Drinnon, *Nowhere at Home*, p. 146). Although she admired Freud personally, she was critical of psychoanalysis, seeing in it "nothing but the old confessional" (EG to Frank Heiner, 24 July 1934, XIV, EG Archive).
4. EG, *Living My Life*, p. 172.
5. Goldman recalled that she had first traveled to the West Coast in 1897. Contemporary anarchist periodicals show that she did not reach California until the spring of 1898. (I am grateful to Blaine McKinley for calling this point to my attention.)
6. *Free Society*, 18 June 1899.
7. *The Firebrand*, 23 May 1897; *Free Society*, 30 July 1899.
8. *Free Society*, 9 January 1898.
9. *Free Society*, 14 November 1897.
10. *Solidarity*, 15 March 1898.
11. EG to Max Metzkow, 2 December 1896, 17 December 1896, 30 December 1896, Ishill Collection.
12. EG to Max Metzkow, 2 December 1896, Ishill Collection.
13. EG to Max Metzkow, 30 December 1896, Ishill Collection.
14. EG, *Living My Life*, p. 967; EG to Van Valkenburgh, 11 December 1927, I1–5, EG Archive; EG to Nunya Seldes, 18 May 1906, EG Papers, Schlesinger Library; Department of Labor, file 11086, No. 52416–43, p. 153, 14 December 1907, National Archives.
15. *Free Society*, 21 October 1900.
16. Ibid.
17. *Free Society*, 5 June 1898.
18. *Free Society*, 15 May 1898.
19. EG, "Anarchism: What It Really Stands For," *Essays*, p. 72.

20. EG, "The Failure of Christianity," in Shulman, *Red Emma Speaks*, p. 187.

21. EG, *Living My Life*, p. 561.

22. Interviews with Ahrne Thorne, 19 May 1983; Clara Solomon, 18 May 1983; Esther Dolgoff and Sam Dolgoff, 13 May 1983; Sonya Farber, 12 September 1979.

23. *Mother Earth*, December 1907, p. 447.

24. EG lecture, February 1908, file 52416-43, U.S. Department of Labor, Immigration and Naturalization Service.

25. EG, "Anarchism," *Essays*, p. 64.

26. Ibid., p. 62.

27. Ibid., pp. 61–62.

28. *New York World*, 17 September 1893.

29. *Free Society*, 13 August 1899.

30. Ibid.

31. *Michigan Daily*, 17 March 1912; EG, "The Element of Sex in Life" (typescript), XXIXA, EG Archive; EG, "The Hypocrisy of Puritanism," *Essays*, pp. 177–78.

32. *Lucifer*, 23 March 1901.

33. *The Firebrand*, 18 July 1897.

34. *Rochester Herald*, 6 December 1897.

35. EG, *Living My Life*, pp. 556–57.

36. Ibid., p. 397.

37. *Free Society*, 23 July 1899.

38. *New York Sun*, 6 January 1901.

39. EG to Frank Heiner, 20 September 1935, XIV, EG Archive.

40. EG, "Minorities versus Majorities," *Essays*, p. 83.

41. *Mother Earth*, January 1913, p. 1.

42. EG, *Essays*, pp. 54, 80, 204.

43. Drinnon, *Rebel*, p. 158.

44. EG, "Minorities versus Majorities," *Essays*, p. 84.

45. George Woodcock, *Anarchism: A History of Libertarian Ideas and Movements* (New York: World, 1962), p. 28.

46. EG, *Essays*, p. 56. "Human beings are pretty much the same to whatever class or creed they belong. They either have character or they have not. I do not believe that their economic status has anything to do with it" (EG to Mark Clevans, 11 December 1925, EG Archive).

47. *New York Sun*, 6 January 1901.

48. *Free Society*, 19 May 1901.

49. EG, "The Individual, Society and the State," in Shulman, *Red Emma Speaks*, p. 97.

50. Alexander Berkman, *A.B.C. of Anarchism* (1929; reprint ed. London: Freedom Press, 1977), p. 35.

51. Shulman, *Red Emma Speaks*, p. 15; EG, *Living My Life*, pp. 131–32.
52. Van Valkenburgh to EG, 25 September 1932, XVA, EG Archive.
53. *San Francisco Call*, quoted in *Free Society*, 22 May 1898.

Chapter 8

CZOLGOSZ

1. *Free Society*, 10 July 1898, 29 April 1900.
2. *New York Sun*, 6 January 1901.
3. EG, "An Open Letter," *Free Society*, 17 February 1901.
4. EG, *Living My Life*, pp. 224–25.
5. *New York Sun*, 6 January 1901.
6. Ibid.
7. EG to Frank Heiner, 13 April 1935, XIV, EG Archive.
8. EG, *Living My Life*, p. 155.
9. Ibid., p. 290.
10. *Free Society*, 1 September 1901.
11. See Sidney Fine, "Anarchism and the Assassination of McKinley," *American Historical Review* 15, no. 4 (July 1955): 777–99.
12. *New York Times*, 8 September 1901.
13. EG, *Living My Life*, p. 296.
14. Ibid., p. 307; also *Chicago Tribune*, 11 September 1901.
15. *New York Times*, 11 September 1901; *Chicago Tribune*, 10, 11 September 1901.
16. *New York Times*, 13 September 1901.
17. *New York Times*, 11 September 1901.
18. *Chicago Tribune*, 13 September 1901.
19. EG to Harry Weinberger, 21 September 1919, Harry Weinberger Papers, Sterling Memorial Library, Yale University, New Haven, Conn.; see Fine, "Assassination of McKinley," p. 780; Wesley A. Johns, *The Man Who Shot McKinley* (South Brunswick, N.J. New York: A. S. Barnes, 1970); Drinnon, *Rebel*, pp. 68–77; EG to Harry Weinberger, 21 September 1919, Weinberger Papers.
20. *New York Times*, 8 September 1901; for a recent but unconvincing reappraisal, see James W. Clarke, *American Assassins* (Princeton, N.J.: Princeton University Press, 1982).
21. Quoted in Drinnon, *Rebel*, pp. 76–77.
22. *Free Society*, 6 October 1901.
23. *Lucifer*, 21 November 1901.
24. *Ibid.*

25. EG, "The Psychology of Political Violence," *Essays*, pp. 79–108.

26. Berkman, *Prison Memoirs*, p. 433.

27. Miller, *Kropotkin*, p. 175; *New York Times*, 8 September 1901; *Chicago Tribune*, 7, 8 September 1901. Johann Most, Carl Nold, and Lucy Parsons all outspokenly condemned the assassination.

28. Voltairine de Cleyre, "McKinley's Assassination from the Anarchist Standpoint," *Mother Earth*, September 1907, pp. 3–4. Goldman later insisted that Czolgosz was indeed "one of us" (EG to "Dear Comrade," 9 April 1929, XVIIC, EG Archive).

29. EG, *Living My Life*, pp. 309–10.

30. EG to Leon Malmed, 29 October 1926, EG Papers, Schlesinger Library, Radcliffe College, Cambridge, Mass.

31. EG to Van Valkenburgh, 29 October 1932, EG Archive.

32. Berkman, *Prison Memoirs*, p. 434.

33. Ibid., p. 435.

34. EG, *Living My Life*, p. 324.

Chapter 9

TOWARD A NEW ANARCHIST COMMUNITY

1. EG, *Living My Life*, p. 318.

2. William Preston, Jr.. *Aliens and Dissenters: Federal Suppression of Radicals, 1903–1933* (New York: Harper & Row, 1963), p. 33.

3. EG, *Living My Life*, p. 328.

4. Ibid., p. 329.

5. EG to Berkman, 18 January 1904, XIIIB, Berkman Archive.

6. EG to AB, [1904], XIIIB, Berkman Archive; see also EG to Ellen Kennan, 21 July 1914, XXVII, EG Archive; EG to Reitman, 26 March [1908], II, f. 140, Reitman Papers.

7. EG to Berkman, [1904], XIIIB, Berkman Archive.

8. EG, *Living My Life*, p. 359.

9. Ibid., p. 552.

10. *Mother Earth*, March 1915, p. 435.

11. *New York Sun*, 6 January 1901.

12. EG, *Living My Life*, p. 377.

13. *Mother Earth*, March 1906, p. 4.

14. On D. H. Lawrence, see EG to Stella Ballantine, 30 March 1919, 23 March 1918, XVI9, EG Archive; on Turgenev, see EG to Michael Cohn, 2 April 1925, XVI4, EG Archive; on Gorky, see EG to Harry Weinberger, 21 September 1919, Weinberger Papers; on Galsworthy, see EG to Stella Bal-

lantine, 15 August 1919, XVI9, EG Archive; on Hemingway, see EG to Frank Heiner, 12 June 1935, XIV, EG Archive. Goldman frequently lectured on Walt Whitman, suggesting that "it was his sex differentiation which enriched his nature, hence enriched his knowledge of and his understanding for human complexities. Walt Whitman's idea of universal comradeship was conditioned in his magnetic response to his own sex" (typescript, Ic, EG Archive). See also EG to Evelyn Scott, 21 November 1927, in Drinnon and Drinnon, *Nowhere at Home*, pp. 140–41.

15. EG to Ellen Kennan, [1920s], XVII, EG Archive.

16. EG to Saxe Commins, 15 February 1935, XVI9, EG Archive.

17. EG to Stella Ballantine, 30 June 1918, XVI9, EG Archive.

18. EG to Reitman, 3 April [1908], II, f. 132, Reitman Papers.

19. EG to Berkman, 22 August 1931, XIIIB, EG Archive.

20. EG, *Living My Life*, pp. 218–19; Paul Avrich, personal communication.

21. See Max Baginski, "The Old and New Drama," *Mother Earth*, April 1906; "Gerhart Hauptmann with the Weavers of Silesia," *Mother Earth*, May 1906.

22. EG to Reitman, 10 April [1909], II, f. 132. Reitman Papers.

23. Ibid., EG to Saxe Commins, 17 May 1931, XVIIA, EG Archive; for a biographical sketch of Havel, see Paul Avrich, *The Modern School Movement: Anarchism and Education in the United States* (Princeton, N.J.: Princeton University Press, 1980), pp. 121–24; also Reichert, *Partisans of Freedom*, pp. 427–32.

24. For biographical sketches of Kelly, see Avrich, *Modern School*, pp. 172–79; Reichert, *Partisans of Freedom*, pp. 441–48; Blaine McKinley, " 'The Quagmires of Necessity': American Anarchists and Dilemmas of Vocation," *American Quarterly* 34, no. 5 (Winter 1982): 503–12.

25. Leonard Abbott to EG, 21 November 1931, IV, EG Archive.

26. Quoted in Avrich, *Modern School*, p. 172.

27. Leonard Abbott, "Emma Goldman as I Knew Her," EG Papers, Tamiment Library, New York University.

28. Leonard Abbott to Agnes Inglis, 20 February 1943, Labadie Collection.

29. Paul Avrich, *An American Anarchist: The Life of Voltairine de Cleyre* (Princeton, N.J.: Princeton University Press, 1978), p. 149; see also Margaret Marsh, *Anarchist Women, 1870–1920* (Philadelphia: Temple University Press, 1981), pp. 122–50; Blaine McKinley, " 'Quagmires of Necessity,' " pp. 512–16.

30. Avrich, *Voltairine de Cleyre*, p. 90.

31. *New York Sun*, 6 January 1901.

32. Marsh, *Anarchist Women*, p. 148.

33. EG, *Living My Life*, p. 158.

34. Berkman, *Prison Memoirs*, pp. 507–08.

35. Ibid., p. 38.

36. Ibid., p. 57.

37. EG to Berkman, 17 March 1907, XVIIB, Berkman Archive.

38. Berkman, *Prison Memoirs*, pp. 511–12.

39. EG, *Living My Life*, p. 393.

40. EG to Berkman, 14 May 1929, in Drinnon and Drinnon, *Nowhere at Home*, p. 148; EG, *Living My Life*, pp. 411–12.

41. EG to Berkman, 17 March 1907, XVIIB, Berkman Archive.

42. Ibid.

43. EG to Berkman, 19 March 1907, XVIIB, Berkman Archive.

44. EG, *Living My Life*, p. 412.

45. EG to Berkman, 19 November 1935, in Drinnon and Drinnon, *Nowhere at Home*, p. 247.

46. Interview with Sam Dolgoff, 13 May 1983; James Joll, *The Anarchists* (London: Eyre & Spottiswood, 1964), pp. 203–5; on the I.W.W. see Melvyn Dubofsky, *We Shall Be All: A History of the Industrial Workers of the World* (Chicago: Quadrangle Books, 1969); also Joseph Conlin, *Bread and Roses: Studies of the Wobblies* (Westport, Conn.: Greenwood Publishers, 1969); Meredith Tax, *The Rising of the Women: Feminist Solidarity and Class Conflict, 1880–1917* (New York: Monthly Review Press, 1980), pp. 125–63; Ann Schoefield, "Rebel Girls and Union Maids: The Woman Question in the Journals of the AFL and IWW, 1905–1920," *Feminist Studies* 9, no. 2 (Summer 1983): 335–58.

47. *International Anarchist Congress, Amsterdam, 26–31 August 1907* (London: Freedom Press, 1907), EG Archive.

48. Joll, *Anarchists*, p. 205; Paul Avrich, *The Russian Anarchists* (Princeton, N.J.: Princeton University Press, 1967), pp. 82–84.

49. Ibid., p. 204; EG, "The International Anarchist Congress," *Mother Earth*, October 1907, p. 312.

50. Dorothy Day, *The Long Loneliness* (1952; reprint ed. Garden City, N.Y.: Doubleday, 1959); Otto Steen to author, 20 July 1980.

51. When Berkman wrote years later that he had "come to the conclusion that work in the unions offers much greater chance of real propaganda and education than just lectures for outside and chance audiences," Goldman replied, "Work in the unions, fine. Whoever objected to going into the unions. The trouble is that most of our comrades who went into them stopped being Anarchists and shouted with the Romans. Even in France where the Anarchists were the originators of revolutionary syndicalism, Pouget, Delasalle, Monatte and the others, what's become of them, what has become of their influence? . . . You are right when you say that unions offer a great field. But they are not the only field, and unions are fertile soil only if they already have some red blood in them." (EG to Berkman, 7

December 1927, in Drinnon and Drinnon, *Nowhere at Home*, p. 78; EG to Berkman, 23 December 1927, XIII, EG Archive.) See also David Porter, ed., *Vision on Fire: Emma Goldman on the Spanish Revolution* (New Paltz, N.Y.: Commonground Press, 1983), pp. 284–85.

52. *Mother Earth*, October 1907, p. 312.

53. William Marion Reedy, "Daughter of the Dream," *Mother Earth*, December 1908; EG, *Living My Life*, p. 401.

54. EG, *Essays*, p. 230.

Chapter 10

"THE SUBLIME MADNESS OF SEX"

1. EG, *Living My Life*, p. 307.
2. EG to Reitman, 4 January 1915, II, f. 128, Reitman Papers.
3. Reitman, "Following the Monkey," pp. 11, 358.
4. Ibid., p. 44.
5. Ibid., p. 144.
6. EG to Jake Margolis, 6 April 1908, X, EG Archive.
7. EG, *Living My Life*, p. 420.
8. Reitman, "Following the Monkey," p. 216.
9. Ibid., p. 187.
10. EG to Reitman, n.d., 5 P.M., II, f. 137, Reitman Papers.
11. EG to Reitman, 25 March 1908, II, [f. 135], Reitman Papers.
12. EG, *Living My Life*, p. 422.
13. EG to Reitman, 26 March, 30 March [1908], II, f. 140, Reitman Papers.
14. EG to Reitman, 1 April [1908], II, [f. 140], Reitman Papers.
15. EG, *Living My Life*, p. 433.
16. *Michigan Daily*, 17 March 1912.
17. "Margaret" to Agnes Inglis, 13 February 1933, Labadie Collection.
18. EG, *Living My Life*, p. 433.
19. EG to Reitman, 29 June [1911], II, f. 109, Reitman Papers.
20. EG to Reitman, 27 September 1911, II, f. 98, Reitman Papers.
21. EG to Reitman, "on the steamer to Ossining," 2 July [1910]; 31 March [1909], 4 P.M., II, [f. 132–146], Reitman Papers.
22. EG to Reitman, 31 March [1909], II [f. 132–146], Reitman Papers.
23. EG to Reitman, 29 June 1911, II, f. 109, Reitman Papers.
24. EG to Reitman, 31 March [1909], 4 P.M., II, [f. 132–146], Reitman Papers.

25. Ibid.

26. EG to Reitman, 13 December 1910, II, f. 108, Reitman Papers.

27. EG to Reitman, 14 August [1910], II, f. 105, Reitman Papers.

28. EG to Reitman, "farm, the pheasant hen waiting for chanticleer," n.d., original accession, f. 20, Reitman Papers.

29. Ibid.

30. EG to Reitman, 31 July 1911, II, f. 110, Reitman Papers.

31. EG to Reitman, 22 October 1910, original accession, f. 15, Reitman Papers.

32. EG to Reitman, n.d., 10 P.M., II, f. 144, Reitman Papers.

33. EG to Reitman, 17 October 1914, II, f. 124, Reitman Papers.

34. Ibid.

35. DG to Reitman, 7 August 1911, II, f. 111, Reitman Papers.

36. EG to Reitman, 2 July [1910], II, [f. 132–146]; EG to Reitman, 3 July, no year, original accession, f. 20, Reitman Papers.

37. EG to Reitman, "on the steamer to Ossining," 2 July [1910], II, [f. 132–146], Reitman Papers.

38. EG to Reitman, 27 June 1910, II, f. 104, Reitman Papers.

39. EG to Reitman, 26 September 1912, II, f. 115, Reitman Papers.

40. EG to Reitman, "the farm, at night," [1910], original accession, f. 20, Reitman Papers.

41. EG to Reitman, 6 September 1910, II, f. 107, Reitman Papers.

42. EG to Reitman, 29 November 1910, original accession, f. 15, Reitman Papers.

43. EG to Reitman, 12 December 1910, II, f. 107, Reitman Papers.

44. EG to Reitman, 27 July 1911, II, f. 110, Reitman Papers.

45. EG to Reitman, 27 June 1910, II, f. 104, Reitman Papers.

46. Lucy Parsons to Carl Nold, 5 May 1930, Labadie Collection.

47. See, for example, Reitman's complaints about Emma keeping "Willie on a starvation diet," and his remark that "if you were not such an Idealist I would come out tonight and drink freely from the T.B. But you don't like to feel that you are a mere wife, you also told me that I was so hard on you the last time that you were rather compelled to give in to me" (Reitman to EG, 3, 4 September 1914, EG Papers, Mugar Memorial Library, Boston University). Years later, Reitman told Emma that he often thought about "your reluctance, or your hesitancy, or your fear, that if I saw much of you that there was danger of your being raped or giving in against your wishes" (Reitman to EG, 11 March 1934, XVIIB, EG Archive).

48. EG to Reitman, 21 July 1910, II, f. 105, Reitman Papers.

49. Eva Langbord to author, 26 December 1980.

50. EG to Reitman, 27 June 1910, II, f. 104, Reitman Papers.

51. EG to Ellen Kennan, [1918], XXVII, EG Archive.

52. EG to Reitman, 29 June 1910, II, f. 104, Reitman Papers.

53. Reitman to EG, [February–March 1914], EG Papers, Mugar Memorial Library.

54. Reitman, "Following the Monkey," p. 357.

55. See Almeda Sperry to EG, 5 January 1914, EG Papers, Mugar Memorial Library; EG to Nunya Seldes, 24 August [1912–13], EG Papers, Schlesinger Library.

56. Reitman to EG, September 1914, III, 1–5b, Reitman Papers, Ben Reitman, "A Visit to London," *Mother Earth*, October 1910.

57. EG to Reitman, 27 March 1911, II, f. 109, Reitman Papers.

58. EG, *Living My Life*, p. 432.

59. Reitman, "Following the Monkey," p. 213.

60. Ibid., pp. 359, 248.

61. Ibid., p. 257.

62. EG to Reitman, 26 September 1908, II, f. 98, Reitman Papers.

63. EG to Reitman, [June 1908], II, f. 98, Reitman Papers.

64. EG, "Love and Marriage," *Essays*, p. 244.

65. EG to Reitman, "en route," 30 March [1908], 9 P.M., II, [f. 134], Reitman Papers.

66. EG to Nunya Seldes, 24 August [1912 or 1913], EG Papers, Schlesinger Library.

67. EG to Reitman, 21 June 1909, II, f. 101, Reitman Papers.

68. EG to Frank Heiner, 22 May 1934, XIV, EG Archive.

69. EG to Nunya Seldes, 24 August [1912 or 1913], EG Papers, Schlesinger Library.

70. EG, "Jealousy: Causes and a Possible Cure," in Shulman, *Red Emma Speaks*, p. 175.

71. EG to Reitman, 13 December 1909, II, f. 102, Reitman Papers.

72. Ibid.

73. EG to Reitman, 14–15 December 1909, II, f. 102, Reitman Papers.

74. EG to Reitman, 16 December 1909, II, f. 102, Reitman Papers.

75. EG to Reitman, 21 December 1902, II, f. 102, Reitman Papers.

76. EG to Reitman, 23 December 1909, II, f. 102, Reitman Papers.

77. EG to Reitman, 30 December 1909, II, f. 103, Reitman Papers.

78. EG to Reitman, 31 July 1911, original accession, f. 16, Reitman Papers; EG to Reitman, 29 August [1912], II, f. 140, Reitman Papers.

79. EG to Reitman, 26 July [1911], 7 P.M., II, f. 110, Reitman Papers.

80. Reitman to EG, [1914], II, f. 96; Reitman to EG, [1914], III, f. 1–5b, Reitman Papers.

81. Reitman to EG, [1914], III, f. 1–6b, Reitman Papers.

82. Reitman to EG, 2 January 1911, II, f. 96, Reitman Papers.

83. EG, *Living My Life*, p. 581.

84. EG to Reitman, 24 July 1910, II, f. 105, Reitman Papers.

85. EG to Reitman, 26 July 1911, II, f. 109, Reitman Papers.

86. Ibid.

87. Ibid.

88. EG to Reitman, 29 July [1911], original accession, f. 16, Reitman Papers.

Chapter 11

"MORE OF A PUBLIC THAN A PRIVATE PERSON"

1. Theodore Dreiser to EG, 15 December 1928, in Robert H. Elias, ed., *Letters of Theodore Dreiser: A Selection* (Philadelphia: University of Pennsylvania Press, 1959), pp. 483–84.

2. See Ben Reitman's reports on Goldman's annual lecture tours—for example, "Three Years: Report of the Manager," *Mother Earth*, July 1911, p. 86; also EG to Harry Weinberger, 16 September 1917, Weinberger Papers; EG to Agnes Inglis, 23 May 1917, Labadie Collection.

3. *Mother Earth*, July 1910, p. 162; September 1915, p. 245; January 1916, pp. 366–69; EG to Alfred Knopf, 12 August 1929, V, EG Archive.

4. Margaret Anderson, "Emma Goldman in Chicago," *Mother Earth*, December 1914, p. 320.

5. Interview with Ahrne Thorne, 19 May 1983.

6. Floyd Dell, *Women as World Builders* (Chicago: Forbes, 1913), p. 60.

7. Sadakichi Hartmann to Reitman, 2 June 1940, EG Papers, New York Public Library.

8. Hutchins Hapgood, A *Victorian in the Modern World* (New York: Harcourt, Brace, 1939), pp. 203–4.

9. EG, *Living My Life*, p. 51.

10. EG, *Essays*, p. 47.

11. John Sloan, *John Sloan's New York Scene: From the Diaries, Notes and Correspondence, 1906–1913*, ed. Bruce St. John (New York: Harper & Row, 1965), pp. 570–71; Reitman, "Following the Monkey," p. 219.

12. Peggy Lamson, *Roger Baldwin, Founder of the American Civil Liberties Union* (Boston: Houghton Mifflin, 1976).

13. *Detroit News*, 1 November 1909, EG scrapbook, Labadie Collection.

14. William Innes Homer, *Robert Henri and His Circle* (Ithaca, N.Y.: Cornell University Press, 1969), p. 180.

15. Sadakichi Hartmann, "Voltairine de Cleyre," *Mother Earth*, April 1915, p. 92; Drinnon, *Rebel*, p. 194.

16. Elizabeth Gurley Flynn, *The Rebel Girl* (New York: International Publishing, 1973), p. 50; Hapgood, *Victorian in Modern World*, pp. 203–04.

17. Joan Norlander to author, 3 September 1980; Agnes Inglis to Ann Lord, 30 April 1934, Labadie Collection.

18. Charles Daniel Frey to Justice Department, 24 April 1917, FBI Files, OG15446, U.S. National Archives.

19. *Mother Earth*, December 1914, pp. 321–22.

20. John Nicholas Beffel, ed., *Art Young, His Life and Times* (New York: Sheridan House, 1939), p. 268.

21. Harry Kelly, "Memorial" (typescript), Labadie Collection.

22. Eva Langbord to author, 26 December 1980.

23. Interview with Sarah Toback, 12 September 1979.

24. *Mother Earth*, "On the Road," passim; see also EG to Agnes Inglis, 13 February 1917, Labadie Collection.

25. Kate Richards O'Hare Memorial Dinner, 17 November 1919, Tamiment Library.

26. EG, "Love and Marriage," *Essays*, p. 242.

27. EG, "Anarchism," *Essays*, p. 70.

28. EG, "Prisons," *Essays*, p. 117.

29. EG, "Hypocrisy of Puritanism," *Essays*, p. 180.

30. Shulman, *Red Emma Speaks*, p. 116.

31. Ibid., p. 187.

32. Ibid., p. 131.

33. EG, "The Tragedy of Woman's Emancipation," *Essays*, p. 220.

34. *Mother Earth*, August 1908, p. 250.

35. Interview with Sarah Toback, 12 September 1979.

36. Reitman, "Following the Monkey," p. 245.

37. *The Gazette*, 16 May 1934.

38. Reitman, "Following the Monkey," p. 245.

39. Daniel Malmed to author, 13 October 1980.

40. Reitman, "Following the Monkey," p. 245.

41. EG, *Living My Life*, p. 213.

42. Eva Langbord to author, 26 December 1980.

43. Reitman, "Following the Monkey," p. 245.

44. Daniel Malmed to author, 26 December 1980; Eva Langbord to author, 26 December 1980.

45. "Margaret" to Agnes Inglis, 13 February 1933, Labadie Collection.

46. Agnes Inglis to Max Metzkow, 2 January 1945, Labadie Collection.

47. Anderson, *My Thirty Years' War*, pp. 71–73.

48. EG to Ruth Olson, 21 March 1911, in possession of author.

49. EG to Reitman, 11 August 1911, II, f. 111, Reitman Papers.

50. *Mother Earth*, May 1907, p. 132.

51. See Reitman, "Three Years," *Mother Earth*, pp. 84–89.

52. EG to Nunya Seldes, 23 February 1911, EG Papers, Schlesinger Library.

53. EG to Hutchins Hapgood, 23 February 1911, Collection of American Literature, Beinecke Rare Book and Manuscript Library, Yale University, New Haven, Conn.

54. EG to Reitman, [1908], EG Papers, Schlesinger Library.

55. *Mother Earth*, January 1909.

56. March 9, 1908, File 52416-43, Department of Labor, U.S. National Archives.

57. Henry D. Cowles to George W. Wickersham, U.S. Attorney General, 15 May 1909, RG 186233-13, File 133149, U.S. National Archives.

58. *Mother Earth*, February 1909.

59. EG to Meyer Simkin and Sophie Simkin, 1 February 1909, II, f. 100, Reitman Papers.

60. EG to Meyer Simkin, 20 February 1909, II, f. 100, Reitman Papers.

61. EG to Reitman, 7 August 1911, II, f. 111, Reitman Papers.

62. Preston, *Aliens and Dissenters*, pp. 72–74.

63. Drinnon, *Rebel*, pp. 126–130.

64. Ibid., p. 138; *Mother Earth*, June 1908. Goldman immediately organized a defense committee for Buwalda, who was pardoned by President Roosevelt ten months later. Buwalda subsequently became involved with the anarchist movement.

65. *Mother Earth*, May 1911, p. 88.

66. See Dubofsky, *We Shall Be All*, pp. 191–97; Grace L. Miller, "The I.W.W. Free Speech Fight: San Diego, 1912," *Southern California Quarterly* 54 (Fall 1972): 211–38; Rosalie Shanks, "The I.W.W. Free Speech Movement, San Diego, 1912," *Journal of San Diego History* 19 (Winter 1973): 25–33.

67. *Mother Earth*, June 1912.

68. Dubofsky, *We Shall Be All*, pp. 151–52; Shanks, "Free Speech Movement," p. 32; Miller, "Free Speech Fight," pp. 230–33.

69. EG to Reitman, "Wed. 1912," II, f. 114, Reitman Papers.

70. EG to Reitman, 29 July 1912, II, f. 116, Reitman Papers.

71. EG, *Living My Life*, pp. 557–59.

72. *New York Sun*, 6 January 1901.

73. Almeda Sperry to EG, [1914], EG Papers, Mugar Memorial Library.

74. EG to Nunya Seldes, "October 4, the woods," [1912], EG Papers, Schlesinger Library.

75. Almeda Sperry to EG, n.d., EG Papers, Mugar Memorial Library.

76. Almeda Sperry to EG, n.d., EG Papers, Mugar Memorial Library.

77. Ibid., 22 October 1912.

78. Ibid., n.d.; see also Ch. 35, n. 12, and Epilogue, n. 10.

79. Agnes Inglis to Alice Furst, 27 May 1934; Agnes Inglis to Ann Lord, 30 April 1934, Labadie Collection.

80. EG to Agnes Inglis, 17 April 1919, Labadie Collection.

81. EG, *Living My Life*, p. 667.

82. Agnes Inglis to Ann Lord, 9 November 1934, Labadie Collection.

83. Agnes Inglis to Ann Lord, 30 April 1934, Labadie Collection.

84. Agnes Inglis to Max Metzkow, 24 December 1944, 3 January 1945, Labadie Collection.

85. Agnes Inglis to Mrs. Edwin Burt, 9 June 1940, Labadie Collection.

86. EG to Leon Malmed, 5 February 1918, EG Papers, Schlesinger Library.

87. See Karen Rosenberg, "An Autumnal Love of Emma Goldman," *Dissent*, Spring 1983; also "The 'Autumnal Love' of Red Emma," *Harvard Magazine*, January–February 1984.

88. Daniel Malmed to author, 13 October 1980.

89. EG to Leon Malmed, 15 March 1916, EG Papers, Schlesinger Library.

90. EG, *Living My Life*, p. 687.

91. EG to Nunya Seldes, n.d., EG Papers, Schlesinger Library; EG to Ellen Kennan, 16 October 1923, XXVII, EG Archive.

92. Agnes Inglis to Pearl Johnson and Bertha Johnson, 26 September 1940, Labadie Collection.

93. Berkman, "Diary," 29 September 1930, XXI, Berkman Archive.

94. EG to Van Valkenburgh, December 1915, EG Papers, Schlesinger Library.

95. "You have at last looked to the soul of EG the public character," wrote Goldman to Hutchins Hapgood in response to his glowing review in *The Bookman* of her 1910 collection of essays (EG to Hapgood, 31 January 1911, Beinecke Library; also EG to Stella Ballantine, 8 June 1919, XVI9, EG Archive). Goldman often expressed her longing "to forget the fact that I am always at the behest of the public; to feel for one brief moment that I belong to myself" (EG to Ellen Kennan, 21 July 1914, XXVII, EG Archive).

96. EG to Reitman, 26 September 1908, II, f. 98, Reitman Papers.

97. EG to "Bob," 11 October 1935, [XVII], EG Archive.

Chapter 12

ANARCHISM, FEMINISM, AND THE INTELLECTUALS

1. Mabel Dodge Luhan, *Intimate Memories* (1936; reprint ed. New York: Kraus Reprint Co., 1971), vol. 3, p. 39.

2. Henry May, *The End of American Innocence* (New York: Alfred A. Knopf, 1959).

3. See Linda Gordon, *Woman's Body*, p. 198.

4. *New York Times*, 29 March 1914.

5. EG, "Intellectual Proletarians," *Mother Earth*, February 1914, pp. 363–70.

6. EG, *Essays*, p. 49.

7. Ibid.

8. Ibid., pp. 61, 68.

9. Ibid., p. 220.

10. Ibid., p. 237.

11. Ibid., p. 222.

12. Ibid., p. 200.

13. Ibid., pp. 227–28.

14. *New York Sun*, 2 May 1909.

15. Ibid.

16. EG, *Essays*, p. 230.

17. Ibid., p. 48.

18. EG, *Living My Life*, p. 556.

19. EG, *Essays*, p. 229.

20. *New York Sun*, 6 January 1901.

21. Ibid.

22. Ibid.

23. EG to Berkman, 4 September 1925, in Drinnon and Drinnon, *Nowhere at Home*, p. 133.

24. Sheila Rowbotham, *Women, Resistance and Revolution* (New York: Pantheon Books, 1972), p. 97.

25. EG, *Essays*, p. 217.

26. *Review of Reviews*, 11 March 1911, p. 382; see also *Current Literature*, February 1911, pp. 176–178; *The Bookman*, February 1911, pp. 639–40; *International Socialist Review*, 8 February 1911; *The Free Comrade*, 1911, pp. 87–92.

27. EG to Hutchins Hapgood, 26 February 1911, Beinecke Collection Library.

28. EG to Leon Malmed, 7 April 1906, EG Papers, Schlesinger Library.

29. Anderson, *My Thirty Years' War*, p. 149.

30. *Mother Earth*, March 1915, p. 435.

31. EG, "Manuscript Outline," XIVA, EG Archive.

32. Anderson, *My Thirty Years' War*, pp. 84–85, 125–27.

33. EG, *Living My Life, p.* 531.

34. Hapgood, *Victorian in Modern World*, p. 203.

35. The attraction between Hapgood and Reitman was mutual. While Hapgood was apparently drawn to Reitman as yet another colorful "character" of a type he cultivated, Emma hints in two letters that Ben was

erotically attracted to Hapgood and that their relationship may have been overtly sexual—a prospect she evidently found more acceptable than Reitman's many affairs with other women. "Yes, I have known for quite some time that if H would sleep with you, you would not need me," she wrote Ben, "also that your passion since you are in NY is due to your association with Hutch and not so much your love for me. I am not eager to act as a substitute and therefore hope H will oblige you. Why not ask him?" (EG to Reitman, "10:30 Friday," n.d., II, f. 132, Reitman Papers). On another occasion she wrote, "You say you wanted Hutch. Believe me dear boy, I do not begrudge you Hutch, I am glad he at least can give you what I can not, peace. . . . What [is] more natural than to go with Hutch when you were not exactly famished for me" (EG to Reitman [November or December 1913], 10 P.M., Reitman Papers). Emma herself had a flirtatious relationship with Hapgood and joked with Reitman about how attractive Hutch was and "how thoroughly married I found him, how absolutely enslaved he is by Neith" (EG to Reitman, 5 January 1912, II, f. 113, Reitman Papers). In his memoirs, written over two decades later, Hapgood describes a sleazy, buffoonish Reitman, while Reitman omits any mention of Hapgood from his. Reitman and Goldman occasionally alluded in their letters to the infatuations of Emma's lesbian admirers, including Margaret Anderson and Almeda Sperry. After meeting Margaret Anderson, Ben wrote Emma that "she is crazy about you. This will be another case of Sperry. Oh your women" (Reitman to EG, 20 September 1914, EG Papers, Mugar Memorial Library). A month later, Goldman wrote back that "yes Margaret is coming and I am glad of that. But—I do not incline that way. I love your damned sex" (EG to Reitman, October 1914, II, f. 125, Reitman Papers). On another occasion, before a visit from Sperry, Ben wrote that he hoped Sperry would not teach Emma any new "technique" that might supplant his (Reitman to EG, 3 September 1914, III, pp. 1–4, Reitman Papers).

36. Lincoln Steffens, *The Autobiography of Lincoln Steffens* (New York: Literary Guild, 1931), pp. 654–55; Luhan, *Memories*, vol. 3, p. 83.

37. Luhan, *Memories*, Vol. 3, p. 58.

38. Ibid., p. 90.

39. Lawrence Veysey, *The Communal Experience: Anarchist and Mystical Counter-Cultures in America* (New York: Harper & Row), 1973, pp. 77–78.

40. Homer, *Robert Henri*, p. 180.

41. Sloan, *New York Scene*, pp. 569–78, 634.

42. Will Durant and Ariel Durant, *A Dual Autobiography* (New York: Simon & Schuster, 1977), p. 40.

43. Max Eastman, *Enjoyment of Living* (New York: Harper & Bros., 1948), p. 423.

44. Margaret Anderson, "The Immutable," *The Little Review*, November 1914, p. 20.

45. EG, "The Ups and Downs of an Anarchist Propagandist," *Mother Earth*, August 1913, p. 173.

46. Ibid.

47. Ben Reitman, "The End of the Tour and a Peep at the Next One," *Mother Earth*, September 1913, pp. 212–13.

48. EG, *The Social Significance of the Modern Drama* (Boston: Richard G. Badger, 1914), p. 186.

49. EG to Evelyn Scott, 21 November 1927, in Drinnon and Drinnon, *Nowhere at Home*, pp. 140–42.

50. EG, *Drama*, pp. 118, 25, 97, 236.

51. *Mother Earth*, December 1914, p. 324; *The Little Review*, October 1914, p. 46.

52. EG, *Drama*, pp. 48–49, 63–68.

53. Jay Martin, *Always Merry and Bright: The Life of Henry Miller* (Santa Barbara, Calif.: Capra Press, 1968), pp. 38–39.

54. *International Socialist Review*, October 1914, p. 250; Van Wyck Brooks, *The Confident Years: 1886–1915* (New York: E. P. Dutton, 1952), p. 375; EG, *Drama*, pp. 4–5. Kenneth Rexroth credits Goldman with helping to inspire the formation of innumerable little theater groups devoted to staging performances of Wedekind, Chekhov, Strindberg, Sudermann, Hauptmann, Shaw, and others. See Rexroth, *An Autobiographical Novel* (Surrey: Whittet Books, 1977), p. 273. Brooks thought no one did more than she to publicize the work of the modern European dramatists (*Confident Years*, p. 375).

55. Harry Kelly, "Anarchism: A Plea for the Impersonal," *Mother Earth*, February 1908, p. 559.

56. *Mother Earth*, December 1910, p. 324.

57. Berkman to EG, 7 December 1927, in Drinnon and Drinnon, *Nowhere at Home*, p. 79; see also EG to Stella Ballantine, 24 April 1919, XVI9, EG Archive: "this lament [that we do not reach the workers] has been S[asha]'s ever since he came out from Pittsburgh. It's an obsession with him."

58. Flynn, *Rebel Girl*, p. 50.

59. EG to Stella Ballantine, 24 April 1919, XVI9, EG Archive.

60. EG to "Dear Dear Friend," "on the farm," 19 August [1907–1908], [II], Reitman Papers.

61. *Mother Earth*, December 1910, pp. 325–27.

62. EG, "The Ups and Downs of an Anarchist Agitator," *Mother Earth*, August 1913, p. 172.

63. EG to Israel Zangwill, 29 November 1924, XIX, EG Archive.

64. Anderson, "The Immutable," p. 21.

65. See Marsh, *Anarchist Women*, p. 105.

Chapter 13

"A GREAT INNER CONFLICT"

1. EG, *Living My Life*, pp. 552–53.

2. David Kennedy, *Birth Control in America: The Career of Margaret Sanger* (New Haven, Conn.: Yale University Press, 1970), pp. 23–24.

3. *Mother Earth*, April 1916, p. 450.

4. Sanger, *Autobiography*, p. 92.

5. EG to Margaret Sanger, 9 April 1914, Margaret Sanger Papers, Library of Congress.

6. EG, *Living My Life*, p. 553.

7. See Gordon, *Woman's Body*, pp. 206–22; also Joan M. Jensen, "The Evolution of Margaret Sanger's 'Family Limitation' Pamphlet, 1914–1921," *Signs* (Spring 1981), pp. 548–67.

8. EG, "My Arrest and Preliminary Hearing," *Mother Earth*, March 1916, p. 426.

9. William Sanger to EG, 14 March 1916, Margaret Sanger Papers; on Sanger's growing conservatism see Drinnon, *Rebel*, pp. 169–72; Gordon, *Woman's Body*, pp. 245–59.

10. Quoted in Drinnon, *Rebel*, p. 168.

11. *Mother Earth*, May 1916, pp. 426–30.

12. Ibid., p. 506.

13. EG to Ellen Kennan, 29 April 1916, XXVII, EG Archive.

14. EG to Jake Margolis, 5 May 1916, X, EG Archive.

15. EG to Agnes Inglis, 18 September 1916, Labadie Collection.

16. *Mother Earth*, December 1916, p. 702; Linda Gordon reiterates this point which many suffragists, socialists, and more conservative birth-control advocates attempted to deny: "The origins of birth control as a woman's movement *were* in free love" (*Woman's Body*, p. 243).

17. *Mother Earth*, October 1916, p. 647.

18. EG to Nunya Seldes, "in the woods, August 29," n.d., II, f. 140, Reitman Papers.

19. EG to Reitman, 13 September 1913, II, f. 116, Reitman Papers.

20. EG to Reitman, 20 September 1913, II, f. 116, Reitman Papers.

21. Ibid.,

22. EG to Reitman, 21 September 1913, II, f. 116, Reitman Papers.

23. Ibid.

24. Reitman to EG, n.d., III, f. 1–6b, Reitman Papers.

25. Reitman, "Following the Monkey," p. 253. Ben never felt comfortable with the immigrant anarchists who were close to Emma. "At the City Hall everyone is so beautiful to me," he wrote her in the spring of 1918, "really little Mommy when I see how I harmonize with the crowd of Americans there and remember the dificulties I always had with the Jews and Russians and other comrades I feel that I am more in my natural element" (FBI Files, OG15466 Reel 87A, U.S. National Archives).

26. Reitman to EG, [1914], II, f. 96, Reitman Papers.

27. EG to Reitman, 24 October [1913], II, f. 125, Reitman Papers.

28. Ibid.

29. EG to Reitman, 1 February [1914], 1:30 A.M., II, f. 139, Reitman Papers.

30. Avrich, *Modern School*, pp. 199–200.

31. *Mother Earth*, July 1914.

32. Avrich, *Modern School*, pp. 199–200.

33. EG, *Living My Life*, p. 536.

34. EG to Reitman, 16 September 1914, II, f. 147, Reitman Papers.

35. EG to Reitman, 25 September 1914, II, f. 122, Reitman Papers.

36. Reitman to EG, 23 September 1914, EG Papers, Mugar Memorial Library.

37. Reitman to EG, [28 September], 16 October 1914, EG Papers, Mugar Memorial Library.

38. EG, *Living My Life*, p. 540.

39. EG to Reitman, 16 September [1914], [II, f. 121–122], Reitman Papers.

40. EG to Reitman, 1 October 1914, II, f. 123, Reitman Papers.

41. Reitman to EG, 12 September 1914, III, f. 1–4b, Reitman Papers.

42. Reitman to EG, 7 October, II, f. 1–5b, Reitman Papers.

43. EG to Reitman, 10 October 1914, II, f. 123, Reitman Papers.

44. EG to Reitman, 25 December 1914, II, f. 126, Reitman Papers.

45. Reitman, "Following the Monkey," pp. 363–64.

46. Reitman to EG, 15 June 1931, XVIIB, EG Archive.

47. Reitman, "Following the Monkey," pp. 359, 366.

48. EG to Agnes Inglis, 14 April 1917, Labadie Collection.

49.. EG to Reitman, 26 July 1911, II, f. 109, Reitman Papers.

50. EG to Ethel Mannin, 15 May 1933, EG Papers, New York Public Library.

51. Reitman, "Following the Monkey," p. 368.

Chapter 14

"THE QUESTION OF CAPITALIST WARS"

1. *New York Times*, 10 June 1917.
2. See H. C. Peterson and Gilbert C. Fite, *Opponents of War, 1917–1918* (Madison: University of Wisconsin Press, 1957).
3. Blanche Wiesen Cook, ed., *Crystal Eastman on Women and Revolution* (New York: Oxford University Press, 1978), p. 264.
4. Randolph Bourne, "War and the Intellectuals," *Seven Arts*, June 1917. See also Christopher Lasch, *The New Radicalism in America, 1889–1963* (New York: Vintage Books, 1965), pp. 207–09, 222–24.
5. EG to Agnes Inglis, April 1917, Labadie Collection.
6. *Mother Earth*, June 1917, pp. 112–14.
7. EG to Agnes Inglis, 23 May 1917, Labadie Collection.
8. Ibid.; EG to Agnes Inglis, 13 June 1917, Labadie Collection.
9. Leonard Abbott, "Emma Goldman as I Knew Her" (typescript), EG Papers, Tamiment Library.
10. *New York Times*, 16 June 1917.
11. *Mother Earth*, July 1917, p. 150; EG to Agnes Inglis, 17 June 1917, Labadie Collection.
12. EG to Agnes Inglis, 20 June 1917, Labadie Collection.
13. William O'Neill, ed., *Echoes of Revolt: The Masses, 1911–1917* (Chicago: Quadrangle Books, 1966), pp. 293–294.
14. Drinnon, *Rebel*, p. 239.
15. *Transcript of Record, Supreme Court of the United States, October Term, 1917. Emma Goldman and Alexander Berkman, plaintiffs-in-error vs. U.S.* (1917), pp. 141–161. Goldman and Berkman also printed part of the trial record in the July 1917 issue of *Mother Earth* and in a pamphlet entitled *Anarchism on Trial: Speeches of Alexander Berkman and Emma Goldman before the United States District Court in the City of New York, July 1917* (New York: Mother Earth Publishing Association, 1917). Goldman's final speech to the jury, as it appeared in *Anarchism on Trial*, also appears in Shulman, *Red Emma Speaks*. The wording in each of these versions differs slightly.
16. *Mother Earth*, July 1917, p. 154.
17. Ibid., p. 140.
18. Ibid., pp. 157–58.
19. Ibid., p. 160.
20. *Anarchism on Trial*, pp. 73–74.
21. EG to Agnes Inglis, 8 July 1917, Labadie Collection.
22. O'Neill, *Revolt*, pp. 293–94.

23. *Mother Earth*, July 1917, p. 170.

24. *Anarchism on Trial*, p. 76.

25. *New York Times*, 11 July 1917.

26. EG to Agnes Inglis, 25 July 1917, Labadie Collection.

27. Richard H. Frost, *The Mooney Case* (Stanford, Calif.: Stanford University Press, 1968), p. 145 ff.

28. EG to Agnes Inglis, 29 September 1917, Labadie Collection.

29. EG to Agnes Inglis, 21 November 1917, Labadie Collection.

30. EG to Agnes Inglis, 29 September 1917, Labadie Collection.

31. EG to Harry Weinberger, 20 April 1919, Weinberger Papers.

32. EG to Agnes Inglis, 31 March 1917, Labadie Collection.

33. EG to Agnes Inglis, 17 April 1917, Labadie Collection.

34. EG, *The Truth about the Boylsheviki* (New York: Mother Earth Publishing Association, 1917).

35. Avrich, *Russian Anarchists*, p. 196.

36. EG to Agnes Inglis, 10 July 1917, Labadie Collection.

Chapter 15

"MY ONE GREAT LOVE—MY IDEAL"

1. EG to Stella Ballantine, 10 February 1918, XVI9, EG Archive.

2. Paul W. Garrett and Austin H. MacCormick, eds., *Handbook of American Prisons and Reformatories* (New York: National Society of Prisons and Reformatories, 1929), p. 539. For a copy of *The Jefftown Journal: Historical Edition* (Summer 1972) and a tour of the facility, I am grateful to Warden Donald Wyrick, Missouri State Penitentiary.

3. For a description of conditions, see Kate Richards O'Hare, *In Prison* (New York: Alfred A. Knopf, 1923), esp. pp. 62–73.

4. EG to Harry Weinberger, 27 October 1918, Weinberger Papers.

5. O'Hare, *Prison*, p. 96.

6. Ibid., p. 115.

7. EG to Stella Ballantine, 15 July 1917, XVI9, EG Archive.

8. EG to Stella Ballantine, 5 September; 6 February 1919, XVI9, EG Archive.

9. EG to Stella Ballantine, 24 February 1918, XVI9, EG Archive.

10. EG to Stella Ballantine, 19 January 1919, XVI9, EG Archive.

11. EG to Agnes Inglis, 21 June 1917, Labadie Collection.

12. *Mother Earth*, July 1911, p. 87.

13. *Mother Earth*, October 1907, p. 325.

14. EG to Frank Harris, 6 September 1925, XVII, EG Archive.

15. EG, *Living My Life*, p. 677.

16. Philip S. Foner and Sally M. Miller, eds., *Kate Richards O'Hare: Selected Writings and Speeches* (Baton Rouge: Louisiana State University Press, 1982), p. 222.

17. Quoted in Drinnon, *Rebel*, p. 201.

18. EG to Stella Ballantine, 30 April 1919, XVI9, EG Archive.

19. Quoted in Drinnon, *Rebel*, p. 202.

20. EG, *Living My Life*, pp. 706–07; Foner and Miller, *O'Hare*, p. 234.

21. EG to Stella Ballantine, 30 April 1919, XVI9, EG Archive.

22. EG to Harry Weinberger, 8 May 1919, Weinberger Papers.

23. Foner and Miller, *O'Hare*, p. 268.

24. EG, *Living My Life*, p. 688.

25. EG to Stella Ballantine, 30 March, 13 April 1919, XVI9, EG Archive.

26. EG to Stella Ballantine, 30 August 1919, XVI9, EG Archive.

27. EG to Stella Ballantine, 23 March 1918, 5 May 1919, XVI9, EG Archive; EG to Harry Weinberger, 11 May 1919, Weinberger Papers.

28. EG to Harry Weinberger, 31 March 1918, Weinberger Papers.

29. EG to Harry Weinberger, 8 September 1918, Weinberger Papers.

30. EG to Stella Ballantine, [May or June 1919], XVI9, EG Archive.

31. EG to Stella Ballantine, 11 March 1919, XVI9, EG Archive.

32. EG to Stella Ballantine, [May or June 1919], XVI9, EG Archive; EG to Harry Weinberger, 6 October [1918], 25 May 1918, Weinberger Papers.

33. EG to Harry Weinberger, 8 September 1918, Weinberger Papers; EG to "Comrade" [Leon Malmed], 17 July 1919, EG Papers, Schlesinger Library.

34. EG to Stella Ballantine, 17 November 1918, XVI9, EG Archive.

35. EG to Stella Ballantine, 7 January 1919, XVI9, EG Archive.

36. EG to Stella Ballantine, 18 February 1919, XVI9, EG Archive.

37. EG to Harry Weinberger, 21 September 1918, Weinberger Papers.

38. EG to Harry Weinberger, 16 February 1919, Weinberger Papers.

39. EG to Stella Ballantine, 13 April 1919, XVI9, EG Archive.

40. EG to Stella Ballantine, 18 March 1919, XVI9, EG Archive.

41. EG to "Babushka" Breshkovskaya, 19 March 1918, XXVII, EG Archive.

42. EG to Stella Ballantine, 4 February 1919, XVI9, EG Archive.

43. EG to Leon Malmed, "Thursday" [1919], EG Papers, Schlesinger Library.

44. EG, *Living My Life*, p. 606.

45. Louis F. Post, *Deportations Delirium of Nineteen-Twenty* (Chicago: Kerr, 1923).

Chapter 16

"CAST OUT AND A STRANGER EVERYWHERE"

The title of this chapter is a quotation from a letter of Emma Goldman to Leon Malmed, 22 February 1927, EG Papers, Schlesinger Library.

1. EG to Ben Capes, 22 October 1919, XVI9, EG Archive; also EG to Leon Malmed, 18 October 1919, EG Papers, Schlesinger Library.

2. Marion Barling, "Report on the Meeting at the Hotel Brevoort, 27 October 1919"; Marion Barling to "Mr. T.," 30 October 1919; Marion Barling to Mr. Turner, 31 October 1919, Lusk Committee Papers, New York State Library, Albany.

3. EG to Miss Scully, 5 November 1919, Lusk Committee Papers.

4. Ibid.

5. Margaret Scully to Mr. Finch, 28 October 1919; Marion [Holmes] to "Chief," 5 November 1919; "Comrade Marion" to Mr. Finch, 6 November 1919, Lusk Committee Papers.

6. Harry Weinberger to EG, 12 July 1919, Weinberger Papers.

7. EG to Harry Weinberger, 20 July 1919, Weinberger Papers.

8. EG to Harry Weinberger, 5 August 1919, Weinberger Papers.

9. EG to Harry Weinberger, 10 August 1919, Weinberger Papers.

10. Harry Weinberger to EG, 12 July, 28 July 1919, Weinberger Papers; see also Drinnon, *Rebel*, pp. 218–20.

11. Saxe Commins to Stella Ballantine, September 1919, Weinberger Papers.

12. EG to Harry Weinberger, 6 September 1919, Weinberger Papers.

13. "Hearing of Emma Goldman," EG Archive.

14. Thomas Elder to Attorney General A. Mitchell Palmer, 7 December 1919, Justice Department, File 186233-13, U.S. National Archives.

15. Anonymous to Justice Department, 10 December 1919, Justice Department, File 186233-13, U.S. National Archives.

16. J. C. Pinckney to Chief of Department of Justice, 6 December 1919, Justice Department, File 186233-13, U.S. National Archives.

17. Anthony Caminetti to Harry Weinberger, 29 November 1919, Weinberger Papers.

18. EG to Leon Malmed, 19 November 1919, EG Papers, Schlesinger Library.

19. EG to Harry Weinberger, 16 August 1919; Harry Weinberger to Anthony Caminetti, 26 November, 4 December 1919, Weinberger Papers.

20. Drinnon, *Rebel*, pp. 216–19; Transcript of Hearing regarding Deportation of Emma Goldman, held before Judge Julius M. Mayer, 8 December 1919, Weinberger Papers.

21. EG to Leon Malmed, 12 December 1919, EG Papers, Schlesinger Library.

22. EG to Reitman, 12 December 1919, original accession, f. 19, Reitman Papers.

23. EG to Eleanor Fitzgerald, 18 December 1919, XVI9, EG Archive.

24. *New York Times*, 22 December 1919.

25. *New York Times*, 23 December 1919.

26. EG, *Living My Life*, p. 594.

27. See EG, "The Two Americas" (typescript of radio talk), V, Berkman Archive.

28. EG to Stella Ballantine, 8 July 1918, XVI9, EG Archive.

29. EG to Stella Ballantine, "aboard *Buford*," 1919, 8 January 1920, XVI9, EG Archive; EG, *Living My Life*, p. 279; EG to Harry Weinberger, 9 January 1920, Weinberger Papers.

EPILOGUE

1. Interview with Bertha Malmed, 15 May 1893; telephone conversation with Ahrne Thorne, 13 June 1983.

2. EG to Stella Ballantine, 18 July 1931, XVII, EG Archive.

3. *The Nation*, 18 November 1931, p. 614.

4. EG to Nunya Seldes, 23 February 1911, EG Papers, Schlesinger Library.

5. EG to Roger Baldwin, 17 January 1934, X8, EG Archive.

6. Kate Rotchek to Carl Nold, 17 April 1932, Labadie Collection.

7. EG to Berkman, 4 September 1925, in Drinnon and Drinnon, *Nowhere at Home*, p. 134.

8. Van Valkenburgh to EG, 25 September 1932, XVA, EG Archive; also Agnes Inglis to Max Metzkow, 24 December 1944, and Agnes Inglis to Pearl Johnson Tucker, 7 March 1943, Labadie Collection.

9. Ibid.

10. Blanche Wiesen Cook, "Female Support Networks and Political Activism: Lillian Wald, Crystal Eastman, Emma Goldman," in Nancy F. Cott and Elizabeth H. Pleck, eds., *A Heritage of Her Own* (New York: Simon & Schuster, 1979), pp. 434–41.

11. *New York Sun*, 6 January 1901.

SELECTED BIBLIOGRAPHY

Manuscript Collections

Arcos, Federico. Private Collection. Windsor, Ont.

Boston University, Mugar Memorial Library. Emma Goldman Papers. Letters of Almeda Sperry, 1912–ca. 1914, and Ben Reitman to Goldman.

Harvard University, Houghton Library, Cambridge, Mass. Joseph Ishill Papers. Extensive correspondence from Goldman to Ishill, an anarchist printer, mainly from the 1920s and 1930s. The Max Metzkow Papers contain Goldman letters, in German, from 1892.

International Institute of Social History, Amsterdam. Emma Goldman–Alexander Berkman Archives. Largest collection of Goldman correspondence and manuscripts, mostly post-1919. Includes nearly complete collection of prison letters from Goldman to Stella Ballantine, 1918–1919.

Library of Congress, Washington, D.C. Margaret Sanger Papers contain Goldman letters about birth control, 1914–1916. Alice Stone Blackwell Papers include several letters from and about Goldman.

National Archives, Washington, D.C. Emma Goldman Files of the Department of State, Department of Labor, Post Office Department, Federal Bureau of Investigation.

New York Public Library. Emma Goldman Papers. Manuscripts of lectures and books; mostly post-1919 correspondence with Stella Ballantine, Roger Baldwin, and others. Rose Pesotta Papers contain Goldman correspondence from 1930s, mainly about Spain.

New York University, Tamiment Library. Emma Goldman Papers. Correspondence with Goldman's lawyer, Arthur Leonard Ross, from 1920s and 1930s; extensive notes of a friend, Jeanne Levey, for an uncompleted biography; tributes from Harry Kelly, Leonard Abbott, and others.

Radcliffe College, Arthur and Elizabeth Schlesinger Library on the History of Women in America, Cambridge, Mass. Emma Goldman Papers. Major collection of Goldman letters to Leon Malmed, 1906–1939, primarily from 1920s. Also correspondence with Nunya Seldes, Sophie Simkin, W. S. Van Valkenburgh. Includes many periodicals, pamphlets, newspapers, and clippings.

Rochester Public Library. City scrapbooks with clippings about Goldman family members.

Southern Illinois University, Morris Library, Carbondale. Theodore Schroeder Papers. A few Goldman letters to attorney for Free Speech League.

University of Illinois, Chicago. Ben L. Reitman Papers. Largest collection of Goldman-Reitman correspondence, mainly 1908–1919, principally in the original accession (9 folders) and in Supplement II, which contains 49 folders of letters donated by Mrs. B. M. Reitman in 1972. Supplement III contains photocopies of Reitman letters housed at the Mugar Memorial Library, some Goldman letters, and Reitman's unpublished autobiographical manuscript, "Following the Monkey." Supplement IV contains a small amount of Goldman correspondence and miscellaneous published and unpublished material.

University of Michigan, Labadie Collection, Ann Arbor. Most important anarchist archive in the United States. The Emma Goldman Papers contain many Goldman letters to Agnes Inglis; also Inglis's correspondence with other anarchists.

University of Texas, Humanities Research Center, Austin. Includes some Goldman letters to Percival Gerson, Frank and Nellie Harris, Havelock Ellis, post-1919.

Yale University, Collection of American Literature, Beinecke Rare Book and Manuscript Library, New Haven, Conn. Hutchins Hapgood Papers. Contains several important letters from Goldman to Hapgood.

Yale University, Sterling Memorial Library, New Haven, Conn. Harry Weinberger Memorial Collection. Major collection of Goldman prison correspondence with her lawyer, 1918–1919; documents relating to 1917 trial, imprisonment, and deportation; letters from 1920s.

Yivo Institute for Jewish Research, New York. A few Goldman letters, post-1919.

Selected Works by Emma Goldman

Anarchism and Other Essays. New York: Mother Earth Publishing Association, 1910.

Anarchism on Trial: Speeches of Alexander Berkman and Emma Goldman Before the United States District Court in the City of New York, July 1917. New York: Mother Earth Publishing Association, 1917.

"Johann Most." *American Mercury*, June 1926, pp. 158–166.

Living My Life. 2 vols. New York: Alfred A. Knopf, 1931. Reprint. New York: Dover Publications, 1970. See also abridged version edited by Richard and Anna Maria Drinnon (New York: New American Library, 1977); unabridged version with an introduction by Candace Falk (Salt Lake City, Utah: Peregrine Smith, 1982).

My Disillusionment in Russia. 1922. Reprint. New York: Thomas Y. Crowell, 1970.

Nowhere at Home: Letters from Exile of Emma Goldman and Alexander Berkman. Edited by Richard and Anna Maria Drinnon. New York: Schocken Books. 1975.

Red Emma Speaks: Selected Writings and Speeches by Emma Goldman. Compiled and edited by Alix Kates Shulman. New York: Random House, 1972.

The Social Significance of the Modern Drama. Boston: Richard G. Badger, 1914.

Voltairine de Cleyre. Berkeley Heights, N.J.: Oriole Press, 1932.

Selected Works about Emma Goldman

Anderson, Margaret. "The Immutable." *The Little Review* 1 (November 1914): 19–22.

Barko, Naomi. "The Emma Goldman You'll Never See in the Movies." *MS*, March 1982, p. 27.

Cook, Blanche Wiesen. "Female Support Networks and Political Activism: Lillian Wald, Crystal Eastman, Emma Goldman. In *A Heritage of Her Own: Towards a New Social History of Women*, edited by Nancy F. Cott and Elizabeth H. Pleck. New York: Simon & Schuster, 1979.

Drinnon, Richard. "Emma Goldman: A Study in American Radicalism." Ph.D. dissertation, University of Minnesota, 1957.

———. *Rebel in Paradise*. Chicago: University of Chicago Press, 1961.

Frank, Waldo. "Elegy for Anarchism." *New Republic*. 30 December 1931, pp. 193–94.

Frazer, Winifred L. *E.G. and E.G.O.: Emma Goldman and "The Iceman Cometh."* Gainesville: University of Florida Press, 1974.

Goldberg, Harold J. "Goldman and Berkman View the Bolshevik Regime." *Slavonic and East European Review* 34 (April 1975): 272–76.

Harris, Frank. "Emma Goldman, the Famous Anarchist." In *Contemporary Portraits*. Fourth Series. London: Grant Richards, 1924.

Kirchwey, Freda. "Emma Goldman." *The Nation*, 2 December 1931, pp. 612–614.

Madison, Charles. "Emma Goldman, Anarchist Rebel." In *Critics and Crusaders*. New York: Holt, 1947–48.

Rosenberg, Karen. "An Autumnal Love of Emma Goldman." *Dissent*, Summer 1983, pp. 380–83.

———. "The 'Autumnal Love' of Red Emma." *Harvard Magazine*, January–February 1984, pp. 52–56.

Shulman, Alix Kates. "Emma Goldman, Anarchist and Feminist." *Women: A Journal of Liberation*, Spring 1980.

———. *To the Barricades: The Anarchist Life of Emma Goldman*. New York: Thomas Y. Crowell, 1971.

———. "Dancing in the Revolution: Emma Goldman's Feminism." *Socialist Review*, March–April 1982, pp. 31–44.

Wexler, Alice. "Emma Goldman on Mary Wollstonecraft." *Feminist Studies* 7 (Spring 1981): 113–33.

———. "Emma Goldman in Love." *Raritan: A Quarterly Review* 1 (Summer 1982): 116–45.
———. "The Early Life of Emma Goldman." *The Psychohistory Review* 8 (Spring 1980): 7–21.

Other Sources

Anderson, Margaret. *My Thirty Years' War*. London: Alfred A. Knopf, 1930.

Ashbaugh, Carolyn. *Lucy Parsons: American Revolutionary*. Chicago: Charles H. Kerr, 1976.

Avrich, Paul. *An American Anarchist: The Life of Voltairine de Cleyre*. Princeton, N.J.: Princeton University Press, 1978.

————. "Bakunin and the United States." *International Review of Social History* 24 (1979): 320–40.

————. "Kropotkin in America." *International Review of Social History* 25 (1980): 1–34.

————. *The Modern School Movement: Anarchism and Education in the United States*. Princeton, N.J.: Princeton University Press, 1980.

————. *The Russian Anarchists*. Princeton, N.J.: Princeton University Press, 1967.

Berkman, Alexander. *Prison Memoirs of an Anarchist*. 1912. Reprint. Pittsburgh, Pa.: Frontier Press, 1970.

————. *The Bolshevik Myth*. New York: Boni & Liveright, 1925.

————. *Now and After: The ABC of Communist Anarchism*. New York: Vanguard Press, 1929.

Berman, Paul. "To Russia with Love: John Reed and the Greenwich Village Revolutionaries." *Voice Literary Supplement*, February 1982.

Brooks, Van Wyck. *The Confident Years: 1885–1915*. New York: E. P. Dutton, 1952.

Buhle, Mari Jo. *Women and American Socialism, 1870–1920*. Urbana: University of Illinois Press, 1981.

Chevigny, Bell Gale. "Daughters Writing: Toward a Theory of Women's Biography." *Feminist Studies* 9 (Spring 1983): 79–102.

Chodorow, Nancy. *The Reproduction of Mothering: Psychoanalysis and the Sociology of Gender*. Berkeley: University of California Press, 1978.

Commins, Dorothy Berliner. *What Is an Editor?* Chicago: University of Chicago Press, 1978.

Conlin, Joseph R. *Big Bill Haywood and the Radical Union Movement.* Syracuse, N.Y.: Syracuse University Press, 1969.

———. *Bread and Roses Too: Studies of the Wobblies.* Westport, Conn.: Greenwood Publishers, 1969.

David, Henry. *A History of the Haymarket Affair.* New York: Farrar & Rinehart, 1936.

———. "Upheaval at Homestead." In *America in Crisis*, edited by Daniel Aaron. New York: Alfred A. Knopf, 1952.

de Leon, David. *The American as Anarchist: Reflections on Indigenous Radicalism.* Baltimore and London: Johns Hopkins University Press, 1978.

Dell, Floyd. *Women as World Builders.* Chicago: Forbes & Co., 1913.

Dubofsky, Melvyn. *We Shall Be All: A History of the Industrial Workers of the World.* Chicago: Quadrangle Books, 1969.

Fine, Sidney. "Anarchism and the Assassination of McKinley." *American Historical Review* 60 (1955): 777–99.

Fishbein, Leslie. *Rebels in Bohemia: The Radicals of the Masses, 1911–1917.* Chapel Hill: University of North Carolina Press, 1982.

Gordon, Linda. *Woman's Body, Woman's Right: A Social History of Birth Control in America.* New York: Penguin Books, 1977.

Gordon, Linda, and Dubois, Ellen. "Seeking Ecstasy on the Battlefield: Danger and Pleasure in Nineteenth Century Feminist Thought." *Feminist Studies* 9 (Spring 1983): 7–25.

Guerin, Daniel. *Anarchism: From Theory to Practice.* New York: Monthly Review Press, 1970.

Gutman, Herbert. *Work, Culture and Society in Industrializing America.* New York: Alfred A. Knopf, 1976.

Hapgood, Hutchins. *A Victorian in the Modern World.* New York: Harcourt Brace, 1939.

Higham, John. *Strangers in the Land: Patterns of American Nativism, 1860–1925.* New York: Atheneum, 1965.

Homer, William Innes. *Robert Henri and His Circle.* Ithaca, N.Y.: Cornell University Press, 1969.

Howe, Irving. *World of Our Fathers.* New York: Harcourt Brace Jovanovich, 1976.

Johns, A. Wesley. *The Man Who Shot McKinley*. South Brunswick and New York: A. S. Barnes, 1970.

Johnson, Donald. *The Challenge to American Freedoms: World War I and the Rise of the American Civil Liberties Union*. Lexington: University Press of Kentucky, 1963.

Joll, James. *The Anarchists*. London: Eyre & Spottiswoode, 1964.

Kazin, Alfred. *On Native Grounds*. New York: Harcourt Brace, 1942.

Kennedy, David. *Birth Control in America: The Career of Margaret Sanger*. New Haven, Conn.: Yale University Press, 1970.

Knight, Amy. "The 'Fritschi': A Study of Female Radicals in the Russian Populist Movement." *Canadian-American Slavic Studies* 9(Spring 1975): 1–17.

Kraut, Grace N. *An Unfinished Symphony: The Story of David Hochstein*. Rochester, N.Y.: Hochstein Music School, 1980.

Kropotkin, Peter. *Kropotkin's Revolutionary Pamphlets*. Edited with an introduction by Roger Baldwin. New York: Benjamin Blom, 1927.

Lasch, Christopher. *The New Radicalism in America, 1889–1963*. New York: Random House, 1965.

Luhan, Mabel Dodge. *Movers and Shakers*. Vol. 3 of *Intimate Memories*. 1936. Reprint. New York: Harcourt Brace, 1971.

Marsh, Margaret. *Anarchist Women, 1870–1920*. Philadelphia: Temple University Press, 1981.

May, Henry F. *The End of American Innocence*. New York: Alfred A. Knopf, 1959.

McKinley, Blaine. "Anarchist Jeremiads: American Anarchists and American History." *Journal of American Culture* 6(Summer 1983): 75–84.

———. " 'The Quagmires of Necessity': American Anarchists and Dilemmas of Vocation." *American Quarterly* 34 (Winter 1982): 503–23.

Miller, Grace L. "The I.W.W. Free Speech Fight: San Diego, 1912." *Southern California Quarterly* 54(Fall 1972): 211–83.

Miller, Martin A. *Kropotkin*. Chicago: University of Chicago Press, 1976.

Miller, Sally. *The Radical Immigrant*. New York: Twayne, 1972.

Nowlin, William. "The Political Thought of Alexander Berkman." Ph.D. Dissertation, Tufts University, 1980.

325

Perlin, Terry M. "Anarchist-Communism in America, 1890–1914." Ph.D. Dissertation, Brandeis University, 1970.

————, ed. *Contemporary Anarchism*. New Brunswick, N.J.: Transaction Books, 1979.

Peterson, H. C., and Fite, Gilbert C. *Opponents of War, 1917–1918*. Madison: University of Wisconsin Press, 1957.

Preston, William, Jr. *Aliens and Dissenters: Federal Suppression of Radicals, 1903–1933*. New York: Harper & Row, 1963.

Reichert, William W. *Partisans of Freedom: A Study of American Anarchism*. Bowling Green, Ohio: Bowling Green University Press, 1976.

Rosenstone, Robert A. *Romantic Revolutionary: A Biography of John Reed*. New York: Alfred A. Knopf, 1975.

Sartre, Jean-Paul. *The Problem of Method*. Translated by Hazel E. Barnes. London: Methuen, 1963.

Sears, Hal D. *The Sex Radicals: Free Love in High Victorian America*. Lawrence: Regents Press of Kansas, 1977.

Shanks, Rosalie. "The I.W.W. Free Speech Movement, San Diego, 1912." *Journal of San Diego History* 19(Winter 1973): 25–33.

Spacks, Patricia Meyer. "Selves in Hiding." In *Women's Autobiography: Essays in Criticism*, edited by Estelle C. Jelinek. Bloomington: Indiana University Press, 1980.

Stansell, Christine. Review of *Nowhere at Home*. *Liberation*, January–February 1977.

Stansell, Christine; Snitow, Ann; and Thompson, Sharon. *Powers of Desire: The Politics of Sexuality*. New York: Monthly Review Press, 1983.

Stites, Richard. *The Women's Liberation Movement in Russia: Feminism, Nihilism, and Bolshevism, 1860–1930*. Princeton, N.J.: Princeton University Press, 1978.

Tax, Meredith. *The Rising of the Women: Feminist Solidarity and Class Conflict, 1880–1917*. New York: Monthly Review Press, 1980.

Venturi, Franco. *Roots of Revolution: A History of the Populist and Socialist Movement in Nineteenth Century Russia*. Translated by Francis Haskell. New York: Grosset & Dunlap, 1966.

Vesey, Laurence. *The Communal Experience: Anarchist and Mystical Counter-cultures in America*. New York: Harper & Row, 1973.

Woodcock, George. *Anarchism: A History of Libertarian Ideas and Movements*. New York: World Publishing Co., 1962.

Zaretsky, Eli. *Capitalism, the Family and Personal Life*. New York: Harper & Row, 1976.

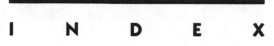

INDEX

A

Abbott, Leonard, 127, 128, 214; on Goldman, 128, 231; and National Free Speech Committee, 179; and No-Conscription League, 230; and Political Prisoners' Amnesty League, 244, 255

Akins, Zoë, 173

Alexander II, 23, 25, 64; attitude of Jews toward, 5–6

anarchism: in America, 44, 45; Bakunin and, 45–46; collectivist, 45–48; as ethical ideal, 92; Goldman on, xv, 90–98, 121–22; individualist, 45, 50–51; Kropotkin on, 47–48; and labor movement in United States, 33–35, 38, 135–37; and Marxism, 45, 46; and morality, 63–64; philosophy of, xv, 45–48; and violence, 51, 64–65

Anarchism and Other Essays (Goldman), 191–98

Anarchist Exclusion Act (1903), 116, 266, 228

anarchists: in Chicago in 1880s, 33–35; and Frick assassination attempt, 64–66; on McKinley assassination, 107–8, 298 *n.*27; 1900 Congress of, 89; 1907 Congress of, 89; persecution of, 42, 116, 176–77; and Russian Revolution, 241–44; and

on, 26, 120, 186, 214, 250, 260–61, 275
Brieux, Eugène, 204
Brisbane, Albert, 78
Brooks, Van Wyck, 205
Brown, John, 275
Bryant, Louise, 202, 256
Buwalda, William, 179

C

Caminetti, Anthony, 270, 274
Cánovas del Castillo, Antonio, 99
Carnegie, Andrew, 61–62
Carnot, Sadi, 64
Carpenter, Edward, 48–49, 94, 127
Caserio, Santo, 79
Chekhov, Anton, 204
Chernyshevsky, Nikolai, 24, 26, 48
Chicago Herald, 62
cloakmakers' strike (1890), 58–59
Cominsky, Lena (*née* Zodikow, half-sister), 12–13, 39, 255
Cominsky, Samuel (brother-in-law), 30, 39
Cominsky, Stella. *See* Ballantine, Stella
Commins, Saxe (nephew), 39, 216, 267, 275, 289 *n*.19
Comstock, Anthony, 49
Comstock Law of 1873, 49, 210–11
Comyn, Stella. *See* Ballantine, Stella
Cook, Blanche, 281
Coryell, John, 123
Craddock, Ida, 215
Crosby, Ernest, 118
Czolgosz, Leon, xvi, 103–12, 116, 117, 129, 270

D

Darrow, Clarence, 119, 201
De Cleyre, Voltairine, 75, 95, 97, 123, 128–30, 206
Debs, Eugene, 229, 257, 275
Dell, Floyd, 123, 167, 191
Dodge, Mabel, 188, 200–1
Dostoyevsky, Fyodor, 125
Dreiser, Theodore, 165, 256
Drinnon, Richard, 96, 233
Dunois, Pierre, 135
Durant, Will, 201, 202–3

E

Eastman, Crystal, 229
Eastman, Max, 124, 190, 203, 257
Edolsohn, Becky, 134, 222
Ego and His Own, The (Stirner), 49–50
Eliot, George, 78
Ellis, Havelock, 48–49
Emerson, Ralph Waldo, 78, 103, 122, 275
Engel, George, 35
Engels, Friedrich, 260

F

feminism, 94–5, 193–98; and free love, 49
Fenichel, Otto, 286 *n*.48
Ferm, Elizabeth and Alexis, 118
Ferrer, Francisco, 192–93
Ferrer Center and School, 201–2
Fielden, Samuel, 33, 34
Figner, Vera, 26
Firebrand, The, 100, 102, 122

331

Gompers, Samuel, 74, 294 *n.*10
Gorky, Maxim, 123, 204, 256
Grandjuan (French anarchist car-
    toonist), 123
Greie, Johanna, 35, 37

H

Hall, Bolton, 118, 213
Hapgood, Hutchins, 167–68, 175–
    76, 199–200, 201, 216; on
    Goldman, 308–9 *n.*35; on
    Reitman, 307 *n.*95
Harman, Lillian, 49, 215
Harman, Moses, 49, 116, 215
Harris, Frank, 67, 123, 256, 285
Harrison, Carter, 34, 106
Hartmann, Sadakichi, 72, 123, 167;
    on Goldman, 167–68
Hauptmann, Gerhardt, 125, 204
Havel, Hippolyte: character, 88; on
    Frick assassination attempt,
    67; and Goldman, 88–90, 126,
    197; and Reitman, 217
Hawthorne, Nathaniel, 78
Haymarket affair, 31–38; impact
    on Goldman, 35–38
Haywood, William, 201
Hecht, Ben, 123
Heine, Heinrich, 123
Helfman, Gesia (Jessie), 26
Henri, Robert, 124; and Goldman,
    xiv, 168, 201, 202
Heyse, Paul, 17
Hillquit, Morris, 190, 238
Hochstein, David (nephew), 39,
    255–56, 289 *n.*18
Hochstein, Helene (*née* Zodikow,
    half-sister), 35, 39, 102–3, 255–

56, 265; character, 11–12, 18;
    influence on Emma, 11–12,
    25, 27
Hochstein, Jacob (brother-in-law),
    39, 255
Homestead steel strike (1892), 61–
    62; impact of Frick assassina-
    tion attempt on, 65–66
Hoover, J. Edgar, 268
Hopkins, Prince, 244, 255
Huneker, James, 72, 205

I

Ibsen, Henrik, 95, 96, 204
Industrial Workers of the World
    (I.W.W.), xvi, 118, 129, 190,
    207; aims and origins, 134–36;
    and birth control, 211–12; de-
    portations of, 266; and Mar-
    garet Sanger, 210, 211; and
    San Diego free speech fight,
    179–82; and World War I, 239–
    40
Inglis, Agnes, 225, 236–41 *passim*;
    and Goldman, 183–84, 186
Inter-Ocean (Chicago), 144
Isaak, Abraham, 100, 116; and
    Czolgosz, 104, 110; and Gold-
    man, 102

J

James, C. L., 123
Jews: in anarchist movement, 44,
    88; and Haskalah, 6; in Königs-
    berg, 16; on New York Lower

East Side, 43–44; in Rochester, N.Y., 9, 29–30; Russian, 4–6, 25, 27; in St. Petersburg, 20; and women, 8
John, Eugenie, 17–18
Joll, James, 136–37
Judith (Biblical personage): as Goldman heroine, 27, 36

K

Kelly, Harry: background and character, 126–27; defense of Allies in World War I, 230; and English-speaking anarchist movement, 205; on Goldman, 169; marriage offer to Goldman, 267, 272
Kennan, Ellen, 214, 225
Kersner, Jacob (first husband), 30–31, 38, 178, 266, 267, 271–72, 288 n.2
Kirchwey, Freda, 279
Königsberg, Prussia, 16
Kropotkin, Peter, 88, 90, 123, 127; anarchism of, 47–48, 92, 95, 96; as Goldman hero, 275; Goldman meeting with, 84; on Nietzsche, 50; opposition to Bolsheviks, 242–44; on sex, 102; on violence, 64, 69, 109; on World War I, 230

L

Labadie, Joseph, 86
Langbord, Eva, 170, 172

Lexington Avenue explosion (1914), 219–22
Liberty, 90
Lindau, Paul, 17
Lindsey, Ben, 173
Lingg, Louis, 35, 65
Lipkin, Dora, 271
Lippman, Walter, 201
Living My Life (Goldman), xvii–xviii
London, Charmian and Jack, 173
Lowell, Amy, 125
Lucifer the Light-bearer, 49, 100, 108, 116
Ludlow massacre (1914), 219–20
Luhan, Mabel Dodge. *See* Dodge, Mabel

M

Maeterlinck, Maurice, 204
Malatesta, Errico, 84, 135–37
Malmed, Daniel, 185
Malmed, Leon, 225, 261, 271, 272; and Goldman, 184–85
Margolis, Jake, 259
Markham, Edwin, 123
Marlitt, Eugenie. *See* John, Eugenie
Marmeladov, Sonya (Dostoyevsky character): as Goldman heroine, 67
Martindale, Anna, 224, 264
Marx, Karl, 46
Marxism, 46, 91, 97–98, 127, 260
Masters, Edgar Lee, 119

May, Henry, 188
Mayer, Julius M., 235–36, 271–72
McKinley, William: assassination of, xvi, 103–4, 110, 115, 121, 139, 144, 270, 271; position of anarchists on assassination, 299 n.27
McNamara brothers, J. J. and J. B., 174, 237–38
McQueen, William, 116
Mencken, H. L., xvi
Metzkow, Max, 86–87
Michel, Louise; Goldman meets, 84; as Goldman role model, 197, 214, 250, 275
Mill, John Stuart, 78
Miller, Henry, 205
Miller, Joaquin, 123
Minkin, Helen, 57
Minor, Robert, 123
Missouri State Penitentiary, 247–51
Modern School. See Ferrer Center and School
Monatte, Pierre, 135, 136, 137
Morris, William, 123, 127
Most, Johann, 43, 44; background and character, 51–52; on Frick assassination attempt, 65–66; death, 116; and *Freiheit*, 35, 37; and Goldman, 52–54, 66, 79, 87, 167–68; and McKinley assassination, 104, 298 n.27; sexual conservatism, 53–54; on violence, 64, 65–66, 290 n.18
Mother Earth, xvi, 190–91, 193, 199, 221–24 *passim*, 232, 238, 240, 279; on black Americans: 251–52; strengths and weaknesses, 121–25

N

Nafe, Gertrude, 123
Narodnaya Volya (The People's Will), 23–25
Natanson, Mark (Uncle Maxim): as Berkman hero, 54, 55; politics of, 291 n.21
Nation, The, 258
National Free Speech Committee, 179
Neo-Malthusians, 89, 209
Nettlau, Max, 66, 123
New Republic, 257
New York Call, 238, 257
New York Sun, 101
New York Times, 74, 76, 105–6, 213; on deportation, 274; Goldman on, 257, 259; on Goldman-Berkman antidraft trial, 236
New York World, 62, 76–77
Nieman. *See* Czolgosz, Leon
Nietzsche, Friedrich, 50–51, 85, 95, 96, 123
Nieuenhuis, Domela, 135
Nihilists, 23–26, 64
No-Conscription League, 230
Nold, Carl, 65, 131, 298 n.27

O

Oerter, Fritz, 58
O'Hare, Kate Richards, 229, 248–49, 252–54
Older, Fremont, 257
Olson, Culbert L., 238
O'Neill, Eugene, xvi, 124, 202
Orleneff, Pavel, 120–21
Ouida. *See* Ramée, Louise de la

P

Palmer, A. Mitchell, 263, 269–70
Palmer, John, 62–63
Paris Commune (1871), 64
Parsons, Albert, 33–35, 105–6, 257
Parsons, Lucy, 95, 151, 298 n.27
Pavlovna, Vera, 26, 40, 60
Pelloutier, Fernand, 123
Perovskaya, Sophia, 26, 40, 275
Peukert, Joseph, 11, 53
Phillips, David Graham, 125, 256
Pinchot, Amos, 201
Populism, 23
Post, Louis B., 271
Pouget, Emile, 123
Pound, Ezra, 125
Prison Memoirs of an Anarchist
(Berkman), 55, 63–64, 67, 134,
200
Progressives, 117–18
prostitution: Goldman on, 194
Proudhon, Pierre-Joseph, 45, 94,
123

R

Rabinowitz, Emmanuel (Man
Ray), 123
racism: Goldman on, 251–52
Rakhmetov (Chernyshevsky char-
acter), 26, 56
Ramée, Louise de la (Ouida), 78
Ravachol (French anarchist), 64
Ray, Man. *See* Rabinowitz, Em-
manuel
Reclus, Elisée, 123
Red Scare (1919), 262–63
Reed, John, 124, 256; and birth
control, 213; at Goldman-

Berkman antidraft trial, 232,
235; as war correspondent, 226
Reedy, William Marion, 173
Reitman, Ben L.: and anarchists,
154, 223–25; and Anna Martindale, 224, 225; arrests, 177,
212; attachment to mother,
142, 159; as birth control advocate, 212, 215; bisexuality,
308–9 n.35; domestic longings,
159–60, 216, 224, 225; early
life, 140–42; and Hutchins
Hapgood, 308–9 n.35; and
Jews, 140, 141, 153–54, 312
n.25; and Lexington Avenue
explosion, 221–22; marriage,
224; police connections, 143–
45, 153; promiscuity, 155–57;
and San Diego free speech
fight (1912), 180–82; self-
doubt, 217–18
AND EMMA GOLDMAN: 68, 150–
51, 250–51, 261, 280, 302 n.47;
attraction to, 139–40, 143–45;
criticisms of, 158–59, 223–24,
225–26; as lover of, 146–48; as
manager of, 145–46, 166, 176;
separation from, 261, 264, 273
Revolutionary Catechism, 56–57,
291 n.28
Rexroth, Kenneth, 310 n.54
Rich, Adrienne, 286
Robeson, Paul, 252
Robinson, Lenox, 204
Rochester, New York, 28–29
Rocker, Rudolph, 123, 135
Roe, Gilbert, 118
Rosenfeld, Morris, 123
Rostand, Edmond, 204
Ruttenberg, Aaron (great-grand-
father), 6

About the Author

Alice Wexler was born in New York City in 1942, and grew up in Tennessee, Kansas, and Los Angeles. She received her B.A. from Stanford and her Ph.D. from Indiana University. A former Fulbright scholar, she has been an associate professor of history at Sonoma State University and a visiting scholar at the University of California, Riverside. She is published in journals such as *Raritan* and *Feminist Studies* and is currently a member of the Venezuela Collaborative Huntington's Disease Project.